HUMAN PROPORTIONS FOR ARTISTS

by

Avard T. Fairbanks,

BFA, MFA, MA, PhD, DFA (Honorary)

Posthumous author

and

Eugene F. Fairbanks, BA, MD

With Best Regards to
Dr. Stephen Marquardt
Eugene F Fairbanks
January 2009

Fairbanks Art and Books

Bellingham, Washington 98226

Human Proportions for Artists
Avard T. Fairbanks, BFA, MFA, MA, PhD, DFA (Honorary), *posthumous author,*
and Eugene F. Fairbanks, BA, MD

Library of Congress Control Number (LCCN): on order
ISBN: 0-9725841-1-0

Editing and proofreading services: Fred Su
Typography, prepress and cover design: Kathleen Weisel

Printed in the U.S.A.

Fairbanks Art and Books
Bellingham, Washington 98226

Illustrations are primarily by Avard T. Fairbanks, or are tracings of illustrations by Avard T. Fairbanks. Additional illustrations are by Eugene F. Fairbanks. X rays of shells were recorded by the Radiology Department of St. Luke's Hospital in Bellingham, Washington. Biology photographs in the section of Symmetry were made by Eugene Fairbanks. These were for inclusion in a marine biology book, *The Sound and the Sea, A Guide to Northwestern Neritic Invertebrate Zoology.* It is an illustrated identification handbook for instructional use in classrooms and field trips on Pacific Northwestern beaches. It was co-authored by Dr. Charles J. Flora of Western Washington University and Eugene Fairbanks.

CONTENTS

ILLUSTRATIONS

HISTORIC

REVIEW OF

HUMAN PROPORTIONS

ANCIENT STUDIES OF HUMAN PROPORTIONS

Of vital interest to any design or work of art is the subject of proportions. Anything out of proportion is always a non-harmony. To achieve the proper proportions is a goal for existence and life—it is fundamental not only to art and design, but to all creation.

In all periods of art, the study of proportions attracted the attention of those needing to have some standard or basis upon which to build their works. Employing an arbitrarily ruled measure was not as suitable as using units that may be compared with parts of the body. As a practical system, when an artist works he cannot constantly refer to tables of measures that are extremely bewildering. He must establish some few basic units that are easy to remember, for comparison to all others. Then charts and measurement tables for recheck can improve accuracy.

The Egyptians developed a system of using the middle finger as the unit of measure. This canon of proportions, along with the cubit, gave an established order to the Egyptian artists. If they had not established some typical figure with its canon of proportions, they would have been at a handicap in making masterpieces, particularly in the production of their colossal statues. With such great figures, the artist would find it impossible to gain a comprehensive idea of the subject upon which he labored, especially when working up close.

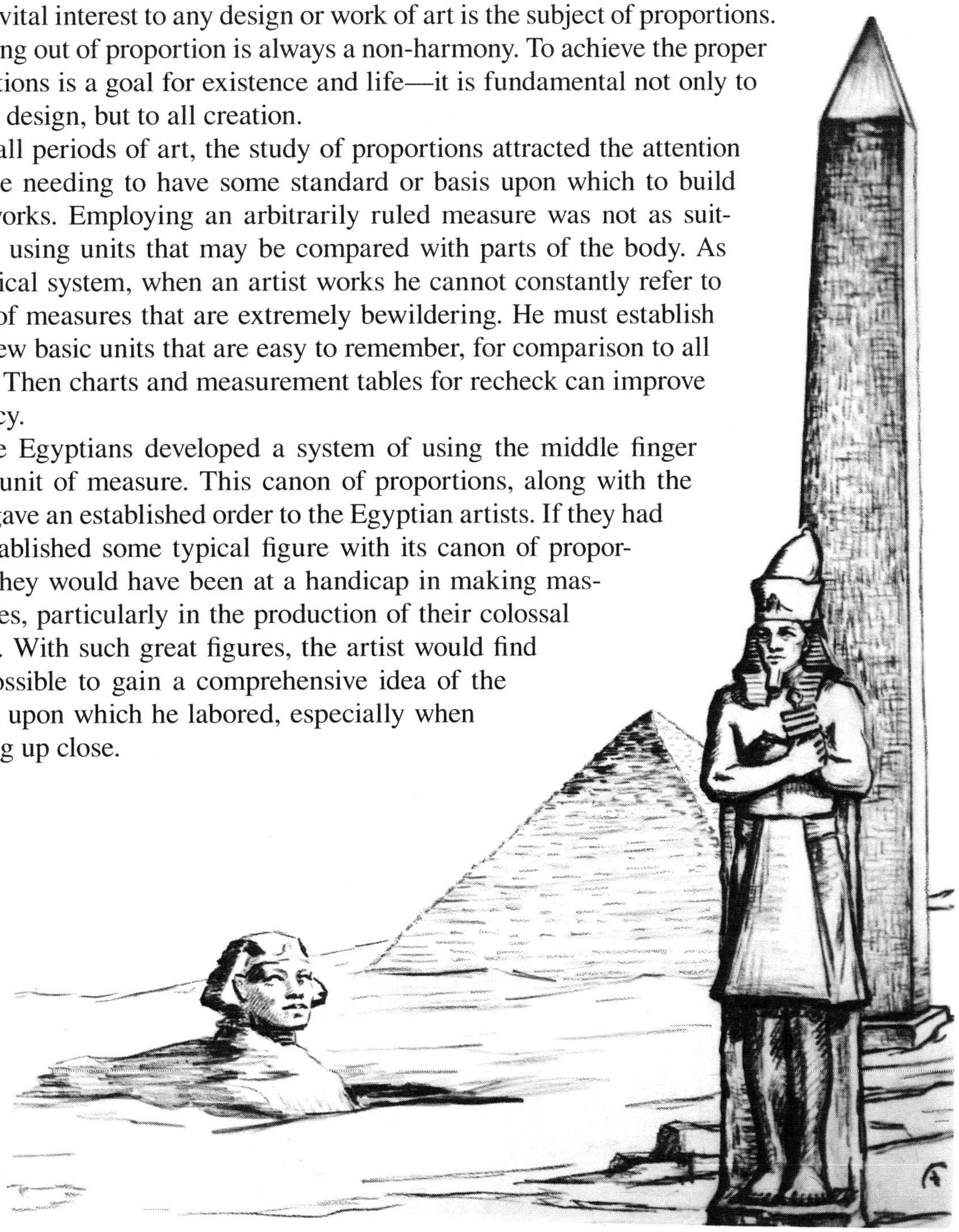

Fig. 1. Illustration representing ancient Egyptian sculpture and colossal structures.

THE GREEK INFLUENCE

With the advent of natural philosophy among the Greeks and an interest in the understanding of the human form throughout the Greek academies, artists strove to gain other measures that could become standard. Myron and Polyclitus, who so eagerly made studies of athletes and warriors, saw in the human form elements of perfection. It was characteristic of the ancient Greek mind to endeavor to reduce natural phenomena to order. The Greek sculptors strove to establish orders of proportions. Polyclitus wrote a book (which has been lost) on proportions, and made a statue to illustrate his typical man. We know that in height it was seven heads to the total figure, but we do not know its other measurements. His bronze statue, Doryphorus, gives us the canon used by the Greeks for a hundred years or more. These proportions were based on geometrical relationships.

Polyclitus and Phidias are considered the leading sculptors of the fifth century B.C. The former excelled in portraiture, but his greatest achievement was the chryselephantine (ivory) statue of Hera, Queen of the Gods, near Argos. Phidias, an Athenian sculptor, made several colossal statues of Athena. His colossal chryselephantine and gold statue of Zeus at Olympia was considered one of the seven wonders of the ancient world The seated figure was sixty feet tall. Phidias was also employed by Pericles as an architect to make Athens the most magnificent city in Greece. The frieze of the Parthenon is generally regarded as his personal creation.

The desire for slenderness and grace supplemented the Greek ideal of the heavy warrior type of man; later Lyssipus established a new canon in the use of eight heads to the body, which persists even to our own times.

There are very few professional schools today where the eight heads measure is not stressed. It is often said that the total height is seven and one-half heads, but in my recent measurements of masculine models, I have found that taking into account the bony structures of the head, and including the skin covering them, the measure becomes eight heads to the total height. This will vary according to individuals, some being more and some being less than eight heads. So a typical eight heads becomes a good, reliable standard. If we figure one-half inch for the hair above the head, and add this increment to the nine inch head height, the ratio changes. When nine and one-half is divided into seventy-two inches or a six foot tall man, it would make the total figure seven and one-half times the head height. The use of either seven and-one half or eight head heights is a reasonable rule to follow.

The Classical ideal of the Greeks remained for many centuries as the best example for ascertaining correct proportion. Later the scientifically inquiring mind of the Renaissance insisted on recognizing truth through demonstration. Many artists of that time were not interested in blindly following the Greek ideal. Such men as Leonardo da Vinci, Michelangelo, and Vesalius were products of this period. They studied human anatomy and recorded proportions. The proportions of Leonardo da Vinci are in constant use even today. He illustrated the human form after the principles of Vitruvius in the geometric

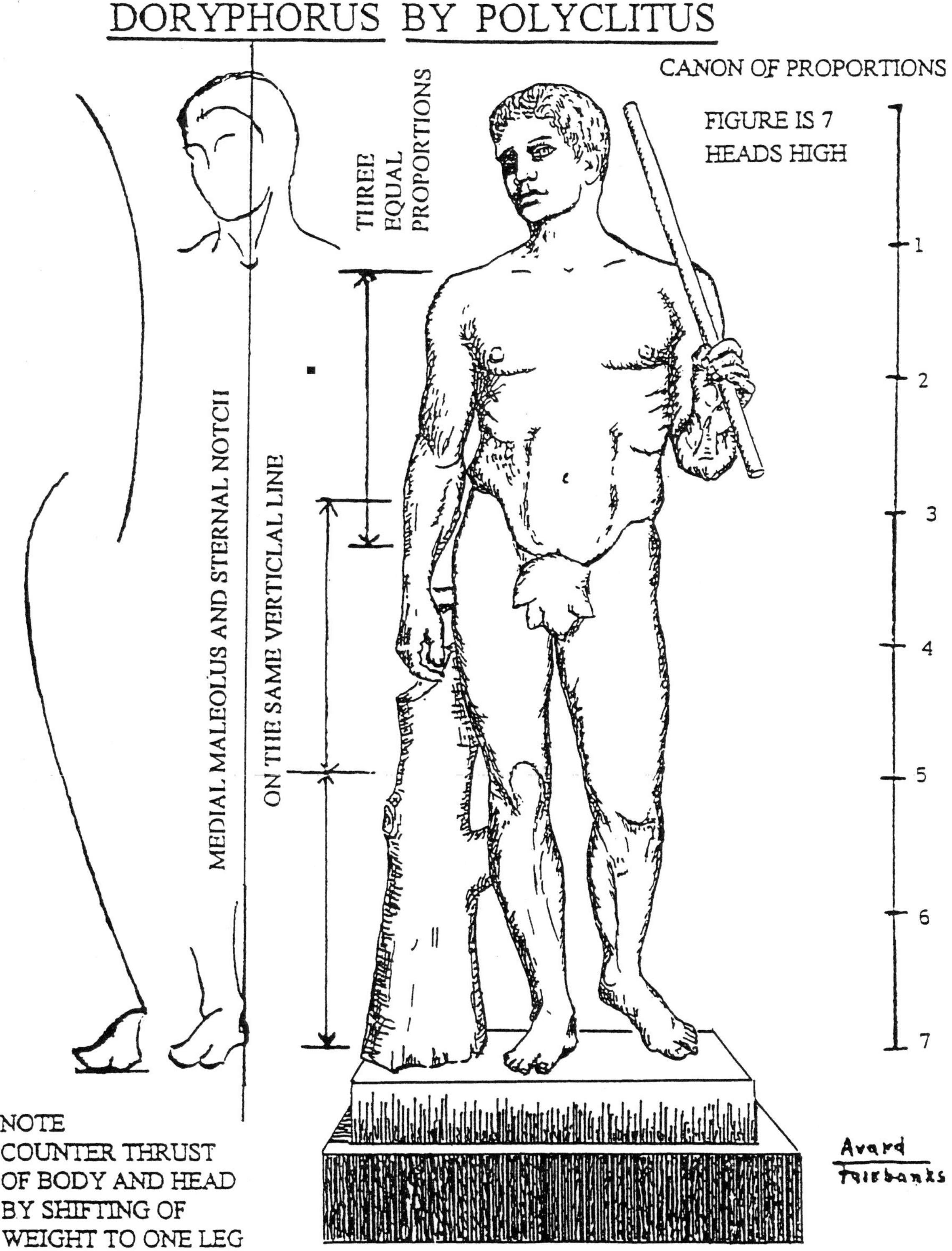

Fig. 2. A sketch representing Doryphorus by Polyclitus showing proportions.

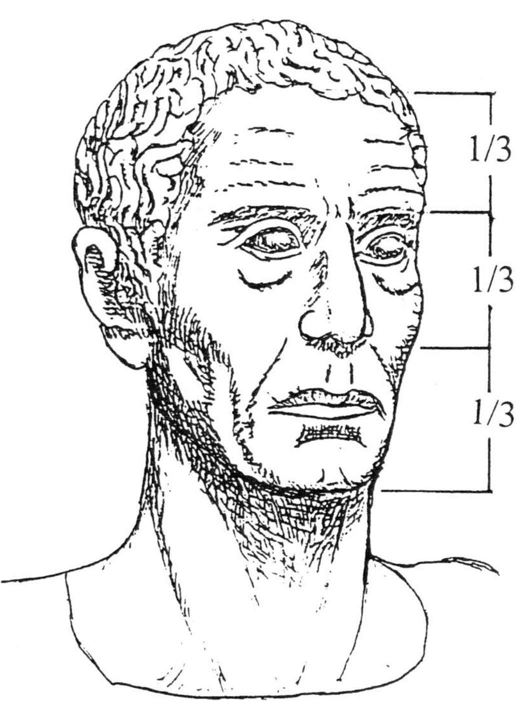

Fig. 3. A pencil-tracing illustration of the portrait of a Roman general living about 50 B.C., showing proportions recognized in that period.

proportions of the circle and the square (the original drawing resided in the Royal Academy in Venice). He also listed a series of relative proportions in his notebooks.

The thorough study of anatomy was born of the desire to serve both the arts and the sciences, and soon both fields benefited from the endeavor. The service to the arts assumed a minor role. Let us hope that the arts will again take up the study of anatomy, to appreciate its most beautiful structures and the fundamental laws for developing designs, evidence of which are manifest in life's growth.

Throughout this discussion, the highest qualities of art and design have been considered to encourage the use of information gained in the study of proportions and human anatomy, and its utilization to produce masterpieces of art. Works thus created should express meaning and reveal true value. Unless there is something to strive for, some objective or purpose, forms, either animate or inanimate, tend to move retrograde. This is not only true of art, but also in natural law. All materials, when agitated and acted upon, strive to achieve the perfection of their order. In the human mind we are conscious of our physical development, and we strive to have life advance to its highest possible attainments. In a like manner, we should strive for cultural development and its optimal attainments.

The significance of good anatomic proportions to art, therefore, is important to make it possible for material forms to be constructed with harmonious design, expressing life and action through art. The very best of proportions and forms should always be used to express the most worthy concepts of the human mind.[1]

The master artists of great ancient civilizations were very concerned about human proportions, even more concerned than some artists today. Indeed, the body provided their units of measurement. The cubit was the distance from the elbow to the tip of the third finger. The palm was the breadth of the extended hand, and the digit was the width of a finger. These were the first recorded units of measure. The Egyptians, Assyrians, Babylonians, Greeks, and Romans carved magnificent statues, and indeed built great cities, using ratios based on human proportions.

The truly remarkable revelation to the student of sculpture is the harmony of the parts of the body to each other and the relations to the whole, including the remarkable flow and grace of the rhythmic lines

[1] Adapted from a doctoral thesis of Avard Fairbanks, 1936, University of Michigan.

and curves of the human figure. Yet all these parts owe their correlations of pattern to measurement because, although this thought may be difficult to grasp, measurements are necessary in both art and science. Measurement implies fact and therefore conveys essential information.

The significant contributions of Greek sculptors were beauty and grace. Their statues were informal with a fluid motion as compared to the static Egyptian statuary. It expressed a culture of democracy and individual importance. When the Romans conquered Greece, they assimilated much of the culture by employing Greek teachers, artists, and physicians. However, the Roman stress was conquest and their preference was sculpture demonstrating victory. The Roman military leaders sought portraits of themselves and this resulted in a refinement of portraiture.[1]

Marcus Vitruvius Pollio, a celebrated Roman architect and engineer, was the superintendent of military engines, the Roman civic buildings, and military edifices for Emperor Augustus Caesar. He wrote a handbook, *De Architectura*, in ten volumes of practical architecture. These manuscripts were lost for fifteen centuries before they were rediscovered in the ancient Swiss monastery of Saint Gall. His writings became influential at the time of the Renaissance. In his handbook he recorded some observations regarding human proportions:

> "For the human body is so designed by nature that the face from the chin to the top of the forehead and the lowest roots of the hair, is a tenth part of the whole height; and the open hand from the wrist to the tip of the middle finger is just the same; the head from the chin to the crown is an eighth, and with the neck and shoulders from the top of the breast to the lowest roots of the hair is a sixth: from the middle of the breast to the summit of the crown is a fourth.
>
> "If we take the height of the face itself, the distance from the bottom of the chin to the underside of the nostrils is one third of it; the nose from the underside of the nostrils to a line between the eyebrows is the same; from there to the lowest roots of hair is also a third, comprising the forehead.
>
> "The length of the foot is one sixth of the height of the body; (the length) of the forearm (is) one fourth, and the breadth of the breast is also one fourth. The other members, too, have their own symmetrical proportions, and it was by employing them that the famous painters and sculptors of antiquity attained great and endless renown." ***Vitruvius.***

Leonardo da Vinci, living about fifteen centuries later, but still prior to modern standardized measurement, recorded in his notebooks many references to Vitruvius, and used a system of comparisons of various parts of the body. He quoted Vitruvius as saying:

> "Four fingers (widths) equal one palm (width); four palms (widths) equal one foot; six palms (widths) equal one cubit; four cubits equal a man's height; four cubits equal one pace (two full steps); 24 palms (widths) equal a man's height. ***Leonardo da Vinci*** #343, p. 182.

Leonardo da Vinci used Vitruvius' observation and quotes from him in composing the familiar drawing, often used in illustrations, #343.

---

[1] Adapted from a doctoral thesis of Avard Fairbanks, 1936, University of Michigan.

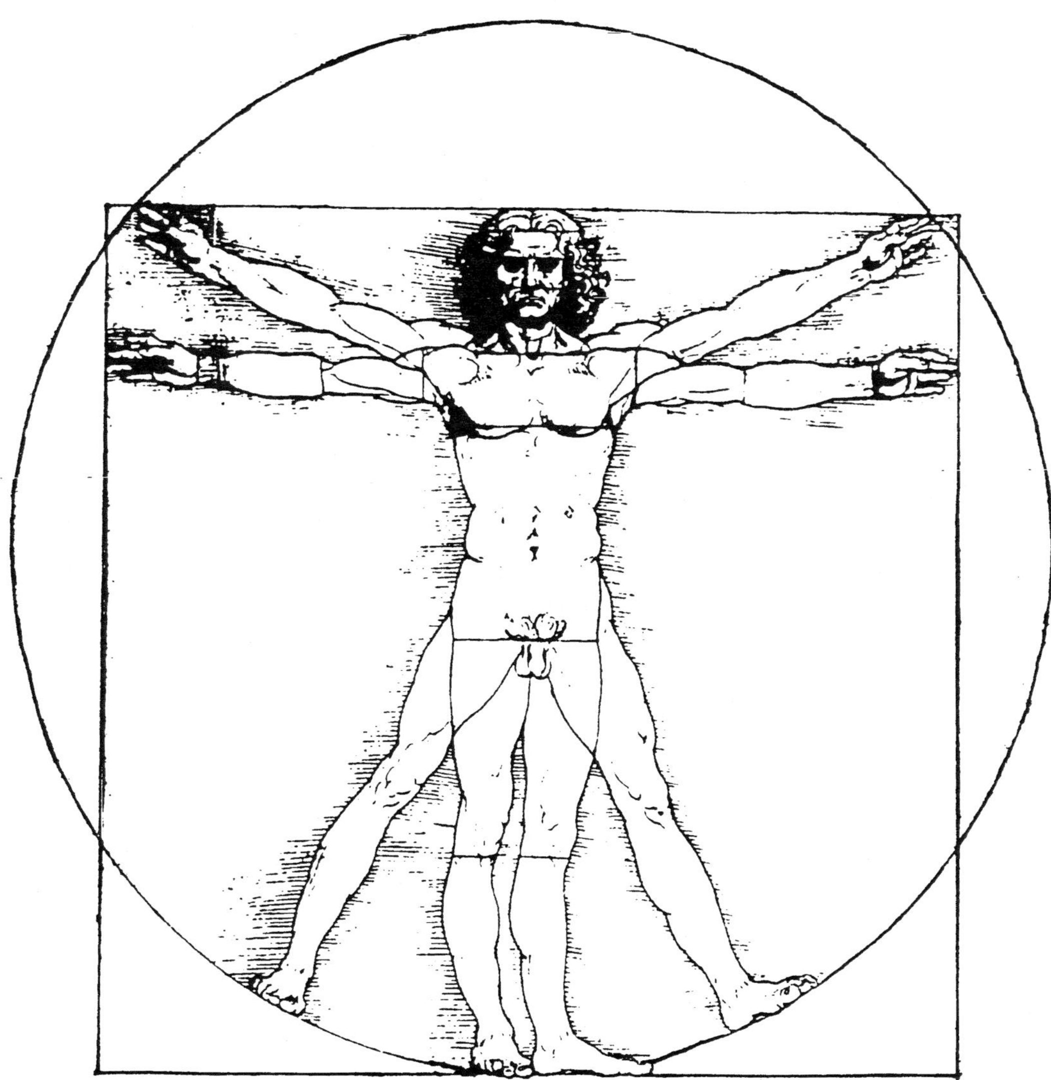

Fig. 4. Leonardo da Vinci's illustration of the human body conforming to the circle and the square.

"Then again, in the human body the central point is naturally the navel (umbilicus). For if a man be placed flat on his back with his hands and feet extended, and a pair of compasses centered at his navel, the fingers and toes of his two hands and feet will touch the circumference of a circle described therefrom. And just as the human body yields a circular outline, so too a square figure may be found from it. For if we measure the distance from the soles of the feet to the top of the head and then apply that measure to the outstretched arms, the breadth will be found to be the same as the height as in the case of plane surfaces which are perfectly square." ***Vitruvius.***

SYSTEMS OF MEASURE

A brief review of the history of measure may be appropriate at this point. An early unit of measure of the ancient Sumerian, Babylonian, and Egyptian culture was the cubit, the length of the forearm and hand from the point of the flexed elbow to the tip of the third finger (18 to 20 inches or 45.7 to 50.8 cm). Another unit was the palm, the width of the outstretched hand at the base of the fingers (about 3 inches or 7.6 cm). A third unit was the digit, the width of a finger (0.72 to 0.75 inches or 1.8 to 1.9 cm). The length of the middle finger was also used.

A unit that the ancient Egyptians used was the Royal Egyptian cubit, 20.62 inches (52.4 cm). The Olympic cubit used by the Greeks was 18.24 inches (46.3 cm). The cubit mentioned in the Bible was slightly less, at 17.5 inches (43.5 cm). The Olympic cubit was divided into two spans of about 9 inches (22.9 cm), six palms of 3 inches each (7.6 cm), and 24 digits, of ¾ inches each (1.9 cm) in length. Later, two-thirds of the Olympic Cubit became the "foot" and was subdivided by the Greeks into twelve thumbnail breadths. The foot unit was passed to Rome and later to Britain where its division of twelfths, *unciae,* became known as inches. Anglo-Saxon measures included the fathom, a span of arms, approximately four cubits. A half a fathom, or about two cubits, was found to be more convenient, especially for measuring cloth, and was called a yard.

Marcus Vitruvius Pollio, the celebrated Roman Architect and contemporary of Augustus Caesar, wrote that the cubit is six palms (palm width) and a foot is four palms or sixteen fingers (finger width). Interestingly, horses are still measured by the number of hands to the withers, the highest part of a horse's back between the shoulder blades.

The foot used as a measure varied with locality. Charlemagne decreed it to be the length of his foot. A German version considered the sum of the left foot of 16 men, standing heel to toe after church, was a rod, and one sixteenth of that was considered a foot. English law later standardized one foot as 36 barley corns taken from the middle ear laid end to end. Therefore, one inch equaled three barley corns. At one time the inch was figured as the span of the knuckles of King Edgar's thumb. A yard was the distance measured on King Henry I, from nose to fingertip of his outstretched arm.

Leonardo da Vinci, in his discussion of proportions, used an old Italian measure called the braccio. This was the length of the arm from the shoulder to the wrist, about 24 inches or 61 cm. He indicated that it was equal to three times the length of the hand. He also referred to the cubit in his notes. The ancient systems suffered from variations, inaccuracies, and a lack of standardization.

Various nations and cultures have developed systems of measure, but most eventually have accepted metric or English systems. An interested reader wishing more information should consult an encyclopedia under Weights and Measures.

When one considers measurement, the question of systems and units must be considered. Currently, most of the world has chosen the metric system as a standard of measure. The United States must inevitably follow, at least in science, since a decimal system has many advantages. However, the metric system is based on a geographic measure. A meter is one millionth the distance of the pole to the equator, and does not conveniently fall into usual human measurements. There are very few men who are two meters, or 6 feet 7 inches, tall.

The English system of inches, feet, and yards is based on human measurements. Body proportions, therefore, conform more to inches and feet. Divisions of a foot by twelve inches and then divisions of inches by sixteen are nevertheless cumbersome, especially when compared to a decimal system. Recognizing the minor disadvantages of either system, a study, later in this book, lists proportions in both systems, and fractions of inches are expressed in decimals. Convenient conversion tables are included.

COMPARATIVE AND RELATIVE PROPORTIONS

A REVIEW OF LEONARDO DA VINCI'S SYSTEM OF PROPORTIONS

Leonardo da Vinci studied Vitruvius' proportions, and about 1490, began to record his own studies in notes in his manuscripts. The publication was later translated into English and entitled: *The Notebooks of Leonardo da Vinci, Compiled and Edited from the Original Manuscripts* by Jean Paul Richter. It was first published in London, 1883. The left column of each page is in Italian and the right column is English translation. Many footnotes help to explain what was written. There are many comparisons and ratios. A few are difficult to understand or to follow, due to translation difficulties or differences in terminology. Many are very detailed, but not finalized by editing as for a publication, even though he may have intended for them to be published.

The work by Jean Paul Richter was a remarkable effort of studying and translating voluminous notes involving sections that had been dispersed in many European nations. He did a monumental task of searching through private, public, and institutional libraries throughout Europe to compile these notes. Some had many sheets, and others had only a few sheets or even one sheet with drawings and manuscript notes. He studied in libraries of fifteen institutions, assisted in many of them by scholars and librarians. In the preface Richter states, "*...and some portions—such as the very important rules for the proportions of the human figure—are wholly wanting; on the other hand they contain passages which, if they are genuine, cannot be verified from any original Manuscript extant.*" (#4 p. XVII)

Leonardo wrote without punctuation and from right to left because he was left handed. Some paragraphs are written without orderly arrangements. Some pages have observations on dissimilar subjects. However, pursuing the subject of the first written notes, he usually intended each observation to be complete by the end of the page. There are a few exceptions. Usually consecutive pages were intended to remain connected. The feature descriptions are in Leonardo's own words with his peculiar symbols, and not as specific as modern anatomical or anthropometric terminology. Many relationships are approximations. Other notations refer to letters or symbols on illustrations that are missing or not available with the published notes. Some of the references are a little conflicting. Nevertheless, the observations are generally very significant.

The initial research and notations were probably recorded between 1490 and 1500 in Milan. Later studies, included in the Notebooks, were done in 1513-14. He pursued anatomical studies with considerable zeal during 1510-16, and these studies may have re-kindled his interest in proportions. He wrote voluminous notes and made many sketches. While the proportions are static, in many sketches he portrayed the human form in vigorous action. His contributions to art, science, and general knowledge are exemplary.

In section VII, of Leonardo's *On the*

Proportions and on the Movements of the Human Figure, about half of the translations by Jean Paul Richter came from the Queen's Library in Windsor, England, but a few were found in manuscripts in the Vatican Library. These notes on proportions have numerous observations and descriptions.

The notes also include some thoughts and findings about childhood proportions, but they are incomplete. Although Leonardo made some paintings portraying women, female proportions are not mentioned in these notes. There may be a few collections of notes in other libraries that were missed in the search. They may have information, and some others may have been lost, since the notes were not saved as one complete set.

Leonardo da Vinci died in 1519. He willed his remarkable collection of manuscripts, of about 5,000 pages, to his young pupil Francesco Melzi, who preserved them with great care. The Melzi descendants were not interested in the old documents, and some were stolen to be sold, while some may have been lost or destroyed. By virtue of fame for "The Last Supper," many were sold to collectors. After the French revolution, a young artillery officer, Napoleon Bonaparte, was appointed General of the French forces in Northern Italy. Under his command the French invaded northern Italy. When he heard that a genius artist had made many plans for military machines, he ordered all of the available manuscripts be acquired and sent to Paris. They were dispatched by an order in 1796 to the Institute of France, where they were classified, edited, and deciphered with some difficulty. Some of the manuscripts were acquired by British royalty and have been secured in the Windsor Library. Other European libraries have collections. Unfortunately, some important parts of his rules for human proportions are missing.

Leonardo da Vinci's student, Luca Paciolo, published a book in 1498, *Divina Proportione*, and in the dedication, acknowledged his master's studies. It was used by many other artists. Another Italian artist, Giovanni Paolo Lomasso of Milan, was interested in proportions and developed a text, *Taratto* or *"A tract containing the Artes of Curious Paintings."* His *Taratto* was influenced by Leonardo's teachings, including proportional information of measurements. This *Taratto* was later translated, in 1598, by an English minister, Richard Haydocke, from Italian to English. It was illustrated with engraved plates and was also influenced by the more complex proportion studies by Albrecht Dürer. This English text was copied, sometimes modified over the next three centuries, and became well known to artists in both the United States and England.

Proportional systems and theory influenced by Leonardo da Vinci were brought to the United States by sculptors studying abroad, as well as by imported books. In 1857, the English sculptors John Gibson and Joseph Bonomi published an illustrated book entitled *Proportions of the Human Figure, as handed down to us by Vitruvius.* It contained references to Leonardo da Vinci and to proportions of ancient Greek statues. This book became popular and went through several printings.

In 1866, the American sculptor, William Wetmore Story, wrote a book that challenged the method of Gibson and Bonomi, entitled *Proportions of the Human Figure According to a New Canon.* Besides being a world-renowned sculptor, Story was a classical scholar, familiar with writings of Pliny the Elder that had offered some insight into the lost *Canon* of proportions by the famous Greek sculptor, Polyclitus. By analyzing the text of Pliny, Story concluded that the sculpture *Doryphoros, the Spear Bearer,* was carved to the propor-

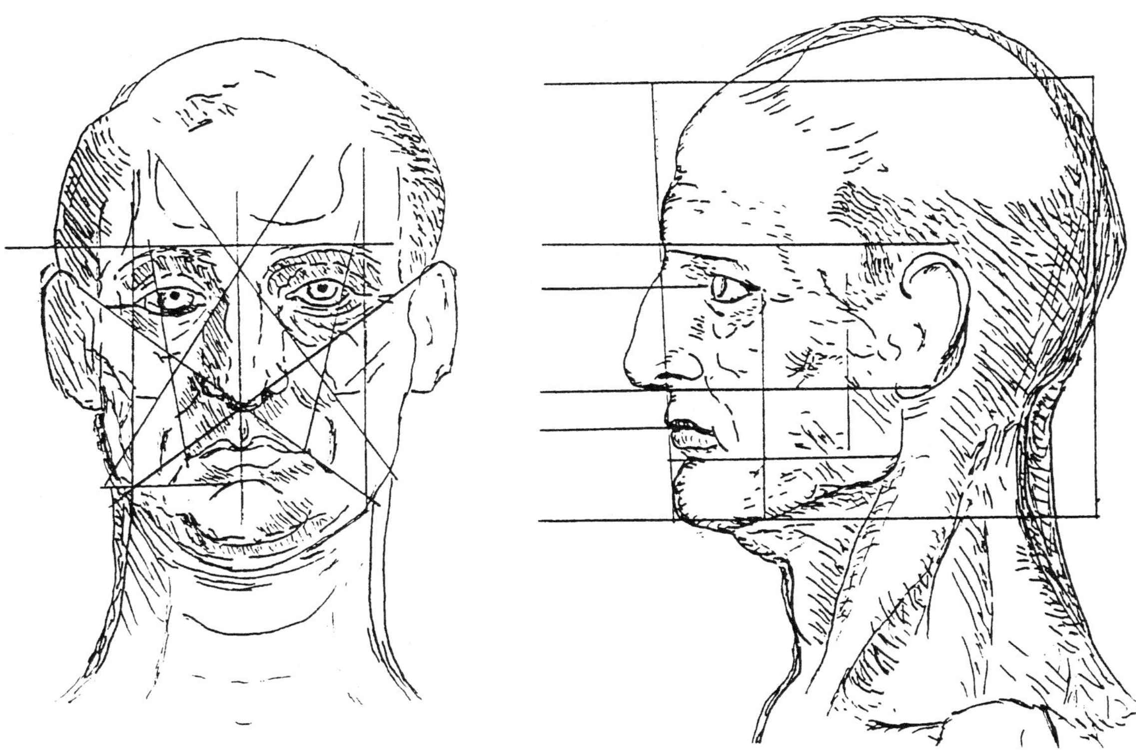

Fig. 5. Tracings of male heads from Leonardo da Vinci's notebook.

tion *canons* of Polyclitus. Story felt that he could restore the *canon* and improve upon it. Instead of human body units as face, head, hand, and feet used by da Vinci, he used a geometric system of circles, squares, and equilateral triangles with significant numerical divisions in these figures. His publication was scholarly, but not practical for studio use.[1]

A review of historical writings may be interesting, but more important is the application of these relative proportions. An effort has been made to organize the salient relationships into categories of body features. Since many of Leonardo's illustrations in the printed notebook translation are small, simple, hand drawings. The illustrations used here in this text are from photostats or adapted by tracings of pencil drawings made by Avard Fairbanks for his doctorate thesis at the University of Michigan in 1936. Details and labels are added to elucidate pertinent features.

Fewer dimensions are applied to individual illustrations, intending to increase ease of comprehension. They are adapted to the notes of Leonardo da Vinci to illustrate the relationships of various body dimensions. It is difficult to determine how many individuals he measured or if he calculated an average set of dimensions. The age of models is not clearly noted. His illustrations appear to be that of older males if the nose, jaw, and facial features are considered.

In proportional studies, whenever small measurements are to be multiplied many times, there is increased opportunity for error, such as "stature equals twenty-four palm widths." Since there is considerable individual variation and opportunity for measurement error, these inaccurate comparisons are omitted from this text.

[1] Fairbanks, Jonathan. Measuring Mankind: Proportions in American Sculpture

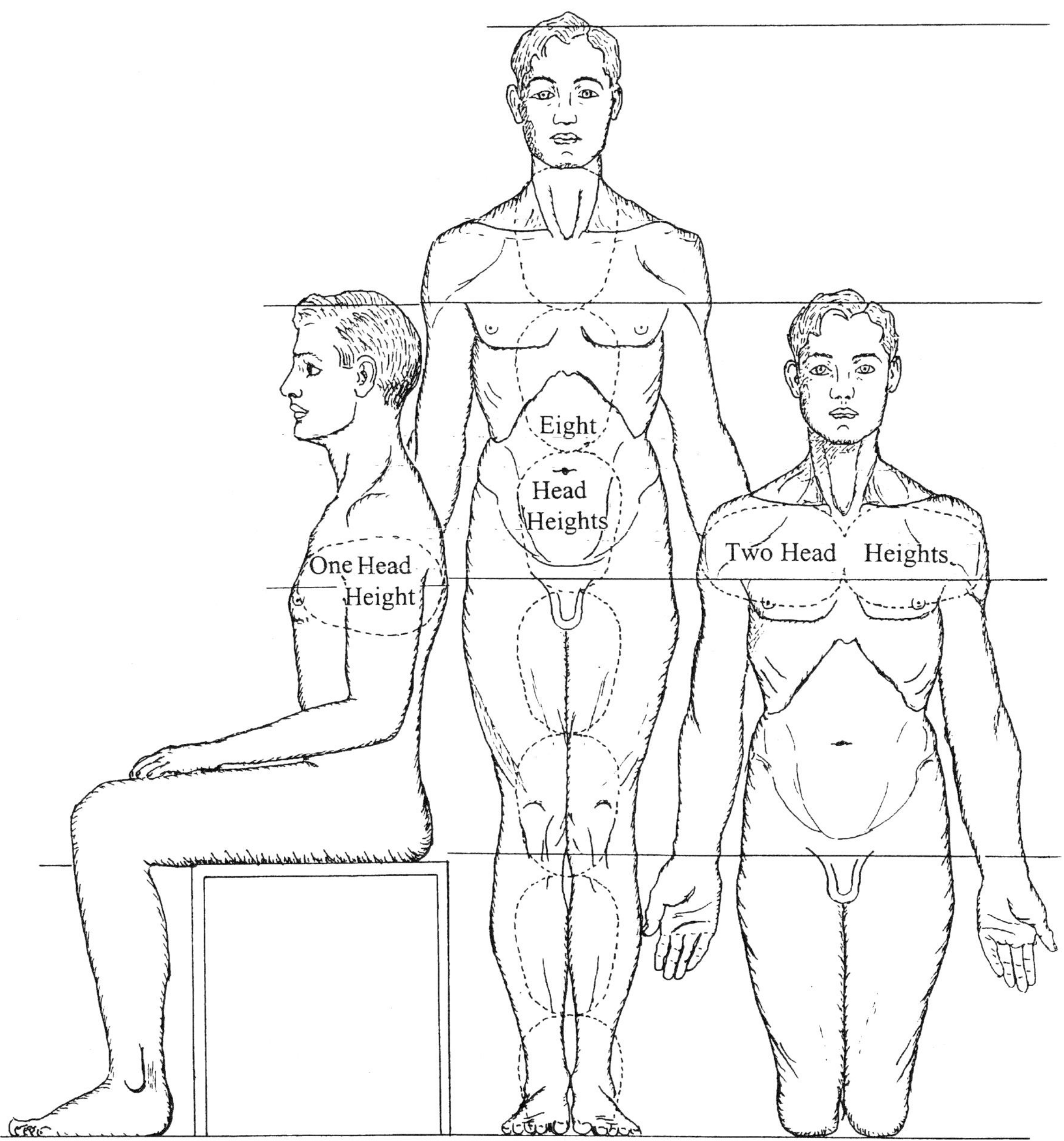

Fig. 6. The male figure of eight head heights.

The male figure of eight head heights is illustrated with kneeling height at three fourths and sitting height at a little more than half of standing height. In the male figure the shoulders are two head heights wide.

When measuring individuals of any given stature, an investigator soon recognizes that there are many individual variations in measurements. Some people have long legs and a short torso. Others may have a long neck and a medium torso. People do not conform to an average or an ideal set of proportions. Most tailors and shoe salesmen can attest to a great variability in form and physique. It is advisable to select a well-proportioned model for fine work, but let the list of proportions

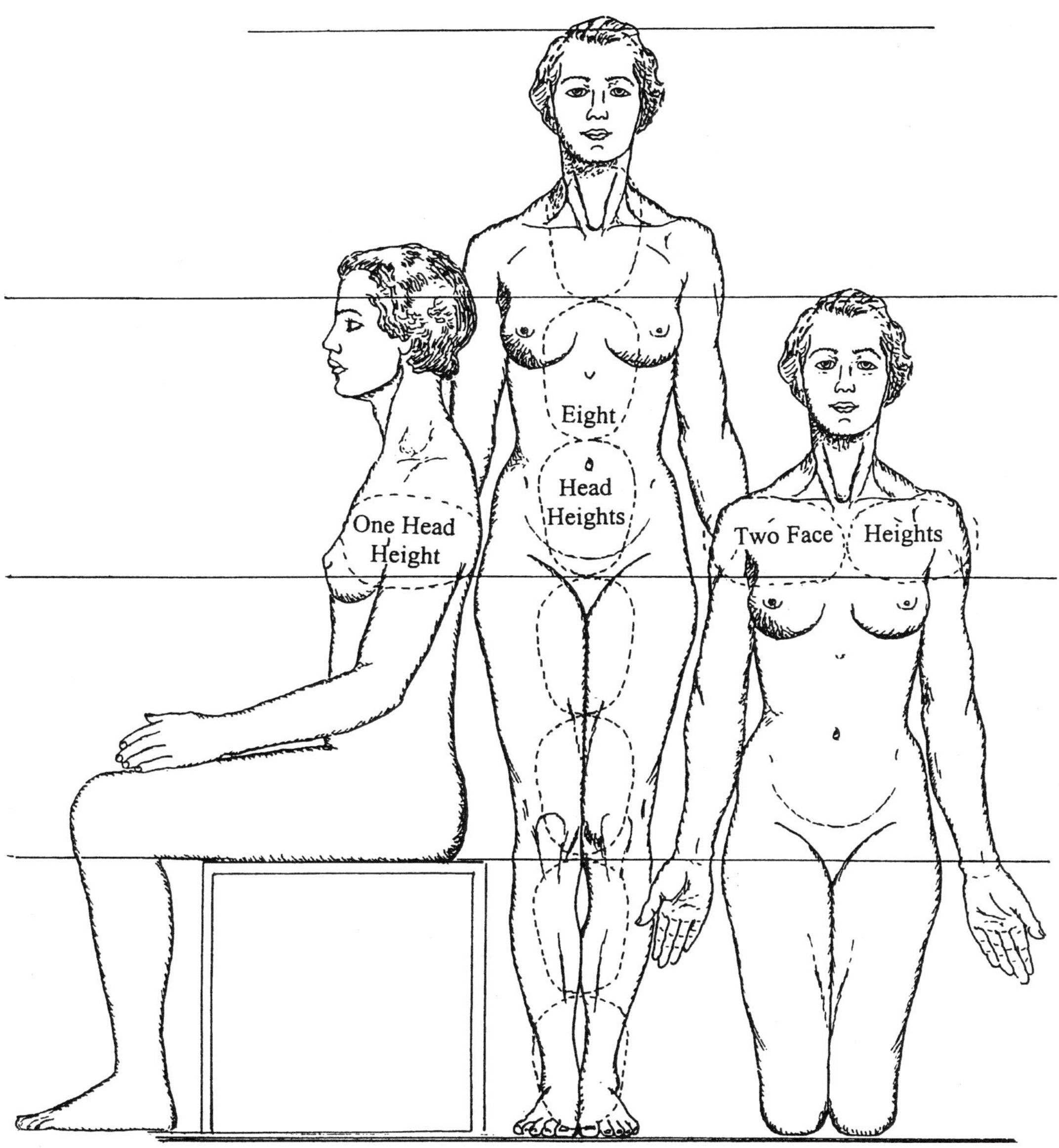

Fig. 7. The female figure of eight head heights.

The female figure is also illustrated with stature at eight head heights. Kneeling height is three fourths standing height, but sitting height is slightly greater than one half standing height since maturation is earlier in females. The long bones of the legs usually do not grow as long as in males. The width of shoulders in females is two face heights.

be used for assistance in preliminary modeling and for recheck. Wherever points of measure in the text are indefinite, variable, or in soft tissues, they may be qualified by a word or phrase, sometimes in parenthesis. (The number of the paragraph quoted in Chapter VII, *On the Proportions and on the Movement of the Human Figure,* are indicated by #__, the paragraph number).

Leonardo recommended: "...take a man of three braccia in height and measure him by the rule I will give you... . Choose one of those who are most graceful and take your measurements." #309. This would presume his concept of ideal proportions would be about a six foot or 183 cm tall man.

The following relative proportions have been extracted from chapter VII in his notebook translation, and appear appropriate and easy to use. The height of a man was considered to be three braccia (an indefinite, variable, archaic Italian term presumed to be the distance from the shoulder to the wrist). In one place he states that the length of a hand, wrist to fingertip (about 8 inches, 20.4 cm) is one third of a braccio. Therefore a braccio would be about 24 inches or 61 cm, resulting in a stature measurement of 3 x 24 = 72 inches, or in metric, 3 x 61 = 183 cm. #309.

Later he states that stature is four cubits (point of the elbow to the tip of the middle finger, about 18 inches or 45.8 cm) resulting in 4 x 18 = 72 inches or 4 x 45.8 = 183.2 cm. #333.

Again he states stature is eight head heights (vertex to chin, about 9 inches or 22 cm), 9 inches x 8 = 72 inches or 22.9 cm x 8 = 183.2 cm. He wrote stature is nine face heights (hairline to chin), 8 inches x 9 = 72 inches or 20.4 cm x 9 = 183.6 cm, #317.

Other comparisons are listed in #343:

The sole to below the knee (tibial point) is one fourth the height.

The sole to the base of the genitals (symphysis pubis) is one half the height.

From the top of the breast (chest at the level of clavicles) to the top of the head is one sixth of the height.

From the nipples (actually anterior axillary fold) to the top of the head is one fourth height.

Kneeling height is three fourths of the standing height.

The umbilicus is at one half the standing height.

Sitting height is a little more than one half the standing height. #332.

The axila is at one half the sitting height. #332.

When standing, the tragus of the ear, the shoulder, the hip joint, and the ankles are in a line perpendicular to the ground. #339.

Leonardo da Vinci's relative proportions of the head, face, and neck are of special interest to the serious artist creating portraits.

HEAD COMPARISON

The head is equal to the length of the foot. According to average figures in a recent study, the head height is about 9 inches, or 22.7 cm, and the foot length is 10 ¾ inches or 27 cm. The chin to vertex nearly equals heel to tip of the toe. #325. The face is equal to the hand, 8 inches or 20.5 cm. The wrist to fingertip equals chin to hairline. The neck, chin to sternal notch, is one-half head height.

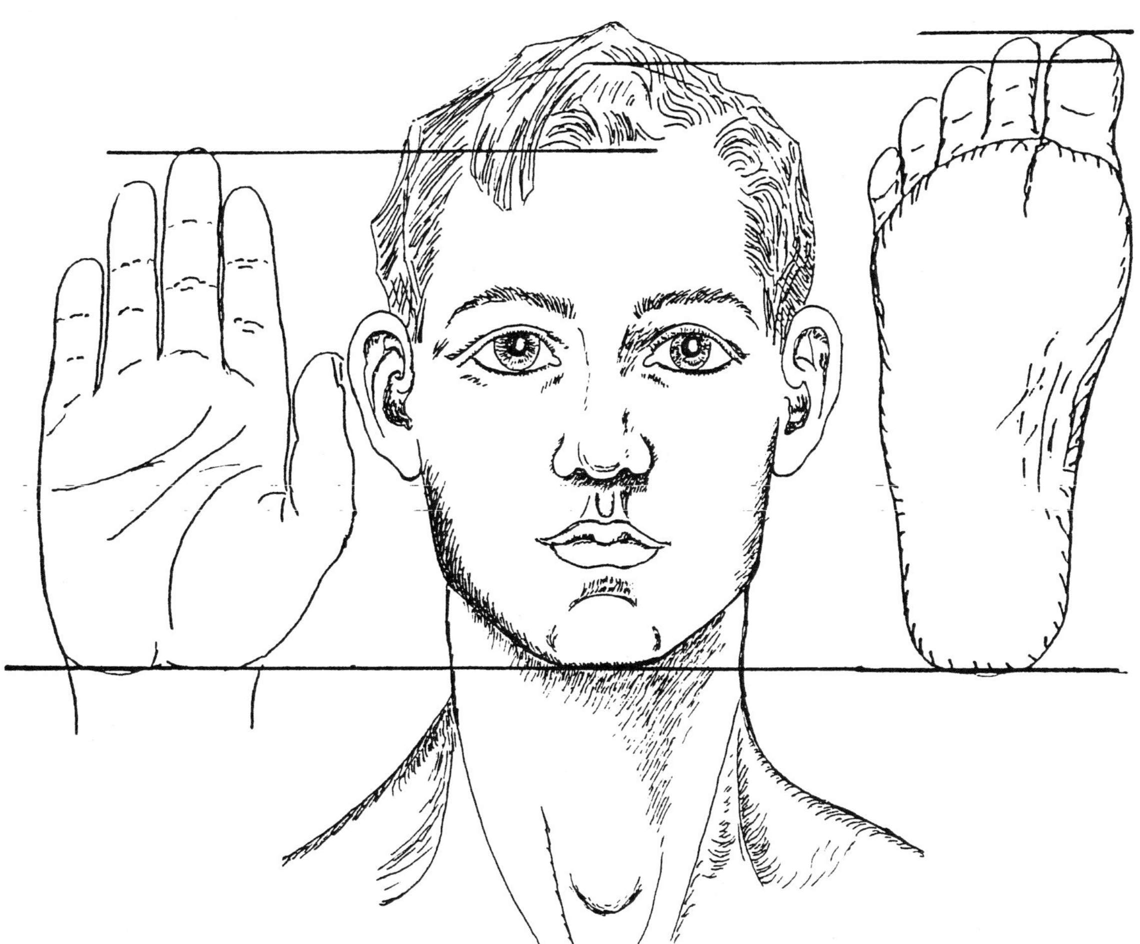

Fig. 8. The masculine head compared to a hand and a foot.

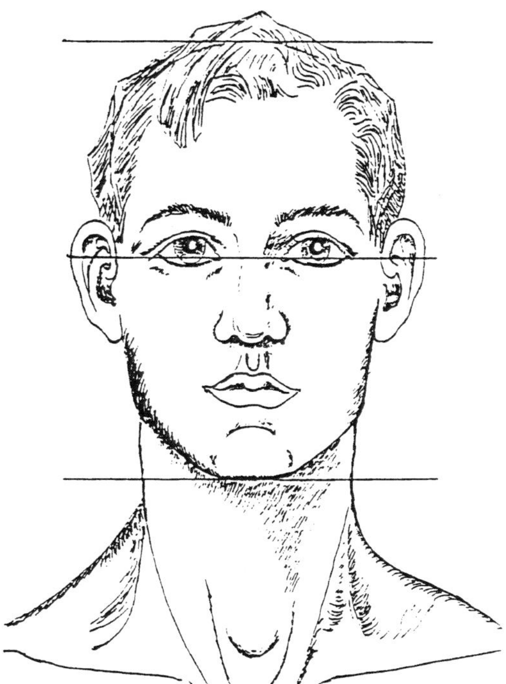

Fig. 9. The head divided into halves.

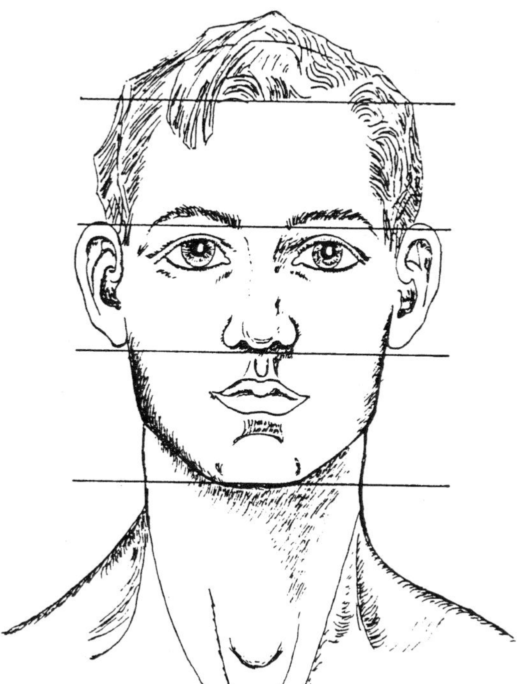

Fig. 10. The face divided into thirds.

The head can be divided in half at the level of the lateral corners of the eyes, and the chin to sternal notch equals ½ head height. The face can be divided into thirds; the chin to base of nose is equal to the base of the nose to the brow, which equals the brow to the hairline. The base of nose to brow equals length of the ear, and the ear is on the same level as the base of the nose to the brow. #310.

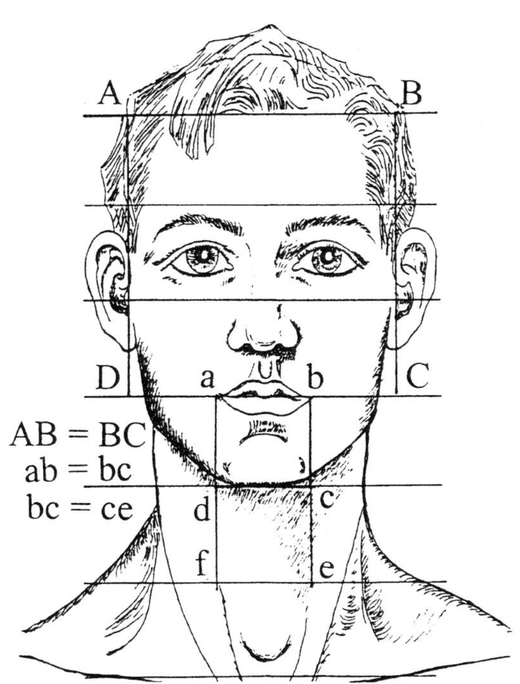

Fig. 11. The face divided into fourths.

MOUTH PROPORTIONS

The mouth aperture, at a line of the parting of the lips, to the chin equals the width of the three middle fingers, #348; equals ¼ face; equals the width of the mouth; equals the chin to throat (at the upper thyroid cartilage of the larynx), a b = b c = c e. The width of the face equals the hairline to mouth aperture or ¾ face height. A B = B C. The mouth aperture to the base of the nose is one seventh face height. #310.

This nearly equals the parting of the lips to the crease below the lower lip. It is also nearly equal (but slightly less) to the distance of that sub-labial crease to the chin. #312. The width of the mouth is equal to the distance between the medial borders of the iris of each of the eyes.

EAR PROPORTIONS

The distance between attach-ments of ears (inter tragion) equals 2/3 the face height. #311.

The opening of the ear canal is over the middle of the neck as seen on lateral view.

The length of the ear equals the length of the thumb.

The width of the ear is ½ thumb length.

The lobe of the ear is ½ thumb length to the angle of the jaw. #317.

The tragus of the ear is ½ the distance between the brow and the nape of the neck. #317, A B = B C.

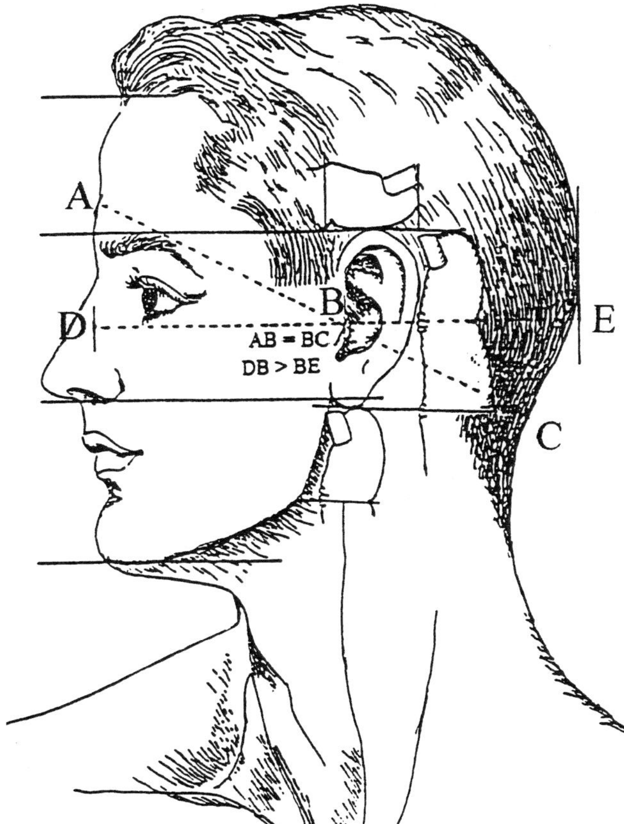

Fig. 12. Proportions of an ear.

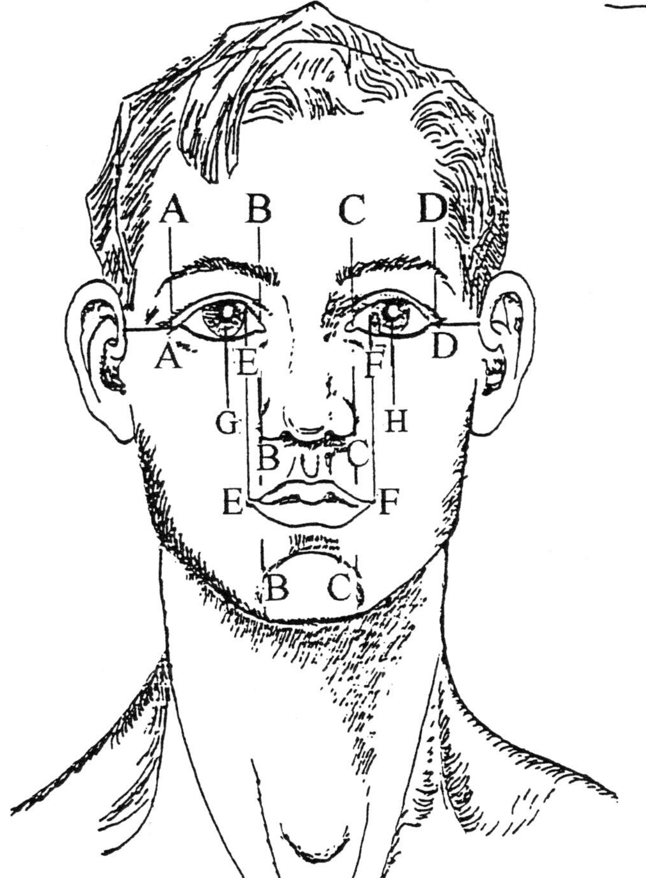

Fig. 13. Proportions of eyes.

EYE PROPORTIONS

The width of an eye equals the width between the eyes. #312, A B = B C = C D.

The space between the center of the pupils of the eyes GH equals 1/3 the face height. #320.

The width between the lateral corners (lateral canthus) A D of the eyes equals 1/2 face height.

The width of the face at eye level equals the distance from hairline to the mouth aperture. #317, 320.

NOSE PROPORTIONS

The width of the nose at the ala, BC, equals the width of an eye, equals the width between the eyes, BC = AD. #319. The ala are wings of the nose.

The nose width equals ½ distance from the tip of nose to brow. The tip of nose to ala, EG, equals the width of the nose at the ala. BC = EG #321.

The junction of the upper lip to the base of the nose is ½ distance of the tip of the nose to the ala, E F = F G.

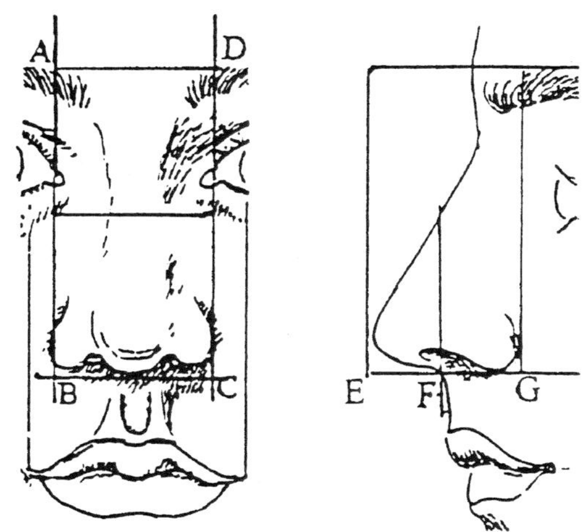

Fig. 14. Nose proportions.

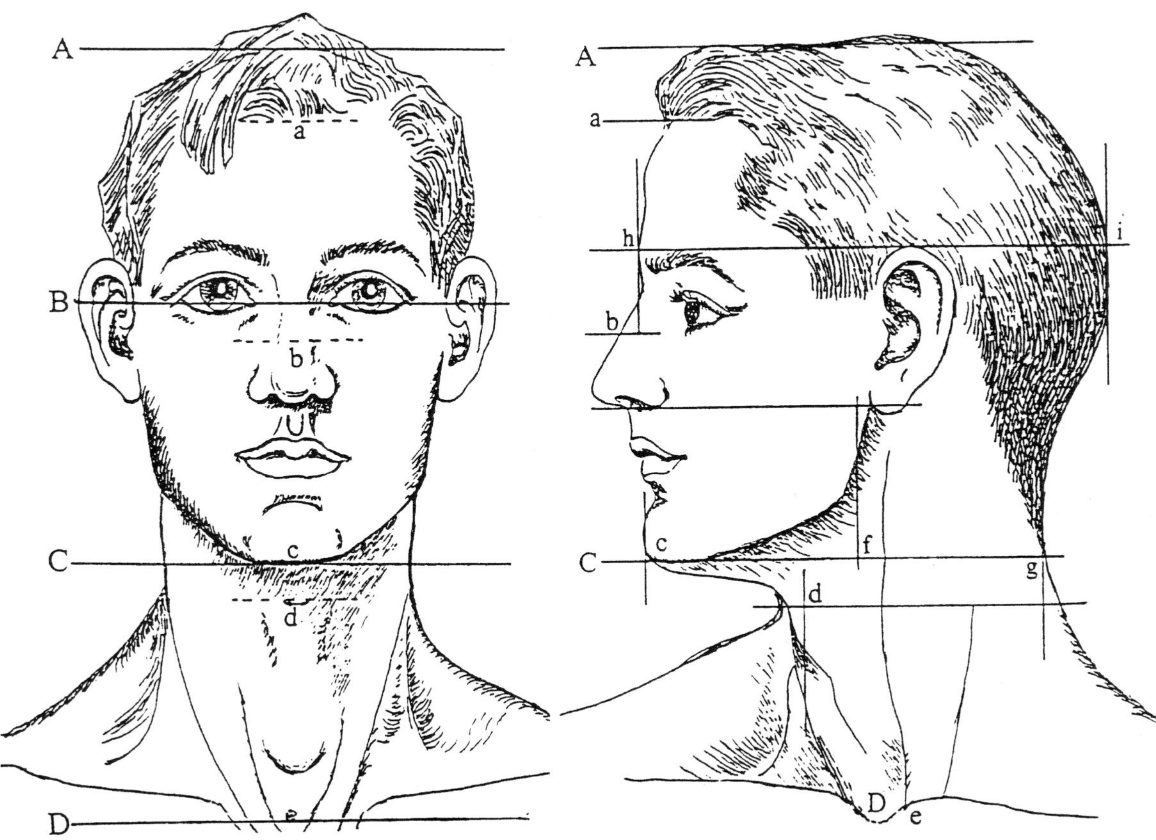

Fig. 15. Neck proportions.

The vertical head proportions of halves are AB = BC = CD. The chin to sternal notch, CD, is half a head height. Vertical face halves are ab = bc, and = de, the larynx to sternal notch. The chin to the back of the neck, Cg, equals ¾ head height, AC. #317. The chin to the angle of the mandible, Cf, nearly equals the thickness of the neck, dg, in profile. The anterior-posterior measurement of the neck, dg, nearly equals ½ head, anterior to posterior measurement, hi, brow to occiput.

RATIOS OF OTHER BODY PROPORTIONS

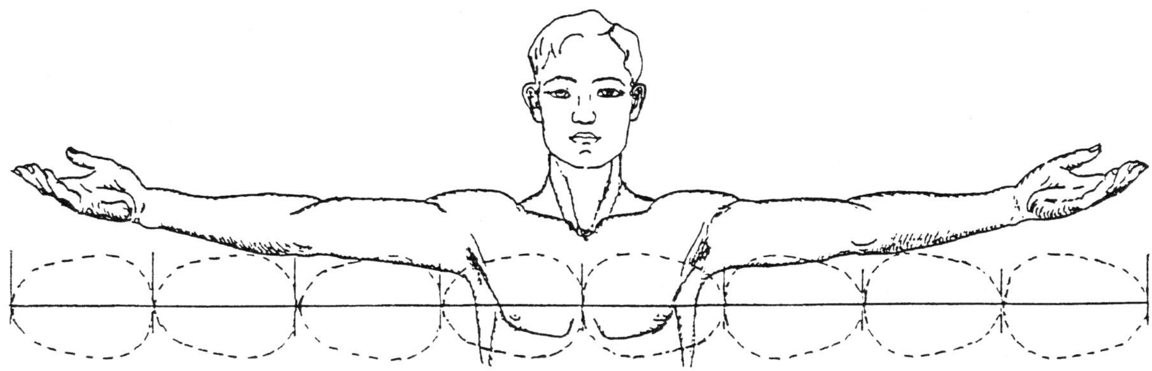

Fig. 16. A man's span equals eight head heights.

The shoulder breadth equals ¼ stature and equals 2 head heights. The anterior to posterior measurement at the level of shoulder equals one head height. #341.

The span, arms outstretched, third fingertip to third fingertip, equals stature and equals eight head heights. #343.

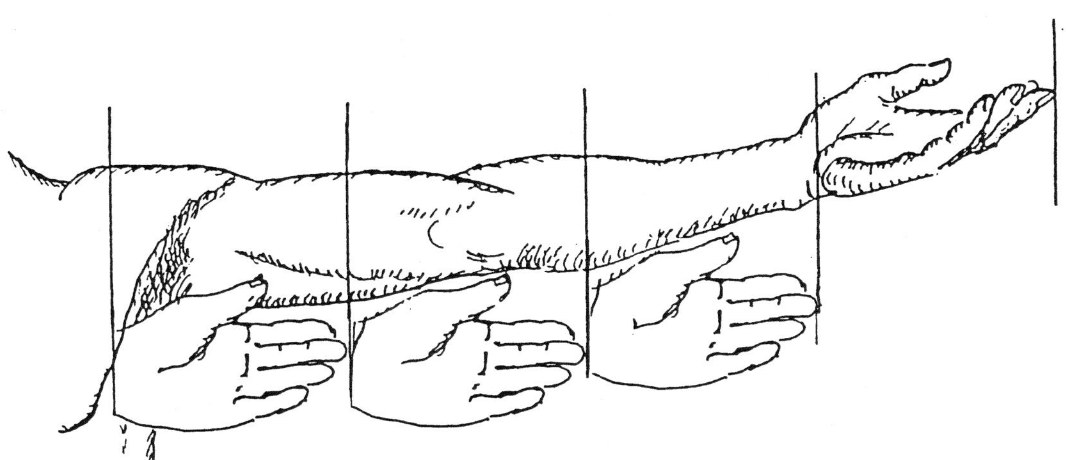

Fig. 17. Shoulder to fingertip is four hand lengths.

The shoulder at the acromion process to the third fingertip of the out-stretched arm equals four face heights or four hand lengths. #345.

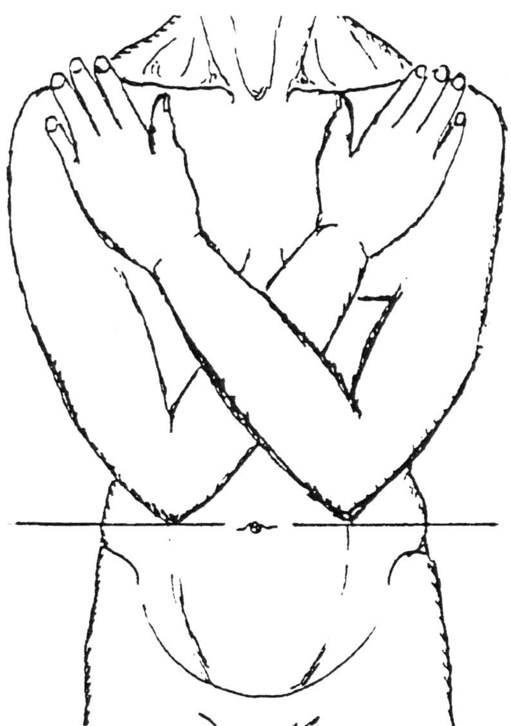

Fig. 18. Arms folded.

When the arms are folded across the chest, the elbow tips are at the level of the umbilicus. #332.

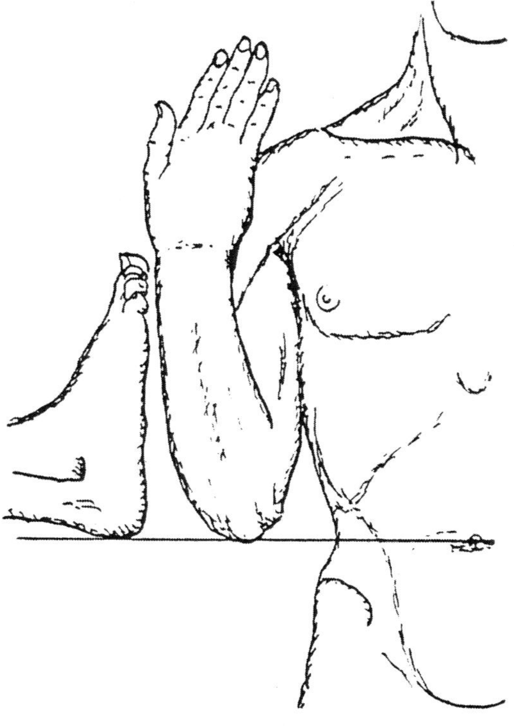

Fig. 19. Wrist to elbow.

The measure from wrist to the tip of the elbow at the olecranon process is equal to a foot length or a head height. #327.

The anterior axillary width of the male figure at armpits equals the hip width, A B = C D, about 14 inches or 35.1 cm. #342.

The thickness of the arm at the shoulder is 1/6 the distance between shoulders, EA = 1/6 EF, 3 inches or 7.5 cm. #334.

The breadth of the thinnest part of the torso, the waist in a lean male figure, equals a foot length, about 11 inches or 21.5 cm. #337.

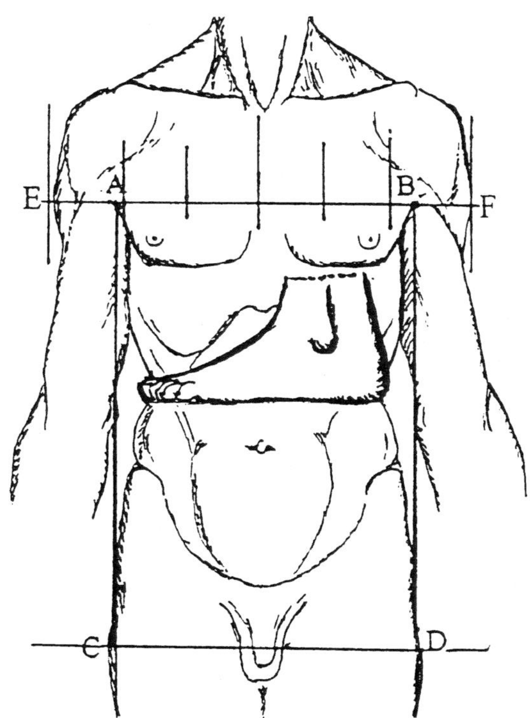

Fig. 20. Anterior axillary width of male.

ARM COMPARISONS

When the arm is flexed at the elbow, the distance from the base of the third finger, metacarpal-phalangeal joint, to the elbow is two hands, and the distance from the elbow to the acromion process (point of the shoulder) is two hand lengths, and the acromion process is nearly at the distal (farthest) inter-phalangeal joint of the thumb. #348.

If one measures the outstretched arm, from the acromion process at the shoulder to the fingertip, and compares it to a sum of the measurements of a flexed arm from the acromion process to the olecranon process (at the point of the elbow) plus the distance of the flexed elbow to the fingertip, it would appear that the sum of the parts is greater than the whole.

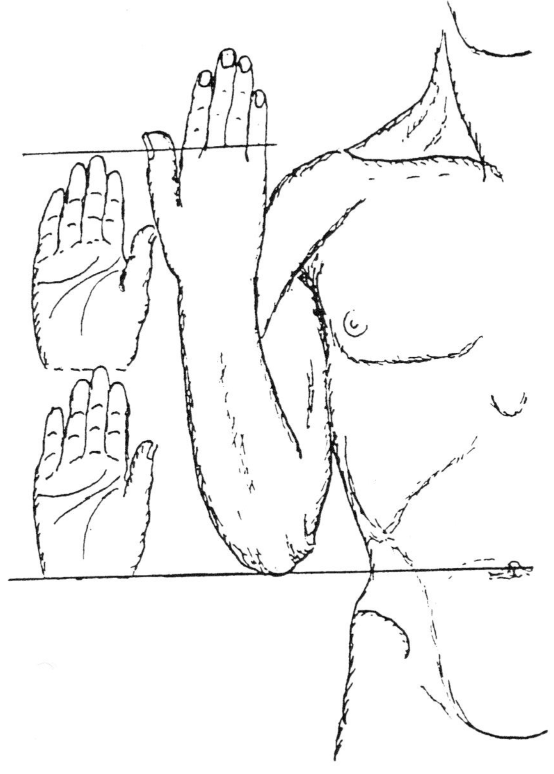

Fig. 21. Arm–hand comparison.

When the arm is extended at the shoulder but the elbow is flexed, the middle finger touches the midline of the sternum. The upper arm from the elbow pivot to axillary pivot to the sternal notch is two head heights. The forearm and hand also equal two head heights. (Since the hand is a face height, the forearm measure is two head heights minus a face height.)

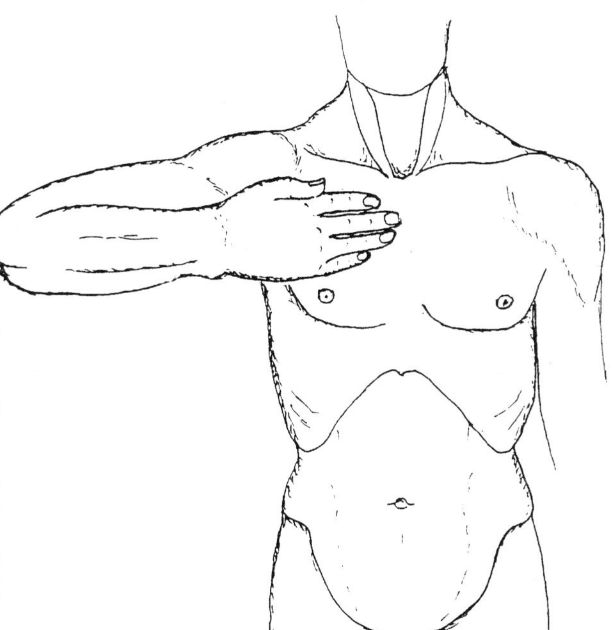

Fig. 22. Fingertip touches sternum.

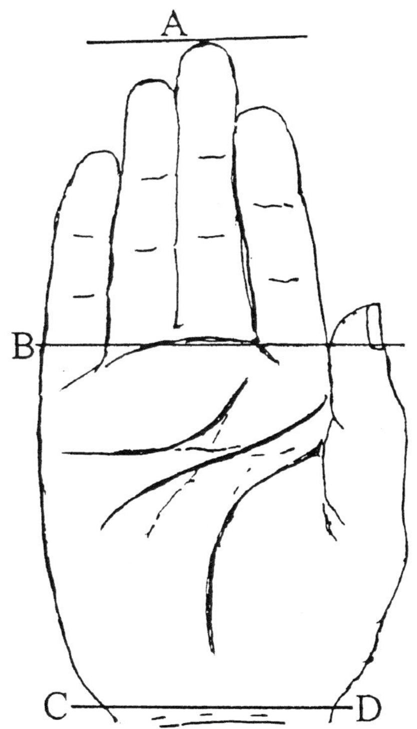

Fig. 23. Hand proportions.

HAND PROPORTIONS

The hand length equals face height. The palm length, BC, approximates ½ hand length, AC, but is slightly longer. The wrist width, CD, equals 1/3 hand length, AC. #348.

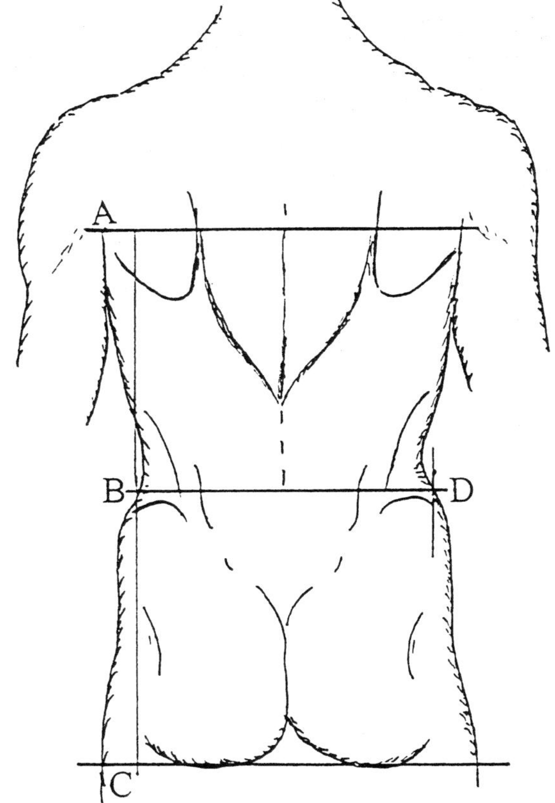

Fig. 24. Back proportions.

BACK PROPORTIONS

The axilla or armpit to the narrow of waist equals the waist to the buttock furrow, AB = BC #342. Note: this is approximate because the narrow of the waist is not well defined, and may be considered above the crest of the ilium or the inferior rib margin. That measurement may equal the crest of ilium to posterior fold of the axilla (arm pit), which is also soft tissue and not well defined. Furthermore, the anterior axillary fold is higher than the posterior axillary fold.

The width across the hips, inter-trochanteric, is nearly equal to the distance from the top of the hips at the crest of the ilium to the bottom of the buttocks at the gluteal furrow, B C to C D. #342.

When the loins or back is flexed, bent forward, the lower border of the breasts are below the level of the lower tips of the scapulae or shoulder blades. If the back is erect, the breasts are on the same level as the lower borders of scapulae, and if the back is extended, or arched backward, the breasts will be above the level of the tips of the scapulae. #357.

FOOT COMPARISONS

The big toe at the web (notch) to toe tip is 1/6 length of the foot. #322.

The hand equals the heel to base of first toe at the joint. It equals ¾ foot length. It also equals the distance from the medial maleolus of the tibia, (the prominence on the inner aspect of the ankle) to the tip of the big toe, that is also ¾ foot length. #324. See Fig. 27.

The width of the hand equals the width of the foot, A B = CD. #324.

The width of the heel equals the width of the wrist, EF = GH. It also equals the width of the narrowest part of the ankle. #324.

The heel to base of the first toe (at the metatarso-phalangeal joint) equals the heel to base of the fifth toe equals a hand length. It also equals ¾ length of the foot.

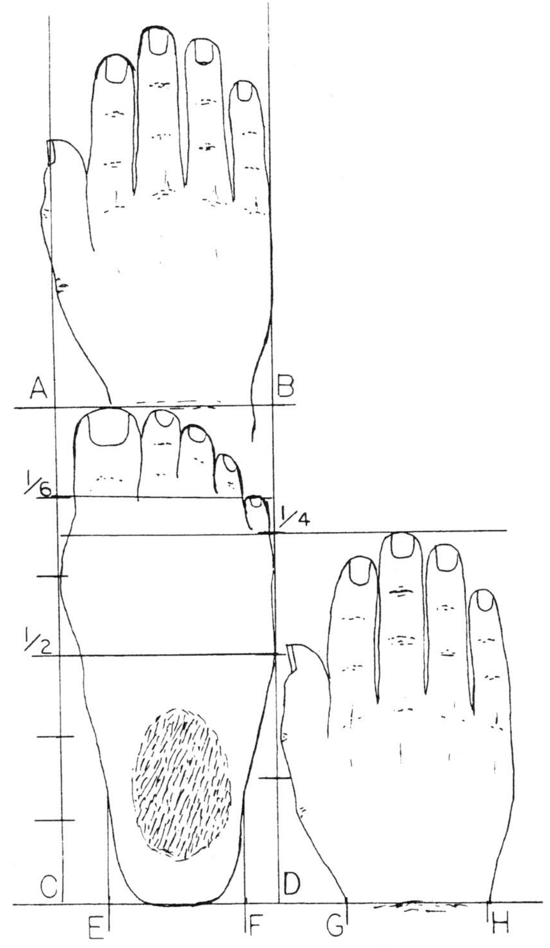

Fig. 25. Foot and hand comparison.

The length of the sole of the foot equals two palm lengths. #324.

The width of the ankle at the maleoli, ankle bony prominences, equals the shortest anterior-posterior ankle diameter. #323.

When joints are flexed the inner tissues of joints become a hollow or concavity. When joints are extended the hollow becomes a fullness or a convexity. #350.

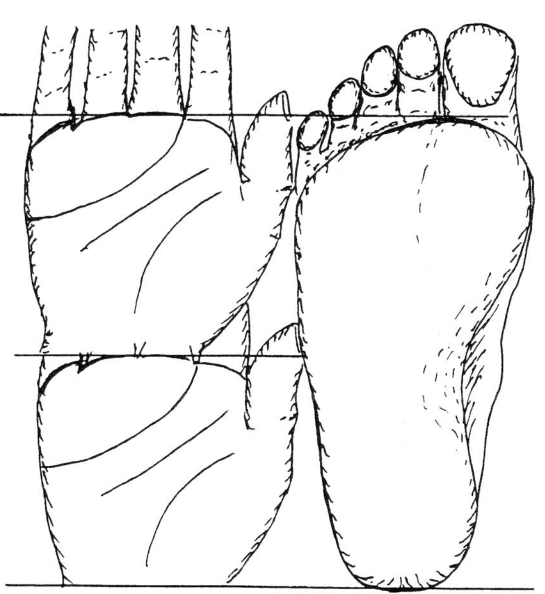

Fig. 26. Palm and sole comparison.

The hand length from the spinous process of the radius to the third finger tip is nearly equal to the distance from the medial maleolus at the ankle of the foot to the tip of the first toe. #323.

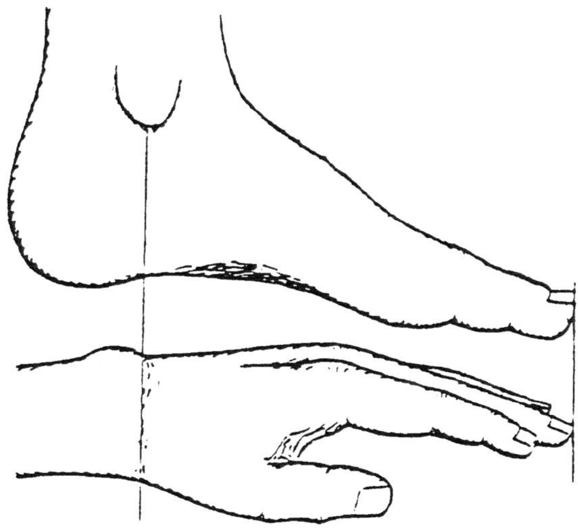

Fig. 27. Hand to foot length comparison.

THE LEG PROPORTIONS

The sole to the knee joint where the fibula meets the femur equals twice the length of the foot. It is usually slightly less than two average foot lengths # 329.

The sole to knee joint equals ¼ stature and equals the knee joint to base of genitals. # 329. This dimension is usually less than four average foot lengths.

The narrowest lateral width of the leg, at the ankle, goes eight times from the sole of the foot to the knee and is the same as the width of the wrist. #331.

Additional hand and foot details are illustrated following the chapter on Symmetry.

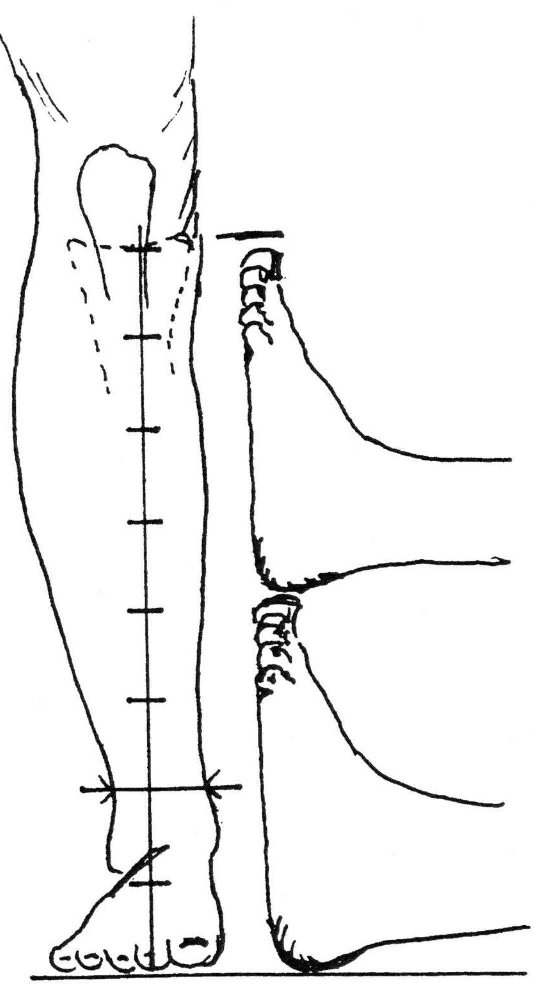

Fig. 28. Foot and leg comparison.

A listing of proportions with comparison of head and of face measurements to other body features may be helpful and easily recalled: Note, in the series of carefully measured proportions listed later in this book, the average foot is 11 inches, or 27.8 cm, for the ideal man of 72 inches or 183 cm height, and the head is 9 inches, or 23 cm. However, da Vinci's observations may serve as a helpful, interesting and approximate guide for quick reference.

LEONARDO DA VINCI'S COMPARISONS

Face height = a hand length.
Face x 1/4 = width of mouth.
Face x 1/4 = mouth aperture to chin.
Face x 1/3 = hairline to brow.
Face x 1/3 = brow to nostrils.
Face x 1/3 = nostrils to chin.
Face x 1/2 = between lateral eye corners.
Face x 1/2 = top of throat (at larynx) to sternal notch.
Face x 2/3 = between attachments of ears.
Face x 3/4 = hairline to mouth aperture.
Face x 4 = outstretched arm, at the point of shoulder to fingertip.
Face x 9 = stature, crown-sole = span fingertip to fingertip.

Head height = a foot length, approximately.
Head x 1/2 = neck length, chin to sternal notch.
Head x 1/2 = neck anterior-posterior.
Head x 3/4 = chin to nape of neck.
Head x 1 = elbow to wrist.
Head x 1 = anterior-posterior of thorax.
Head x 2 = sole to tibia at knee.
Head x 2 = tibia at knee to base of genitals, and genital base- to sternal notch.
Head x 2 = shoulder width at acromion process, point of shoulder.
Head x 4 = sternal notch to fingertip.
Head x 8 = stature, crown-sole = span, fingertip to fingertip.

A recumbent man's vertical measurement of the chest, posterior to anterior, is 1/9 his vertical stature. #338.

Albrecht Dürer, who lived in Nuremberg, Germany, was a prolific artist and became famous for his woodcuts. He also had a special interest in human proportions, made many sketches with notes, and in 1528 prepared manuscripts entitled *Four Books On Human Proportions.* It was published as an illustrated book after his death, entitled the *Dresden Sketchbook.* It has been recently republished as *The Human Figure By Albrecht Dürer, The Complete Dresden Sketchbook.* It is interesting to review, but has fewer comparisons, and is more difficult to follow than da Vinci's studies. It has not been used in this study.

REFERENCES

Douglas, R. Langton. *Leonardo da Vinci, His Life and His Pictures.* Chicago: The University of Chicago Press, 1944.

Fabri, Ralph. "The Art of Ancient Greece, II Self-Limitations in Greek Sculpture," *Today's Art.* Summer 1957:V-7: 7.

Fairbanks, Avard F. *Anatomical Design: A Dissertation Submitted in Partial Fulfillment of the Requirements of Doctor of Philosophy Degree at the University of Michigan.* Ann Arbor, Michigan: 1936.

Fairbanks, Jonathan L. *America's Measure of Mankind: Proportions and Harmonics Sculpture. 1800-1940.* Smithsonian Studies in American Art. 2.1, 1988: 73-87.

"How Long Is a Rod?" *Historical Review of the Measurement of Length.* Ford Motor Company. 7126, 3-39.

Richter, Jean Paul. *The Notebooks of Leonardo da Vinci.* Compiled and edited from the original manuscripts, in two volumes. London: Sampson Low, Marston, Searle, & Rivington, 1883. New York: Dover Publications, 1970.

Strauss, Walter L. *The Human Figure by Albrecht Dürer, The Complete Dresden Sketchbook.* New York: Dover Publications, 1972.

Translated by Morris Hickey Morgan. New York: Dover Publications, 1960.

Van Loon, Hendrik Willem. *The Arts.* New York: Simon and Schuster, 1937: 286-292.

Vitruvius, (Marcus Vitruvius Pollio). *Vitruvius, The Ten Books on Architecture.* Translated by Morris Hickey Morgan. New York: Dover Publications, 1960.

Weaver, Kenneth F. "How Soon Will We Measure in Metric?" *National Geographic*, July 1977: 287-294.

ANATOMIC RATIO MEASUREMENTS IN HUMAN PROPORTIONS

ANATOMIC RATIOS IN HUMAN PROPORTIONS

The proportions of the human body, as found in a typical 72 inches, 183 cm male figure and a 66 inches, 168 cm female figure, will be considered as representational.

Note: These are not average heights, which are slightly less. All measurements given here and shown in the illustrations in this text are these representative types, slightly more robust, and are considered the author's concept of representational.

Artists using these proportions are advised that the basis for measurements listed was a tabulation of about fifty individuals, selected by the preferred heights. They were primarily of Northwestern European descent, since this population was more available to the sculptor.

Twenty-five each of young, mature adult males and females were chosen with stature near to the height to be considered representational. For greater consistency and correlation of the details, careful measurements were made to calculate the average of these measurements. Further measurements were gathered from articulated skeletons of near representational stature in the medical laboratories of the University of Michigan.

To consider the measurements of averages would approach the subject differently and could lead to an entirely different conclusion. However, on the subject of averages, very exhaustive researches have been made by Quetelet of Belgium. In his book *Anthropometrie*, he gives us tables on averages and selected models. Ales Hrdlicka's book, *Old Americans*, gives excellent data on the measurement of Americans. I have consulted both of these books while developing the typical figure that I present here.

There is a general conception that to divide a design into halves or thirds causes the design to lose certain subtleties. The ease with which a form is readily analyzed this way might seem to lessen the interest in the object, a fact that is quite noticeable in very simple geometric patterns, such as square shapes. Plastic design such as in sculpture cannot actually move in a manner that many other forms of expression are able to do, since the maintenance of interest on a fixed surface becomes very important.

A rather interesting corollary may be noticed in studies of the entire figure and of the face. Halves and thirds seem to be prevalent. The head is 1/8th of the total, just as the hair above the forehead is 1/8th of the vertical head length. The figure, excluding the head, is then divided into thirds to gain the leg length. This process establishes three main lengths: those of the lower leg, sole to knee; at the patella or knee cap, the knee to the crest of ilium; and of the body, crest of ilium to chin. An inverted arch in the pelvis is a repetition in reverse of the dome of the thorax and the arch of the rib margins. It creates a drop of one-half head height. This is compensated by neck height, which is also one-half head height. This results in a torso measurement from the pubis to the pit of the neck, or sternal notch, of a similar length. In establishing vertical measures of head, face, nose, leg, or other feature for a typical figure, all one needs to know, to begin modeling, is the proposed overall height of the statue to be created. Illustrations of these proportions are included later in the text for finer details, along with tables for several different fractions of life size. There are subtle differences in the torso proportions of male and female as listed on the following pages.

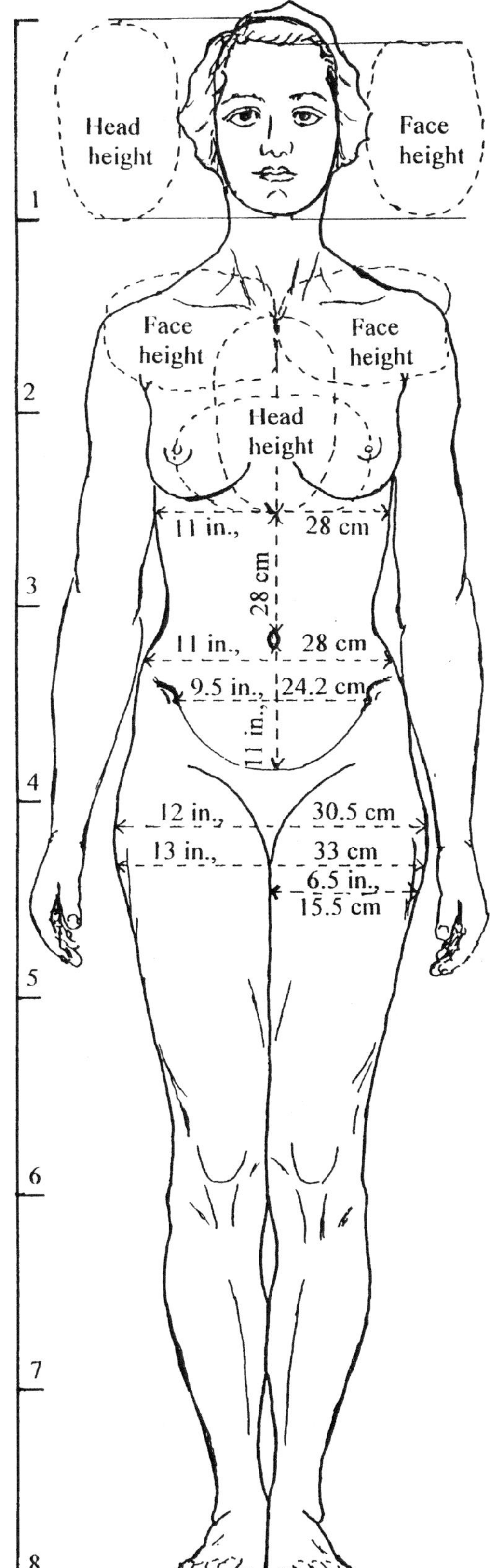

Fig. 29. Female proportions.

FEMALE PROPORTIONS

The distance from the sternal notch to the tip of the xiphoid process of the sternum or breast bone is one head height: 8 in., 20.4 cm.

The width between the nipples is one head height: 8 in., 20.4 cm.

The depth from sternum at the level of the nipple to scapula is one head height: 8 in., 20.4 cm.

The vertical distance of the abdomen from the tip of the xiphoid process of the sternum or breast bone to the pubis is 1/6 total height: 11 in., 28.0 cm.

The umbilicus is 1/2 the distance between xiphoid and pubis. This measurement is equal to 1/12 total height: 5.5 in., 14.0 cm.

The breadth of the shoulders is two face heights: 14 in., 35.6 cm.

The breadth of the thorax equals the width between anterior superior spines of ilium equals the vertical length of the abdomen, xiphoid to pubis, and is 1/7 height: 9.5 in., 24.2 cm.

The breadth between the anterior superior spines of the ilium is 1/7 stature: 9.5 in., 24.2 cm.

The breadth between the crests of the ilium is approximately 1/6 stature: 9.5 in., 24.2 cm.

The depth of the thigh at the gluteal region is one head height: 8 in., 20.3 cm.

The breadth between the greater trochanters of both femurs: 12 in., 30.5 cm.

The breadth between fleshy portions just below greater trochanters: 13 in., 33 cm.

The diameter of one thigh is: 6.5 in., 16.5 cm.

MALE PROPORTIONS

The distance from the sternal notch to the tip of the xiphoid process of the sternum breast bone is one head height: 9 in., 22.9 cm.

The width between the nipples is one head height: 9 in., 22.9 cm.

The depth from sternum at the level of the nipple to scapula is one head height: 9 in., 22.9 cm.

The vertical distance of the abdomen from the tip of the xiphoid process of the sternum breast bone to the pubis is 1/6 total height: 12 in. 30.5 cm.

The umbilicus is 1/2 distance between xiphoid and pubis. This measurement is equal to 1/12 total height: 6 in. 15.3 cm.

The breadth of the shoulders is two head heights: 18 in., 45.8 cm.

The breadth of the thorax equals the height of the abdomen, xiphoid to pubis, which equals the breadth between iliac crests and is 1/6 height: 12 in., 30.5 cm.

The breadth between the anterior superior spines of the ilium is 1/7 stature: 10 in., 25.4 cm.

The breadth between the crests of the ilium is approximately 1/6 stature: 12 in., 30.5 cm.

The depth of the thigh at the gluteal region is one face height: 8 in., 20.3 cm.

The breadth between the greater trochanters of both femurs: 13 in., 33 cm.

The breadth between fleshy portions just below greater trochanters: 14 in., 35.5 cm.

The diameter of one thigh is 7 in., 17.8 cm.

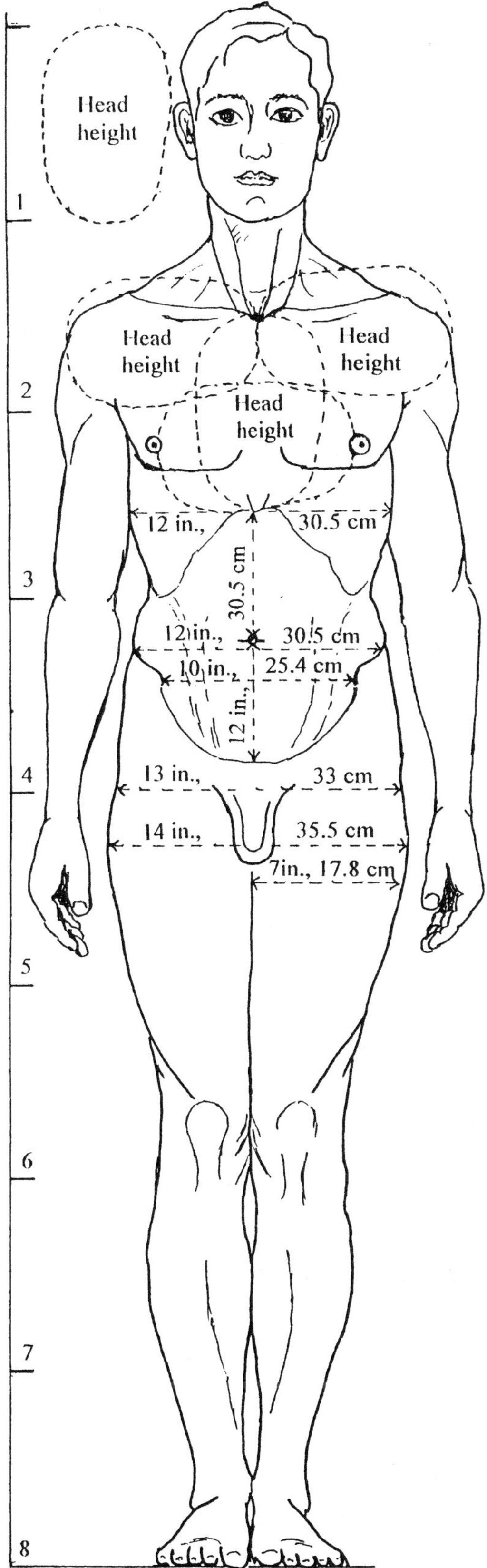

Fig. 30. Male proportions.

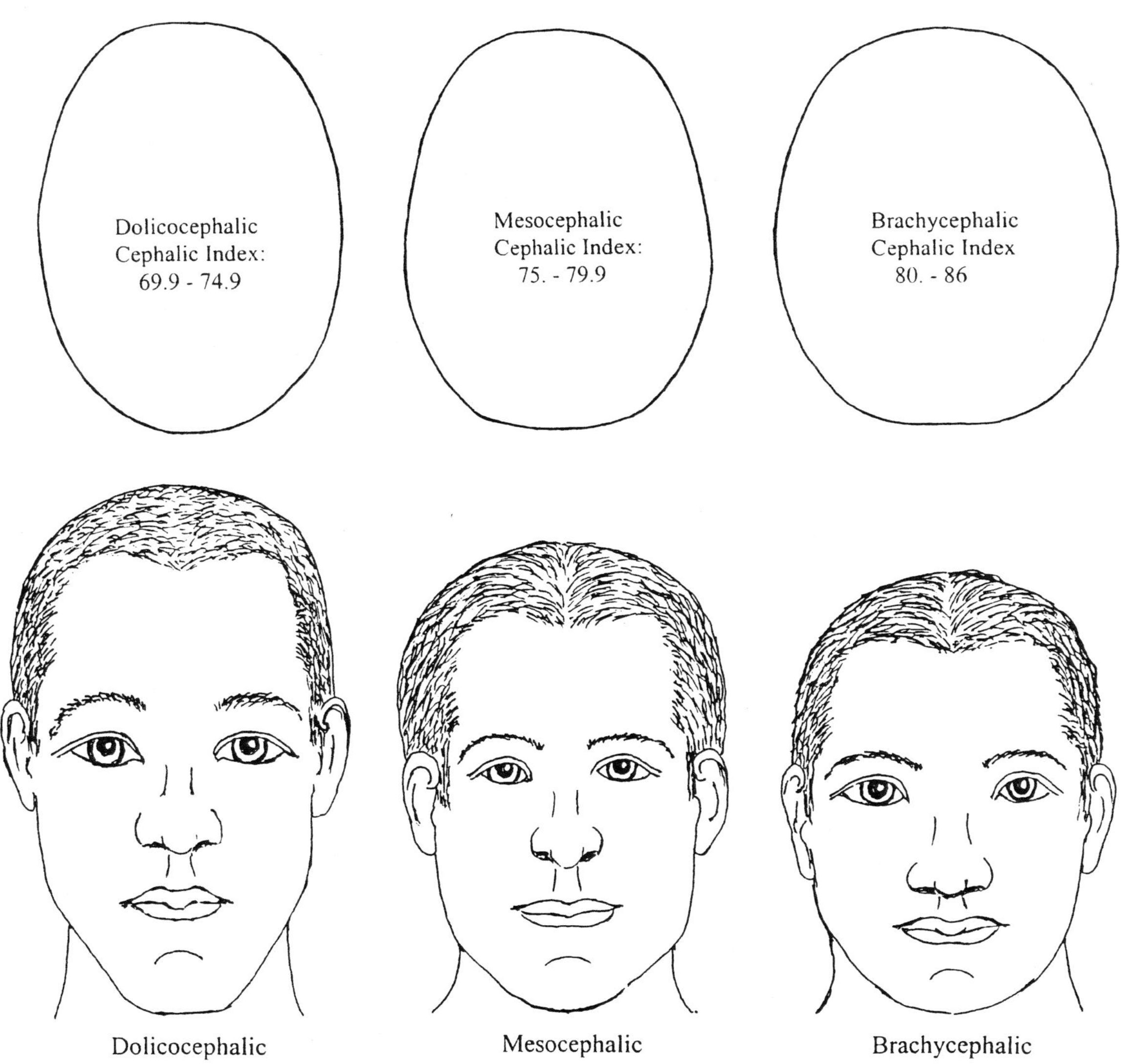

Fig. 31. Cephalic, Head, indices.

There are some ethnic differences and minor difference of measurements when portrayals of Native Americans, African Americans, or Asian Americans are considered. However, the relative proportions are similar with only minor variations. The most common observed differences involve the ratios of individual head proportions. These ratios are called cephalic indices; cephalic refers to skull. They are expressed like a percentage of breadth to anterior-posterior measurement by a formula: Cephalic Index = breadth x 100 divided by the anterior-posterior measure.

An index of 70 to 74.9 is called dolicocephalic; an index of 75 to 79.9 is termed mesochephalic; and an index of 80 to 80.5 is called brachycephalic. Many African Americans and Caucasian of Nordic descent have heads considered to be dolico-cephalic, meaning longer anterior-posterior and vertical measurements. Most Caucasians are mesocephalic, while many Native Americans and Asian Americans are brachycephalic. The cephalic index has no relation to skin color.

When creating art of any culture, a living model is recommended, and careful

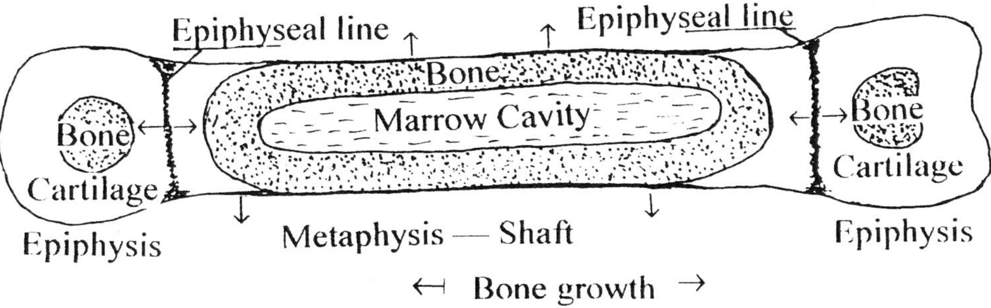

Fig. 32. A growing infant long bone.

measurements with attention to details is important. The tabulated proportions that are included serve as a guide, an example, but not as a stereotyped format. Individuals vary considerably. Just as there are practically no persons that are average, there are none that are typical or representative. The skillful artist will make alterations to suit the expression desired. Other alterations are needed for demonstration of age, robust physical development as an athlete or laborer, and any individual characteristic of the subject to be portrayed. Efforts should be made to avoid creating art with multiple repetitions of a prototype, but rather include variety to render a natural realism.

Variations of heights in human form are related to the period of rapid bone growth in youth before maturity. The long bones of the leg, the tibia, fibula, and femur, contribute nearly two thirds of height. During development in puberty, these bones grow lengthwise at the epiphyses near the bone ends. Lateral bone growth results in bone tissue created by the periostium, a tough membrane adherent to the shaft. The longer the person's period of bone growth before maturity, the longer these bones grow, and the taller the person becomes. As a result there may be considerable variations from the listed, representative, proportions.

Another variable in growth is that not all epiphyses grow at the same rate. Some epiphyses in one individual fuse earlier than others and there are variations in maturation of the bones of individuals.

Body types are classified as dolicomorphic, a tall and slender body configuration; mesomorphic, a medium body configuration; and brachymorphic, a short and stocky body configuration. The body configurations, illustrated in these studies of human proportions are essentially mesomorphic types. Another body configuration modifier is the distribution of fatty deposits that can affect all body somatic types. Body types are generally inherited characteristics. There are also some changes in body fat distribution and skeletal structure with advancing age. These factors are not addressed in this study of young adults.

The longitudinal body and leg proportions of the figure charts may be thought of in the following simple illustrated explanations: to find the leg height, sole to knee, divide the distance from the sole to chin by three.

BODY DIVISION OF THIRDS

The head is 1/8th of the total figure, and the neck is one half head height

Subtract this head height. It leaves 7/8ths from the chin to the sole

Divide this 7/8ths into three parts.

1/3rd is the torso vertical measure from the sternal notch to the symphysis pubis.

1/3rd is thigh length from the anterior superior spine of the ilium to the anterior prominence of the patella or knee-cap.

1/3rd is lower leg length from patella to the sole of the foot.

It should be noted that the torso measure was not from the chin to the hip, but from sternal notch to pubis. It is, however, the same distance as the chin to the anterior superior spine of the ilium.

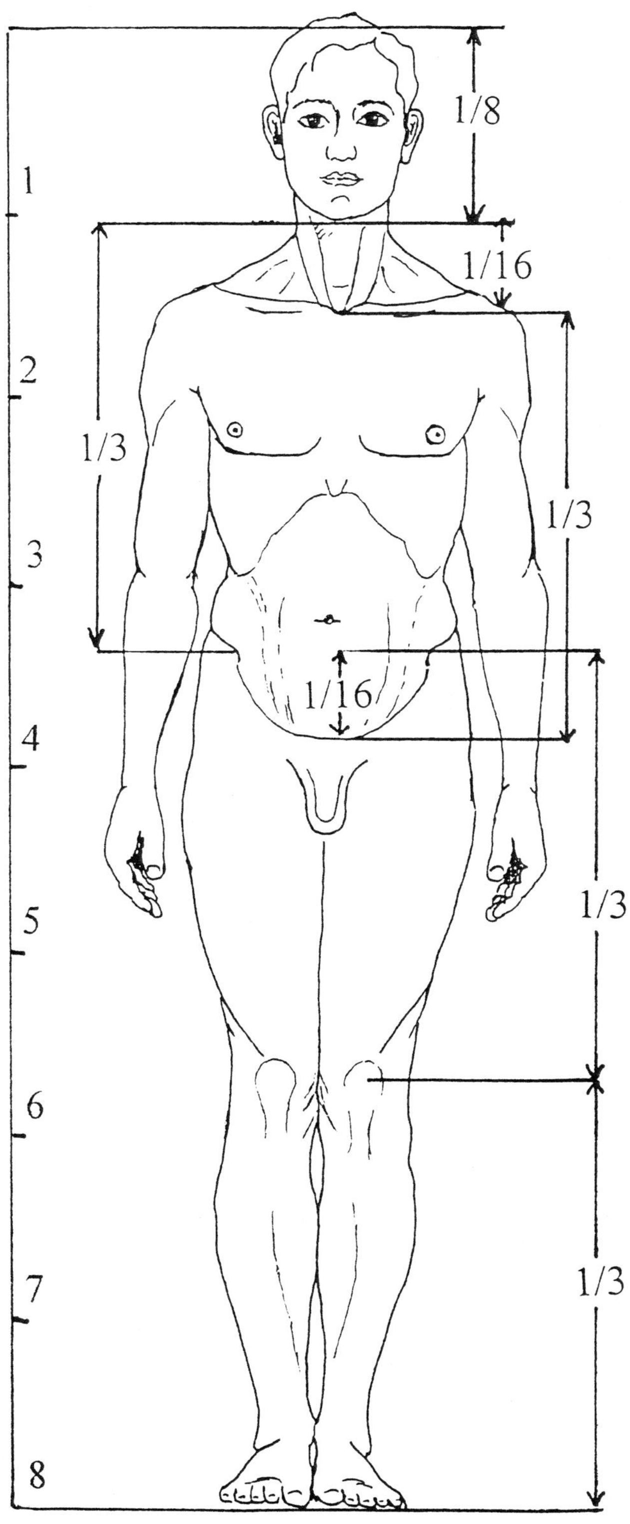

Fig. 33. Body proportions are divided into thirds.

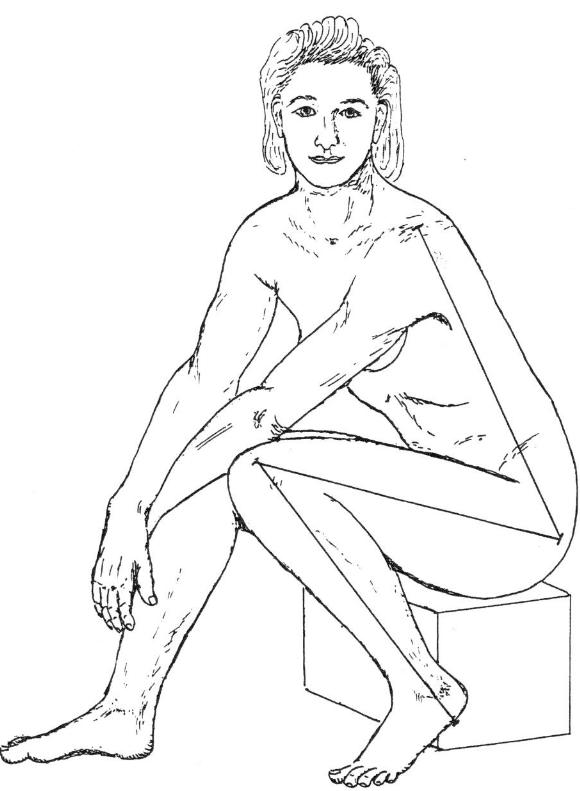

Fig. 34a. The human figure folds into thirds.

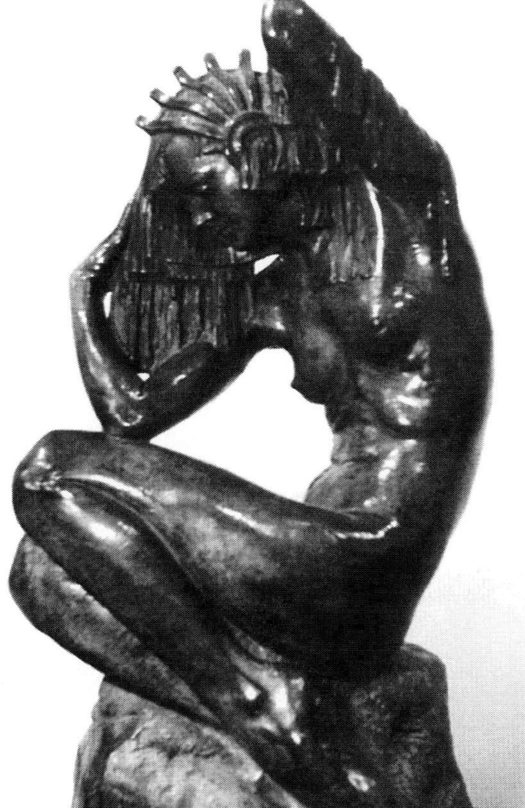

Fig. 34b. Rain, a bronze sculpture by Avard Fairbanks, also illustrates the human figure folding into thirds.

An illustration with flexion of the knees and hips demonstrates how the human figure may fold into approximate thirds. The torso is about the same measure as the thigh and the lower leg. This flexion into thirds is even more apparent when a human assumes a squatting position. Sitting is more familiar to persons in modernized and developed nations, but squatting is frequently observed in primitive populations during leisure periods as a means of rest.

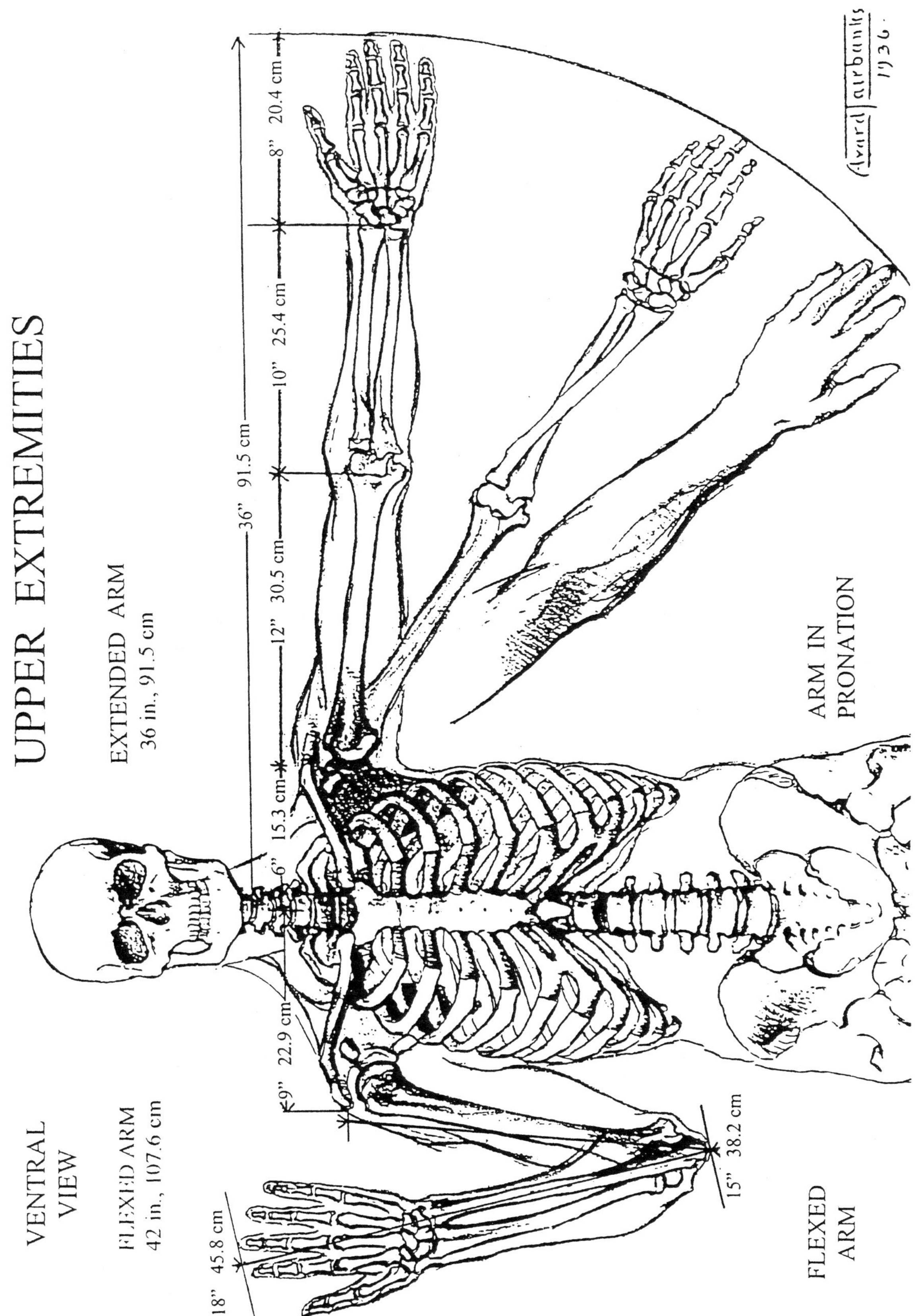

Fig. 35. Upper extremity measurments.

MEASUREMENTS OF THE UPPER EXTREMITIES

Determining the correct proportions of the arms has always been a troublesome problem to the artist. The sum of the measurements of all the segments of a flexed arm would become a few inches longer than the measurement of the fully extended arm. It may be noticed in the drawing on proportions by Leonardo da Vinci that the two extended arms have the same measurement as the total height of the figure, making the square of the human form. A six foot male figure, according to his plan, would have for one outstretched arm length, from the sternal notch, a measurement of 36 in., 91.4 cm. Generally, when making measurements of the flexed arm of a six foot figure, one discovers that the various units are the following lengths:

From **sternal notch** to the **acromion process** of scapula, 9 in., 22.9 cm
From **acromion process** to **flexed elbow** at **olecranon process**, 15 in., 38.1 cm
From **olecranon process** to the **third fingertip**, 18 in., 45.8 cm

The total of all of these measurements is 42 in., 106.7 cm, which may be compared to the 36 in., 91.4 cm, of the arm extended out to the side. We may readily see there is about a 6 in., 15.3 cm, difference between these two measurements. It appears that the sum of the parts are greater than the whole. This is due to the shoulder pivot being closer to the midline than the olecranon process, and the elbow pivot is about two inches from the olecranon process of the elbow. Leonardo da Vinci recognized this difference in his notes and suggested a factor for correction. In practice, to obtain some basis for measuring the arm has been a constant problem in the field of art. The most generally accepted relative measurement of the upper arm, shoulder to elbow, is the length from the sternal notch to the umbilicus. The approximate measurement is equivalent to two hands or two face heights.

Because of numerous contradictions as to the proportions of the arm, we sought a definitive solution. When measuring cadavers in the anatomy laboratory, the manner in which bones fit into each other at the joints was noted. Measurements were then made using the pivots of the joints at the shoulder, the elbow, and the wrist. This demonstrated a constant distance between pivots, regardless of the flexion or extension. When measuring at the bony prominences, at acromion process and olecranon process, instead of at the pivots, the sum demonstrates significant discrepancies found in arm measurement. By determining a pivot at the glenoid fossa or arm socket of the shoulder, the axillary pivot is at the lesser tuberosity of the humerus, which is palpable at the anterior shoulder below the acromion process of the scapula. The elbow pivot is at the lateral epicondyle of the humerus. The measure of flexion and extension would become constant except for the slight arc caused by the raising of the clavicle when the arm is outstretched in extension. This causes the entire shoulder to be lifted slightly.

The distance from the tip of the elbow, the olecranon process, to the outstretched third fingertip (a cubit) does not change on flexion or extension. When flexing the arm, the shoulder to the point of the elbow increases by a distance about equal to the depth of the wrist, dorsal to palmar measurement. #348. This increase of sum of measurements of the flexed arm is due to the olecranon process or point of the elbow moving through an arc when the arm is flexed.

By considering the pivots, a more accurate and new form of arm measurement is possible. On a 6 foot, 183 cm, male figure, utilizing the pivots, the measure of one arm from the sternal notch to the axillary pivot is approximately 6 in., 15.2 cm; the axillary pivot to the elbow pivot is approximately 12 in., 30.5 cm; from the elbow pivot to the wrist pivot or carpal pivot is about 10 in., 25.4 cm; and from the carpal pivot of the wrist at the styloid process of the radius of the forearm to the tip of the middle finger is approximately 8 in., 20.3 cm. The total measure of the flexed arm from the sternal notch to fingertip is 36 in., 91.4 cm, the same as the extended arm would be according to Leonardo da Vinci's system.

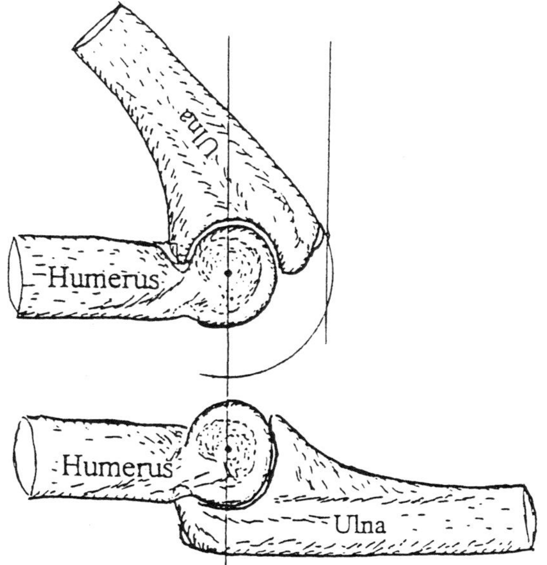

Fig 36. The elbow straight and flexed.

The same is found in the flexed arm.

The illustrations of the masculine figure and the feminine figure, in a later chapter with the proportion tables, graphically shows the results of these measurements. Details of the hands may be noted in the

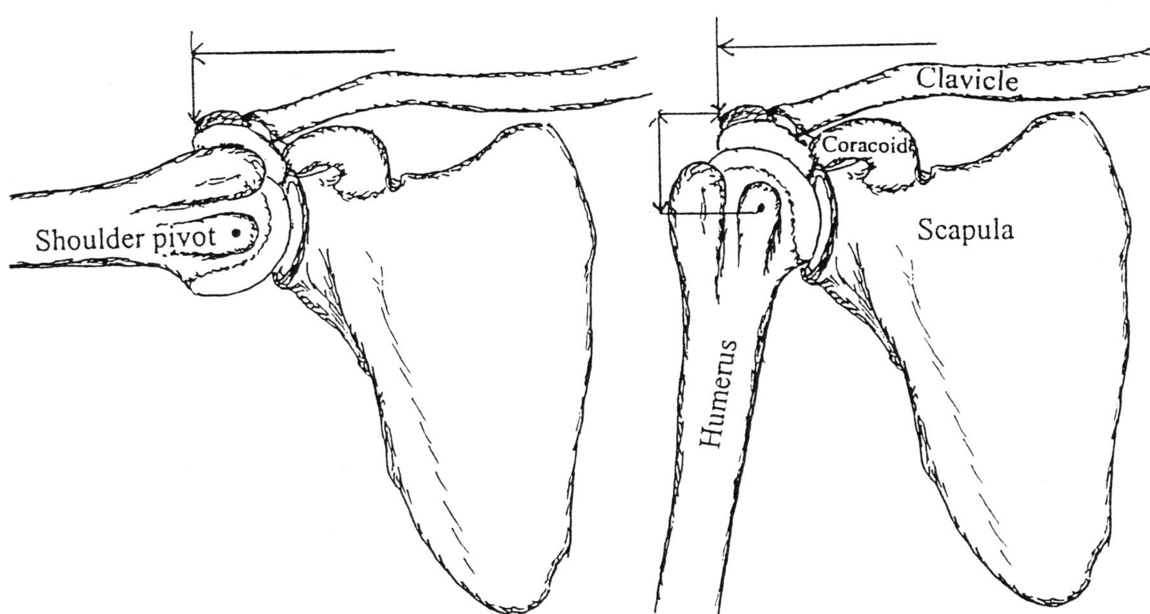

Fig. 37. When the arm hangs vertically, there is a gain in measured length.

illustrations, but for general considerations the middle finger, measured at the dorsal aspect from metacarpal-phalangeal joint to fingertip is 1/2 the hand length. When the hand is 8-in., 20.4 cm, the middle finger from its base to tip would be 4 in., 10.2 cm. The thumb length from its base, first metacarpo-phalangeal joint to tip, is one-half the distance from the carpal pivot to thumb tip, about 5 in., 12.7 cm. In addition the thumb length, proximal and distal phalanx, is nearly equal to the nose length, tip to brow, and vertical length of the ear. Additional hand features are more completely discussed in a later chapter.

ANATOMICAL DESIGN

It is the knowledge of law and order that leads the mind of man from chaos into the realm of reason, from confusion and mental bondage to freedom, and from mystery to understanding. Design in itself implies order.

Cells, the units of life, arrange themselves into forms that become structural and functional organisms. They develop according to design arrangements. Organic construction is based upon principles, much the same as those that determine the orderly arrangements of inorganic forms as crystals. However, because of the increased functions of living organisms, the laws governing their forms and arrangements become more complex. Through analysis and study, one finds that organic and inorganic structures are based upon laws that have shaped them into definite patterns creating orderly design forms.

Just as the scientist is deeply concerned with morphology, which is the study of forms and structure of organized beings, so also artists and the designers should concern themselves with the study of structures and principles governing their arrangement. The understanding of human growth and development can be of great value to artists, not only in knowing life and in presenting its functional arrangements, but also in making the objects of art express significance and bespeak our cultural outlook. The primary purpose of a subject, Anatomical Design, is to correlate the artistic concepts of design with the scientific study of the human form.

The artist, in the study of anatomical charts, sees a conglomeration of muscles and bones together with an innumerable list of unfamiliar and unintelligible names. The drawing together of all these into designs is at first not very interesting. The study is seen as aids to knowing why there are bumps and hollows on the external surface of the human form.

For the artist to know the human body as a structural harmony is quite as necessary as it is for an architect to understand the relationship between the inner structure and the significance and beauty of a house of worship. The human body, considered from a standpoint of science is a structural and functional organism. The artist needs to see it aesthetically as an object of beauty, and to be studied from this latter standpoint. Objectively, the artist has the opportunity to see the human body containing the most subtle and the most highly proportional form of design of any type of creation. Subjectively, the artist may appreciate the human form as the means of expressing the highest concepts of the human consciousness. With the use of the human form as an objective pattern, the artist strives to make lives of people more significant by placing

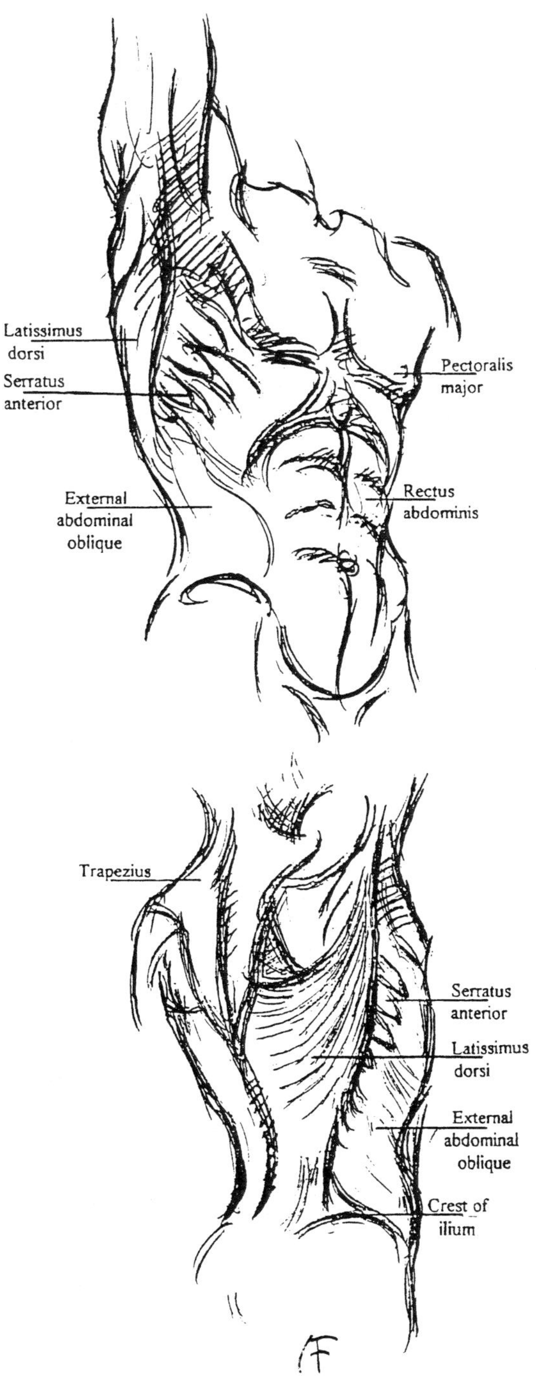

Fig. 38. Muscle forms in action.

examples of aesthetic harmony in creative master-pieces of art for the public to see and appreciate.

The human structure is not particularly an object of beauty when it is in the process of dissection, or when it is considered only in light of anatomical analysis. However, when it is considered from the point of harmony, the arrangement and pattern by which cells form into organs, the organs into systems, the systems into forms, and finally into a human being capable of finer feelings, then the whole is a complete design. It has developed from units built into parts and finally into an individual, an object for aesthetic appreciation like a beautiful temple worthy of our admiration. The harmony of the whole entity is an expression of a unity of all the parts becoming the design, and any complete design must result from the harmony of all of its parts. This leads to a definition of design: the structural basis of forms as they are organized into harmonies, including development, growth, and action.

The typical anatomical diagrams and charts have been recorded by scientific observation much as a building might be designed without particular regard to aesthetic features. To this splendid physical structure, illustrated by the efforts of science, the artist has the opportunity of adding harmonic orders of beautiful forms. The artist's work should lead to a realization that the human form is something beautiful and significant, the dwelling place of man's most treasured concepts.

The artist must so organize his masterpieces, in beautiful proportions, with such orderly lines, masses, and forms that anyone in the presence of the artistic masterpiece feels a sense of reverence, appreciating the elevated harmonic orders of truth and beauty.

Illustration of major muscle masses of the torso are included to demonstrate form in action, manifest by arcs, reversal curves, three dimensional curvilinear triangles, and other geometric figures. The drawing of Rhythmic Analysis demonstrates curved lines that depend on the forms of muscles and bones. There are also grace-

THE LIVING DESIGN

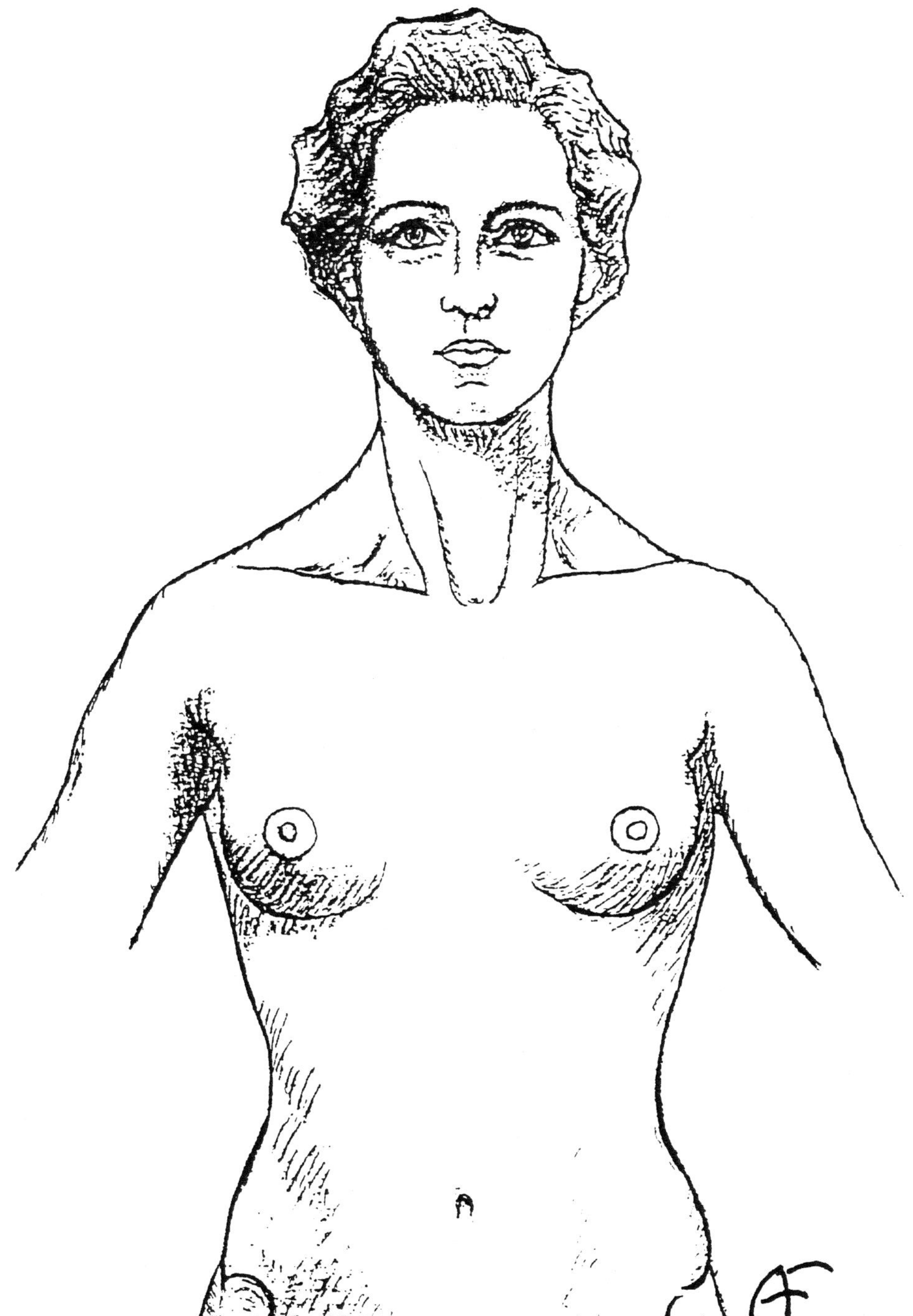

Fig. 39. The living design, female torso.

ful lines and curves in the extremities. The absence of illustrations of underlying muscle masses here should not detract from the beauty of forms. The observant artist will recognize their contribution to harmonic design of the human physique.

Illustrations 39, 40, and 41were adapted from the doctoral thesis of Avard Fairbanks.

A RHYTHMIC ANALYSIS OF THE HEAD AND TORSO

In a geometric analysis, there is a dominance of straight line measurements. Yet the human body is a dynamic entity graced with curved lines and prominent arcs that are modified by "C" and "S" type curves. The three scalenius muscles on each side of the neck give the vertebra lateral stability like guy wires for a telephone pole. They are crossed by the sternocleidomastoid muscles that are active in turning the head. This graceful muscle divides the neck on each side into the anterior and posterior triangles. The anterior triangles are further defined by the border of the mandibles and the midline. It contain the larynx, the thyroid gland, and other tissue. The posterior triangle is bounded by the sternocleidomastoid muscle, the clavicle below and the massive trapezius muscle posteriorly. The clavicles have a gentle "S" or reversal configuration. A sulcus or channel on each side of the clavicles descends from the neck between the scalenius muscles and the upper portion of the trapezius muscle in the posterior and lateral aspects of the neck. These channels continue, under the clavicles or collar bones, providing space for nerves and blood vessels. Continuing, they pass under the anterior borders of the three-dimensional, curvilinear triangles of the deltoid muscles, and on down the arms.

The female breasts overlie the pectoralis muscles and are hemispherical, but assume a tear drop form when the person is erect. The maiden breast extends from the anterior aspect of the second to the sixth rib and from the sternum, or breast bone, laterally to the mid-axillary line, a vertical line starting in the middle of the armpit. Breast tissue lies on the deep fascia, a tendinous membrane, covering the prominent pectoralis major muscle of the upper chest. A lateral extension of the breast tissue turns around the border of the pectoralis major muscle to just below the armpit. Much of the form of the breasts is related to the amount of fat overlying the mammary tissue. Breasts are suspended by a broad fascia, a connective tissue ligament, from the clavicles and pectoral fascia. Since breasts enlarge during lactation, the weight may cause the fascia to stretch. Advancing age may result in relaxation. An increase or decrease in fat, superficial to the disk of mammary tissue, may further alter breast contours. An artist may adjust modeling of a breast to a more youthful and graceful form

There are other graceful forms with configurations that flow and may be parallel, or they may be intersected by other features. There are three-dimensional forms as cylindroid-shaped muscles with tendinous attachments at both ends. Other muscles are strap-like, while abdominal muscles are broad membranes. The rectus muscles of the anterior abdomen have segments with fibrous transverse bands and demonstrate repetition, with the arched tendinous attachments.

The rib margins form an arch above the abdomen, while the pelvis has an inverted arch that complements and reflects the form of the rib margin arch. The inherent beauty of these features is partly obscured by skin and underlying fatty tissue, but the skilled artist recognizes their concealed presence and models them subtly into the masterpiece.

RHYTHMIC ANALYSIS

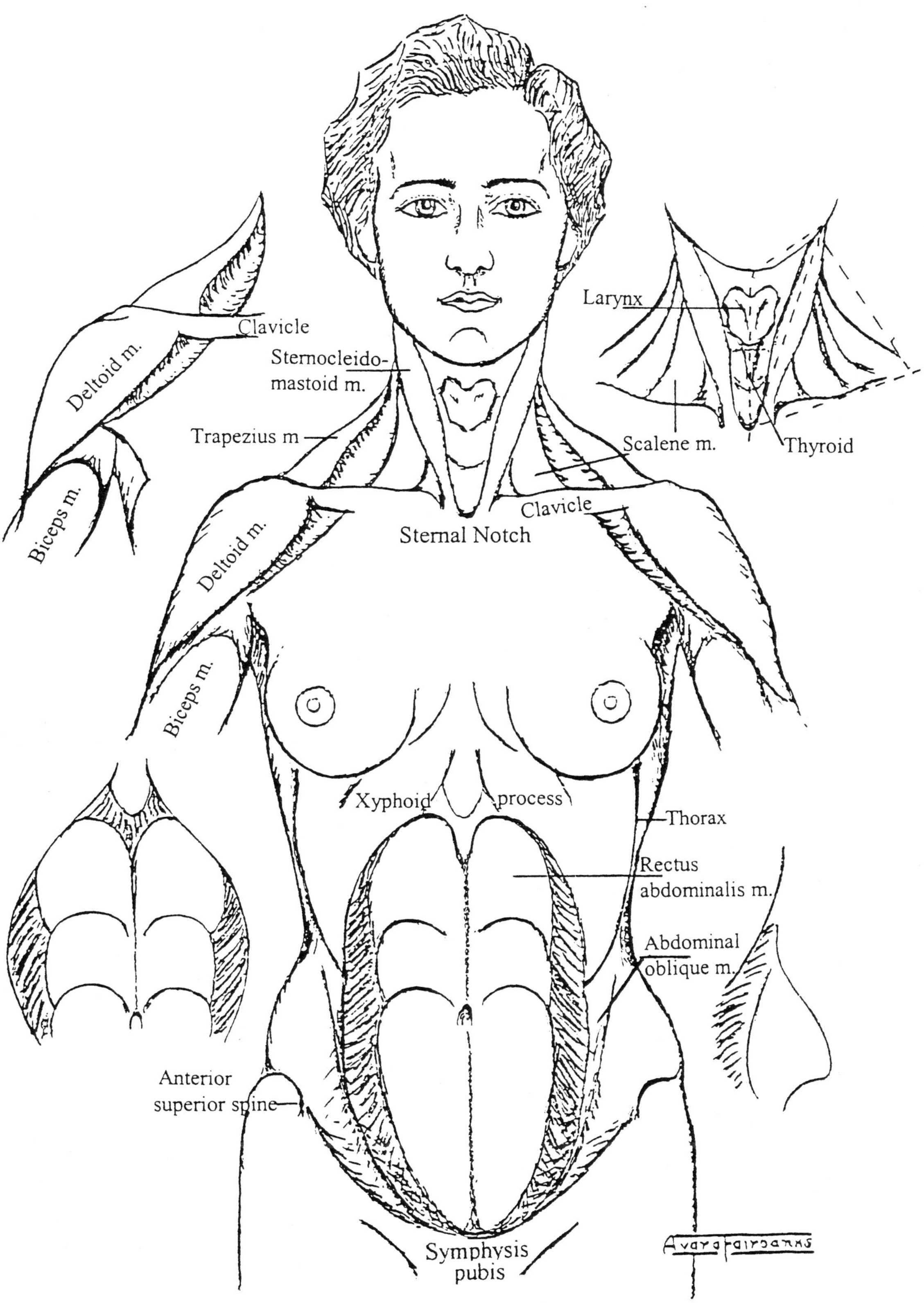

Fig. 40. Rhythmic analysis.

A GEOMETRIC ANALYSIS OF THE FEMALE HEAD AND TORSO

When studying the face, there are many interesting relationships of measurements that may be vertical, horizontal, or in combinations. Certain strength is achieved by the use of halves and thirds in the human face. In the female head, general proportions are expressed in the typical height of 8 inches or 20.3 cm and a breadth of 5 1/2 inches or 14 cm. The vertical measure of the head is divided in half at the eye level, particularly at the lateral corners or canthus of the eyes. The symmetry of the face divides it again vertically into two equal halves, and with the transverse division, four similar rectangles result.

The head breadth at the zygomatic arches is a little greater than one-half head height. The chin to the sternal notch is one-half head height. That divides the head and neck into thirds. This division into thirds resembles the face, which may also be divided into thirds; chin to lip-nose juncture, nose to brow, and brow to hairline. In analyzing the human face one discovers that the most pleasing arrangement is a division of thirds: the forehead from the hairline to the brow; the brow to the nose-lip juncture, near the nostrils; and the nose to chin. The proportions listed here are in part a repetition of the teachings of Leonardo da Vinci. These proportions are beautiful in effect, strong yet sufficiently subtle to maintain interest. Furthermore, the width between the lateral eye corners equals the neck breadth and is one-half face height. The width of the mouth equals one-half the breadth between lateral eye corners. The mouth corners are below the medial borders of the irises of the eyes.

Each of the modialis are junctions of muscles of expression just lateral to mouth corners, and sometimes underlie dimples. They are directly below the pupils of the eyes. The width of the eyes and the distance between the eyes are three equal spaces. The muscles of expression are active in smiling or frowning. The space between the inner canthus, corners of the eyes, is equal to an eye width, measured from the medial to lateral corners. The measure is also equal to the width between the lateral ala (wings) of the nose, and to the lateral corners of the chin. Similar ratios are present in the face of the male. The main differences are the heavier brow ridges, more prominent nose and chin, and more angular features. It seems by analysis that halves and thirds are quite prevalent throughout the head and facial design in a similar manner to the body and the extremities. In the illustration, *Geometric Analysis,* one can note proportions corresponding to triangles, squares, and rectangles.

The breadth between angles of mandibles, jaw, is slightly greater than one half-head height. The breadth of the brow ridges is slightly less than one-half head height.

The torso has some interesting relationships. The sternal notch to the xiphoid process of the sternum, or breast bone, is one head height. The shoulder breadth is two face heights in females. From these points of the shoulder to the umbilicus, an isosceles triangle is formed, and the lines from the shoulder cross over the nipples in the female. In the male torso, the shoulders are two head heights and the nipples are lateral to these isosceles triangle lines. The level of the nipples to the umbilicus is a head height.

The breadth of the inter-anterior axilla, arm pits, equals the breadth at the crest of the ilium and equals the height of the abdomen, xiphoid process to symphysis pubis.

The breadth of the shoulders of a female equals two face heights and the hip breadth

GEOMETRIC ANALYSIS

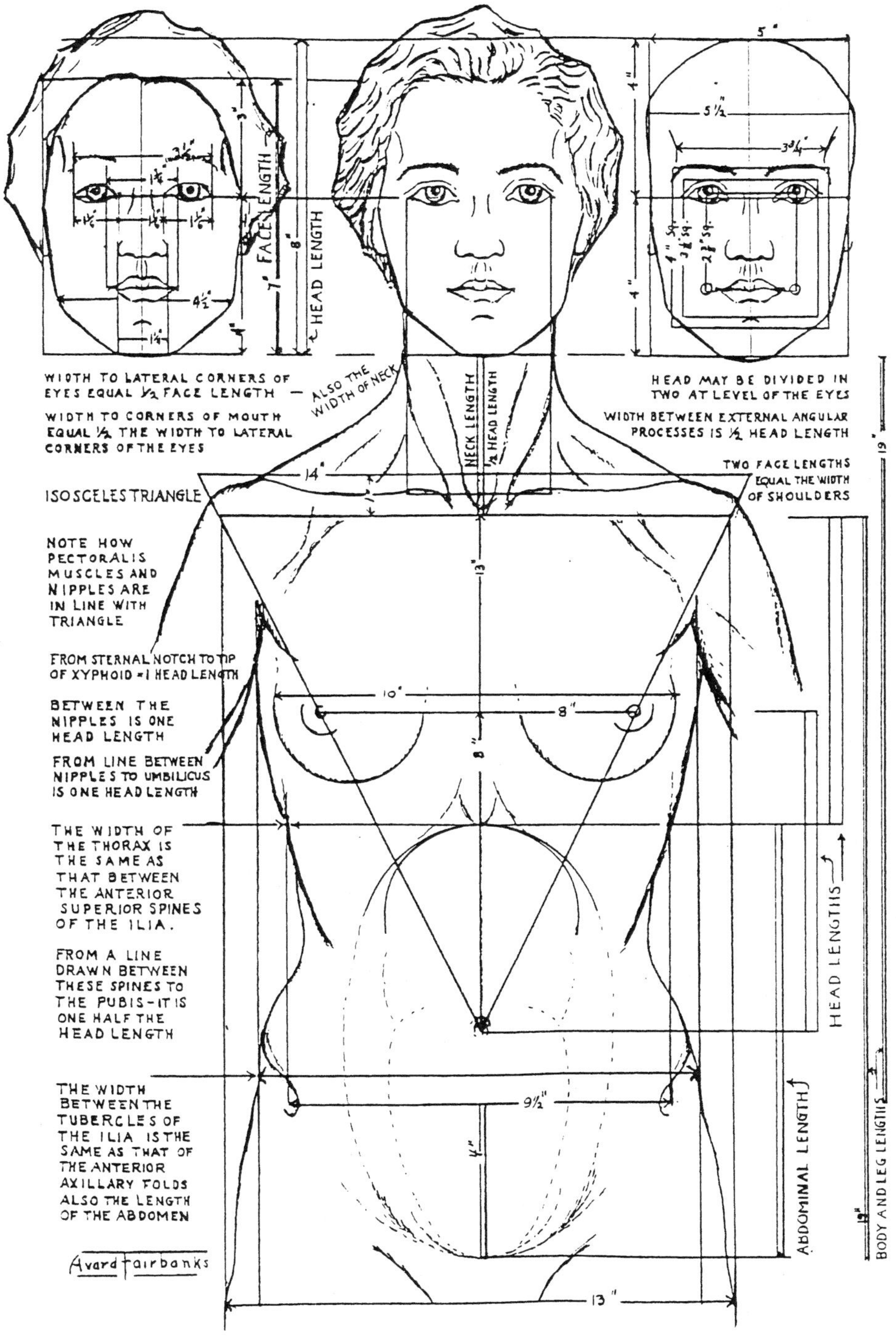

Fig. 41. Geometric analysis.

at the greater trochanters is slightly less but is nearly equal. The breadth of the mid-thorax is similar to the breadth between the anterior superior spines of the ilia. The distance from the symphysis pubis to a line between the anterior spines of the ilia is one-half head height. The breadth of the crests of the ilia is equal to the abdominal height, symphysis pubis to xiphoid process, and to the breadth of the inter-anterior axillary folds.

ANATOMICAL PLANES

Fundamental to anatomical description of the human body are the anatomical planes. These are based on an erect figure facing the observer. They are compared to the planes in another vertebrate, a fish whose central axis is horizontal.

A **sagittal plane** is any vertical plane going from front to back, anterior-posterior, or ventral-dorsal. The mid-sagittal plane goes through the center of the figure, midline anterior to midline posterior, while a parasagittal plane is to one side and is parallel to the mid sagittal plane. *Sagitta* is a Latin word for arrow. During ancient armed conflicts some foot soldiers received arrow wounds proceeding from front to back, hence sagittal plane.

A **frontal plane** is any plane intersecting the erect figure from side to side vertically. These planes would be at right angles to the sagittal planes.

Transverse planes are any planes intersecting the erect figure horizontally. These planes would be at right angles to sagittal and frontal planes. Although oblique planes are possible to consider, they are not officially recognized or described. All planes are in reference to the bony structures of the human body in the erect posture. Other designations of location are important to recognize and list in the biological terms.

Anterior = Ventral: the front of a standing human figure or the inferior aspect of quadrupeds or fish.

Posterior = Dorsal: the back of a standing human figure or the superior aspect of quadrupeds or fish.

Medial: toward the midsagittal plane.

Central: toward the center axis, the vertebral column, which is vertical in erect humans and horizontal in most other vertebrates. It is generally but not entirely central. The central axis is a theoretical line nearly on a plane, but it is not a plane.

Lateral: away from the midsagittal plane.

Superficial: toward the surface.

Deep: in from the surface toward the center.

In this proportion study, depth is also construed as an antero-posterior (ventral-dorsal) measure to avoid confusion with a non-definite use of the word, "length" for measurement.

Cephalic: toward the head, also up or superior in erect humans.

Caudal: toward a tail; in erect humans toward the coccyx or down in the erect human.

Proximal: a part of an extremity nearest the origin or point of attachment to the body.

Distal: a part of an extremity remote or away from the origin or point of attachment to the body.

ANATOMICAL PLANES

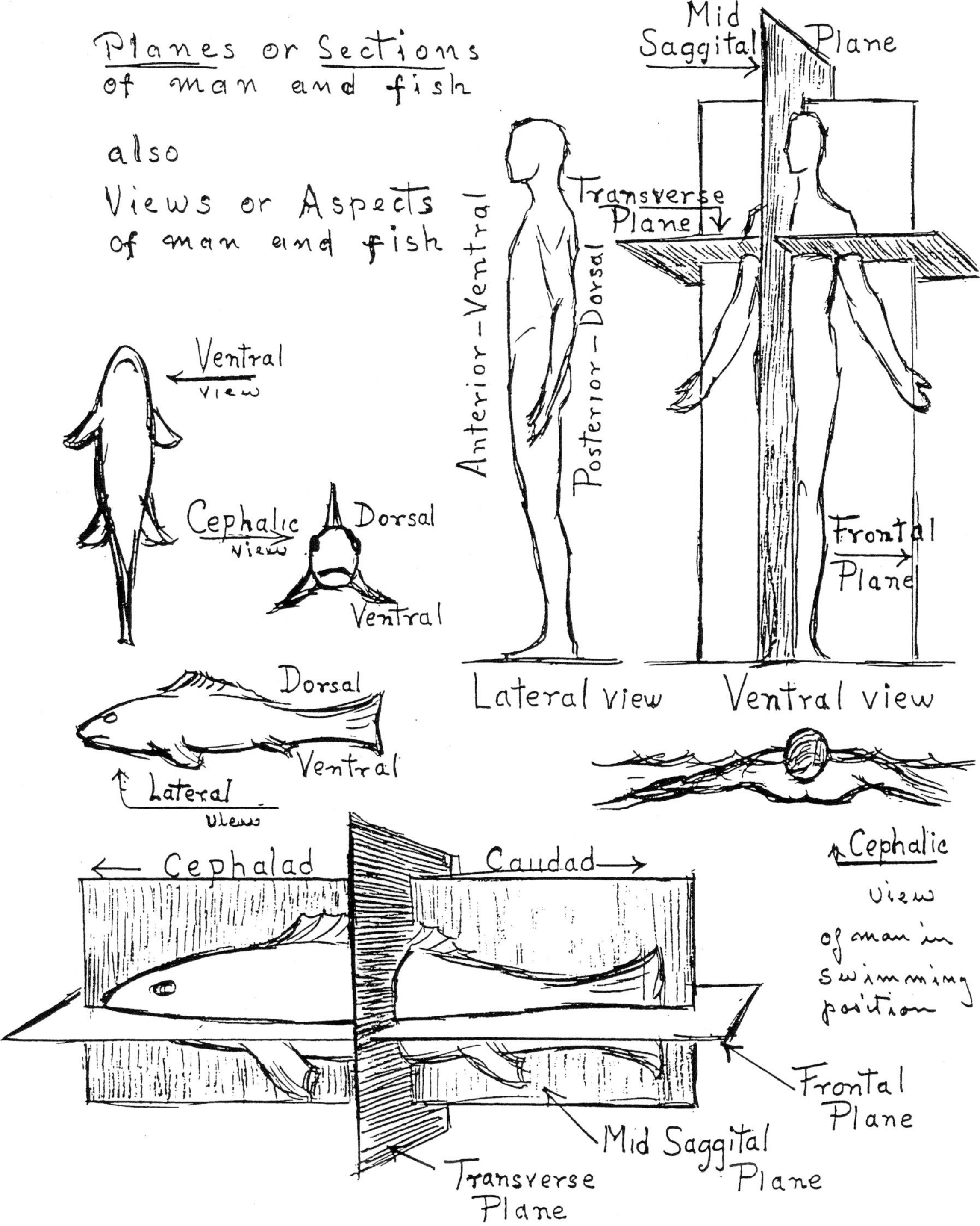

Fig. 42. Anatomic planes of the human figure.

SKELETAL TERMINOLOGY

A drawing of a human skeleton is included with a list of anatomic features for better comprehension. This list will attempt to correlate the common names of these bones with anatomic designations, starting from the neck and moving down. Not all of the bones will be listed. It is intended to be limited to those referred to in the discussion of proportions. Joints are designated by the bones they join, and the bone closest to the central body is usually named first.

The **clavicle** is known as the collar bone. It is attached to the sternum, or breast bone, near the midline and to the acromion process of the scapula, or shoulder blade, near the point of the shoulder.

The **sternum** is an anterior midline bone of the chest, called the breast bone. The upper ribs attach to it.

The **sternal notch** is an indentation of the upper end of the sternum between articulations of the sterno-clavicular joints.

The **acromioclavicular** joint is at the shoulder joining the clavicle, or collar bone, with the acromion process, a projection of the scapula, shoulder blade.

The **acromion process** is a forward projection of the scapula, or the shoulder blade, at the shoulder. It is part of the socket of the shoulder.

The **shoulder pivot** is on the lesser tuberosity, an anterior prominence at the head of the humerus, or arm bone. It can be felt at the anterior aspect of the humerus at the shoulder.

The **humerus** is the upper arm bone with joints at the shoulder and at the elbow with the forearm bones, the radius and ulna. The **medial epicondyle** is medial and the **lateral epicondyle** is lateral on the humerus near the elbow joint.

The **xiphoid** process is a small bone, of variable size, at the lower end of the sternum. It is firmly attached and serves as an attachment for abdominal muscles.

The **inferior costal margin**, or rib margin, is the lower border of the rib cage. The lateral border is the 10th and 11th ribs.

The **lateral epicondyle of the humerus** is a palpable prominence on the lower end of the humerus at the elbow that serves to locate the elbow pivot.

The **radius** and **ulna** are forearm bones.

The **spine of the ulna** is a prominence on the lateral aspect of the wrist

The **spine of the radius** is a palpable prominence at the wrist, proximal to the thumb. It is the location of wrist pivot. See details in the section on hands and feet.

The **pelvic girdle** is composed of the **sacrum,** the lower portion of the spine, at the posterior aspect that attaches to both **ilia** at the **sacroiliac joints**.

Each **ilium** is fused to the **pubis** and **ischium** bones early in development. Although these fused bones appear like one bone, the parts retain their individual names. The two pelvic bones join anteriorly at a firm, fibrous joint, the **symphysis pubis**. The upper border of the **symphysis** is a significant point of reference. Leonardo da Vinci called it the base of the genitals. The **crest of the ilium** is lateral, easily palpable, and is just below the belt line.

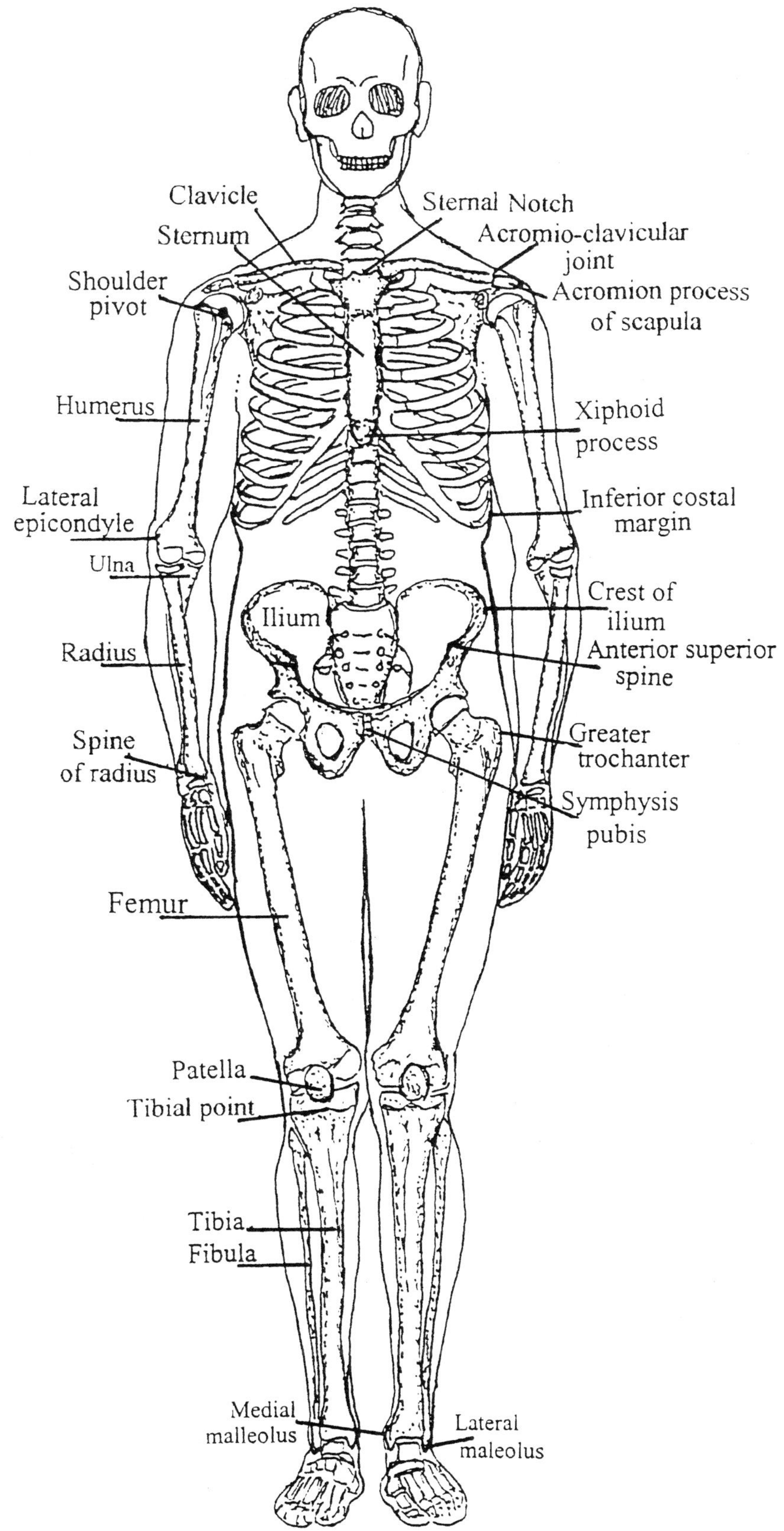

Fig. 43. Human skeleton anterior view.

The **anterior superior spine of the ilium** is a prominence, anterior to, medial to, and a little below the level of the crest. It is easily palpable.

The **femur** is the thigh bone. The **greater trochanter** is easily palpated on the lateral aspect and is about on the level of the hip pivot. The distance between the trochanters is the widest measurement of the hips.

The **patella** is the knee cap. On a straight leg, the patella center is at the pivot.

The **tibial point** is the palpable ridge of the tibia at the knee joint. The measurement from this point is more accurate than measuring from the patella, since the patella moves on flexing the knee

The **tibia** and **fibula** are lower leg bones.

The **medial maleolus** is a prominence of the tibia at the ankle joint. The **lateral maleolus** is the lower tip of the fibula.

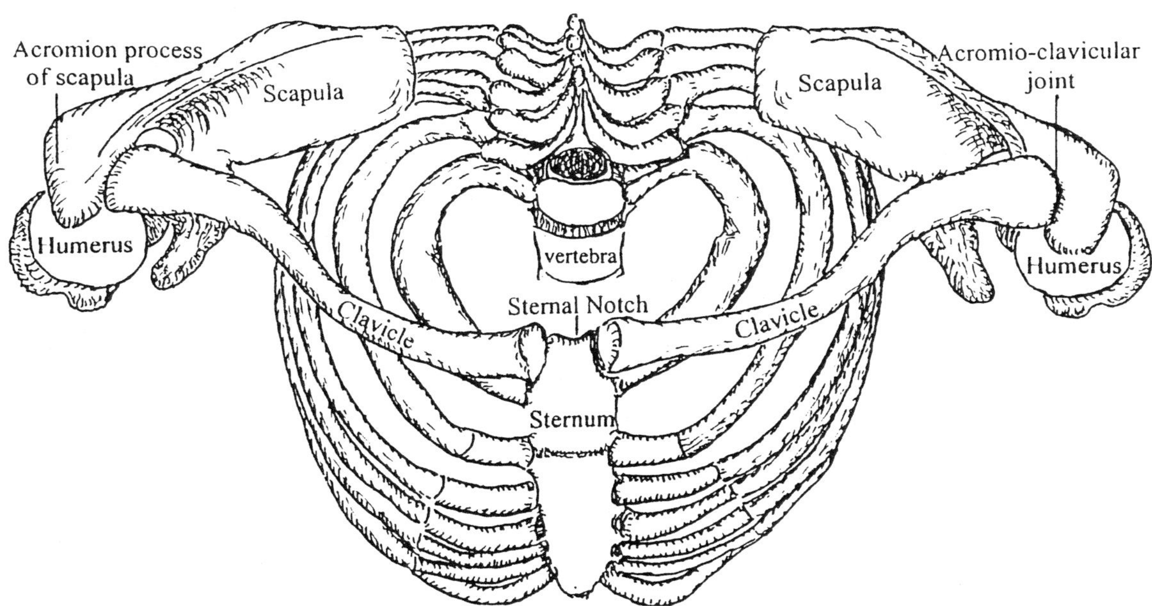

Fig. 44. The thorax and shoulder girdle viewed from above.

REFERENCES

Backhouse, Kenneth M., Hutchings, Kenneth M. *Color Atlas of Surface Anatomy.* Baltimore: Williams and Wilkins, 1986.

Huber, G. Carl. *Piersol's Human Anatomy.* Philadelphia: J.B. Lippincott Company, 1930.

Lockhart, R.D., Hamilton, G.F., Fyfe, F.D. *Anatomy of The Human Body.* Philadelphia: J.B. Lippincott Company, 1972.

Sbotta, Johanes, McMurric, J. Playfair. *Atlas of Human Anatomy.* New York: G.E. Strechert & Co., 1930.

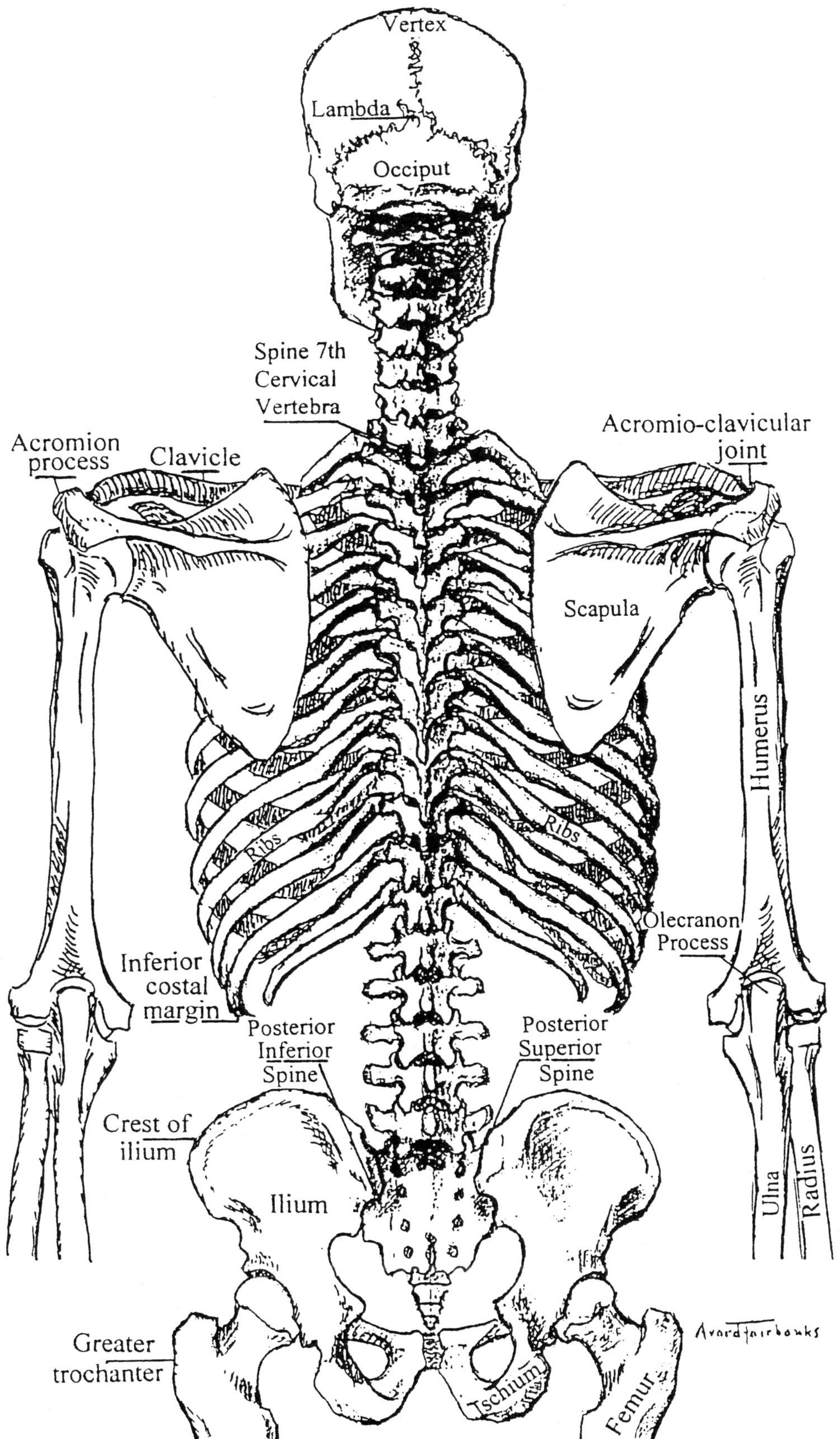

Fig. 45. Human skeleton posterior view of trunk.

ANTHROPOMETRY POINTS OF REFERENCE ON THE HEAD

Physical anthropologists are also interested in the measurements of the human body. A subspecialty of anthropology is titled anthropometry, and it is designated for human measurement. Terms have been used to describe various points of reference to standardize information. When considering the skull, references are now made to the neurocranium, the portion containing the brain, and the viscerocranium, essentially the face. For simplicity, in this study, the skull will be construed to mean both the neurocranium and the viscerocranium. Precise points can often be determined by observing junctions of suture lines on some ancient skull. Sculptors deal with live human form and must try to use reference points that are covered with soft tissues. To facilitate understanding, these points will be described and illustrated in depicting a skull. It is interesting to note that Leonardo da Vinci chose many points that are now in use by anthropologists. Of prime interest to the serious artist is the human head. Beginning the list is the top of the head, the vertex.

Vertex is the uppermost portion of the skull vault in the midline, a little posterior to a vertical line to the ear.

Bregma is the junction of the midsaggital suture and the coronal sutures joining the frontal and parietal bones. It is anterior to the vertex and is often in a groove or depression. It is the soft spot or anterior fontanel, a quadrangle, of an infant skull until bone fusion occurs by growth.

Parietal Prominences are indefinite prominence of the parietal bones at the widest part of the cranium, posterior and above the ears. Biparietal measurement is between these two prominences.

Glabella is the midpoint of the frontal bones above the nasal root, essentially the midline of the brow.

Zygoma, or **zygomatic arch**, cheek bone, is at the greatest breadth of the face. It is about the same breadth as the biparietal breadth of the upper part of the skull.

Nasion or **Selion** is the point at which the nasal bones join the frontal bones, commonly called the bridge of the nose. It is usually an indentation below the brow. The exception is in some ethnic groups with a high nasal bridge. In sculpture history, it is noted as the classic Greek nose.

Ala nasae, or wings of the nose, these semicircular structures are supported by cartilage and outline the nostrils.

The **subnasal point** is at the upper lip juncture and the nose. On a skull, it is a definite projection that supports the cartilage of the nasal septum in the midline.

Gonion is the angle of the jaw. Rather than a definite point, it is rounded, but it is a bony landmark that is easily palpable.

Menton is a designation for the bony border of the chin in the midline. Soft tissues on living subjects serve as a cushion in front and below the bone.

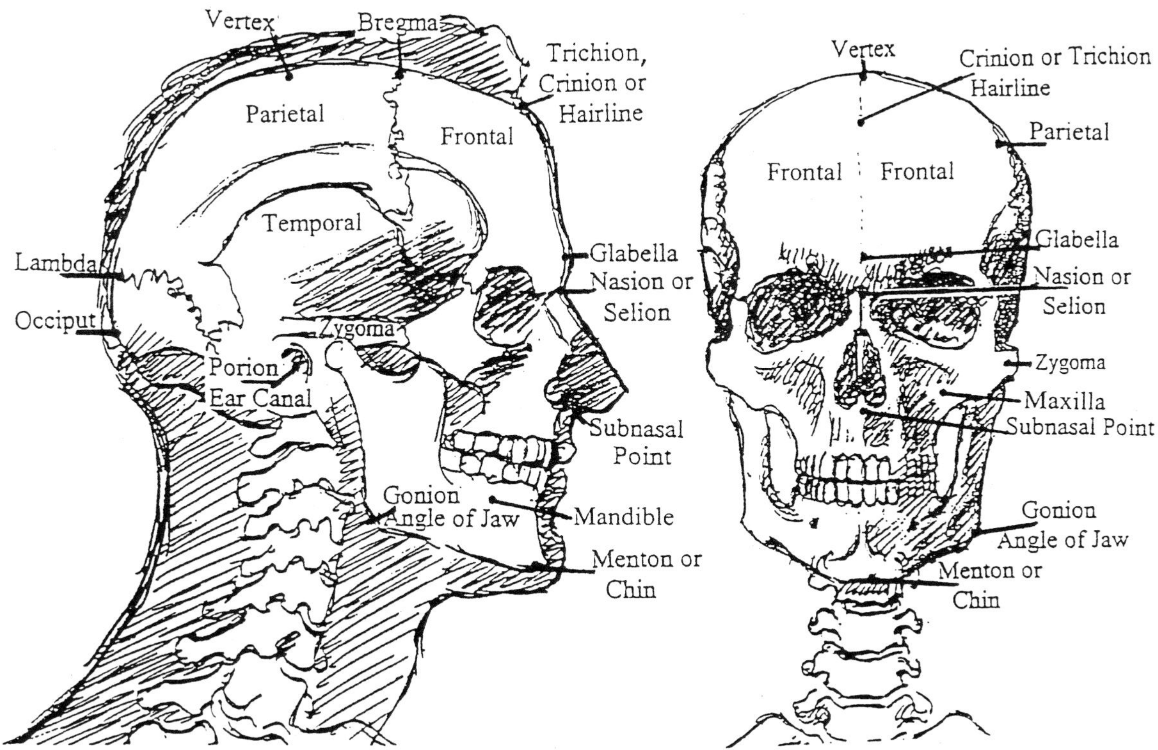

Fig. 46. Anthropometry reference points on the head.

Porion is the ear canal. On living subjects, the tragus, the cartilaginous flap just anterior to the ear canal, is essentially the same point for anterior-posterior measurement.

Lambda of the posterior skull, so named for a Greek letter of three intersecting lines, is a slight indentation at the posterior skull, the location of three sutures that join. It is a remnant of the posterior or triangular fontanel of infancy.

Occiput is the maximum posterior point of the skull.

There are other designated points for measurements of interest to anthropologists but of less significance to artists and therefore will not be listed. Many soft tissue features are supported by bony features and the localization of these need to be recognized. Other soft tissue features of living subjects have common names. They need the attention of serious students and amateurs, and are indicated in illustrations.

REFERENCES

Hrdlicka, Arles. *Practical Anthropometry.* Philadelphia: Wistar Institute of Biology and Physiology, 1939, 122-125.

DESIGNATIONS OF MEASUREMENTS FOR TABLES OF HUMAN PROPORTIONS

In order to compile information about human proportions, Avard Fairbanks made a comprehensive study of about 25 adult females and 25 adult males, predominantly descendants of northwestern Europeans, which was the dominant population in his community at that time. He selected those with what he considered a preferred stature and calculated average measurements of them. These are not a general population average, but are about the 75th percentile. He has arbitrarily considered a stature of six feet, 72 inches or 180.3 cm, for the male figure and five-and-one-half-feet, 66 inches or 167.6 cm, for women to be representative or near the preferred heights.

An extensive review has been made of other anthropometry studies of large series of different populations to compare his data for any significant differences. The results are very comparable. For those who would like to collect data on other ethnic groups and have a sufficient number of volunteer subjects, they are hereby welcome to use this format in any study with the authors' approval and encouragement.

This study is not intended to replace a live model, but rather as a guide and another check of accuracy and quality in art. It can be helpful in the construction of an armature and in the roughed-in modeling for a figurine, statuette, or a statue. Public monuments are usually placed on pedestals so that the figure is above eye level. If a life size figure is erected, the honored person looks too small. Consequently, artists prefer heroic statues of either one and one-third, 4/3, or one and one-half, 3/2, life size. For colossal statues, the life size tables can be multiplied by the intended enlargement.

The tables of proportions presented in this book need both brevity and an adequate definition. For rapid comprehension, brief descriptions are on the same line as the human measurements and the fractional data. The extended explanation of proportion measurements are listed here so that they can be used as a reference in the event of question or misunderstanding.

A line is copied from a page as an example:

Example

HUMAN PROPORTIONS ADULT FEMALE

3/2 Life Heroic inch	4/3 Life Heroic inch	**LIFE SIZE inch**		Inch measurements	3/4 Life inch	2/3 Life inch	1/2 Life inch
				Example			
12.00	10.67	**8.0**	H1V	Stature, Height, Vertex to Sole	6.0	5.3	4.00

In the **designation** of a measurement of human proportions, a **feature**, is considered to be a representational measurement, and is written in the center column of each page, with abbreviated names for prompt and easy reference. The terminology, briefly listed, is a combination of common, anthropometric (human physical measurement), and anatomic names in an attempt to carefully define measurements, allowing easy comprehension for a novice who may need a more adequate descriptions in these lists of designations.

A study of the lists may familiarize the reader with technical terms. The first three columns and the last three columns on any page are proportional measurements. Heroic proportions, larger than life, of three-halves and four-thirds, are in the first and second columns respectively. Life size measurements are printed in bold type in the third column of the left side on the left page. Other columns to the right hand side of the left page and on the right page are in fractions of life size.

The fourth column is a combination of numbers and letters, that serves as an index or a reference guide to designations or names of the itemized proportional measurements. The numbers indicate the serial category of measurement. The first capital letter designates the body portion being considered. The number refers to the list in a series of measurements. The following capital letter indicates the direction of measurement, as listed.

H. Head and neck measurements.
B. Body or Torso measurements.
U. Upper extremity: measurements of arms and hands.
L. Lower extremity: measurements of legs and feet.
'00'. Numbers indicate reference in the order of listing for various groupings of the features of the head and neck, body, upper extremity, or lower extremity. After the numbers are letters designating the direction of measurement.
V. **Vertical measurements**, heights: Assuming erect posture, and longitudinal measurements of the extremities.
T. **Transverse measurements**: Usually breadth, horizontal measurements on a frontal, side to side, plane.
D. **Depth: Measurements** in the anterior-posterior direction on a midsagittal, center-line plane or a parasagittal plane, a parallel anterior-posterior plane.

These serve as a code for referring to a more complete description of the location of measurements listed in the center column. The format of three columns, separated by the designations, followed by the next three rows, is intended to facilitate use and render easy comprehension. Rows are separated by a space every five lines, because the mind has less chance for confusion with a small series of numbers.

For ease of comprehension, common names are often used in conjunction with scientific terms of anatomy and anthropometry (the physical measurement of humans) to more accurately describe points of reference. Underlined words on the following pages appear in the center columns of the tables. Vertical measurements will be termed heights. Transverse measurements on a frontal plane will be termed breadth or occasionally width. Anterior-posterior, front to back (ventral to dorsal), measurements, will be termed depth, except when applied to flexed extremities. Length and width are very good terms, but may be construed differently by various people and therefore have usually been avoided in this study.

GENERAL VERTICAL BODY MEASUREMENTS

1V Height or **stature**; vertex or crown of the head to the sole of the foot.
2V Sternal notch or **Acromion process** at shoulder **to the sole.**
3V **Anterior superior spine of ilium** of the pelvis **to the sole.**
4V The superior border of the **symphysis pubis** of the pelvis **to the sole.**
5V The **crotch to** the **sole** of the foot.

6V **Knee** at upper border of the knee cap, or patella, **to the sole** of the foot.
7V **Head and neck**; **vertex** of head **to the sternal notch**, or pit of the neck.
8V **Sternal notch** or acromion process at the shoulder (being nearly at the same level, the sternal notch is 1/4 inch, lower) **to the anterior superior spine** of the ilium.
9V **Sternal notch to** the superior border of the **symphysis pubis** of the pelvis.
10V **Anterior superior spine** of the ilium of pelvis **to the knee** at the knee cap, patella.

11V **Kneeling height**; vertex to the flexed knee while kneeling erect.
12V **Erect sitting height**; vertex of the head to the buttocks.
13V **Buttocks, straight leg to sole**, while sitting with straight, horizontal leg.
14V **Buttocks to a flexed knee** at patella, while sitting.
15V **Flexed knee to the sole** of a foot while sitting.

VERTICAL HEAD AND NECK MEASUREMENTS

H1V Head height; **vertex** of the head **to the chin.**
H2V Face height; from **hairline to chin**, trichion to menton.
H3V **Vertex** of the head **to the lateral corner of an eye**; vertex to lateral canthus of an eye, which is one half of head height.
H4V Vertex of the head to the tragus of an ear; just anterior to the ear canal; **vertex to tragion of an ear.**
H5V **Hairline to** the upper border of an eye **brow**; trichion to glabella, about one third of the face height.

H6V **Hairline to the infranasal** point at the junction of nostrils with the upper lip; trichion to infranasal, which is two thirds of face height.
H7V **Brow to infranasal point**; glabella to infranasal point, at juncture with the upper lip, which is one third of face height.
H8V Bridge of nose to infranasal point; **selion** or nasion to **infranasal point** at the upper lip.
H9V Bridge of nose to chin, lower face height; **selion** or nasion **to chin** or menton.

H10V **Infranasal** point **to** the lower border of the **chin**; infranasal to menton.
H11V **Infranasal** point **to the lip** or mouth **aperture**; infranasal to stomion.
H12V **Lip aperture** of the mouth to **sublabial crease** below the lower lip and above the chin; stomion to sublabial crease. This crease is semicircular and is arching up.
H13V **Sublabial crease to the chin**; sublabial crease to menton.

TRANSVERSE HEAD MEASUREMENTS

H14T Maximum transverse breadth of head is between the parietal prominences above and posterior to the ear; **bi-parietal**.
H15T Width of cheek at zygoma or cheek bones; **bi-zygomatic**.
H16T Breadth of forehead at the junctions of frontal and temporal bones, just a little above and posterior to the lateral brow near to the hairline; **bi-frontotemporal**.
H17T Breadth between the lateral brow ridges as they turn down; inter-supercilliary arch, **inter-brow ridge**.
H18T Breadth between the tragus of both ears just anterior to ear canals; **inter-tragion**.

H19T Breadth between angles of the mandibles; **inter-angle of mandible**, inter-gonion.
H20T Breadth between the lateral canthus of both eyes; **inter-lateral corners of eyes**.
H21T **Width of an eye**, breadth of palpebral fissure or opening between the lids of one eye, measured between each corner or canthus.
H22T Width between inner canthus of eyes; **inter-inner corners of eyes**.

H23T **Breadth of nose** lateral to the flare of nostrils or wings of nose, ala nasae.
H24T **Breadth of mouth** between corners of mouth, the lip aperture.
H25T **Breadth of the chin**, at borders of the arc of the sublabial crease.
H26T **Breadth of neck** at level of the thyroid cartilage of the larynx (Adam's apple).

ANTERIOR POSTERIOR HEAD MEASUREMENTS

H27D Maximum anterior posterior measurement; **brow** or glabella, **to occiput** at the back of the head, head depth.
H28D **Brow to the tragus** of an ear anterior to the ear canal; glabella to tragion, the anterior cranium.
H29D Bridge of nose to tragus of ear; **selion** or nasion to **tragus**.
H30D Posterior cranium; **tragus** of an ear **to the occiput**.
H31V **Tragus** of an ear to the **angle of a mandible**; tragion to gonion.

H32D **Angle of a mandible** to the anterior **chin**; gonion to menton.
H33V **Length of ear, vertical** measurement of helix at top of the ear to the lobe.
H34D **Width of ear, anterior-posterior** measurement of the tragus to the helix border.
H35D **Anterior-posterior of neck** at a level of the thyroid cartilage of the larynx.

VERTICAL BODY MEASUREMENTS

B1 V **Chin** with the face looking straight ahead **to the sternal notch**, the pit of the neck at the top of the breast bone or sternum in the midline of the chest. Since the head is very mobile, the neck is not a reliable measure, but it must be considered.

B2 V The pit of the neck to the anterior level of an armpit; **sternal notch to axilla.**

B3 V **Sternal notch to** the level of **the nipples.** Breasts being soft tissues are therefore variable in measurements. These are approximate measurements.

B4 V **Sternal notch to the** lower tip of the breast bone or **xyphoid process**. There is considerable variation in size and length of the xyphoid process of the sternum.

B5 V **Sternal notch to umbilicus** or belly button. Some variation is recognized.

B6 V **Sternal notch to** the level of **the crest of the ilium** of the pelvis at the hip.

B7 V **Sternal notch to anterior superior spine of the ilium** of the pelvis, a prominence anterior to the crest of the ilium.

B8 V **Sternal notch to** the symphysis **pubis** of the pelvis, above the base of the genitals. This is the **anterior trunk measurement**.

B9 V **Sternal notch to the crotch**. Since the crotch is composed of soft tissue, considerable variation is recognized.

B10V **Xyphoid** process of the sternum **to the umbilicus** or belly button.

B11V **Umbilicus to** the symphysis **pubis** in the midline of the pelvis above the base of the genitals.

B12V **Umbilicus to the crotch**. Both are soft tissue locations and are therefore variable.

TRANSVERSE BODY MEASUREMENTS

B13T **Shoulder breadth**; the maximum measurements between the deltoid muscles below the point of the shoulder. The muscles are soft tissue and measurements are variable.

B14T Sternal notch to the point of shoulder; **clavicle to the acromion process**.

B15T Breadth, between point of both shoulders; **bi-acromion process breadth**.

B16T Breadth between the joints of the collar bones, clavicles, to the acromion of the shoulder blades; **inter-acromioclavicular joints.**

B17T Distance between armpits seen anteriorly; **inter-anterior axillary folds.**

B18T Distance between the nipples; **inter-nipples**; soft tissue is variable.

B19T **Breadth of thorax**, or chest at the mid thorax at about the eighth rib and below the axilla.

B20T Breadth of chest at the lower rib margin; **inter-costal margin.**

B21T Upper pelvis breadth; **inter-crest of ilium** of the pelvis.

B22T **Inter-anterior superior spines** of the ilium of the pelvis.

B23T Breadth of hips, **inter-greater trochanters** of the **femurs**. These points are considered the pivots of the hip joint.

ANTERIOR-POSTERIOR BODY MEASUREMENTS

B24D Depth of upper chest or thorax; **sternal notch to dorsal thorax** at the back.
B25D Sternal **manubrium** joint, at level of second rib, **to dorsal spines** of thorax.
B26D **Xyphoid process to** the posterior scapula, shoulder blade; xyphoid-dorsal.

B27D **Umbilicus to dorsum**, the belly button to the low back. This involves soft tissue, and measurements are variable.
B28D **Pubis to buttock**, the symphysis pubis of pelvis to the posterior buttock.
B29D Anterior **thigh to the gluteal furrow** below the buttock.

VERTICAL BACK MEASUREMENTS

B30V **Vertex** of the head **to the seventh cervical vertebra spinous process**. This is a prominence at the base of the neck posteriorly at the upper thorax. Measurements are then made from the seventh cervical process to other features of the back.
B31V Seventh cervical vertebra spinous process **to the posterior axillary folds**.
B32V Seventh cervical spinous process to the **to the inferior tip of scapulae**, or shoulder blades.
B33V Seventh cervical spinous process **to posterior superior spines** of the **ilium**, recognized as a dimple on both sides of the posterior pelvis.

B34V Seventh cervical spinous process **to the upper buttocks crease in the midline**, essentially near inferior tip of the coccyx.
B35V Seventh cervical spinous process **to the gluteal furrow**, an inverted arc-shaped crease below the buttocks.
B36V Seventh cervical spinous process **to the popliteal crease** behind **the knee**.
B37V Seventh cervical spinous process **to the sole of the foot** at the heel.

TRANSVERSE BACK MEASUREMENTS

B38T Breadth between the armpits in back, **inter-posterior axillary folds**, which is wider than anterior armpits.
B39T **Inter scapulae** breadth between the **median borders** of both scapulae.
B40T Breadth between, **inter posterior superior spines** of the ilium, recognized as between dimples.
B41T Breadth between, **inter posterior inferior spines of the ilium** at lower border of the dimples.
B42T Breadth of buttocks between the lateral borders of the gluteus maximus muscles, **inter gluteus maximus muscles**. Being soft tissue, the measure is variable.

UPPER EXTREMITIES MEASUREMENTS

U1 T **Span of** outstretched **arms** and hands to the fingertips.
U2 T **Sternal notch to the acromion process** of the scapula.
U3 T **Sternal notch to the shoulder pivot** at the head of the humerus.
U4 V The shoulder to elbow, **humerus pivot to elbow pivot**, at the lateral epicondyle of the humerus at the elbow.

U5 V The **shoulder to flexed elbow** from acromion process to the olecranon process.
U6 V Shoulder at **acromion** process to **lateral epicondyle** of the humerus at the **elbow**.
U7 V With an elbow **flexed, elbow to fingertip**, the measurement from the olecranon process of ulna to tip of the third finger (a cubit).
U8 V **Flexed elbow** at the pivot, or lateral epicondyle of humerus, **to wrist at pivot**, the styloid process of the radius.

U9 V **Wrist** at the pivot, radial styloid process, **to the fingertip** of the third finger.
U10V **Wrist** at pivot **to the tip of the thumb**.
U11V **Length of palm** from the wrist skin crease to the palmar crease of the third finger.
U12V **Length of third finger**, from the palmar finger crease to the finger tip.

U13V **Thumb crotch to the third finger** tip.
U14V **Thumb crotch to the tip of the thumb**.
U15D **Anterior-posterior** depth of an **upper arm at biceps** muscle at mid humerus.
U16D **Anterior- posterior** of a **forearm** at mid forearm.

U17D **Depth of wrist**, volar (palmar) to dorsal (back of hand and wrist).
U18T **Breadth of wrist** between the spines of radius and ulna.
U19T **Breadth of hand** including thumb, either outstretched or clenched.
U20T **Breadth of the palm** of the hand.

LOWER EXTREMITY MEASUREMENTS

L1 V **Crest of the ilium** of the pelvis **to the sole** of a foot.
L2 V **Anterior superior spine of the ilium to the sole** of a foot.
L3 V **Greater trochanter of the femur to the sole** of a foot.
L4 V **Crotch to sole of foot**.

L5 V **Gluteal furrow** of buttock **to the sole** of a foot.
L6 V **Posterior knee crease** at the popliteal fossa or concavity, **to the sole** of a foot.
L7 V **Anterior superior spine of an ilium, to the knee** at its patella or knee cap.
L8 V **Pubis** of the pelvis **to the knee at its patella**.

L9 V The **knee at the patella to the sole** of a foot.
L10V **Tibia** at quadriceps tendon insertion below knee cap, **to sole** of the foot; tibial height.
L11V **Medial malleolus** of ankle, the point tibia at the ankle near the foot, **to the sole** of the foot.
L12V **Lateral malleolus** of ankle **to the sole** of a foot, which is less than the medial malleolus to sole measure.

L13T Breadth of both thighs at mid thigh, **inter both mid thighs**.
L14T **Breadth of both knees**.
L15T **Breadth of both calves** at the gastrocnemius muscles.
L16T **Breadth of a single ankle at** the level of the **malleoli**.

L17D **Mid thigh, anterior-posterior**.
L18D **Knee** at patella, **anterior-posterior**.
L19D **Mid calf anterior-posterior**, at the gastrocnemius muscle.
L20D **Ankle** at its least diameter, **anterior-posterior**.
L21D **Ankle at malleoli, anterior-posterior**.

L22D **Length of foot**; heel to the tip of a first or second toe.
L23D Measurement from the **heel to** the base of **the fifth toe**.
L24T **Breadth of a foot, relaxed**, pointing down, in plantar flexion.
L25T **Breadth of a foot** when **standing**.
L26T **Width of a heel** below the malleolus.

ADULT HUMAN FEMALE PROPORTIONS

INCH MEASUREMENTS

Conversions of Inch Fraction in 1/16ths to Inch Decimal

Inch fraction	1/16	1/8	3/16	1/4	5/16	3/8	7/16	1/2
Inch decimal	.06	.13	.19	.25	.31	.38	.44	.50

Inch fraction	9/16	5/8	11/16	3/4	13/16	7/8	15/16
Inch decimal	.56	.63	.69	.75	.81	.88	.94

Fig. 47. Conversions of inch fractions in 1/16ths to inch decimal.

Facing page, Fig. 48a.
Feminine figure, height 5 ft., 6 inches. Shows inch and centimeter measurements.

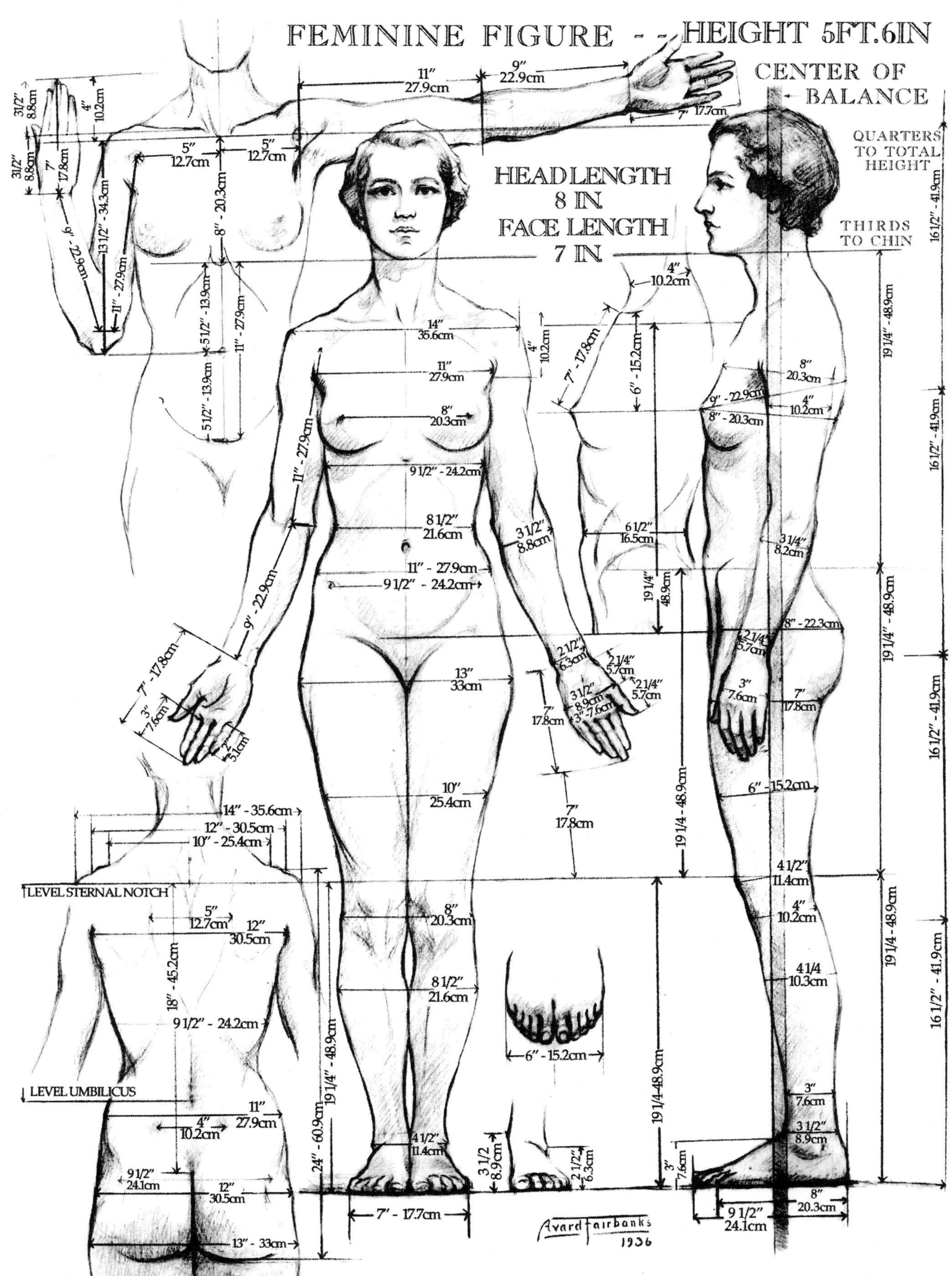
FEMININE FIGURE - - HEIGHT 5FT.6IN
CENTER OF BALANCE
QUARTERS TO TOTAL HEIGHT
THIRDS TO CHIN
HEAD LENGTH 8 IN.
FACE LENGTH 7 IN.
LEVEL STERNAL NOTCH
LEVEL UMBILICUS
Avard Fairbanks 1936

FEMININE HAND DETAILS

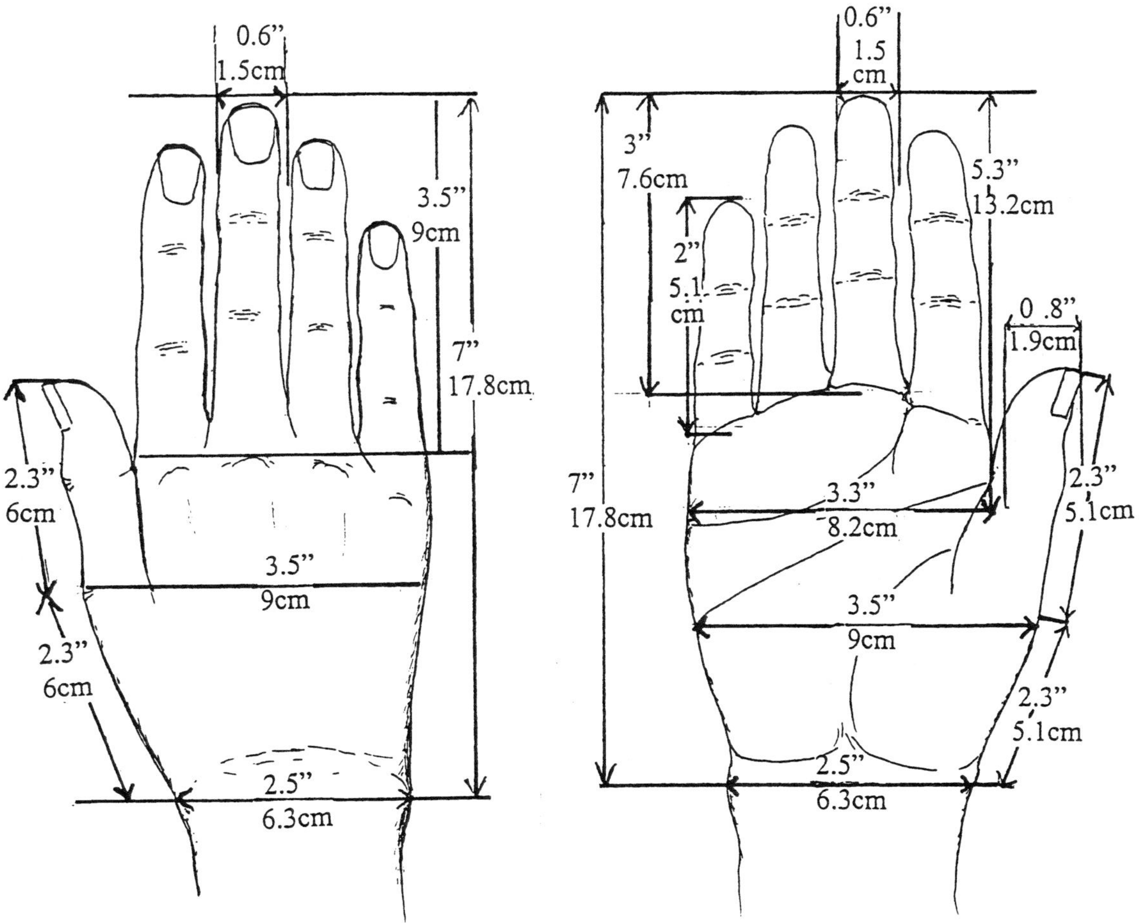

Fig. 48b. Feminine hand details.

FEMININE FOOT DETAILS

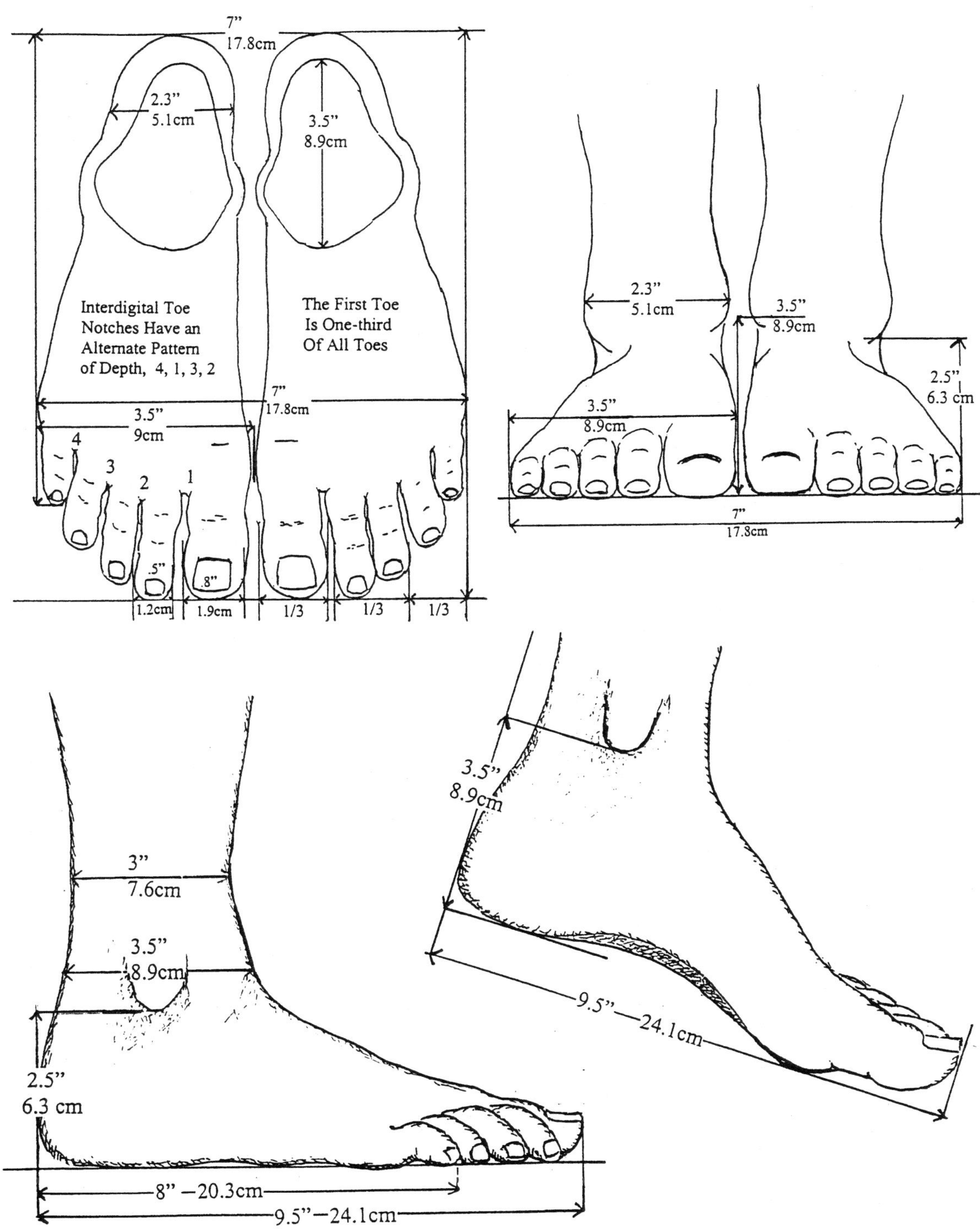

Fig. 48c. Feminine foot details.

FEMININE HEAD, LENGTH 8 INCHES

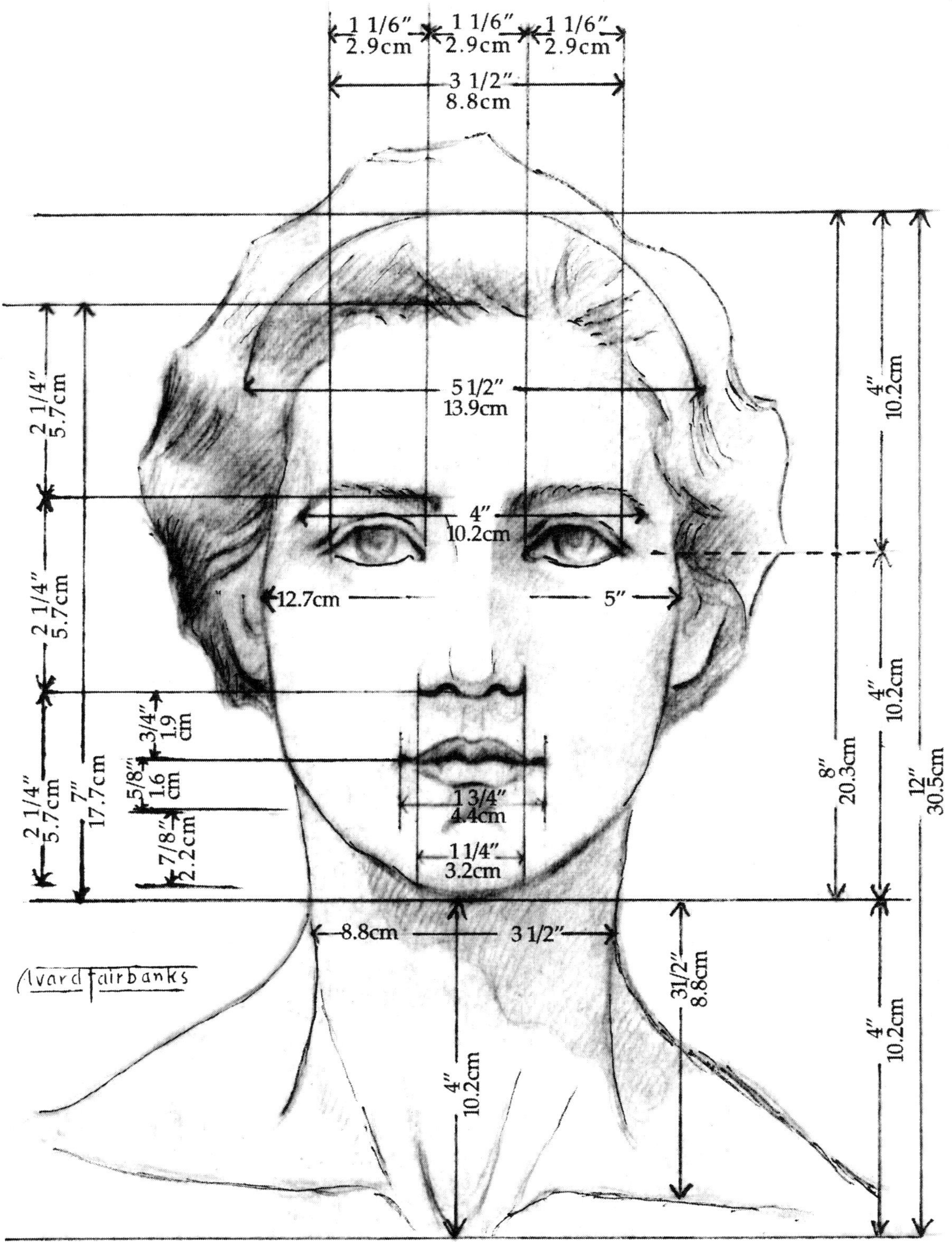

Fig. 49. The feminine head, detailed proportions, anterior view. The head is divided in two at the level of the eyes. One half face height = distance between lateral corners of eyes. The mouth width = one half distance between the lateral corners of eyes.

FEMININE HEAD, LENGTH 8 INCHES

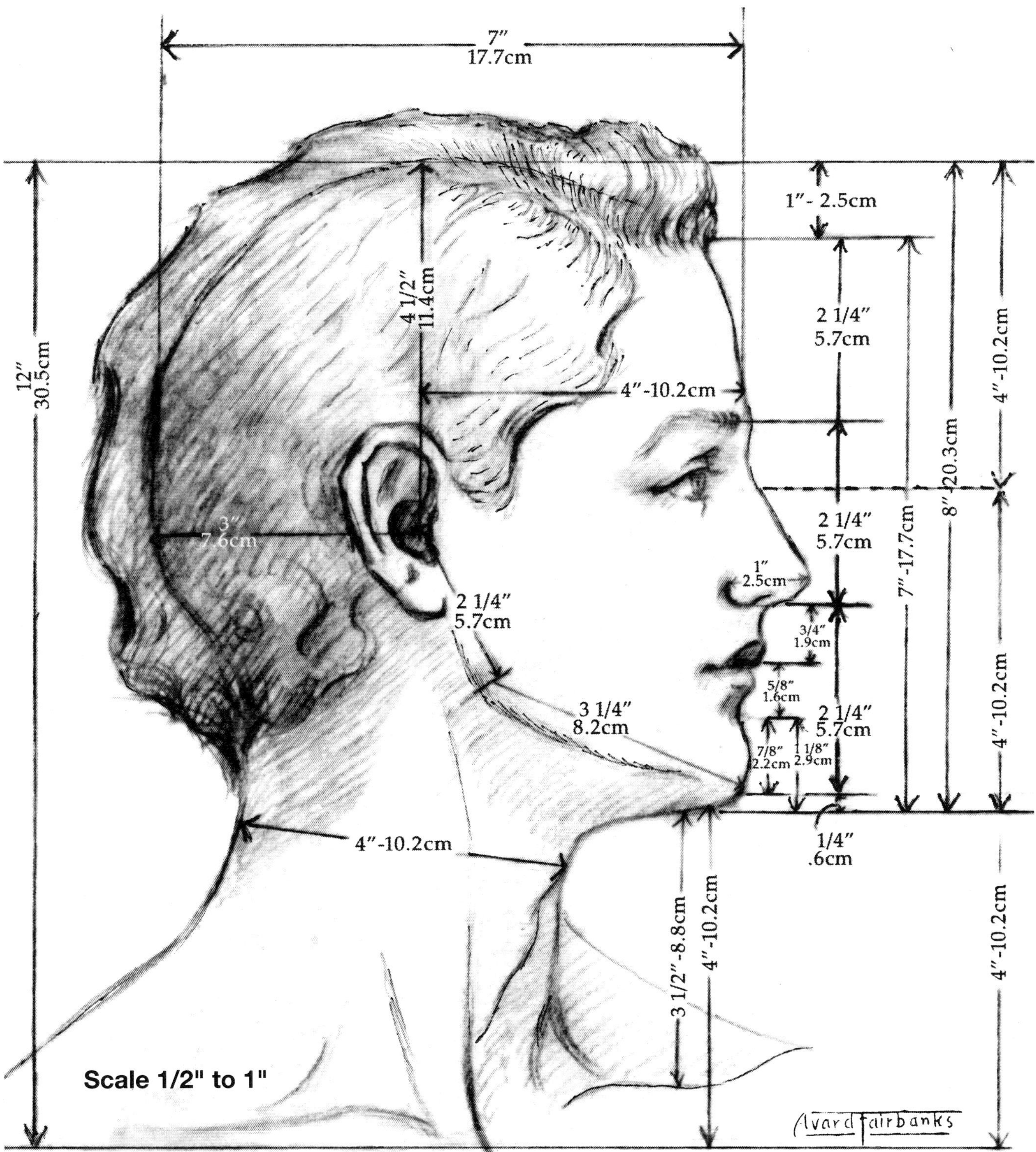

Fig. 50. The feminine head, detailed proportions, right lateral view. Head and neck are divided into three equal proportions: Sternal notch to chin; to corner of eye; to top of head. The face also is divided into three equal proportions, commonly known as nose lengths.

ADULT FEMALE
INCH MEASUREMENTS

3/2 Life	4/3 Life (Heroic)	LIFE SIZE			3/4 Life	2/3 Life	1/2 Life
				VERTICAL MEASUREMENTS			
Inch	Inch	Inch			Inch	Inch	Inch
99.0	88.0	**66.0**	1 V	Stature, Height, Vertex to Sole	49.5	44.0	33.0
80.6	71.7	**53.8**	2 V	Shoulder at Acromion to Sole	40.3	35.8	26.9
57.8	51.3	**38.5**	3 V	Ant. Sup. Spine of Ilium to Sole	28.9	25.7	19.3
51.8	46.0	**34.5**	4 V	Symphysis Pubis to Sole	25.9	23.0	17.3
48.0	42.7	**32.0**	5 V	Crotch to Sole	24.0	21.3	16.0
28.9	25.7	**19.2**	6 V	Knee at Patella to Sole	14.4	12.8	9.6
18.4	16.3	**12.2**	7 V	Head & Neck, Vertex-St. Notch	9.2	8.2	6.1
22.9	20.3	**15.2**	8 V	St. Notch, Shoulder-Ant. Sup. Sp.	11.4	10.2	7.6
28.9	25.7	**19.2**	9 V	Sternal Notch to Symph. Pubis	14.4	12.8	9.6
28.9	25.7	**19.2**	10 V	Ant. Sup. Spine of Ilium-Knee	14.4	12.8	9.6
74.3	66.0	**49.5**	11 V	Kneeling Height	37.1	33.0	24.8
52.5	46.7	**35.0**	12 V	Sitting Height	26.3	23.3	17.5
59.3	52.7	**39.5**	13 V	Buttock Straight Leg to Sole	29.6	26.3	19.8
34.9	31.0	**23.2**	14 V	Buttock to Flexed Knee	17.4	15.5	11.6
30.3	26.9	**20.2**	15 V	Flexed Knee to Sole	15.2	13.5	10.1
				VERTICAL HEAD MEASUREMENTS			
Inch	Inch	Inch			Inch	Inch	Inch
12.0	10.7	**8.0**	H1 V	Vertex to Chin	6.0	5.3	4.0
10.5	9.3	**7.0**	H2 V	Hairline to Chin	5.3	4.7	3.5
6.0	5.3	**4.0**	H3 V	Vertex-Lateral Corner of Eye	3.0	2.7	2.0
6.4	5.7	**4.3**	H4 V	Vertex to Tragion of Ear	3.2	2.9	2.1
3.4	3.0	**2.2**	H5 V	Hairline to Brow	1.7	1.5	1.1
6.8	6.0	**4.5**	H6 V	Hairline to Infranasal	3.4	3.0	2.3
3.4	3.0	**2.2**	H7 V	Brow to Infranasal	1.7	1.5	1.1
3.0	2.7	**2.0**	H8 V	Selion-Infranasal	1.5	1.3	1.0
6.5	5.7	**4.3**	H9 V	Selion to Chin	3.2	2.9	2.2
3.8	3.3	**2.5**	H10 V	Infranasal to Chin	1.9	1.7	1.3
1.1	1.0	**0.8**	H11 V	Infranasal-Lip Aperature	0.6	0.5	0.4
0.9	0.8	**0.6**	H12 V	Lip Ap. to Sublabial Crease	0.5	0.4	0.3
1.6	1.5	**1.1**	H13 V	Sublabial Crease to Chin	0.8	0.7	0.5

ADULT FEMALE
INCH MEASUREMENTS

VERTICAL MEASUREMENTS

3/8 Life	1/3 Life	1/4 Life			1/6 Life	1/8 Life	1/12 Life
Inch	Inch	Inch			Inch	Inch	Inch
24.8	22.0	16.5	1 V	Stature, Height, Vertex to Sole	11.0	8.3	5.5
20.2	17.9	13.4	2 V	Shoulder at Acromion to Sole	9.0	6.7	4.5
14.4	12.8	9.6	3 V	Ant. Sup. Spine of Ilium to Sole	6.4	4.8	3.2
12.9	11.5	8.6	4 V	Symphysis Pubis to Sole	5.8	4.3	2.9
12.0	10.7	8.0	5 V	Crotch to Sole	5.3	4.0	2.7
7.2	6.4	4.8	6 V	Knee at Patella to Sole	3.2	2.4	1.6
4.6	4.1	3.1	7 V	Head & Neck, Vertex-St. Notch	2.0	1.5	1.0
5.7	5.1	3.8	8 V	St. Notch, Shoulder-Ant. Sup. Sp.	2.5	1.9	1.3
7.2	6.4	4.8	9 V	Sternal Notch to Symph. Pubis	3.2	2.4	1.6
7.2	6.4	4.8	10 V	Ant. Sup. Spine of Ilium-Knee	3.2	2.4	1.6
18.6	16.5	12.4	11 V	Kneeling Height	8.3	6.2	4.1
13.1	11.7	8.8	12 V	Sitting Height	5.8	4.4	2.9
14.8	13.2	9.9	13 V	Buttock Straight Leg to Sole	6.6	4.9	3.3
8.7	7.8	5.8	14 V	Buttock to Flexed Knee	3.9	2.9	1.9
7.6	6.7	5.1	15 V	Flexed Knee to Sole	3.4	2.5	1.7

VERTICAL HEAD MEASUREMENTS

Inch	Inch	Inch			Inch	Inch	Inch
3.0	2.7	2.0	H1 V	Vertex to Chin	1.3	1.0	0.7
2.6	2.3	1.8	H2 V	Hairline to Chin	1.2	0.9	0.6
1.5	1.3	1.0	H3 V	Vertex-Lateral Corner of Eye	0.7	0.5	0.3
1.6	1.4	1.1	H4 V	Vertex to Tragion, Ear	0.7	0.5	0.4
0.8	0.8	0.6	H5 V	Hairline to Brow	0.4	0.3	0.2
1.7	1.5	1.1	H6 V	Hairline to Infranasal	0.8	0.6	0.4
0.8	0.8	0.6	H7 V	Brow to Infranasal	0.4	0.3	0.2
0.8	0.7	0.5	H8 V	Selion-Infranasal	0.3	0.3	0.2
1.6	1.4	1.1	H9 V	Selion to Chin	0.7	0.5	0.4
0.9	0.8	0.6	H10 V	Infranasal to Chin	0.4	0.3	0.2
0.3	0.3	0.2	H11 V	Infranasal-Lip Aperature	0.1	0.1	0.1
0.2	0.2	0.2	H12 V	Lip Ap. to Sublabial Crease	0.1	0.1	0.1
0.4	0.4	0.3	H13 V	Sublabial Crease to Chin	0.2	0.1	0.1

ADULT FEMALE
INCH MEASUREMENTS

TRANSVERSE HEAD MEASUREMENTS

3/2 Life	4/3 Life (Heroic)	LIFE SIZE			3/4 Life	2/3 Life	1/2 Life
Inch	Inch	Inch			Inch	Inch	Inch
8.3	7.3	**5.5**	H14 T	Biparietal	4.1	3.7	2.8
7.5	6.7	**5.0**	H15 T	Bizygomatic	3.8	3.3	2.5
6.9	6.2	**4.6**	H16 T	Bifronto Temporal	3.5	3.1	2.3
6.0	5.3	**4.0**	H17 T	Inter Brow Ridge	3.0	2.7	2.0
8.3	7.3	**5.5**	H18 T	Inter Tragion, Ear	4.1	3.7	2.8
6.9	6.2	**4.6**	H19 T	Inter Angle of Mandible	3.5	3.1	2.3
5.3	4.7	**3.5**	H20 T	Inter Lateral Corners of Eyes	2.6	2.3	1.8
1.8	1.6	**1.2**	H21 T	Width of Eye	0.9	0.8	0.6
1.8	1.6	**1.2**	H22 T	Inter Inner Corners of Eyes	0.9	0.8	0.6
1.9	1.7	**1.2**	H23 T	Breadth of Nose	0.9	0.8	0.6
2.6	2.3	**1.8**	H24 T	Breadth of Mouth	1.3	1.2	0.9
1.9	1.7	**1.2**	H25 T	Breadth of Chin	0.9	0.8	0.6
5.3	4.7	**3.5**	H26 T	Breadth of Neck	2.6	2.3	1.8

ANTERIOR-POSTERIOR HEAD MEASUREMENTS

Inch	Inch	Inch			Inch	Inch	Inch
11.1	9.9	**7.4**	H27 D	Brow to Occiput	5.6	4.9	3.7
6.3	5.6	**4.2**	H28 D	Brow to Tragus	3.2	2.8	2.1
5.4	4.8	**3.6**	H29 D	Selion to Tragus	2.7	2.4	1.8
4.8	4.3	**3.2**	H30 D	Tragus to Occiput	2.4	2.1	1.6
3.4	3.0	**2.2**	H31 D	Tragus to Angle of Mandible	1.7	1.5	1.1
4.9	4.3	**3.2**	H32 D	Angle Mandible to Chin	2.4	2.2	1.6
3.7	3.3	**2.5**	H33 V	Length Ear, Vertical	1.8	1.6	1.2
2.0	1.7	**1.3**	H34 D	Width of Ear, Anterior-Posterior	1.0	0.9	0.7
6.0	5.3	**4.0**	H35 D	Anterior Posterior of Neck	3.0	2.7	2.0

ADULT FEMALE
INCH MEASUREMENTS

TRANSVERSE HEAD MEASUREMENTS

3/8 Life Inch	1/3 Life Inch	1/4 Life Inch			1/6 Life Inch	1/8 Life Inch	1/12 Life Inch
2.1	1.8	1.4	H14 T	Biparietal	0.9	0.7	0.5
1.9	1.7	1.3	H15 T	Bizygomatic	0.8	0.6	0.4
1.7	1.5	1.2	H16 T	Bifronto Temporal	0.8	0.6	0.4
1.5	1.3	1.0	H17 T	Inter Brow Ridge	0.7	0.5	0.3
2.1	1.8	1.4	H18 T	Inter Tragion, Ear	0.9	0.7	0.5
1.7	1.5	1.2	H19 T	Inter Angle of Mandible	0.8	0.6	0.4
1.3	1.2	0.9	H20 T	Inter Lateral Corners of Eyes	0.6	0.4	0.3
0.5	0.4	0.3	H21 T	Width of Eye	0.2	0.1	0.1
0.5	0.4	0.3	H22 T	Inter Inner Corners of Eyes	0.2	0.1	0.1
0.5	0.4	0.3	H23 T	Breadth of Nose	0.2	0.2	0.1
0.7	0.6	0.4	H24 T	Breadth of Mouth	0.3	0.2	0.1
0.5	0.4	0.3	H25 T	Breadth of Chin	0.2	0.2	0.1
1.3	1.2	0.9	H26 T	Breadth of Neck	0.6	0.4	0.3

ANTERIOR-POSTERIOR HEAD MEASUREMENTS

Inch	Inch	Inch			Inch	Inch	Inch
2.8	2.5	1.9	H27 D	Brow to Occiput	1.2	0.9	0.6
1.6	1.4	1.1	H28 D	Brow to Tragus	0.7	0.5	0.4
1.4	1.2	0.9	H29 D	Selion to Tragus	0.6	0.5	0.3
1.2	1.1	0.8	H30 D	Tragus to Occiput	0.5	0.4	0.3
0.8	0.8	0.6	H31 D	Tragus to Angle Mandible	0.4	0.3	0.2
1.2	1.1	0.8	H32 D	Angle Mandible-Chin	0.5	0.4	0.3
0.9	0.8	0.6	H33 V	Length Ear, Vertical	0.4	0.3	0.2
0.5	0.4	0.3	H34 D	Width of Ear, Anterior-Posterior	0.2	0.2	0.1
1.5	1.3	1.0	H35 D	Anterior Post. Neck	0.7	0.5	0.3

ADULT FEMALE
INCH MEASUREMENTS

3/2 Life (Heroic)	4/3 Life	LIFE SIZE			3/4 Life	2/3 Life	1/2 Life
				VERTICAL BODY MEASUREMENTS			
Inch	Inch	Inch			Inch	Inch	Inch
6.0	5.3	**4.0**	B1 V	Chin to Sternal Notch	3.0	2.7	2.0
4.5	4.0	**3.0**	B2 V	Sternal Notch to Anterior Axilla	2.3	2.0	1.5
9.0	8.0	**6.0**	B3 V	Sternal Notch to Nipples	4.5	4.0	3.0
12.0	10.7	**8.0**	B4 V	Sternal Notch to Xyphoid	6.0	5.3	4.0
20.3	18.0	**13.5**	B5 V	Sternal Notch to Umbilicus	10.1	9.0	6.8
21.2	18.9	**14.2**	B6 V	Sternal Notch to Crest of Ilium	10.6	9.4	7.1
22.9	20.3	**15.2**	B7 V	St. Notch to Ant. Sup. Spine Ilium	11.4	10.2	7.6
28.9	25.7	**19.2**	B8 V	Sternal Notch to Pubis	14.4	12.8	9.6
36.0	32.0	**24.0**	B9 V	Sternal Notch to Crotch	18.0	16.0	12.0
8.3	7.3	**5.5**	B10 V	Xyphoid to Umbilicus	4.1	3.7	2.8
8.3	7.3	**5.5**	B11 V	Umbilicus to Pubis	4.1	3.7	2.8
15.8	14.0	**10.5**	B12 V	Umbilicus to Crotch	7.9	7.0	5.3
				TRANSVERSE BODY MEASUREMENTS			
Inch	Inch	Inch			Inch	Inch	Inch
24.0	21.3	**16.0**	B13 T	Shoulder Breadth	12.0	10.7	8.0
9.0	8.0	**6.0**	B14 T	Clavicle to Acromion Process	4.5	4.0	3.0
21.0	18.7	**14.0**	B15 T	Bi-acromial Process Breadth	10.5	9.3	7.0
18.0	16.0	**12.0**	B16 T	Inter Achromioclavicular Joint	9.0	8.0	6.0
16.5	14.7	**11.0**	B17 T	Inter Anterior Axillary Fold	8.3	7.3	5.5
12.0	10.7	**8.0**	B18 T	Inter Nipples	6.0	5.3	4.0
14.3	12.7	**9.5**	B19 T	Breadth of Thorax	7.1	6.3	4.8
12.8	11.3	**8.5**	B20 T	Inter Costal Margin	6.4	5.7	4.3
16.5	14.7	**11.0**	B21 T	Inter Crest of Illium	8.3	7.3	5.5
14.3	12.7	**9.5**	B22 T	Inter Ant. Superior Spine of Ilium	7.1	6.3	4.8
19.5	17.3	**13.0**	B23 T	Inter Greater Trocanter of Femur	9.8	8.7	6.5

ADULT FEMALE
INCH MEASUREMENTS

VERTICAL BODY MEASUREMENTS

3/8 Life	1/3 Life	1/4 Life			1/6 Life	1/8 Life	1/12 Life
Inch	Inch	Inch			Inch	Inch	Inch
1.5	1.3	1.0	B1 V	Chin to Sternal Notch	0.7	0.5	0.3
1.1	1.0	0.8	B2 V	Sternal Notch to Anterior Axilla	0.5	0.4	0.3
2.3	2.0	1.5	B3 V	Sternal Notch to Nipples	1.0	0.8	0.5
3.0	2.7	2.0	B4 V	Sternal Notch to Xyphoid	1.3	1.0	0.7
5.1	4.5	3.4	B5 V	Sternal Notch to Umbilicus	2.3	1.7	1.1
5.3	4.7	3.5	B6 V	Sternal Notch to Crest of Ilium	2.4	1.8	1.2
5.7	5.1	3.8	B7 V	St. Notch to Ant. Sup. Spine Ilium	2.5	1.9	1.3
7.2	6.4	4.8	B8 V	Sternal Notch to Pubis	3.2	2.4	1.6
9.0	8.0	6.0	B9 V	Sternal Notch to Crotch	4.0	3.0	2.0
2.1	1.8	1.4	B10 V	Xyphoid to Umbilicus	0.9	0.7	0.5
2.1	1.8	1.4	B11 V	Umbilicus to Pubis	0.9	0.7	0.5
3.9	3.5	2.6	B12 V	Umbilicus to Crotch	1.8	1.3	0.9

TRANSVERSE BODY MEASUREMENTS

Inch	Inch	Inch			Inch	Inch	Inch
6.0	5.3	4.0	B13 T	Shoulder Breadth	2.7	2.0	1.3
2.3	2.0	1.5	B14 T	Clavicle to Acromion Process	1.0	0.8	0.5
5.3	4.7	3.5	B15 T	Bi-acromial Process Breadth	2.3	1.8	1.2
4.5	4.0	3.0	B16 T	Inter Achromioclavicular Joint	2.0	1.5	1.0
4.1	3.7	2.8	B17 T	Inter Anterior Axillary Fold	1.8	1.4	0.9
3.0	2.7	2.0	B18 T	Inter Nipples	1.3	1.0	0.7
3.6	3.2	2.4	B19 T	Breadth of Thorax	1.6	1.2	0.8
3.2	2.8	2.1	B20 T	Inter Costal Margin	1.4	1.1	0.7
4.1	3.7	2.8	B21 T	Inter Crest of Illium	1.8	1.4	0.9
3.6	3.2	2.4	B22 T	Inter Ant. Superior Spine of Ilium	1.6	1.2	0.8
4.9	4.3	3.3	B23 T	Inter Greater Trocanter Femur	2.2	1.6	1.1

ADULT FEMALE
INCH MEASUREMENTS

3/2 Life	4/3 Life (Heroic)	LIFE SIZE			3/4 Life	2/3 Life	1/2 Life
				ANTERIOR-POSTERIOR BODY MEASUREMENTS			
Inch	Inch	Inch			Inch	Inch	Inch
8.6	7.7	**5.8**	B24 D	Sternal Notch to Dorsal Spine	4.3	3.8	2.9
12.0	10.7	**8.0**	B25 D	Manubrium to Dorsal Spine	6.0	5.3	4.0
12.4	11.0	**8.2**	B26 D	Xyphoid-Sternum to Scapula	6.2	5.5	4.1
9.8	8.7	**6.5**	B27 D	Umbilicus to Dorsum	4.9	4.3	3.3
14.4	12.8	**9.6**	B28 D	Pubis to Buttock	7.2	6.4	4.8
10.5	9.3	**7.0**	B29 D	Thigh to Gluteal Furrow	5.3	4.7	3.5
				VERTICAL BACK MEASUREMENTS			
Inch	Inch	Inch			Inch	Inch	Inch
14.3	12.7	**9.5**	B30 V	Vertex to 7th Cervical Spine	7.1	6.3	4.8
				7th Cervical Vertebra Spine to:			
9.6	8.5	**6.4**	B31 V	Posterior Axillary Fold	4.8	4.3	3.2
11.6	10.3	**7.7**	B32 V	Inferior Tip of Scapula	5.8	5.1	3.9
25.7	22.8	**17.1**	B33 V	Post. Sup. Spines of Ilium	12.8	11.4	8.6
31.1	27.7	**20.8**	B34 V	Upper Buttock Midline Crease	15.6	13.8	10.4
38.7	34.4	**25.8**	B35 V	Gluteal Furrow	19.4	17.2	12.9
57.8	51.3	**38.5**	B36 V	Popliteal Crease Behind Knee	28.9	25.7	19.3
83.3	74.0	**55.5**	B37 V	Sole of the Foot	41.6	37.0	27.8
				TRANSVERSE BACK MEASUREMENTS			
Inch	Inch	Inch			Inch	Inch	Inch
18.0	16.0	**12.0**	B38 T	Inter Posterior Axillary Folds	9.0	8.0	6.0
7.5	6.7	**5.0**	B39 T	Inter Scapulae Medial Borders	3.8	3.3	2.5
6.0	5.3	**4.0**	B40 T	Inter Post. Sup. Spines Sacrum	3.0	2.7	2.0
4.5	4.0	**3.0**	B41 T	Inter Post. Inf. Spines Sacrum	2.3	2.0	1.5
13.9	12.3	**9.2**	B42 T	Inter Gluteus Maximus Muscle	6.9	6.2	4.6

ADULT FEMALE
INCH MEASUREMENTS

ANTERIOR-POSTERIOR BODY MEASUREMENTS

3/8 Life Inch	1/3 Life Inch	1/4 Life Inch			1/6 Life Inch	1/8 Life Inch	1/12 Life Inch
2.2	1.9	1.4	B24 D	Sternal Notch to Dorsal Spine	1.0	0.7	0.5
3.0	2.7	2.0	B25 D	Manubrium to Dorsal Spine	1.3	1.0	0.7
3.1	2.8	2.1	B26 D	Xyphoid-Sternum to Scapula	1.4	1.0	0.7
2.4	2.2	1.6	B27 D	Umbilicus to Dorsum	1.1	0.8	0.5
3.6	3.2	2.4	B28 D	Pubis to Buttock	1.6	1.2	0.8
2.6	2.3	1.8	B29 D	Thigh-Gluteal Furrow	1.2	0.9	0.6

VERTICAL BACK MEASUREMENTS

Inch	Inch	Inch			Inch	Inch	Inch
3.6	3.2	2.4	B30 V	Vertex to 7th Cervical Spine	1.6	1.2	0.8
				7th Cervical Vertebra Spine to:			
2.4	2.1	1.6	B31 V	Posterior Axillary Fold	1.1	0.8	0.5
2.9	2.6	1.9	B32 V	Inferior Tip of Scapula	1.3	1.0	0.6
6.4	5.7	4.3	B33 V	Post. Sup. Spines of Ilium	2.9	2.1	1.4
7.8	6.9	5.2	B34 V	Upper Buttock Midline Crease	3.5	2.6	1.7
9.7	8.6	6.5	B35 V	Gluteal Furrow	4.3	3.2	2.2
14.4	12.8	9.6	B36 V	Popliteal Crease Behind Knee	6.4	4.8	3.2
20.8	18.5	13.9	B37 V	Sole of the Foot	9.3	6.9	4.6

TRANSVERSE BACK MEASUREMENTS

Inch	Inch	Inch			Inch	Inch	Inch
4.5	4.0	3.0	B38 T	Inter Posterior Axillary Folds	2.0	1.5	1.0
1.9	1.7	1.3	B39 T	Inter Scapulae Medial Borders	0.8	0.6	0.4
1.5	1.3	1.0	B40 T	Inter Post. Sup. Spines Sacrum	0.7	0.5	0.3
1.1	1.0	0.8	B41 T	Inter Post. Inf. Spines Sacrum	0.5	0.4	0.3
3.5	3.1	2.3	B42 T	Inter Gluteus Maximus Muscle	1.5	1.2	0.8

ADULT FEMALE
INCH MEASUREMENTS

UPPER EXTREMITY MEASUREMENTS

3/2 Life	4/3 Life (Heroic)	LIFE SIZE			3/4 Life	2/3 Life	1/2 Life
Inch	Inch	Inch			Inch	Inch	Inch
96.0	85.3	**64.0**	U1 T	Span of Arms	48.0	42.7	32.0
10.5	9.3	**7.0**	U2 T	Sternum to Acromian Process	5.3	4.7	3.5
7.5	6.7	**5.0**	U3 T	Sternum-Shoulder Pivot	3.8	3.3	2.5
16.5	14.7	**11.0**	U4 V	Humerus-Elbow Pivot	8.3	7.3	5.5
20.6	18.3	**13.7**	U5 V	Shoulder-Elbow Flexed	10.3	9.1	6.9
18.8	16.7	**12.5**	U6 V	Acromian to Lat. Condyl Elbow	9.4	8.3	6.3
26.4	23.5	**17.6**	U7 V	Flexed Elbow to Finger Tip	13.2	11.7	8.8
13.5	12.0	**9.0**	U8 V	Flexed Elbow to Wrist	6.8	6.0	4.5
10.5	9.3	**7.0**	U9 V	Wrist to Finger Tip	5.3	4.7	3.5
6.8	6.0	**4.5**	U10 V	Wrist to Thumb	3.4	3.0	2.3
6.0	5.3	**4.0**	U11 V	Length of Palm	3.0	2.7	2.0
4.5	4.0	**3.0**	U12 V	Length 3rd Finger	2.3	2.0	1.5
7.3	6.5	**4.9**	U13 V	Thumb Crotch to 3rd Finger Tip	3.7	3.3	2.4
3.6	3.2	**2.4**	U14 V	Thumb Crotch to Thumb Tip	1.8	1.6	1.2
6.0	5.3	**4.0**	U15 D	Anterior Post. Arm at Biceps	3.0	2.7	2.0
4.8	4.3	**3.2**	U16 D	Anterior Posterior at Forearm	2.4	2.1	1.6
2.3	2.0	**1.5**	U17 D	Depth of Wrist	1.1	1.0	0.8
3.3	2.9	**2.2**	U18 T	Breadth of Wrist	1.7	1.5	1.1
5.6	5.0	**3.8**	U19 T	Breadth of Hand	2.8	2.5	1.9
4.5	4.0	**3.0**	U20 T	Breadth of Palm	2.3	2.0	1.5

ADULT FEMALE INCH MEASUREMENTS

UPPER EXTREMITY MEASUREMENTS

3/8 Life	1/3 Life	1/4 Life			1/6 Life	1/8 Life	1/12 Life
Inch	Inch	Inch			Inch	Inch	Inch
24.0	21.3	16.0	U1 T	Span of Arms	10.7	8.0	5.3
2.6	2.3	1.8	U2 T	Sternum to Acromian Process	1.2	0.9	0.6
1.9	1.7	1.3	U3 T	Sternum-Shoulder Pivot	0.8	0.6	0.4
4.1	3.7	2.8	U4 V	Humerus-Elbow Pivot	1.8	1.4	0.9
5.1	4.6	3.4	U5 V	Shoulder-Elbow Flexed	2.3	1.7	1.1
4.7	4.2	3.1	U6 V	Acromian to Lat. Condyl Elbow	2.1	1.6	1.0
6.6	5.9	4.4	U7 V	Flex ed Elbow to Finger Tip	2.9	2.2	1.5
3.4	3.0	2.3	U8 V	Flexed Elbow to Wrist	1.5	1.1	0.8
2.6	2.3	1.8	U9 V	Wrist to Finger Tip	1.2	0.9	0.6
1.7	1.5	1.1	U10 V	Wrist to Thumb	0.8	0.6	0.4
1.5	1.3	1.0	U11 V	Length of Palm	0.7	0.5	0.3
1.1	1.0	0.8	U12 V	Length 3rd Finger	0.5	0.4	0.3
1.8	1.6	1.2	U13 V	Thumb Crotch to 3rd Finger Tip	0.8	0.6	0.4
0.9	0.8	0.6	U14 V	Thumb Crotch to Thumb Tip	0.4	0.3	0.2
1.5	1.3	1.0	U15 D	Anterior Post. Arm at Biceps	0.7	0.5	0.3
1.2	1.1	0.8	U16 D	Anterior Posterior at Forearm	0.5	0.4	0.3
0.6	0.5	0.4	U17 D	Depth of Wrist	0.3	0.2	0.1
0.8	0.7	0.6	U18 T	Breadth of Wrist	0.4	0.3	0.2
1.4	1.3	0.9	U19 T	Breadth of Hand	0.6	0.5	0.3
1.1	1.0	0.8	U20 T	Breadth of Palm	0.5	0.4	0.3

ADULT FEMALE
INCH MEASUREMENTS

LOWER EXTREMITY MEASUREMENTS

3/2 Life (Heroic)	4/3 Life	LIFE SIZE			3/4 Life	2/3 Life	1/2 Life
Inch	Inch	Inch			Inch	Inch	Inch
60.9	54.1	**40.6**	L1 V	Crest of Ilium to Sole	30.5	27.1	20.3
57.0	50.7	**38.0**	L2 V	Ant. Sup. Spine of Ilium to Sole	28.5	25.3	19.0
50.6	44.9	**33.7**	L3 V	Greater Trochanter Femur-Sole	25.3	22.5	16.9
45.0	40.0	**30.0**	L4 V	Crotch to Sole	22.5	20.0	15.0
46.5	41.3	**31.0**	L5 V	Gluteal Furrow to Sole	23.3	20.7	15.5
25.5	22.7	**17.0**	L6 V	Posterior Knee Crease to Sole	12.8	11.3	8.5
28.5	25.3	**19.0**	L7 V	Ant. Sup. Spine of Ilium to Knee	14.3	12.7	9.5
22.9	20.3	**15.2**	L8 V	Pubis to Knee at Patella	11.4	10.2	7.6
28.9	25.7	**19.2**	L9 V	Knee at Patella to Sole	14.4	12.8	9.6
25.5	22.7	**17.0**	L10 V	Tibia to Sole	12.8	11.3	8.5
5.3	4.7	**3.5**	L11 V	Medial Malleolus to Sole	2.6	2.3	1.8
3.8	3.3	**2.5**	L12 V	Lateral Malleolus to Sole	1.9	1.7	1.3
15.0	13.3	**10.0**	L13 T	Inter Both Mid Thighs	7.5	6.7	5.0
12.4	11.0	**8.2**	L15 T	Breadth Both Knees	6.2	5.5	4.1
12.8	11.3	**8.5**	L15 T	Breadth Both Calves	6.4	5.7	4.3
3.4	3.0	**2.2**	L16 T	Breadth One Ankle at Maleoli	1.7	1.5	1.1
9.0	8.0	**6.0**	L17 D	Mid Thigh, Anterior-Posterior	4.5	4.0	3.0
6.8	6.0	**4.5**	L18 D	Knee, Anterior-Posterior.	3.4	3.0	2.3
6.4	5.7	**4.2**	L19 D	Mid Calf, Anterior-Posterior	3.2	2.8	2.1
4.5	4.0	**3.0**	L20 D	Ankle, Anterior-Posterior	2.3	2.0	1.5
5.3	4.7	**3.5**	L21 D	Ankle at Maleoli, Anterior-Post	2.6	2.3	1.8
14.4	12.8	**9.6**	L22 V	Length of Foot	7.2	6.4	4.8
12.0	10.7	**8.0**	L23 V	Heel to 5th Toe	6.0	5.3	4.0
5.3	4.7	**3.5**	L24 T	Breadth Foot at Rest	2.6	2.3	1.8
6.0	5.3	**4.0**	L25 T	Breadth Foot Standing	3.0	2.7	2.0
3.4	3.0	**2.2**	L26 T	Width of Heel	1.7	1.5	1.1

ADULT FEMALE INCH MEASUREMENTS

LOWER EXTREMITY MEASUREMENTS

3/8 Life	1/3 Life	1/4 Life			1/6 Life	1/8 Life	1/12 Life
Inch	Inch	Inch			Inch	Inch	Inch
15.2	13.5	10.2	L1 V	Crest of Ilium to Sole	6.8	5.1	3.4
14.3	12.7	9.5	L2 V	Ant. Sup. Spine of Ilium to Sole	6.3	4.8	3.2
12.6	11.2	8.4	L3 V	Greater Trochanter Femur-Sole	5.6	4.2	2.8
11.3	10.0	7.5	L4 V	Crotch to Sole	5.0	3.8	2.5
11.6	10.3	7.8	L5 V	Gluteal Furrow to Sole	5.2	3.9	2.6
6.4	5.7	4.3	L6 V	Posterior Knee Crease to Sole	2.8	2.1	1.4
7.1	6.3	4.8	L7 V	Ant. Sup. Spine of Ilium to Knee	3.2	2.4	1.6
5.7	5.1	3.8	L8 V	Pubis to Knee at Patella	2.5	1.9	1.3
7.2	6.4	4.8	L9 V	Knee at Patella to Sole	3.2	2.4	1.6
6.4	5.7	4.3	L10 V	Tibia to Sole	2.8	2.1	1.4
1.3	1.2	0.9	L11 V	Medial Malleolus to Sole	0.6	0.4	0.3
0.9	0.8	0.6	L12 V	Lateral Malleolus to Sole	0.4	0.3	0.2
3.8	3.3	2.5	L13 T	Inter Both Mid Thighs	1.7	1.3	0.8
3.1	2.8	2.1	L15 T	Breadth Both Knees	1.4	1.0	0.7
3.2	2.8	2.1	L15 T	Breadth Both Calves	1.4	1.1	0.7
0.9	0.8	0.6	L16 T	Breadth One Ankle at Maleoli	0.4	0.3	0.2
2.3	2.0	1.5	L17 D	Mid Thigh, Anterior-Posterior	1.0	0.8	0.5
1.7	1.5	1.1	L18 D	Knee, Anterior-Posterior.	0.8	0.6	0.4
1.6	1.4	1.1	L19 D	Mid Calf, Anterior-Posterior	0.7	0.5	0.4
1.1	1.0	0.8	L20 D	Ankle, Anterior-Posterior	0.5	0.4	0.3
1.3	1.2	0.9	L21 D	Ankle at Maleoli, Anterior-Post	0.6	0.4	0.3
3.6	3.2	2.4	L22 V	Length of Foot	1.6	1.2	0.8
3.0	2.7	2.0	L23 V	Heel to 5th Toe	1.3	1.0	0.7
1.3	1.2	0.9	L24 T	Breadth Foot at Rest	0.6	0.4	0.3
1.5	1.3	1.0	L25 T	Breadth Foot Standing	0.7	0.5	0.3
0.8	0.8	0.6	L26 T	Width of Heel	0.4	0.3	0.2

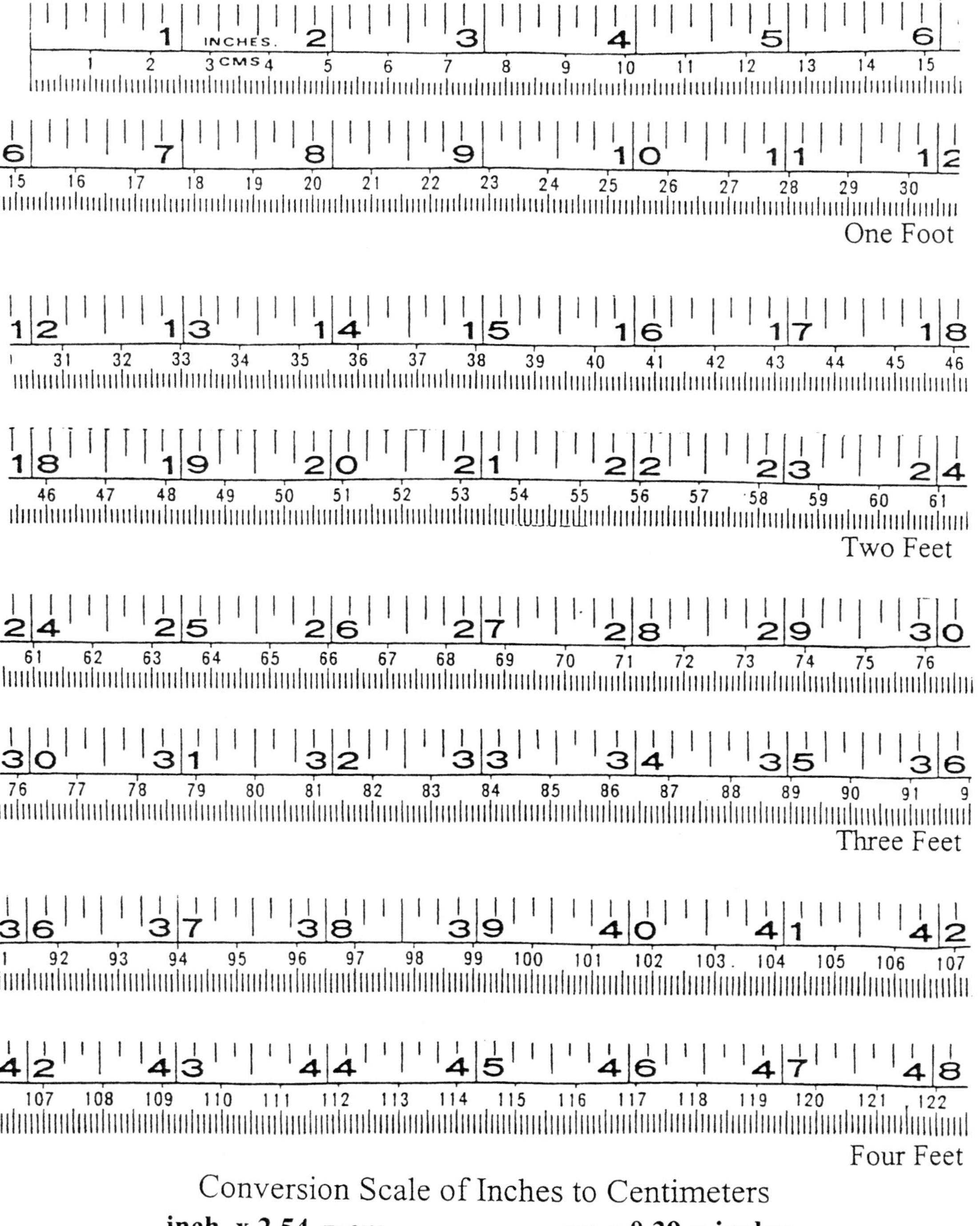

Fig. 51. Conversion scale of inches to centimeters.

ADULT HUMAN

FEMALE

PROPORTIONS

METRIC MEASUREMENTS

ADULT FEMALE METRIC MEASUREMENTS

3/2 Life	4/3 Life (Heroic)	LIFE SIZE			3/4 Life	2/3 Life	1/2 Life
				VERTICAL MEASUREMENTS			
cm	cm	cm			cm	cm	cm
251.4	223.5	**167.6**	1 V	Stature, Height, Vertex to Sole	125.7	111.7	83.8
204.8	182	**136.5**	2 V	Shoulder at Acromion to Sole	102.4	91	68.3
146.7	130.4	**97.8**	3 V	Ant. Sup. Spine of Ilium to Sole	73.4	65.2	48.9
131.7	117.1	**87.8**	4 V	Symphysis Pubis to Sole	65.9	58.5	43.9
122	108.4	**81.3**	5 V	Crotch to Sole	61	54.2	40.7
73.4	65.2	**48.9**	6 V	Knee at Patella to Sole	36.7	32.6	24.5
45.8	40.7	**30.5**	7 V	Head & Neck, Vertex-St. Notch	22.9	20.3	15.3
58.1	51.6	**38.7**	8 V	St. Notch, Shoulder-Ant. Sup. Sp.	29	25.8	19.4
73.4	65.2	**48.9**	9 V	Sternal Notch to Symph. Pubis	36.7	32.6	24.5
73.4	65.2	**48.9**	10 V	Ant. Sup. Spine of Ilium-Knee	36.7	32.6	24.5
188.6	167.6	**125.7**	11 V	Kneeling Height	94.3	83.8	62.9
133.5	118.7	**89.0**	12 V	Sitting Height	66.8	59.3	44.5
150.5	133.7	**100.3**	13 V	Buttock Straight Leg to Sole	75.2	66.9	50.2
88.7	78.8	**59.1**	14 V	Buttock to Flexed Knee	44.3	39.4	29.6
77.6	68.9	**51.7**	15 V	Flexed Knee to Sole	38.8	34.5	25.9
				VERTICAL HEAD MEASUREMENTS			
cm.	cm.	cm.			cm.	cm.	cm.
30.6	27.2	**20.4**	H1 V	Vertex to Chin	15.3	13.6	10.2
26.7	23.7	**17.8**	H2 V	Hairline to Chin	13.4	11.9	8.9
15.3	13.6	**10.2**	H3 V	Vertex-Lateral Corner of Eye	7.7	6.8	5.1
17.1	15.2	**11.4**	H4 V	Vertex to Tragion, Ear	8.6	7.6	5.7
8.6	7.6	**5.7**	H5 V	Hairline to Brow	4.3	3.8	2.9
17.3	15.3	**11.5**	H6 V	Hairline to Infranasal	8.6	7.7	5.8
8.6	7.6	**5.7**	H7 V	Brow to Infranasal	4.3	3.8	2.9
7.7	6.8	**5.1**	H8 V	Selion-Infranasal	3.8	3.4	2.6
16.4	14.5	**10.9**	H9 V	Selion to Chin	8.2	7.3	5.5
9.5	8.4	**6.3**	H10 V	Infranasal to Chin	4.7	4.2	3.2
3	2.7	**2.0**	H11 V	Infranasal-Lip Aperature	1.5	1.3	1
2.4	2.1	**1.6**	H12 V	Lip Ap. to Sublabial Crease	1.2	1.1	0.8
4.2	3.7	**2.8**	H13 V	Sublabial Crease to Chin	2.1	1.9	1.4

ADULT FEMALE METRIC MEASUREMENTS

VERTICAL MEASUREMENTS

3/8 Life	1/3 Life	1/4 Life			1/6 Life	1/8 Life	1/12 Life
cm	cm	cm			cm	cm	cm
62.9	55.9	41.9	1 V	Stature, Height, Vertex to Sole	27.9	21	14
51.2	45.5	34.1	2 V	Shoulder at Acromion to Sole	22.8	17.1	11.4
36.7	32.6	24.5	3 V	Ant. Sup. Spine of Ilium to Sole	16.3	12.2	8.2
32.9	29.3	22	4 V	Symphysis Pubis to Sole	14.6	11	7.3
30.5	27.1	20.3	5 V	Crotch to Sole	13.6	10.2	6.8
18.3	16.3	12.2	6 V	Knee at Patella to Sole	8.2	6.1	4.1
11.4	10.2	7.6	7 V	Head & Neck, Vertex-St. Notch	5.1	3.8	2.5
14.5	12.9	9.7	8 V	St. Notch, Shoulder-Ant. Sup. Sp.	6.5	4.8	3.2
18.3	16.3	12.2	9 V	Sternal Notch to Symph. Pubis	8.2	6.1	4.1
18.3	16.3	12.2	10 V	Ant. Sup. Spine of Ilium-Knee	8.2	6.1	4.1
47.1	41.9	31.4	11 V	Kneeling Height	21	15.7	10.5
33.4	29.7	22.3	12 V	Sitting Height	14.8	11.1	7.4
37.6	33.4	25.1	13 V	Buttock Straight Leg to Sole	16.7	12.5	8.4
22.2	19.7	14.8	14 V	Buttock to Flexed Knee	9.9	7.4	4.9
19.4	17.2	12.9	15 V	Flexed Knee to Sole	8.6	6.5	4.3

VERTICAL HEAD MEASUREMENTS

cm.	cm.	cm.			cm.	cm.	cm.
7.7	6.8	5.1	H1 V	Vertex to Chin	3.4	2.6	1.7
6.7	5.9	4.5	H2 V	Hairline to Chin	3	2.2	1.5
3.8	3.4	2.6	H3 V	Vertex-Lateral Corner of Eye	1.7	1.3	0.9
4.3	3.8	2.9	H4 V	Vertex to Tragion, Ear	1.9	1.4	1
2.1	1.9	1.4	H5 V	Hairline to Brow	1	0.7	0.5
4.3	3.8	2.9	H6 V	Hairline to Infranasal	1.9	1.4	1
2.1	1.9	1.4	H7 V	Brow to Infranasal	1	0.7	0.5
1.9	1.7	1.3	H8 V	Selion-Infranasal	0.9	0.6	0.4
4.1	3.6	2.7	H9 V	Selion to Chin	1.8	1.4	0.9
2.4	2.1	1.6	H10 V	Infranasal to Chin	1.1	0.8	0.5
0.8	0.7	0.5	H11 V	Infranasal-Lip Aperature	0.3	0.3	0.2
0.6	0.5	0.4	H12 V	Lip Ap. to Sublabial Crease	0.3	0.2	0.1
1.1	0.9	0.7	H13 V	Sublabial Crease to Chin	0.5	0.4	0.2

ADULT FEMALE METRIC MEASUREMENTS

3/2 Life	4/3 Life (Heroic)	LIFE SIZE			3/4 Life	2/3 Life	1/2 Life
				TRANSVERSE HEAD MEASUREMENTS			
cm.	cm.	cm.			cm.	cm.	cm.
21	18.7	**14.0**	H14 T	Biparietal	10.5	9.3	7
19.1	16.9	**12.7**	H15 T	Bizygomatic	9.5	8.5	6.4
17.7	15.7	**11.8**	H16 T	Bifronto Temporal	8.9	7.9	5.9
15.3	13.6	**10.2**	H17 T	Inter Brow Ridge	7.7	6.8	5.1
19.1	16.9	**12.7**	H18 T	Inter Tragion, Ear	9.5	8.5	6.4
17.7	15.7	**11.8**	H19 T	Inter Angle of Mandible	8.9	7.9	5.9
13.5	12	**9.0**	H20 T	Inter Lateral Corners of Eyes	6.8	6	4.5
4.5	4	**3.0**	H21 T	Width of Eye	2.3	2	1.5
4.5	4	**3.0**	H22 T	Inter Inner Corners of Eyes	2.3	2	1.5
4.7	4.1	**3.1**	H23 T	Breadth of Nose	2.3	2.1	1.6
6.6	5.9	**4.4**	H24 T	Breadth of Mouth	3.3	2.9	2.2
4.8	4.3	**3.2**	H25 T	Breadth of Chin	2.4	2.1	1.6
13.4	11.9	**8.9**	H26 T	Breadth of Neck	6.7	5.9	4.5
				ANTERIOR-POSTERIOR HEAD MEASUREMENTS			
cm.	cm.	cm.			cm.	cm.	cm.
27.8	24.7	**18.5**	H27 D	Brow to Occiput	13.9	12.3	9.3
15.3	13.6	**10.2**	H28 D	Brow to Tragus	7.7	6.8	5.1
13.8	12.3	**9.2**	H29 D	Selion to Tragus	6.9	6.1	4.6
11.4	10.1	**7.6**	H30 D	Tragus to Occiput	5.7	5.1	3.8
8.6	7.6	**5.7**	H31 D	Tragus-Angle Mandible	4.3	3.8	2.9
12.5	11.1	**8.3**	H32 D	Angle Mandible-Chin	6.2	5.5	4.2
9	8	**6.0**	H33 V	Length Ear	4.5	4	3
5	4.4	**3.3**	H34 D	Width of Ear	2.5	2.2	1.7
15.3	13.6	**10.2**	H35 D	Anterior Post. Neck	7.7	6.8	5.1

ADULT FEMALE METRIC MEASUREMENTS

TRANSVERSE HEAD MEASUREMENTS

3/8 Life	1/3 Life	1/4 Life			1/6 Life	1/8 Life	1/12 Life
cm.	cm.	cm.			cm.	cm.	cm.
5.3	4.7	3.5	H14 T	Biparietal	2.3	1.8	1.2
4.8	4.2	3.2	H15 T	Bizygomatic	2.1	1.6	1.1
4.4	3.9	3	H16 T	Bifronto Temporal	2	1.5	1
3.8	3.4	2.6	H17 T	Inter Brow Ridge	1.7	1.3	0.9
4.8	4.2	3.2	H18 T	Inter Tragion, Ear	2.1	1.6	1.1
4.4	3.9	3	H19 T	Inter Angle of Mandible	2	1.5	1
3.4	3	2.3	H20 T	Inter Lateral Corners of Eyes	1.5	1.1	0.8
1.1	1	0.8	H21 T	Width of Eye	0.5	0.4	0.3
1.1	1	0.8	H22 T	Inter Inner Corners of Eyes	0.5	0.4	0.3
1.2	1	0.8	H23 T	Breadth of Nose	0.5	0.4	0.3
1.7	1.5	1.1	H24 T	Breadth of Mouth	0.7	0.6	0.4
1.2	1.1	0.8	H25 T	Breadth of Chin	0.5	0.4	0.3
3.3	3	2.2	H26 T	Breadth of Neck	1.5	1.1	0.7

ANTERIOR-POSTERIOR HEAD MEASUREMENTS

cm.	cm.	cm.			cm.	cm.	cm.
6.9	6.2	4.6	H27 D	Brow to Occiput	3.1	2.3	1.5
3.8	3.4	2.6	H28 D	Brow to Tragus	1.7	1.3	0.9
3.5	3.1	2.3	H29 D	Selion to Tragus	1.5	1.2	0.8
2.9	2.5	1.9	H30 D	Tragus to Occiput	1.3	1	0.6
2.1	1.9	1.4	H31 D	Tragus-Angle Mandible	1	0.7	0.5
3.1	2.8	2.1	H32 D	Angle Mandible-Chin	1.4	1	0.7
2.3	2	1.5	H33 V	Length Ear	1	0.8	0.5
1.2	1.1	0.8	H34 D	Width of Ear	0.6	0.4	0.3
3.8	3.4	2.6	H35 D	Anterior Post. Neck	1.7	1.3	0.9

ADULT FEMALE METRIC MEASUREMENTS

3/2 Life (Heroic)	4/3 Life	LIFE SIZE			3/4 Life	2/3 Life	1/2 Life
				VERTICAL BODY MEASUREMENTS			
cm.	cm.	cm.			cm	cm.	cm.
15.3	13.6	**10.2**	B1 V	Chin to Sternal Notch	7.7	6.8	5.1
10.5	9.3	**7.0**	B2 V	Sternal Notch to Anterior Axilla	5.3	4.7	3.5
22.8	20.3	**15.2**	B3 V	Sternal Notch to Nipples	11.4	10.1	7.6
30.6	27.2	**20.4**	B4 V	Sternal Notch to Xyphoid	15.3	13.6	10.2
51.5	45.7	**34.3**	B5 V	Sternal Notch to Umbilicus	25.7	22.9	17.2
49.5	44	**33.0**	B6 V	Sternal Notch to Crest of Ilium	24.8	22	16.5
57.9	51.5	**38.6**	B7 V	St. Notch to Ant. Sup. Spine Ilium	29	25.7	19.3
73.2	65.1	**48.8**	B8 V	Sternal Notch to Pubis	36.6	32.5	24.4
84	74.7	**56.0**	B9 V	Sternal Notch to Crotch	42	37.3	28
21	18.7	**14.0**	B10 V	Xyphoid to Umbilicus	10.5	9.3	7
21	18.7	**14.0**	B11 V	Umbilicus to Pubis	10.5	9.3	7
32.4	28.8	**21.6**	B12 V	Umbilicus to Crotch	16.2	14.4	10.8
				TRANSVERSE BODY MEASUREMENTS			
cm.	cm.	cm.			cm.	cm.	cm.
61.1	54.3	**40.7**	B13 T	Shoulder Breadth	30.5	27.1	20.4
22.8	20.3	**15.2**	B14 T	Clavicle to Acromion Process	11.4	10.1	7.6
53.4	47.5	**35.6**	B15 T	Bi-acromial Process Breadth	26.7	23.7	17.8
45.8	40.7	**30.5**	B16 T	Inter Achromioclavicular Joint	22.9	20.3	15.3
42	37.3	**28.0**	B17 T	Inter Anterior Axillary Fold	21	18.7	14
30.3	26.9	**20.2**	B18 T	Inter Nipples	15.2	13.5	10.1
36.2	32.1	**24.1**	B19 T	Breadth of Thorax	18.1	16.1	12.1
33	29.3	**22.0**	B20 T	Inter Costal Margin	16.5	14.7	11
42	37.3	**28.0**	B21 T	Inter Crest of Illium	21	18.7	14
36.2	32.1	**24.1**	B22 T	Inter Ant. Superior Spine of Ilium	18.1	16.1	12.1
49.7	44.1	**33.1**	B23 T	Inter Greater Trocanter Femur	24.8	22.1	16.6

ADULT FEMALE METRIC MEASUREMENTS

VERTICAL BODY MEASUREMENTS

3/8 Life	1/3 Life	1/4 Life			1/6 Life	1/8 Life	1/12 Life
cm.	cm.	cm.			cm	cm.	cm.
3.8	3.4	2.6	B1 V	Chin to Sternal Notch	1.7	1.3	0.9
2.6	2.3	1.8	B2 V	Sternal Notch to Anterior Axilla	1.2	0.9	0.6
5.7	5.1	3.8	B3 V	Sternal Notch to Nipples	2.5	1.9	1.3
7.7	6.8	5.1	B4 V	Sternal Notch to Xyphoid	3.4	2.6	1.7
12.9	11.4	8.6	B5 V	Sternal Notch to Umbilicus	5.7	4.3	2.9
12.4	11	8.3	B6 V	Sternal Notch to Crest of Ilium	5.5	4.1	2.8
14.5	12.9	9.7	B7 V	St.Notch to Ant. Sup. Spine Ilium	6.4	4.8	3.2
18.3	16.3	12.2	B8 V	Sternal Notch to Pubis	8.1	6.1	4.1
21	18.7	14	B9 V	Sternal Notch to Crotch	9.3	7	4.7
5.3	4.7	3.5	B10 V	Xyphoid to Umbilicus	2.3	1.8	1.2
5.3	4.7	3.5	B11 V	Umbilicus to Pubis	2.3	1.8	1.2
8.1	7.2	5.4	B12 V	Umbilicus to Crotch	3.6	2.7	1.8

TRANSVERSE BODY MEASUREMENTS

cm.	cm.	cm.			cm.	cm.	cm.
15.3	13.6	10.2	B13 T	Shoulder Breadth	6.8	5.1	3.4
5.7	5.1	3.8	B14 T	Clavicle to Acromion Process	2.5	1.9	1.3
13.4	11.9	8.9	B15 T	Bi-acromial Process Breadth	5.9	4.5	3
11.4	10.2	7.6	B16 T	Inter Achromioclavicular Joint	5.1	3.8	2.5
10.5	9.3	7	B17 T	Inter Anterior Axillary Fold	4.7	3.5	2.3
7.6	6.7	5.1	B18 T	Inter Nipples	3.4	2.5	1.7
9	8	6	B19 T	Breadth of Thorax	4	3	2
8.3	7.3	5.5	B20 T	Inter Costal Margin	3.7	2.8	1.8
10.5	9.3	7	B21 T	Inter Crest of Illium	4.7	3.5	2.3
9	8	6	B22 T	Inter Ant. Superior Spine of Ilium	4	3	2
12.4	11	8.3	B23 T	Inter Greater Trocanter Femur	5.5	4.1	2.8

ADULT FEMALE
METRIC MEASUREMENTS

3/2 Life (Heroic)	4/3 Life	LIFE SIZE			3/4 Life	2/3 Life	1/2 Life
				ANTERIOR-POSTERIOR BODY MEASUREMENTS			
cm.	cm.	cm.			cm.	cm.	cm.
21.9	19.5	**14.6**	B24 D	Sternal Notch to Dorsal Spine	11	9.7	7.3
30.6	27.2	**20.4**	B25 D	Manubrium to Dorsal Spine	15.3	13.6	10.2
31.4	27.9	**20.9**	B26 D	Xyphoid-Sternum to Scapula	15.7	13.9	10.5
24.8	22	**16.5**	B27 D	Umbilicus to Dorsum	12.4	11	8.3
36.6	32.5	**24.4**	B28 D	Pubis to Buttock	18.3	16.3	12.2
26.7	23.7	**17.8**	B29 D	Thigh-Gluteal Furrow	13.4	11.9	8.9
				VERTICAL BACK MEASUREMENTS			
cm.	cm.	cm.			cm.	cm.	cm.
36.2	32.1	**24.1**	B30 V	Vertex to 7th Cervical Spine	18.1	16.1	12.1
				7th Cervical Vertebra Spine to:			
24	21.3	**16.0**	B31 V	Posterior Axillary Fold	12	10.7	8
29.3	26	**19.5**	B32 V	Inferior Tip of Scapula	14.6	13	9.8
65.3	58	**43.5**	B33 V	Post. Sup. Spines of Ilium	32.6	29	21.8
78	69.3	**52.0**	B34 V	Upper Buttock Midline Crease	39	34.7	26
92.4	82.1	**61.6**	B35 V	Gluteal Furrow	46.2	41.1	30.8
141	125.3	**94.0**	B36 V	Popliteal Crease Behind Knee	70.5	62.7	47
210.6	187.2	**140.4**	B37 V	Sole of the Foot	105.3	93.6	70.2
				TRANSVERSE BACK MEASUREMENTS			
cm.	cm.	cm.			cm.	cm.	cm.
45.8	40.7	**30.5**	B38 T	Inter Posterior Axillary Folds	22.9	20.3	15.3
19.1	16.9	**12.7**	B39 T	Inter Scapulae Medial Borders	9.5	8.5	6.4
15.3	13.6	**10.2**	B40 T	Inter Post. Sup. Spines Sacrum	7.7	6.8	5.1
8.3	7.3	**5.5**	B41 T	Inter Post. Inf. Spines Sacrum	4.1	3.7	2.8
35.3	31.3	**23.5**	B42 T	Inter Gluteus Maximus Muscle	17.6	15.7	11.8

ADULT FEMALE METRIC MEASUREMENTS

3/8 Life	1/3 Life	1/4 Life			1/6 Life	1/8 Life	1/12 Life
				ANTERIOR-POSTERIOR BODY MEASUREMENTS			
cm.	cm.	cm.			cm.	cm.	cm.
5.5	4.9	3.7	B24 D	Sternal Notch to Dorsal Spine	2.4	1.8	1.2
7.7	6.8	5.1	B25 D	Manubrium to Dorsal Spine	3.4	2.6	1.7
7.8	7	5.2	B26 D	Xyphoid-Sternum to Scapula	3.5	2.6	1.7
6.2	5.5	4.1	B27 D	Umbilicus to Dorsum	2.8	2.1	1.4
9.2	8.1	6.1	B28 D	Pubis to Buttock	4.1	3.1	2
6.7	5.9	4.5	B29 D	Thigh-Gluteal Furrow	3	2.2	1.5
				VERTICAL BACK MEASUREMENTS			
cm.	cm.	cm.			cm.	cm.	cm.
9	8	6	B30 V	Vertex to 7th Cervical Spine	4	3	2
				7th Cervical Vertebra Spine to:			
6	5.3	4	B31 V	Posterior Axillary Fold	2.7	2	1.3
7.3	6.5	4.9	B32 V	Inferior Tip of Scapula	3.3	2.4	1.6
16.3	14.5	10.9	B33 V	Post. Sup. Spines of Ilium	7.3	5.4	3.6
19.5	17.3	13	B34 V	Upper Buttock Midline Crease	8.7	6.5	4.3
23.1	20.5	15.4	B35 V	Gluteal Furrow	10.3	7.7	5.1
35.3	31.3	23.5	B36 V	Popliteal Crease Behind Knee	15.7	11.8	7.8
52.7	46.8	35.1	B37 V	Sole of the Foot	23.4	17.6	11.7
				TRANSVERSE BACK MEASUREMENTS			
cm.	cm.	cm.			cm.	cm.	cm.
11.4	10.2	7.6	B38 T	Inter Posterior Axillary Folds	5.1	3.8	2.5
4.8	4.2	3.2	B39 T	Inter Scapulae Medial Borders	2.1	1.6	1.1
3.8	3.4	2.6	B40 T	Inter Post. Sup. Spines Sacrum	1.7	1.3	0.9
2.1	1.8	1.4	B41 T	Inter Post. Inf. Spines Sacrum	0.9	0.7	0.5
8.8	7.8	5.9	B42 T	Inter Gluteus Maximus Muscle	3.9	2.9	2

ADULT FEMALE METRIC MEASUREMENTS

UPPER EXTREMITY MEASUREMENTS

3/2 Life	4/3 Life (Heroic)	LIFE SIZE			3/4 Life	2/3 Life	1/2 Life
cm.	cm.	cm.			cm.	cm.	cm.
243.6	216.5	**162.4**	U1 T	Span of Arms	121.8	108.3	81.2
26.7	23.7	**17.8**	U2 T	Sternum to Acromion Process	13.4	11.9	8.9
19.1	16.9	**12.7**	U3 T	Sternum-Shoulder Pivot	9.5	8.5	6.4
41.9	37.2	**27.9**	U4 V	Humerus-Elbow Pivot	20.9	18.6	14
51.5	45.7	**34.3**	U5 V	Shoulder-Elbow Flexed	25.7	22.9	17.2
47.6	42.3	**31.7**	U6 V	Acromion to Lat. Condyl Elbow	23.8	21.1	15.9
64.5	57.3	**43.0**	U7 V	Flex ed Elbow to Finger Tip	32.3	28.7	21.5
34.2	30.4	**22.8**	U8 V	Flexed Elbow to Wrist	17.1	15.2	11.4
26.7	23.7	**17.8**	U9 V	Wrist to Finger tip	13.4	11.9	8.9
17.3	15.3	**11.5**	U10 V	Wrist to Thumb	8.6	7.7	5.8
15.3	13.6	**10.2**	U11 V	Length of Palm	7.7	6.8	5.1
11.4	10.1	**7.6**	U12 V	Length 3rd Finger	5.7	5.1	3.8
18.3	16.3	**12.2**	U13 V	Thumb Crotch to 3rd Finger tip	9.2	8.1	6.1
9.3	8.3	**6.2**	U14 V	Thumb Crotch to Thumb Tip	4.7	4.1	3.1
15.3	13.6	**10.2**	U15 D	Anterior Post. Arm at Biceps	7.7	6.8	5.1
12.3	10.9	**8.2**	U16 D	Anterior Posterior at Forearm	6.2	5.5	4.1
5.9	5.2	**3.9**	U17 D	Depth of Wrist	2.9	2.6	2
8.6	7.6	**5.7**	U18 T	Breadth of Wrist	4.3	3.8	2.9
13.4	11.9	**8.9**	U19 T	Breadth of Hand	6.7	5.9	4.5
11.4	10.1	**7.6**	U20 T	Breadth of Palm	5.7	5.1	3.8

ADULT FEMALE METRIC MEASUREMENTS

UPPER EXTREMITY MEASUREMENTS

3/8 Life	1/3 Life	1/4 Life			1/6 Life	1/8 Life	1/12 Life
cm.	cm.	cm.			cm.	cm.	cm.
60.9	54.1	40.6	U1 T	Span of Arms	27.1	20.3	13.5
6.7	5.9	4.5	U2 T	Sternum to Acromion Process	3	2.2	1.5
4.8	4.2	3.2	U3 T	Sternum-Shoulder Pivot	2.1	1.6	1.1
10.5	9.3	7	U4 V	Humerus-Elbow Pivot	4.7	3.5	2.3
12.9	11.4	8.6	U5 V	Shoulder-Elbow Flexed	5.7	4.3	2.9
11.9	10.6	7.9	U6 V	Acromion to Lat. Condyl Elbow	5.3	4	2.6
16.1	14.3	10.8	U7 V	Flex ed Elbow to Finger Tip	7.2	5.4	3.6
8.6	7.6	5.7	U8 V	Flexed Elbow to Wrist	3.8	2.9	1.9
6.7	5.9	4.5	U9 V	Wrist to Finger tip	3	2.2	1.5
4.3	3.8	2.9	U10 V	Wrist to Thumb	1.9	1.4	1
3.8	3.4	2.6	U11 V	Length of Palm	1.7	1.3	0.9
2.9	2.5	1.9	U12 V	Length 3rd Finger	1.3	1	0.6
4.6	4.1	3.1	U13 V	Thumb Crotch to 3rd Finger tip	2	1.5	1
2.3	2.1	1.6	U14 V	Thumb Crotch to Thumb Tip	1	0.8	0.5
3.8	3.4	2.6	U15 D	Anterior Post. Arm at Biceps	1.7	1.3	0.9
3.1	2.7	2.1	U16 D	Anterior Posterior at Forearm	1.4	1	0.7
1.5	1.3	1	U17 D	Depth of Wrist	0.7	0.5	0.3
2.1	1.9	1.4	U18 T	Breadth of Wrist	1	0.7	0.5
3.3	3	2.2	U19 T	Breadth of Hand	1.5	1.1	0.7
2.9	2.5	1.9	U20 T	Breadth of Palm	1.3	1	0.6

ADULT FEMALE METRIC MEASUREMENTS

3/2 Life	4/3 Life (Heroic)	LIFE SIZE			3/4 Life	2/3 Life	1/2 Life
				LOWER EXTREMITY MEASUREMENTS			
cm.	cm.	cm.			cm.	cm.	cm.
154.8	137.6	**103.2**	L1 V	Crest of Ilium to Sole	77.4	68.8	51.6
144.8	128.7	**96.5**	L2 V	Ant. Sup. Spine of Ilium to Sole	72.4	64.3	48.3
128.6	114.3	**85.7**	L3 V	Greater Trochanter Femur-Sole	64.3	57.1	42.9
114.3	101.6	**76.2**	L4 V	Crotch to Sole	57.2	50.8	38.1
118.2	105.1	**78.8**	L5 V	Gluteal Furrow-Sole	59.1	52.5	39.4
64.8	57.6	**43.2**	L6 V	Posterior Knee Crease to Sole	32.4	28.8	21.6
72.3	64.3	**48.2**	L7 V	Ant. Sup. Spine of Ilium to Knee	36.2	32.1	24.1
57.9	51.5	**38.6**	L8 V	Pubis to Knee at Patella	29	25.7	19.3
73.4	65.2	**48.9**	L9 V	Knee at Patella to Sole	36.7	33.2	24.5
64.8	57.6	**43.2**	L10 V	Tibia to Sole	32.4	28.8	21.6
13.5	12	**9.0**	L11 V	Medial Malleolus to Sole	6.8	6	4.5
9.6	8.5	**6.4**	L12 V	Lateral Malleolus to Sole	4.8	4.3	3.2
38.1	33.9	**25.4**	L13 T	Inter Both Mid Thighs	19.1	16.9	12.7
31.5	28	**21.0**	L15 T	Breadth Both Knees	15.8	14	10.5
36.2	32.1	**24.1**	L15 T	Breadth Both Calves	18.1	16.1	12.1
8.6	7.6	**5.7**	L16 T	Breadth one Ankle at Maleoli	4.3	3.8	2.9
22.8	20.3	**15.2**	L17 D	Mid Thigh, Anterior-Posterior	11.4	10.1	7.6
17.3	15.3	**11.5**	L18 D	Knee, Anterior-Posterior.	8.6	7.7	5.8
17.3	15.3	**11.5**	L19 D	Mid Calf, Anterior-Posterior	8.6	7.7	5.8
10.7	9.5	**7.1**	L20 D	Ankle, Anterior-Posterior	5.3	4.7	3.6
13.4	11.9	**8.9**	L21 D	Ankle at Maleoli, Anterior-Post	6.7	5.9	4.5
36.6	32.5	**24.4**	L22 V	Length of Foot	18.3	16.3	12.2
30.6	27.2	**20.4**	L23 V	Heel to 5th Toe	15.3	13.6	10.2
13.5	12	**9.0**	L24 T	Breadth Foot at Rest	6.8	6	4.5
15	13.3	**10.0**	L25 T	Breadth Foot Standing	7.5	6.7	5
7.7	6.8	**5.1**	L26 T	Width of Heel	3.8	3.4	2.6

ADULT FEMALE METRIC MEASUREMENTS

LOWER EXTREMITY MEASUREMENTS

3/8 Life	1/3 Life	1/4 Life			1/6 Life	1/8 Life	1/12 Life
cm.	cm.	cm.			cm.	cm.	cm.
38.7	34.4	25.8	L1 V	Crest of Ilium to Sole	17.2	12.9	8.6
36.2	32.2	24.1	L2 V	Ant. Sup. Spine of Ilium to Sole	16.1	12.1	8
32.1	28.6	21.4	L3 V	Greater Trochanter Femur-Sole	14.3	10.7	7.1
28.6	25.4	19.1	L4 V	Crotch to Sole	12.7	9.5	6.4
29.6	26.3	19.7	L5 V	Gluteal Furrow-Sole	13.1	9.9	6.6
16.2	14.4	10.8	L6 V	Posterior Knee Crease to Sole	7.2	5.4	3.6
18.1	16.1	12.1	L7 V	Ant. Sup. Spine of Ilium to Knee	8	6	4
14.5	12.9	9.7	L8 V	Pubis to Knee at Patella	6.4	4.8	3.2
18.3	16.3	12.2	L9 V	Knee at Patella to Sole	8.2	6.1	4.1
16.2	14.4	10.8	L10 V	Tibia to Sole	7.2	5.4	3.6
3.4	3	2.3	L11 V	Medial Malleolus to Sole	1.5	1.1	0.8
2.4	2.1	1.6	L12 V	Lateral Malleolus to Sole	1.1	0.8	0.5
9.5	8.5	6.4	L13 T	Inter Both Mid Thighs	4.2	3.2	2.1
7.9	7	5.3	L15 T	Breadth Both Knees	3.5	2.6	1.8
9	8	6	L15 T	Breadth Both Calves	4	3	2
2.1	1.9	1.4	L16 T	Breadth one Ankle at Maleoli	1	0.7	0.5
5.7	5.1	3.8	L17 D	Mid Thigh, Anterior-Posterior	2.5	1.9	1.3
4.3	3.8	2.9	L18 D	Knee, Anterior-Posterior.	1.9	1.4	1
4.3	3.8	2.9	L19 D	Mid Calf, Anterior-Posterior	1.9	1.4	1
2.7	2.4	1.8	L20 D	Ankle, Anterior-Posterior	1.2	0.9	0.6
3.3	3	2.2	L21 D	Ankle at Maleoli, Anterior-Post	1.5	1.1	0.7
9.2	8.1	6.1	L22 V	Length of Foot	4.1	3.1	2
7.7	6.8	5.1	L23 V	Heel to 5th Toe	3.4	2.6	1.7
3.4	3	2.3	L24 T	Breadth Foot at Rest	1.5	1.1	0.8
3.8	3.3	2.5	L25 T	Breadth Foot Standing	1.7	1.3	0.8
1.9	1.7	1.3	L26 T	Width of Heel	0.9	0.6	0.4

ADULT HUMAN

MALE

PROPORTIONS

INCH MEASUREMENTS

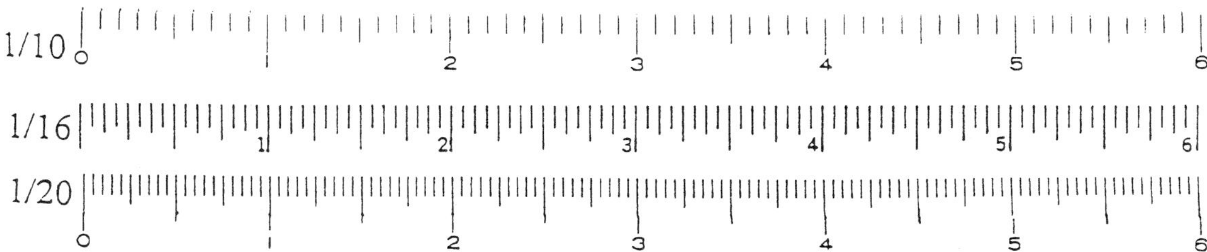

Conversions of Inch Fraction in 1/16ths to Inch Decimal

Inch fraction	1/16	1/8	3/16	1/4	5/16	3/8	7/16	1/2
Inch decimal	.06	.13	.19	.25	.31	.38	.44	.50

Inch fraction	9/16	5/8	11/16	3/4	13/16	7/8	15/16
Inch decimal	.56	.63	.69	.75	.81	.88	.94

Fig. 52. Conversions of inch fractions in 1/16ths to inch decimal.

Facing page, Fig. 53a.
Masculine figure, height 6 ft. Shows inch and centimeter measurements.

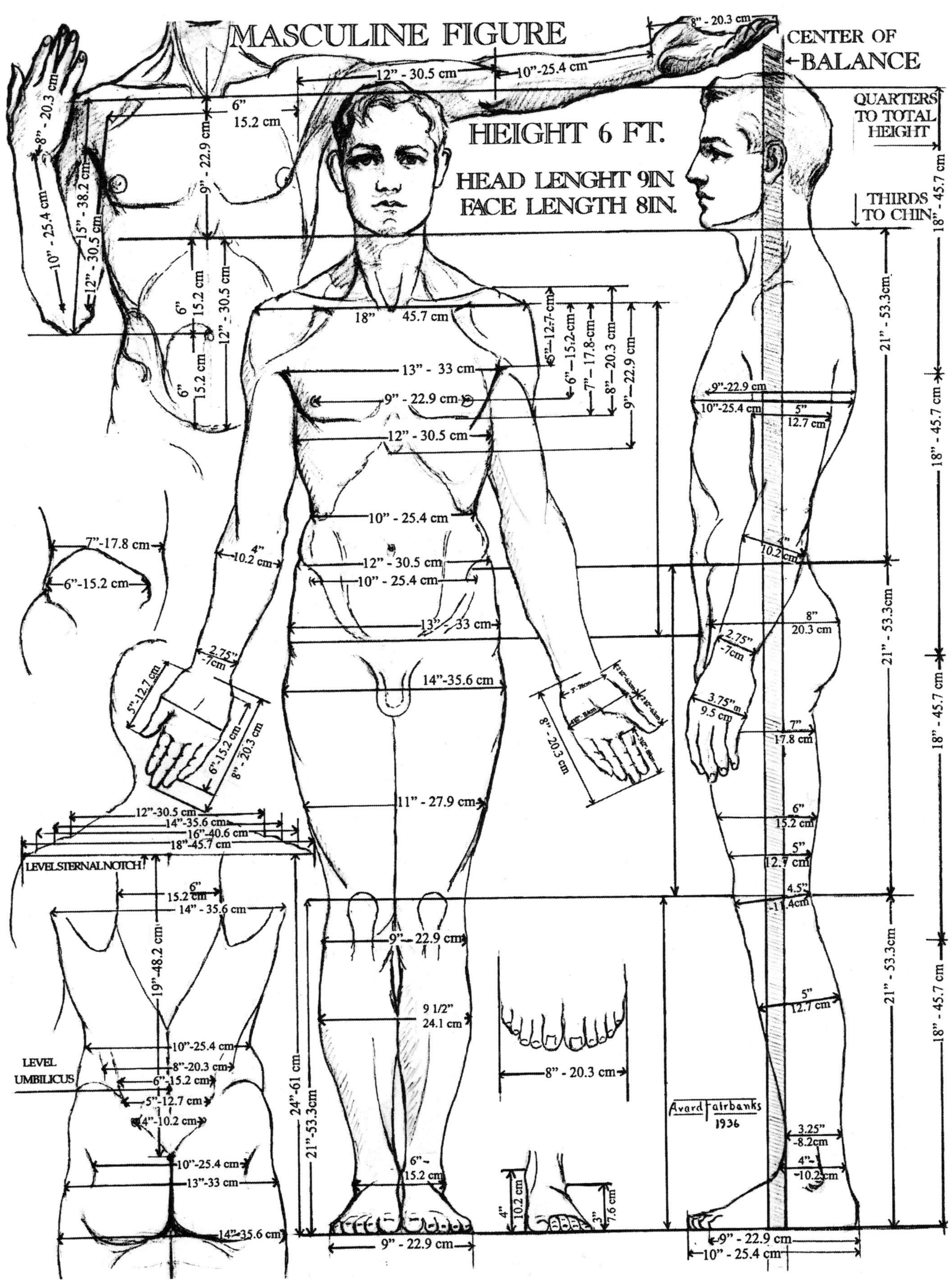
MASCULINE FIGURE
HEIGHT 6 FT.
HEAD LENGHT 9IN.
FACE LENGTH 8IN.
CENTER OF BALANCE
QUARTERS TO TOTAL HEIGHT
THIRDS TO CHIN
LEVEL STERNAL NOTCH
LEVEL UMBILICUS
Avard Fairbanks 1936

MASCULINE HAND DETAILS

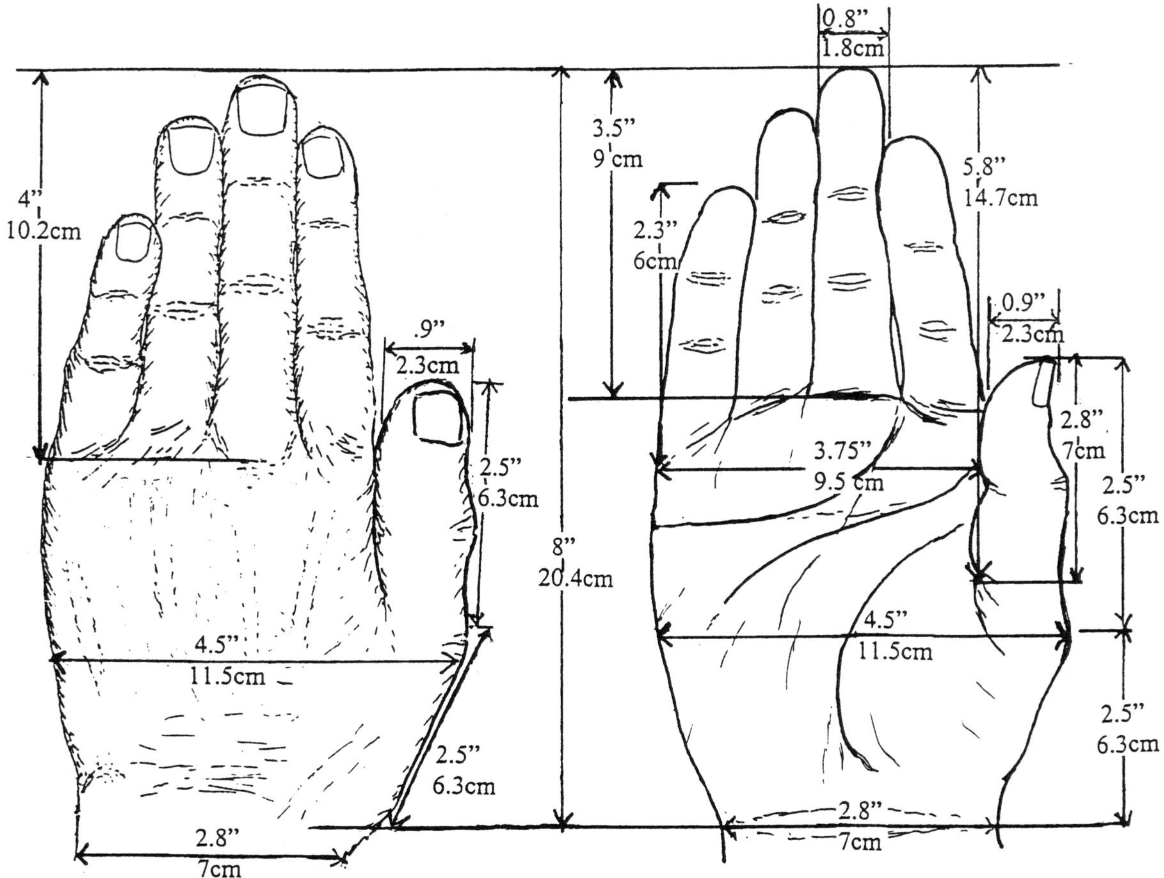

Fig. 53b. Masculine hand details.

MASCULINE FOOT DETAILS

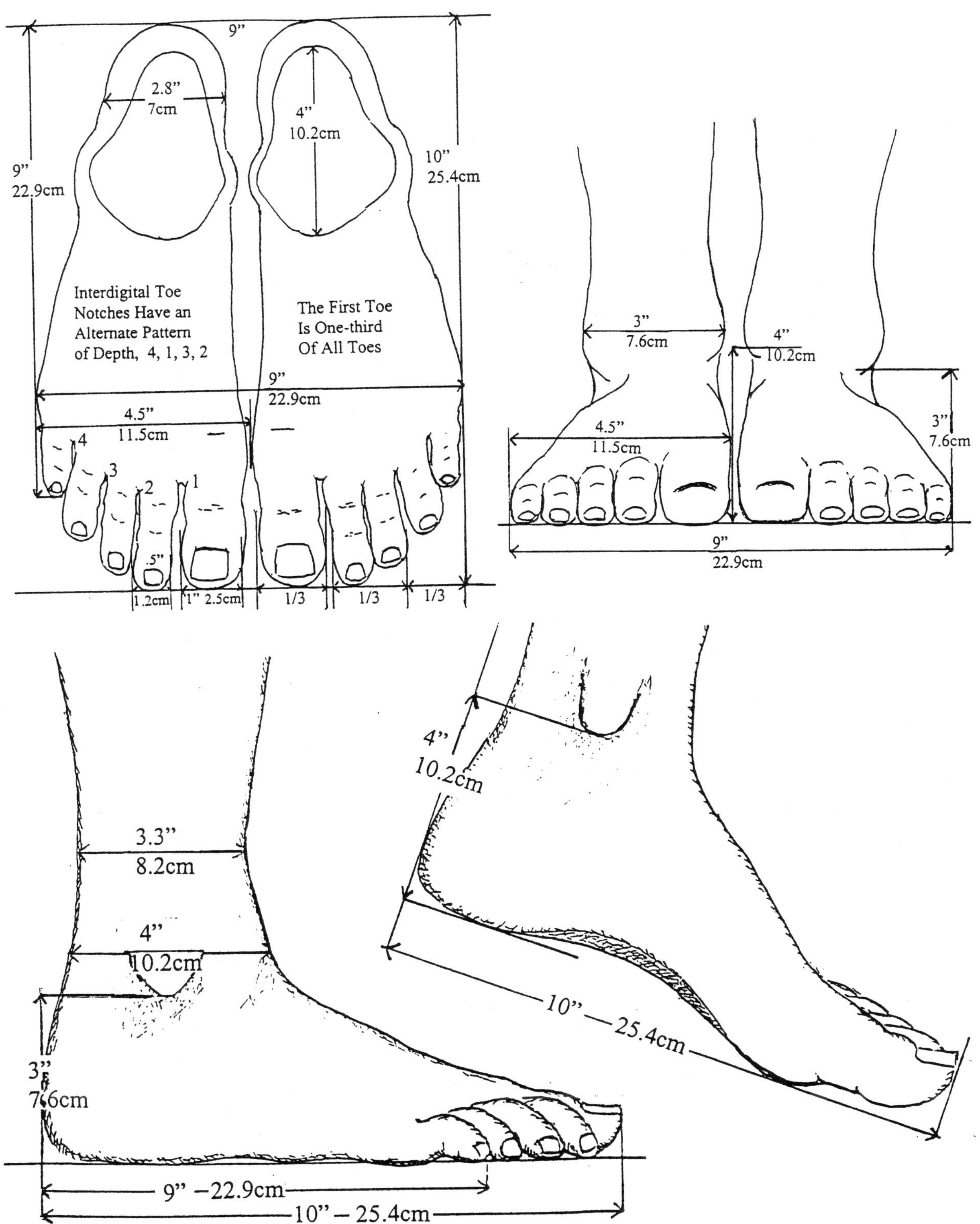

Fig. 53c. Masculine foot details.

MASCULINE HEAD, LENGTH 9 INCHES

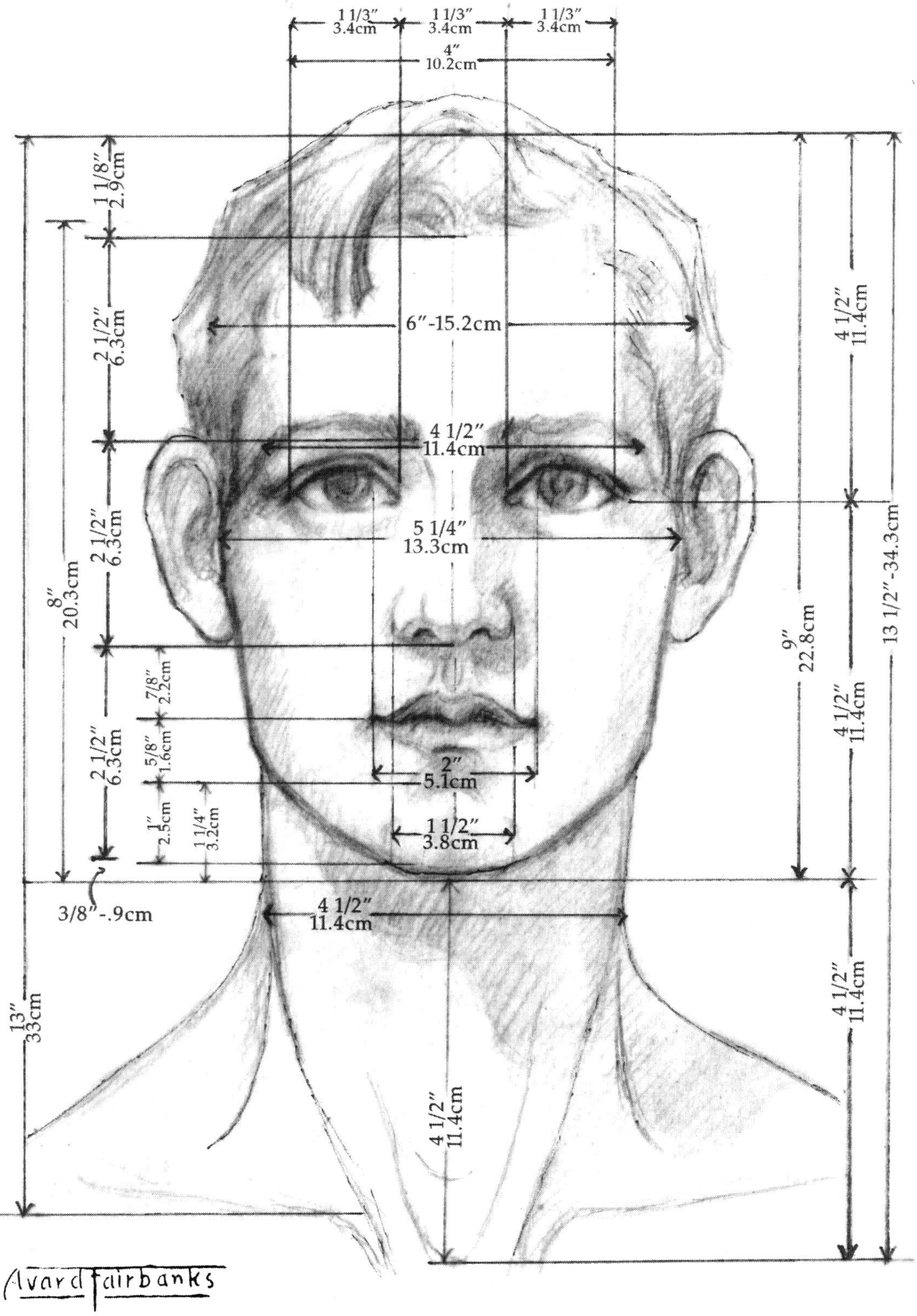

Fig. 54. The masculine head, detailed proportions, anterior view. The head is divided in two at the level of the eyes. One half face height = distance between lateral corners of eyes. The mouth width = one half distance between the lateral corners of eyes.

MASCULINE HEAD, LENGTH 9 INCHES

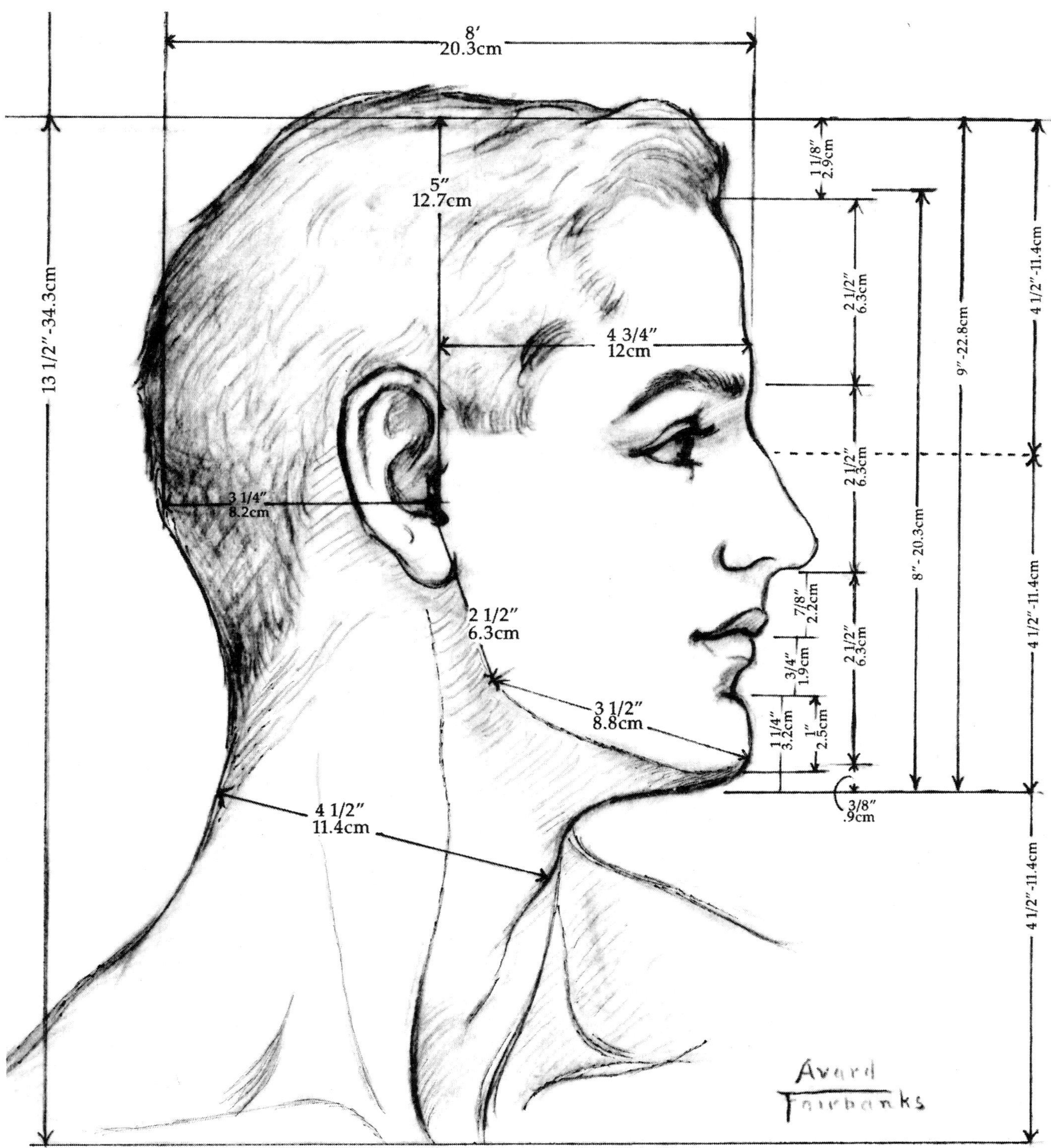

Fig. 55. The masculine head, detailed proportions, right lateral view. The face is divided into three equal proportions: Sternal notch to chin; to corner of eye; to top of head. The ear is on the same horizontal level as the nose and length is equal. The eye is one half the distance from the top of the head to the chin.

ADULT MALE
INCH MEASUREMENTS

3/2 Life	4/3 Life (Heroic)	LIFE SIZE			3/4 Life	2/3 Life	1/2 Life
				VERTICAL MEASUREMENTS			
Inch	Inch	Inch			Inch	Inch	Inch
108.0	96.0	**72.0**	1 V	Stature, Height, Vertex to Sole	54.0	48.0	36.0
87.8	78.0	**58.5**	2V	Shoulder at Acromion to Sole	43.9	39.0	29.2
63.0	56.0	**42.0**	3V	Ant. Sup. Spine of Ilium to Sole	31.5	28.0	21.0
56.1	49.9	**37.4**	4V	Symphysis Pubis to Sole	28.1	24.9	18.7
49.0	43.6	**32.7**	5V	Crotch to Sole	24.5	21.8	16.4
31.5	28.0	**21.0**	6V	Knee to Sole	15.8	14.0	10.5
20.2	18.0	**13.5**	7V	Head & Neck, Vertex – St. Notch	10.1	9.0	6.8
24.8	22.0	**16.5**	8V	St.Notch, Shoulder – Ant. Sup. Sp.	12.4	11.0	8.2
40.2	35.7	**26.8**	9V	Sternal Notch to Crotch	20.1	17.9	13.4
31.5	28.0	**21.0**	10V	Ant. Sup. Spine of Ilium to Knee	15.8	14.0	10.5
81.0	72.0	**54.0**	11V	Kneeling Height	40.5	36.0	27.0
57.0	50.7	**38.0**	12V	Sitting Height	28.5	25.3	19.0
63.8	56.7	**42.5**	13V	Buttock, Straight Leg to Sole	31.9	28.3	21.2
37.1	32.9	**24.7**	14V	Buttock to Flexed Knee	18.5	16.5	12.3
35.4	31.5	**23.6**	15V	Flexed Knee to Sole	17.7	15.7	11.8
				VERTICAL HEAD MEASUREMENTS			
Inch	Inch	Inch			Inch	Inch	Inch
13.5	12.0	**9.0**	H1 V	Vertex to Chin	6.8	6.0	4.5
12.0	10.7	**8.0**	H2 V	Hairline to Chin	6.0	5.3	4.0
6.8	6.0	**4.5**	H3 V	Vertex to Lateral Corner of Eye	3.4	3.0	2.2
8.2	7.3	**5.5**	H4 V	Vertex to Tragion of Ear	4.1	3.7	2.8
3.8	3.3	**2.5**	H5 V	Hairline to Brow	1.9	1.7	1.2
7.5	6.7	**5.0**	H6 V	Hairline to infranasal	3.8	3.3	2.5
3.8	3.3	**2.5**	H7 V	Brow to Infranasal	1.9	1.7	1.2
3.2	2.8	**2.1**	H8 V	Selion to Infranasal	1.6	1.4	1.1
7.7	6.8	**5.1**	H9 V	Selion to Chin	3.9	3.4	2.6
3.8	3.3	**2.5**	H10 V	Infranasal to Chin	1.9	1.7	1.2
1.3	1.2	**0.9**	H11 V	Infranasal to Lip Aperature	0.7	0.6	0.4
1.1	1.0	**0.8**	H12 V	Lip Aperat. to Sublabial Crease	0.6	0.5	0.4
1.9	1.7	**1.2**	H13 V	Sublabial Crease to Chin	0.9	0.8	0.6

ADULT MALE
INCH MEASUREMENTS

VERTICAL MEASUREMENTS

3/8 Life	1/3 Life	1/4 Life			1/6 Life	1/8 Life	1/12 Life
Inch	Inch	Inch			Inch	Inch	Inch
27.0	24.0	18.0	1 V	Stature, Height, Vertex to Sole	12.0	9.0	6.0
21.9	19.5	14.6	2 V	Shoulder at Acromion to Sole	9.8	7.3	4.9
15.8	14.0	10.5	3 V	Ant. Sup. Spine of Ilium to Sole	7.0	5.2	3.5
14.0	12.5	9.3	4 V	Symphysis Pubis to Sole	6.2	4.7	3.1
12.3	10.9	8.2	5 V	Crotch to Sole	5.5	4.1	2.7
7.9	7.0	5.2	6 V	Knee to Sole	3.5	2.6	1.8
5.1	4.5	3.4	7 V	Head & Neck, Vertex to St. Notch	2.2	1.7	1.1
6.2	5.5	4.1	8 V	St.Notch, Shoulder – Ant. Sup.Sp.	2.8	2.1	1.4
10.1	8.9	6.7	9 V	Sternal Notch to Crotch	4.5	3.4	2.2
7.9	7.0	5.2	10 V	Ant. Sup. Spine of Ilium to Knee	3.5	2.6	1.8
20.2	18.0	13.5	11 V	Kneeling Height	9.0	6.8	4.5
14.2	12.7	9.5	12 V	Sitting Height	6.3	4.8	3.2
15.9	14.2	10.6	13 V	Buttock, Straight Leg to Sole	7.1	5.3	3.5
9.3	8.2	6.2	14 V	Buttock to Flexed Knee	4.1	3.1	2.1
8.8	7.9	5.9	15 V	Flexed Knee to Sole	3.9	2.0	1.0

VERTICAL HEAD MEASUREMENTS

Inch	Inch	Inch			Inch	Inch	Inch
3.4	3.0	2.2	H1 V	Vertex to Chin	1.5	1.1	0.8
3.0	2.7	2.0	H2 V	Hairline to Chin	1.3	1.0	0.7
1.7	1.5	1.1	H3 V	Vertex to Lateral Corner of Eye	0.8	0.6	0.4
2.1	1.8	1.4	H4 V	Vertex to Tragion of Ear	0.9	0.7	0.5
0.9	0.8	0.6	H5 V	Hairline to Brow	0.4	0.3	0.2
1.9	1.7	1.2	H6 V	Hairline to infranasal	0.8	0.6	0.4
0.9	0.8	0.6	H7 V	Brow to Infranasal	0.4	0.3	0.2
0.8	0.7	0.5	H8 V	Selion to Infranasal	0.4	0.3	0.2
1.9	1.7	1.3	H9 V	Selion to Chin	0.9	0.6	0.4
0.9	0.8	0.6	H10 V	Infranasal to Chin	0.4	0.3	0.2
0.3	0.3	0.2	H11 V	Infranasal to Lip Aperature	0.1	0.1	0.1
0.3	0.2	0.2	H12 V	Lip Aperat. to Sublabial Crease	0.1	0.1	0.1
0.5	0.4	0.3	H13 V	Sublabial Crease to Chin	0.2	0.2	0.1

ADULT MALE
INCH MEASUREMENTS

3/2 Life (Heroic)	4/3 Life	LIFE SIZE			3/4 Life	2/3 Life	1/2 Life
				TRANSVERSE HEAD MEASUREMENTS			
Inch	Inch	Inch			Inch	Inch	Inch
9.0	8.0	**6.0**	H14 T	Bi-Parietal	4.5	4.0	3.0
7.9	7.0	**5.2**	H15 T	Bi-Zygomatic	3.9	3.5	2.6
6.8	6.0	**4.5**	H16 T	Bi-Fronto Temporal	3.4	3.0	2.2
6.4	5.7	**4.2**	H17 T	Inter Brow Ridge	3.2	2.8	2.1
7.9	7.0	**5.2**	H18 T	Inter Tragion of Ears	3.9	3.5	2.6
7.1	6.3	**4.8**	H19 T	Inter Angle of Mandible	3.6	3.2	2.4
6.0	5.3	**4.0**	H20 T	Inter Lateral Corners of Eyes	3.0	2.7	2.0
2.0	1.8	**1.3**	H21 T	Width of Eye	1.0	0.9	0.7
2.0	1.8	**1.3**	H22 T	Inter Inner Corner of eyes	1.0	0.9	0.7
2.2	2.0	**1.5**	H23 T	Breadth of Nose	1.1	1.0	0.8
3.0	2.7	**2.0**	H24 T	Breadth of Mouth	1.5	1.3	1.0
2.2	2.0	**1.5**	H25 T	Breadth of Chin	1.1	1.0	0.8
6.8	6.0	**4.5**	H26 T	Breadth of Neck	3.4	3.0	2.2
				ANTERIOR-POSTERIOR HEAD			
Inch	Inch	Inch			Inch	Inch	Inch
12.0	10.7	**8.0**	H27 D	Brow to Occiput	6.0	5.3	4.0
7.1	6.3	**4.8**	H28 D	Brow to Tragus	3.6	3.2	2.4
6.8	6.0	**4.5**	H29 D	Selion to Tragus	3.4	3.0	2.2
4.9	4.3	**3.2**	H30 D	Tragus to Occiput	2.4	2.2	1.6
3.8	3.3	**2.5**	H31 D	Tragus to Angle Mandible	1.9	1.7	1.2
5.2	4.7	**3.5**	H32 D	Angle of Mandible to Chin	2.6	2.3	1.8
4.3	3.8	**2.9**	H33 V	Length of Ear, Vertical	2.2	1.9	1.4
2.2	2.0	**1.5**	H34 D	Width of Ear, Anterior-Posterior	1.1	1.0	0.8
6.8	6.0	**4.5**	H35 D	Anterior to Posterior of Neck	3.4	3.0	2.2

ADULT MALE
INCH MEASUREMENTS

TRANSVERSE HEAD MEASUREMENTS

3/8 Life	1/3 Life	1/4 Life			1/6 Life	1/8 Life	1/12 Life
Inch	Inch	Inch			Inch	Inch	Inch
2.2	2.0	1.5	H14 T	Bi-Parietal	1.0	0.8	0.5
1.0	1.8	1.3	H15 T	Bi-Zygomatic	0.9	0.7	0.4
1.7	1.5	1.1	H16 T	Bi-Fronto Temporal	0.8	0.6	0.4
1.6	1.4	1.1	H17 T	Inter Brow Ridge	0.7	0.5	0.3
1.0	1.8	1.3	H18 T	Inter Tragion of Ears	0.9	0.7	0.4
1.8	1.6	1.2	H19 T	Inter Angle of Mandible	0.8	0.6	0.4
1.5	1.3	1.0	H20 T	Inter Lateral Corners of Eyes	0.7	0.5	0.3
0.5	0.4	0.3	H21 T	Width of Eye	0.2	0.2	0.1
0.5	0.4	0.3	H22 T	Inter Inner Corner of eyes	0.2	0.2	0.1
0.6	0.5	0.4	H23 T	Breadth of Nose	0.2	0.2	0.1
0.8	0.7	0.5	H24 T	Breadth of Mouth	0.3	0.2	0.2
0.6	0.5	0.4	H25 T	Breadth of Chin	0.2	0.2	0.1
1.7	1.5	1.1	H26 T	Breadth of Neck	0.8	0.6	0.4

ANTERIOR-POSTERIOR HEAD

Inch	Inch	Inch			Inch	Inch	Inch
3.0	2.7	2.0	H27 D	Brow to Occiput	1.3	1.0	0.7
1.8	1.6	1.2	H28 D	Brow to Tragus	0.8	0.6	0.4
1.7	1.5	1.1	H29 D	Selion to Tragus	0.8	0.6	0.4
1.2	1.1	0.8	H30 D	Tragus to Occiput	0.5	0.4	0.3
0.9	0.8	0.6	H31 D	Tragus to Angle Mandible	0.4	0.3	0.2
1.3	1.2	0.9	H32 D	Angle of Mandible to Chin	0.6	0.4	0.3
1.1	0.0	0.7	H33 V	Length of Ear, Vertical	0.5	0.4	0.2
0.6	0.5	0.4	H34 D	Width of Ear, Anterior-Posterior	0.2	0.2	0.1
1.7	1.5	1.1	H35 D	Anterior to Posterior of Neck	0.8	0.6	0.4

ADULT MALE
INCH MEASUREMENTS

3/2 Life (Heroic)	4/3 Life	LIFE SIZE			3/4 Life	2/3 Life	1/2 Life
				VERTICAL BODY MEASUREMENTS			
Inch	Inch	Inch			Inch	Inch	Inch
6.8	6.0	**4.5**	B1 V	Chin to Sternal Notch	3.4	3.0	2.2
6.0	5.3	**4.0**	B2 V	Sternal Notch to Axilla	3.0	2.7	2.0
9.0	8.0	**6.0**	B3 V	Sternal Notch to Nipples	4.5	4.0	3.0
13.5	12.0	**9.0**	B4 V	Sternal Notch to Xyphoid	6.8	6.0	4.5
22.5	20.0	**15.0**	B5 V	Sternal Notch to Umbilicus	11.2	10.0	7.5
22.5	20.0	**15.0**	B6 V	Strernal Notch to Crest Ilium	11.2	10.0	7.5
24.8	22.0	**16.5**	B7 V	Sternal Notch to Ant. S. Sp. Ilium	12.4	11.0	8.2
31.5	28.0	**21.0**	B8 V	Sternal Notch to Pubis	15.8	14.0	10.5
40.5	36.0	**27.0**	B9 V	Sternal Notch to Crotch	20.2	18.0	13.5
9.0	8.0	**6.0**	B10 V	Xyphoid to Umbilicus	4.5	4.0	3.0
9.0	8.0	**6.0**	B11 V	Umbilicus to Pubis	4.5	4.0	3.0
18.0	16.0	**12.0**	B12 V	Umbilicus to Crotch	9.0	8.0	6.0
				TRANSVERSE BODY MEASUREMENTS			
Inch	Inch	Inch			Inch	Inch	Inch
28.5	25.3	**19.0**	B13 T	Shoulder Breadth	14.2	12.7	9.5
12.4	11.0	**8.2**	B14 T	Clavicle to Acromion Process	6.2	5.5	4.1
27.0	24.0	**18.0**	B15 T	Biacromial Process Breadth	13.5	12.0	9.0
24.0	21.3	**16.0**	B16 T	Inter Acroioclavicular Joints	12.0	10.7	8.0
19.5	17.3	**13.0**	B17 T	Inter Anterior Axillary Fold	9.8	8.7	6.5
13.5	12.0	**9.0**	B18 T	Inter Nipples	6.8	6.0	4.5
18.0	16.0	**12.0**	B19 T	Breadth of Thorax	9.0	8.0	6.0
15.0	13.3	**10.0**	B20 T	Inter Costal Margin	7.5	6.7	5.0
18.0	16.0	**12.0**	B21 T	Inter Crest of Illium	9.0	8.0	6.0
15.0	13.3	**10.0**	B22 T	Inter Anterior Superior Spine	7.5	6.7	5.0
21.0	18.7	**14.0**	B23 T	Inter Greater Trochanter Femur	10.5	9.3	7.0

ADULT MALE
INCH MEASUREMENTS

VERTICAL BODY MEASUREMENTS

3/8 Life	1/3 Life	1/4 Life			1/6 Life	1/8 Life	1/12 Life
Inch	Inch	Inch			Inch	Inch	Inch
1.7	1.5	1.1	B1 V	Chin to Sternal Notch	0.8	0.6	0.4
1.5	1.3	1.0	B2 V	Sternal Notch to Axilla	0.7	0.5	0.3
2.2	2.0	1.5	B3 V	Sternal Notch to Nipples	1.0	0.8	0.5
3.4	3.0	2.2	B4 V	Sternal Notch to Xyphoid	1.5	1.1	0.8
5.6	5.0	3.8	B5 V	Sternal Notch to Umbilicus	2.5	1.9	1.2
5.6	5.0	3.8	B6 V	Strernal Notch to Crest Ilium	2.5	1.9	1.2
6.2	5.5	4.1	B7 V	Sternal Notch to Ant. S. Sp. Ilium	2.8	2.1	1.4
7.9	7.0	5.2	B8 V	Sternal Notch to Pubis	3.5	2.6	1.8
10.1	9.0	6.8	B9 V	Sternal Notch to Crotch	4.5	3.4	2.2
2.2	2.0	1.5	B10 V	Xyphoid to Umbilicus	1.0	0.8	0.5
2.2	2.0	1.5	B11 V	Umbilicus to Pubis	1.0	0.8	0.5
4.5	4.0	3.0	B12 V	Umbilicus to Crotch	2.0	1.5	1.0

TRANSVERSE BODY MEASUREMENTS

Inch	Inch	Inch			Inch	Inch	Inch
7.1	6.3	4.8	B13 T	Shoulder Breadth	3.2	2.4	1.6
3.1	2.8	2.1	B14 T	Clavicle to Acromion Process	1.4	1.0	0.7
6.8	6.0	4.5	B15 T	Biacromial Process Breadth	3.0	2.2	1.5
6.0	5.3	4.0	B16 T	Inter Acroioclavicular Joints	2.7	2.0	1.3
4.9	4.3	3.2	B17 T	Inter Anterior Axillary Fold	2.2	1.6	1.1
3.4	3.0	2.2	B18 T	Inter Nipples	1.5	1.1	0.8
4.5	4.0	3.0	B19 T	Breadth of Thorax	2.0	1.5	1.0
3.8	3.3	2.5	B20 T	Inter Costal Margin	1.7	1.2	0.8
4.5	4.0	3.0	B21 T	Inter Crest of Illium	2.0	1.5	1.0
3.8	3.3	2.5	B22 T	Inter Anterior Superior Spine	1.7	1.2	0.8
5.2	4.7	3.5	B23 T	Inter Greater Trochanter Femur	2.3	1.8	1.2

ADULT MALE
INCH MEASUREMENTS

3/2 Life	4/3 Life (Heroic)	LIFE SIZE			3/4 Life	2/3 Life	1/2 Life
				ANTERIOR-POSTERIOR BODY MEASUREMENTS			
Inch	Inch	Inch			Inch	Inch	Inch
9.0	8.0	**6.0**	B24 D	Sternal Notch to Dorsal Spine	4.5	4.0	3.0
12.9	11.5	**8.6**	B25 D	Manubrium Dorsal Spine	6.5	5.8	4.3
15.0	13.3	**10.0**	B26 D	Xyphoid Process to Scapula	7.5	6.7	5.0
10.5	9.3	**7.0**	B27 D	Umbilicus to Dorsum	5.2	4.7	3.5
13.5	12.0	**9.0**	B28 D	Pubis to Buttock	6.8	6.0	4.5
10.5	9.3	**7.0**	B29 D	Thigh to Gluteal Furrow	5.2	4.7	3.5
				VERTICAL BACK MEASUREMENTS			
Inch	Inch	Inch			Inch	Inch	Inch
15.0	13.3	**10.0**	B28 V	Vertex to 7th Cervical Spine	7.5	6.7	5.0
				7th Cervical Spine to:			
10.1	8.9	**6.7**	B29 V	Posterior Axillary Fold	5.0	4.5	3.4
12.6	11.2	**8.4**	B30 V	Inferior Tip of Scapula	6.3	5.6	4.2
28.1	25.0	**18.8**	B31 V	Post. Superior Spine Ilium	14.1	12.5	9.4
34.2	30.4	**22.8**	B32 V	Upp. Buttock Crease Midline	17.1	15.2	11.4
40.1	35.7	26.8	B33 V	Gluteal Furrow	20.1	17.8	13.4
62.6	55.7	41.8	B34 V	Popliteal Crease of Knee	31.3	27.8	20.9
93.0	82.7	62.0	B35 V	Sole of Foot	46.5	41.3	31.0
				TRANSVERSE BACK MEASUREMENTS			
Inch	Inch	Inch			Inch	Inch	Inch
21.0	18.7	**14.0**	B36 T	Inter Posterior Axillary Fold	10.5	9.3	7.0
9.0	8.0	**6.0**	B37 T	Inter Scapulae Medial Border	4.5	4.0	3.0
7.5	6.7	**5.0**	B38 T	Inter Post. Sup. Spines Sacrum	3.8	3.3	2.5
6.0	5.3	**4.0**	B39 T	Inter Post. Inf. Spines of Sacrum	3.0	2.7	2.0
15.0	13.3	**10.0**	B40 T	Inter Gluteus Maximus Muscle	7.5	6.7	5.0

ADULT MALE
INCH MEASUREMENTS

3/8 Life	1/3 Life	1/4 Life			1/6 Life	1/8 Life	1/12 Life
				ANTERIOR-POSTERIOR BODY MEASUREMENTS			
Inch	Inch	Inch			Inch	Inch	Inch
2.2	2.0	1.5	B24 D	Sternal Notch to Dorsal Spine	1.0	0.8	0.5
3.2	2.9	2.2	B25 D	Manubrium Dorsal Spine	1.4	1.1	0.7
3.8	3.3	2.5	B26 D	Xyphoid Process to Scapula	1.7	1.2	0.8
2.6	2.3	1.8	B27 D	Umbilicus to Dorsum	1.2	0.9	0.6
3.4	3.0	2.2	B28 D	Pubis to Buttock	1.5	1.1	0.8
2.6	2.3	1.8	B29 D	Thigh to Gluteal Furrow	1.2	0.9	0.6
				VERTICAL BACK MEASUREMENTS			
Inch	Inch	Inch			Inch	Inch	Inch
3.8	3.3	2.5	B28 V	Vertex to 7th Cervical Spine	1.7	1.2	0.8
				7th Cervical Spine to:			
2.5	2.2	1.7	B29 V	Posterior Axillary Fold	1.1	0.8	0.6
3.1	2.8	2.1	B30 V	Inferior Tip of Scapula	1.4	1.1	0.7
7.0	6.2	4.7	B31 V	Post. Superior Spine Ilium	3.1	2.3	1.6
8.6	7.6	5.7	B32 V	Upp. Buttock Crease Midline	3.8	2.9	1.9
10.0	8.9	6.7	B33 V	Gluteal Furrow	4.5	3.3	2.2
15.7	13.9	10.4	B34 V	Popliteal Crease of Knee	6.0	5.2	3.5
23.2	20.7	15.5	B35 V	Sole of Foot	10.3	7.8	5.2
				TRANSVERSE BACK MEASUREMENTS			
Inch	Inch	Inch			Inch	Inch	Inch
5.2	4.7	3.5	B36 T	Inter Posterior Axillary Fold	2.3	1.8	1.2
2.2	2.0	1.5	B37 T	Inter Scapulae Medial Border	1.0	0.8	0.5
1.9	1.7	1.2	B38 T	Inter Post. Sup. Spines Sacrum	0.8	0.6	0.4
1.5	1.3	1.0	B39 T	Inter Post. Inf. Spines of Sacrum	0.7	0.5	0.3
3.8	3.3	2.5	B40 T	Inter Gluteus Maximus Muscle	1.7	1.2	0.8

ADULT MALE
INCH MEASUREMENTS

3/2 Life	4/3 Life (Heroic)	LIFE SIZE			3/4 Life	2/3 Life	1/2 Life
				UPPER EXTREMITY MEASUREMENTS			
Inch	Inch	Inch			Inch	Inch	Inch
108.0	96.0	**72.0**	U1 T	Span of Arms	54.0	48.0	36.0
13.5	12.0	**9.0**	U2 T	Sternum to Acromion Process	6.8	6.0	4.5
9.0	8.0	**6.0**	U3 T	Sternum to Shoulder Pivot	4.5	4.0	3.0
18.0	16.0	**12.0**	U4 V	Humerus Pivot to Elbow Pivot	9.0	8.0	6.0
22.5	20.0	**15.0**	U5 V	Shoulder to Elbow Flexed	11.2	10.0	7.5
21.0	18.7	**14.0**	U6 V	Acromion to Lat. Condyle Elbow	10.5	9.3	7.0
27.0	24.0	**18.0**	U7 V	Flexed Elbow to Finger Tip	13.5	12.0	9.0
15.0	13.3	**10.0**	U8 V	Flexed Elbow to Wrist Pivot	7.5	6.7	5.0
12.0	10.7	**8.0**	U9 V	Wrist to Finger Tip	6.0	5.3	4.0
7.5	6.7	**5.0**	U10 V	Wrist to Thumb	3.8	3.3	2.5
6.8	6.0	**4.5**	U11 V	Length of Palm	3.4	3.0	2.2
5.2	4.7	**3.5**	U12 V	Length 3rd Finger	2.6	2.3	1.8
8.6	7.7	**5.8**	U13 V	Thumb Crotch to 3rd Finger	4.3	3.8	2.9
4.3	3.8	**2.9**	U14 V	Thumb Crotch to Thumb Tip	2.2	1.9	1.4
7.5	6.7	**5.0**	U15 D	Anterior-Post. Arm at Biceps	3.8	3.3	2.5
6.0	5.3	**4.0**	U16 D	Anterior-Posterior at Forearm	3.0	2.7	2.0
2.6	2.3	**1.8**	U17 D	Depth of Wrist	1.3	1.2	0.9
4.1	3.7	**2.8**	U18 T	Breadth of Wrist	2.1	1.8	1.4
6.8	6.0	**4.5**	U19 T	Breadth of Hand	3.4	3.0	2.2
5.6	5.0	**3.8**	U20 T	Breadth of Palm	2.8	2.5	1.9

ADULT MALE
INCH MEASUREMENTS

UPPER EXTREMITY MEASUREMENTS

3/8 Life	1/3 Life	1/4 Life			1/6 Life	1/8 Life	1/12 Life
Inch	Inch	Inch			Inch	Inch	Inch
27.0	24.0	18.0	U1 T	Span of Arms	12.0	9.0	6.0
3.4	3.0	2.2	U2 T	Sternum to Acromion Process	1.5	1.1	0.8
2.2	2.0	1.5	U3 T	Sternum to Shoulder Pivot	1.0	0.8	0.5
4.5	4.0	3.0	U4 V	Humerus Pivot to Elbow Pivot	2.0	1.5	1.0
5.6	5.0	3.8	U5 V	Shoulder to Elbow Flexed	2.5	1.9	1.2
5.2	4.7	3.5	U6 V	Acromion to Lat. Condyle Elbow	2.3	1.8	1.2
6.8	6.0	4.5	U7 V	Flexed Elbow to Finger Tip	3.0	2.2	1.5
3.8	3.3	2.5	U8 V	Flexed Elbow to Wrist Pivot	1.7	1.2	0.8
3.0	2.7	2.0	U9 V	Wrist to Finger Tip	1.3	1.0	0.7
1.9	1.7	1.2	U10 V	Wrist to Thumb	0.8	0.6	0.4
1.7	1.5	1.1	U11 V	Length of Palm	0.8	0.6	0.4
1.3	1.2	0.9	U12 V	Length 3rd Finger	0.6	0.4	0.3
2.2	1.9	1.4	U13 V	Thumb Crotch to 3rd Finger	0.0	0.7	0.5
1.1	0.0	0.7	U14 V	Thumb Crotch to Thumb Tip	0.5	0.4	0.2
1.9	1.7	1.2	U15 D	Anterior-Post. Arm at Biceps	0.8	0.6	0.4
1.5	1.3	1.0	U16 D	Anterior-Posterior at Forearm	0.7	0.5	0.3
0.7	0.6	0.4	U17 D	Depth of Wrist	0.3	0.2	0.1
1.0	0.9	0.7	U18 T	Breadth of Wrist	0.5	0.3	0.2
1.7	1.5	1.1	U19 T	Breadth of Hand	0.8	0.6	0.4
1.4	1.2	0.9	U20 T	Breadth of Palm	0.6	0.5	0.3

ADULT MALE
INCH MEASUREMENTS

3/2 Life (Heroic)	4/3 Life	LIFE SIZE			3/4 Life	2/3 Life	1/2 Life
				LOWER EXTREMITY MEASUREMENTS			
Inch	Inch	Inch			Inch	Inch	Inch
65.2	58.0	**43.5**	L1 V	Crest of Ilium to Sole	32.6	29.0	21.8
63.0	56.0	**42.0**	L2 V	Ant. Sup. Spine of Ilium to Sole	31.5	28.0	21.0
55.9	49.7	**37.2**	L3 V	Greater Trochanter Femur-Sole	27.9	24.8	18.6
49.1	43.7	**32.8**	L4 V	Crotch to Sole	24.6	21.8	16.4
51.8	46.0	**34.5**	L5 V	Gluteal Furrow to Sole	25.9	23.0	17.2
30.4	27.0	**20.2**	L6 V	Posterior Knee Crease-Sole	15.2	13.5	10.1
31.5	28.0	**21.0**	L7 V	Ant. Sup. Spine of Ilium-Knee	15.8	14.0	10.5
24.8	22.0	**16.5**	L8 V	Pubis to Knee at Patella	12.4	11.0	8.2
31.5	28.0	**21.0**	L9 V	Knee at Patella to sole	15.8	14.0	10.5
28.5	25.3	**19.0**	L10 V	Tibia to Sole	14.2	12.7	9.5
6.0	5.3	**4.0**	L11 V	Med. Malleolus to Sole	3.0	2.7	2.0
4.5	4.0	**3.0**	L12 V	Lat. Malleolus to Sole	2.2	2.0	1.5
21.0	18.7	**14.0**	L13 T	Inter Both Mid Thighs	10.5	9.3	7.0
13.5	12.0	**9.0**	L14 T	Breadth of Both Knees	6.8	6.0	4.5
14.2	12.7	**9.5**	L15 T	Breadth of Both Calves	7.1	6.3	4.8
4.5	4.0	**3.0**	L16 T	Breadth One Ankle at Malleoli	2.2	2.0	1.5
9.0	8.0	**6.0**	L17 D	Mid Thigh, Anterior-Posterior	4.5	4.0	3.0
6.8	6.0	**4.5**	L18 D	Knee, Anterior-Posterior	3.4	3.0	2.2
7.5	6.7	**5.0**	L19 D	Mid Calf, Anterior-Posterior	3.8	3.3	2.5
4.9	4.3	**3.2**	L20 D	Ankle, Anterior-Posterior	2.4	2.2	1.6
6.0	5.3	**4.0**	L21 D	Ankle at Malleoli, Anterior-Post.	3.0	2.7	2.0
16.5	14.7	**11.0**	L22 D	Length of Foot	8.2	7.3	5.5
13.5	12.0	**9.0**	L23 D	Heel to 5th Toe	6.8	6.0	4.5
6.0	5.3	**4.0**	L24 T	Breadth Foot at Rest	3.0	2.7	2.0
6.8	6.0	**4.5**	L25 T	Breadth Foot Standing	3.4	3.0	2.2
4.1	3.7	**2.8**	L26 T	Width of Heel	2.1	1.8	1.4

ADULT MALE
INCH MEASUREMENTS

LOWER EXTREMITY MEASUREMENTS

3/8 Life	1/3 Life	1/4 Life			1/6 Life	1/8 Life	1/12 Life
Inch	Inch	Inch			Inch	Inch	Inch
16.3	14.5	10.9	L1 V	Crest of Ilium to Sole	7.2	5.4	3.6
15.8	14.0	10.5	L2 V	Ant. Sup. Spine of Ilium to Sole	7.0	5.2	3.5
13.0	12.4	9.3	L3 V	Greater Trochanter Femur-Sole	6.2	4.7	3.1
12.3	10.9	8.2	L4 V	Crotch to Sole	5.5	4.1	2.7
12.9	11.5	8.6	L5 V	Gluteal Furrow to Sole	5.8	4.3	2.9
7.6	6.8	5.1	L6 V	Posterior Knee Crease to Sole	3.4	2.5	1.7
7.9	7.0	5.2	L7 V	Ant. Sup. Spine of Ilium to Knee	3.5	2.6	1.8
6.2	5.5	4.1	L8 V	Pubis to Knee at Patella	2.8	2.1	1.4
7.9	7.0	5.2	L9V	Knee at Patella to sole	3.5	2.6	1.8
7.1	6.3	4.8	L10 V	Tibia to Sole	3.2	2.4	1.6
1.5	1.3	1.0	L11 V	Med. Malleolus to Sole	0.7	0.5	0.3
1.1	1.0	0.8	L12 V	Lat. Malleolus to Sole	0.5	0.4	0.2
5.2	4.7	3.5	L13 T	Inter Both Mid Thighs	2.3	1.8	1.2
3.4	3.0	2.2	L14 T	Breadth of Both Knees	1.5	1.1	0.8
3.6	3.2	2.4	L15 T	Breadth of Both Calves	1.6	1.2	0.8
1.1	1.0	0.8	L16 T	Breadth One Ankle at Malleoli	0.5	0.4	0.2
2.2	2.0	1.5	L17 D	Mid Thigh, Anterior-Posterior	1.0	0.8	0.5
1.7	1.5	1.1	L18 D	Knee, Anterior-Posterior	0.8	0.6	0.4
1.9	1.7	1.2	L19 D	Mid Calf, Anterior-Posterior	0.8	0.6	0.4
1.2	1.1	0.8	L20 D	Ankle, Anterior-Posterior	0.5	0.4	0.3
1.5	1.3	1.0	L21 D	Ankle at Malleoli, Anterior-Post.	0.7	0.5	0.3
4.1	3.7	2.8	L22 D	Length of Foot	1.8	1.4	0.9
3.4	3.0	2.2	L23 D	Heel to 5th Toe	1.5	1.1	0.8
1.5	1.3	1.0	L24 T	Breadth Foot at Rest	0.7	0.5	0.3
1.7	1.5	1.1	L25 T	Breadth Foot Standing	0.8	0.6	0.4
1.0	0.9	0.7	L26 T	Width of Heel	0.5	0.3	0.2

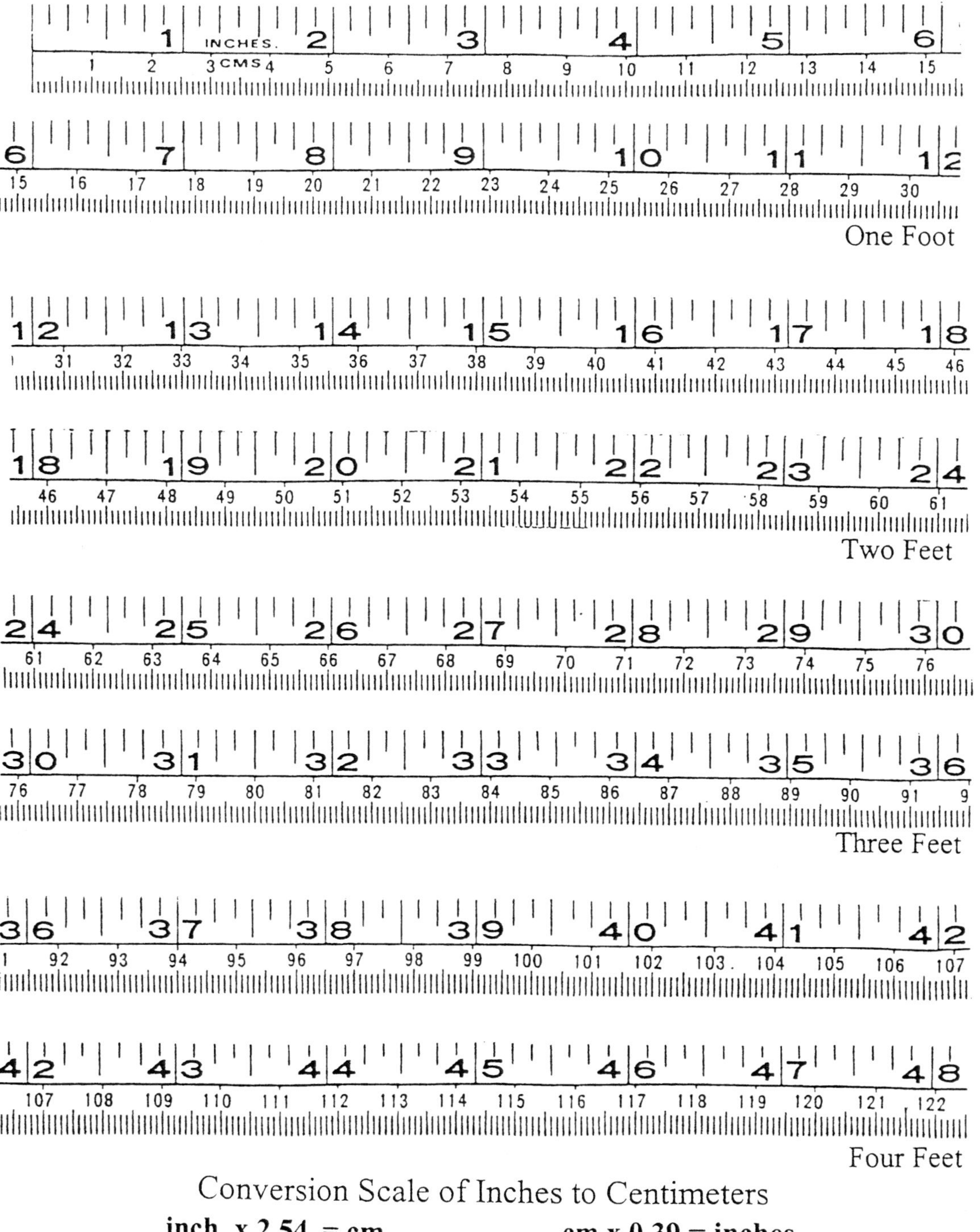

Fig. 56. Conversion scale of inches to centimeters.

ADULT HUMAN

MALE

PROPORTIONS

METRIC MEASUREMENTS

ADULT MALE METRIC MEASUREMENTS

VERTICAL MEASUREMENTS

3/2 Life (Heroic)	4/3 Life	LIFE SIZE			3/4 Life	2/3 Life	1/2 Life
cm	cm	cm			cm	cm	cm
274.5	244	**183**	1 V	Stature, Height, Vertex to Sole	137.3	122	91.5
222.9	198.1	**148.6**	2V	Shoulder at Acromion to Sole	111.5	99.1	74.3
160.1	142.3	**106.7**	3V	Ant.Sup.Spine of Ilium to Sole	80	71.1	53.4
142.5	126.7	**95**	4V	Symphysis Pubis to Sole	71.3	63.3	47.5
124.5	110.7	**83**	5V	Crotch to Sole	62.3	55.3	41.5
80	71.1	**53.3**	6V	Knee at Patella to Sole	40	35.5	26.7
51.5	45.7	**34.3**	7V	Head & Neck, Vertex-St. Notch	25.7	22.9	17.2
62.9	55.9	**41.9**	8V	St. Notch, Shoulder-Ant. Sup.Sp.	31.4	27.9	21
102.2	90.8	**68.1**	9V	Sternal Notch to Crotch	51.1	45.4	34.1
80	71.1	**53.3**	10V	Ant. Sup. Spine of Ilium to Knee	40	35.5	26.7
207	184	**138**	11V	Kneeling Height	103.5	92	69
144.3	128.3	**96.2**	12V	Sitting Height	72.2	64.1	48.1
162	144	**108**	13V	Buttock, Straight Leg to Sole	81	72	54
94.5	84	**63**	14V	Buttock to Flexed Knee	47.3	42	31.5
88.5	78.7	**59**	15V	Flexed Knee to Sole	44.3	39.3	29.5

VERTICAL HEAD MEASUREMENTS

cm	cm	cm			cm	cm	cm
34.4	30.5	**22.9**	H1 V	Vertex to Chin	17.2	15.3	11.5
30.5	27.1	**20.3**	H2 V	Hairline to Chin	15.2	13.5	10.2
17.1	15.2	**11.4**	H3 V	Vertex to Lateral Corner of Eye	8.6	7.6	5.7
20.7	18.4	**13.8**	H4 V	Vertex to Tragion of Ear	10.4	9.2	6.9
9.6	8.5	**6.4**	H5 V	Hairline to Brow	4.8	4.3	3.2
19.1	16.9	**12.7**	H6 V	Hairline to infranasal	9.5	8.5	6.4
9.6	8.5	**6.4**	H7 V	Brow to Infranasal	4.8	4.3	3.2
8.1	7.2	**5.4**	H8 V	Selion to Infranasal	4.1	3.6	2.7
19.5	17.3	**13**	H9 V	Selion to Chin	9.8	8.7	6.5
9.6	8.5	**6.4**	H10 V	Infranasal to Chin	4.8	4.3	3.2
3.3	2.9	**2.2**	H11 V	Infranasal to Lip Aperature	1.7	1.5	1.1
2.4	2.1	**1.6**	H12 V	Lip Aperat. to Sublabial Crease	1.2	1.1	0.8
3.8	3.3	**2.5**	H13 V	Sublabial Crease to Chin	1.9	1.7	1.3

ADULT MALE METRIC MEASUREMENTS

VERTICAL MEASUREMENTS

3/8 Life	1/3 Life	1/4 Life			1/6 Life	1/8 Life	1/12 Life
cm	cm	cm			cm	cm	cm
68.6	61	45.8	1 V	Stature, Height, Vertex to Sole	30.5	22.9	15.3
55.7	49.5	37.2	2V	Shoulder at Acromion to Sole	24.8	18.6	12.4
40	35.6	26.7	3V	Ant.Sup.Spine of Ilium to Sole	17.8	13.3	8.9
35.6	31.7	23.8	4V	Symphysis Pubis to Sole	15.8	11.9	7.9
31.1	27.7	20.8	4V	Crotch to Sole	13.8	10.4	6.9
20	17.8	13.3	5V	Knee at Patella to Sole	8.9	6.7	4.4
12.9	11.4	8.6	6V	Head & Neck, Vertex- St. Notch	5.7	4.3	2.9
15.7	14	10.5	7V	St. Notch, Shoulder-Ant. Sup.Sp.	7	5.2	3.5
25.5	22.7	17	8V	Sternal Notch to Crotch	11.4	8.5	5.7
20	17.8	13.3	9V	Ant. Sup. Spine of Ilium to Knee	8.9	6.7	4.4
51.8	46	34.5	10V	Kneeling Height	23	17.3	11.5
36.1	32.1	24.1	11V	Sitting Height	16	12	8
40.5	36	27	12V	Buttock, Straight Leg to Sole	18	13.5	9
23.6	21	15.8	13V	Buttock to Flexed Knee	10.5	7.9	5.3
22.1	19.7	14.8	14V	Flexed Knee to Sole	9.8	7.4	4.9

VERTICAL HEAD MEASUREMENTS

cm	cm	cm			cm	cm	cm
8.6	7.6	5.7	H1 V	Vertex to Chin	3.8	2.9	1.9
7.6	6.8	5.1	H2 V	Hairline to Chin	3.4	2.5	1.7
4.3	3.8	2.9	H3 V	Vertex to Lateral Corner of Eye	1.9	1.4	1
5.2	4.6	3.5	H4 V	Vertex to Tragion of Ear	2.3	1.7	1.2
2.4	2.1	1.6	H5 V	Hairline to Brow	1.1	0.8	0.5
4.8	4.2	3.2	H6 V	Hairline to infranasal	2.1	1.6	1.1
2.4	2.1	1.6	H7 V	Brow to Infranasal	1.1	0.8	0.5
2	1.8	1.4	H8 V	Selion to Infranasal	0.9	0.7	0.5
4.9	4.3	3.3	H9 V	Selion to Chin	2.2	1.6	1.1
2.4	2.1	1.6	H10 V	Infranasal to Chin	1.1	0.8	0.5
0.8	0.7	0.6	H11 V	Infranasal to Lip Aperature	0.4	0.3	0.2
0.6	0.5	0.4	H12 V	Lip Aperat. to Sublabial Crease	0.3	0.2	0.1
0.9	0.8	0.6	H13 V	Sublabial Crease to Chin	0.4	0.3	0.2

ADULT MALE
METRIC MEASUREMENTS

3/2 Life	4/3 Life (Heroic)	LIFE SIZE			3/4 Life	2/3 Life	1/2 Life
				TRANSVERSE HEAD MEASUREMENTS			
cm	cm	cm			cm	cm	cm
22.8	20.3	**15.2**	H14 T	Bi-Parietal	11.4	10.1	7.6
20	17.7	**13.3**	H15 T	Bi-Zygomatic	10	8.9	6.7
17.1	15.2	**11.4**	H16 T	Bi-Fronto Temporal	8.6	7.6	5.7
16.1	14.3	**10.7**	H17 T	Inter Brow Ridge	8.0	7.1	5.3
20.6	18.3	**13.7**	H18 T	Inter Tragion of Ears	10.3	9.1	6.9
18.2	16.1	**12.1**	H19 T	Inter Angle of Mandible	9.1	8.1	6.1
15.3	13.6	**10.2**	H20 T	Inter Lateral Corners of Eyes	7.7	6.8	5.1
5	4.4	**3.3**	H21 T	Width of Eye	2.5	2.2	1.7
5	4.4	**3.3**	H22 T	Inter Inner Corner of Eyes	2.5	2.2	1.7
5.7	5.1	**3.8**	H23 T	Breadth of Nose	2.9	2.5	1.9
7.7	6.8	**5.1**	H24 T	Breadth of Mouth	3.8	3.4	2.6
5.7	5.1	**3.8**	H25 T	Breadth of Chin	2.9	2.5	1.9
17.1	15.2	**11.4**	H26 T	Breadth of Neck	8.6	7.6	5.7
				ANTERIOR-POSTERIOR HEAD MEASUREMENTS			
cm	cm	cm			cm	cm	cm
30.6	27.2	**20.4**	H27 D	Brow to Occiput	15.3	13.6	10.2
18.2	16.1	**12.1**	H28 D	Brow to Tragus	9.1	8.1	6.1
17.7	15.7	**11.8**	H29 D	Selion to Tragus	8.9	7.9	5.9
12.6	11.2	**8.4**	H30 D	Tragus to Occiput	6.3	5.6	4.2
9.8	8.7	**6.5**	H31 D	Tragus to Angle Mandible	4.9	4.3	3.3
12.9	11.5	**8.6**	H32 D	Angle of Mandible to Chin	6.5	5.7	4.3
11	9.7	**7.3**	H33 V	Length of Ear, Vertical	5.5	4.9	3.7
5.6	4.9	**3.7**	H34 D	Width of Ear, Anterior-Posterior	2.8	2.5	1.9
17.3	15.3	**11.5**	H35 D	Anterior to Posterior of Neck	8.6	7.7	5.8

ADULT MALE
METRIC MEASUREMENTS

TRANSVERSE HEAD MEASUREMENTS

3/8 Life	1/3 Life	1/4 Life			1/6 Life	1/8 Life	1/12 Life
cm	cm	cm			cm	cm	cm
5.7	5.1	3.8	H14 T	Bi-Parietal	2.5	1.9	1.3
5	4.4	3.3	H15 T	Bi-Zygomatic	2.2	1.7	1.1
4.3	3.8	2.9	H16 T	Bi-Fronto Temporal	1.9	1.4	1
4.0	3.6	2.7	H17 T	Inter Brow Ridge	1.8	1.3	0.1
5.1	4.6	3.4	H18 T	Inter Tragion of Ears	2.3	1.7	1.1
4.5	4	3	H19 T	Inter Angle of Mandible	2	1.5	1
3.8	3.4	2.6	H20 T	Inter Lateral Corners of Eyes	1.7	1.3	0.9
1.2	1.1	0.8	H21 T	Width of Eye	0.6	0.4	0.3
1.2	1.1	0.8	H22 T	Inter Inner Corner of Eyes	0.6	0.4	0.3
1.4	1.3	1	H23 T	Breadth of Nose	0.6	0.5	0.3
1.9	1.7	1.3	H24 T	Breadth of Mouth	0.9	0.6	0.4
1.4	1.3	1	H25 T	Breadth of Chin	0.6	0.5	0.3
4.3	3.8	2.9	H26 T	Breadth of Neck	1.9	1.4	1

ANTERIOR-POSTERIOR HEAD MEASUREMENTS

3/8 Life	1/3 Life	1/4 Life			1/6 Life	1/8 Life	1/12 Life
cm	cm	cm			cm	cm	cm
7.7	6.8	5.1	H27 D	Brow to Occiput	3.4	2.6	1.7
4.5	4	3	H28 D	Brow to Tragus	2	1.5	1
4.4	3.9	3	H29 D	Selion to Tragus	2	1.5	1
3.2	2.8	2.1	H30 D	Tragus to Occiput	1.4	1.1	0.7
2.4	2.2	1.6	H31 D	Tragus to Angle Mandible	1.1	0.8	0.5
3.2	2.9	2.2	H32 D	Angle of Mandible to Chin	1.4	1.1	0.7
2.7	2.4	1.8	H33 V	Length of Ear, Vertical	1.2	0.9	0.6
1.4	1.2	0.9	H34 D	Width of Ear, Anterior-Posterior	0.6	0.5	0.3
4.3	3.8	2.9	H35 D	Anterior to Posterior of Neck	1.9	1.4	1

ADULT MALE
METRIC MEASUREMENTS

3/2 Life (Heroic)	4/3 Life	LIFE SIZE			3/4 Life	2/3 Life	1/2 Life
				VERTICAL BODY MEASUREMENTS			
cm	cm	cm			cm	cm	cm
17.1	15.2	**11.4**	B1 V	Chin to Sternal Notch	8.6	7.6	5.7
15.3	13.6	**10.2**	B2 V	Sternal Notch to Axilla	7.6	6.8	5.1
23	20.4	**15.3**	B3 V	Sternal Notch to Nipples	11.5	10.2	7.7
34.4	30.5	**22.9**	B4 V	Sternal Notch to Xyphoid	17.2	15.3	11.5
57	50.7	**38**	B5 V	Sternal Notch to Umbilicus	28.5	25.3	19
57	50.7	**38**	B6 V	Strernal Notch to Crest ilium	28.4	25.3	19
63.0	56.0	**42.0**	B7 V	Sternal Notch to Ant. S. Sp. Ilium	31.5	28.0	21.0
80	71.1	**53.3**	B8 V	Sternal Notch to Pubis	40	35.5	26.7
102.2	90.8	**68.1**	B9 V	Sternal Notch to Crotch	51.1	45.4	34.1
23	20.4	**15.3**	B10 V	Xyphoid to Umbilicus	11.5	10.2	7.7
23	20.4	**15.3**	B11 V	Umbilicus to Pubis	11.5	10.2	7.7
45.2	40.1	**30.1**	B12 V	Umbilicus to Crotch	22.6	20.1	15.1
				TRANSVERSE BODY MEASUREMENTS			
cm	cm	cm			cm	cm	cm
72.3	64.3	**48.2**	B13 T	Shoulder Breadth	64.3	32.1	24.1
31.5	28.0	**21.0**	B14 T	Clavicle to Acromion Process	15.8	14.0	10.5
68.6	60.9	**45.7**	B15 T	Bi-acromial Process Breadth	34.3	30.5	22.9
61.1	54.3	**40.7**	B16 T	Inter Achroioclavicular Joints	30.5	27.1	20.4
49.5	44	**33**	B17 T	Inter Anterior Axillary Fold	24.8	22	16.5
34.4	30.5	**22.9**	B18 T	Inter Nipples	17.2	15.3	11.5
45.8	40.7	**30.5**	B19 T	Breadth of Thorax	22.9	20.3	15.3
38.1	33.9	**25.4**	B20 T	Inter Costal Margin	19.1	16.9	12.7
45.8	40.7	**30.5**	B21 T	Inter Crest of Illium	22.9	20.3	15.3
38.1	33.9	**25.4**	B22 T	Inter Anterior Superior Spine	19.1	16.9	12.7
53.2	47.3	**35.5**	B23 T	Inter Greater Trchanter Femur	26.6	23.7	17.8

ADULT MALE METRIC MEASUREMENTS

3/8 Life	1/3 Life	1/4 Life			1/6 Life	1/8 Life	1/12 Life
				VERTICAL BODY MEASUREMENTS			
cm	cm	cm			cm	cm	cm
4.3	3.8	2.9	B1 V	Chin to Sternal Notch	1.9	1.4	1
3.8	3.4	2.5	B2 V	Sternal Notch to Axilla	1.7	1.3	0.8
5.7	5.1	3.8	B3 V	Sternal Notch to Nipples	2.6	1.9	1.3
8.6	7.6	5.7	B4 V	Sternal Notch to Xyphoid	3.8	2.9	1.9
14.3	12.7	9.5	B5 V	Sternal Notch to Umbilicus	6.3	4.8	3.2
14.2	12.6	9.5	B6 V	Strernal Notch to Crest ilium	6.3	4.7	3.2
15.8	14.0	10.5	B7 V	Sternal Notch to Ant. S. Sp. Ilium	7.0	5.2	3.5
20	17.8	13.3	B8 V	Sternal Notch to Pubis	8.9	6.7	4.4
25.5	22.7	17	B9 V	Sternal Notch to Crotch	11.4	8.5	5.7
5.7	5.1	3.8	B10 V	Xyphoid to Umbilicus	2.6	1.9	1.3
5.7	5.1	3.8	B11 V	Umbilicus to Pubis	2.6	1.9	1.3
11.3	10.0	7.5	B12 V	Umbilicus to Crotch	5.0	3.8	2.5
				TRANSVERSE BODY MEASUREMENTS			
cm	cm	cm			cm	cm	cm
18.1	16.1	12.1	B13 T	Shoulder Breadth	8.0	6.0	4.0
7.9	7.0	5.2	B14 T	Clavicle to Acromion Process	3.5	2.6	1.7
17.1	15.2	11.4	B15 T	Bi-acromial Process Breadth	7.6	5.7	3.8
15.3	13.6	10.2	B16 T	Inter Achroioclavicular Joints	6.8	5.1	3.4
12.4	11	8.3	B17 T	Inter Anterior Axillary Fold	5.5	4.1	2.8
8.6	7.6	5.7	B18 T	Inter Nipples	3.8	2.9	1.9
11.4	10.2	7.6	B19 T	Breadth of Thorax	5.1	3.8	2.5
9.5	8.5	6.4	B20 T	Inter Costal Margin	4.2	3.2	2.1
11.4	10.2	7.6	B21 T	Inter Crest of Illium	5.1	3.8	2.5
9.5	8.5	6.4	B22 T	Inter Anterior Superior Spine	4.2	3.2	2.1
13.2	11.7	8.9	B23 T	Inter Greater Trchanter Femur	5.9	4.4	2.9

ADULT MALE METRIC MEASUREMENTS

3/2 Life	4/3 Life (Heroic)	LIFE SIZE			3/4 Life	2/3 Life	1/2 Life
				ANTERIOR-POSTERIOR BODY MEASUREMENTS			
cm	cm	cm			cm	cm	cm
23.3	20.7	**15.5**	B24 D	Sternal Notch to Dorsal Spine	11.6	10.3	7.8
33	29.3	**22**	B25 D	Manubrium to Dorsal Spine	16.5	14.7	11
38.1	33.9	**25.4**	B26 D	Xyphoid Process to Scapula	19.1	16.9	12.7
26.7	23.7	**17.8**	B27 D	Umbilicus to Dorsum	13.4	11.9	8.9
34.3	30.5	**22.9**	B28 D	Pubis to Buttock	17.2	15.3	11.4
26.7	23.7	**17.8**	B29 D	Thigh to Gluteal Furrow	13.4	11.9	8.9
				VERTICAL BACK MEASUREMENTS			
cm	cm	cm			cm	cm	cm
38.1	33.9	**25.4**	B30 V	Vertex to 7th Cervical Spine	19.1	16.9	12.7
				7th Cervical Spine to:			
25.5	22.7	**17**	B31 V	Posterior Axillary Fold	12.8	11.3	8.5
32	28.4	**21.3**	B32 V	Inferior Tip of Scapula	16	14.2	10.7
71.3	63.3	**47.5**	B33 V	Post. Superior Spine Ilium	35.6	31.7	23.8
87	77.3	**58**	B34 V	Upp. Buttock Crease Midline	43.5	38.7	29
101.9	90.5	**67.9**	B35 V	Gluteal Furrow	50.9	45.3	34
159.2	141.5	**106.1**	B36 V	Popliteal Crease of Knee	79.6	70.7	53.1
236.4	210.1	**157.6**	B37 V	Sole of Foot	118.2	105.1	78.8
				TRANSVERSE BACK MEASUREMENTS			
cm	cm	cm			cm	cm	cm
53.2	47.3	**35.5**	B38 T	Inter Posterior Axillary Fold	26.6	23.7	17.8
22.8	20.3	**15.2**	B39 T	Inter Scapulae Medial Border	11.4	10.1	7.6
19.1	16.9	**12.7**	B40 T	Inter Post. Sup. Spines Sacrum	9.5	8.5	6.4
15.3	13.6	**10.2**	B41 T	Inter Post. Inf. Spines of Sacrum	7.7	6.8	5.1
38.1	33.9	**25.4**	B42 T	Inter Gluteus Maximus Muscle	19.1	16.9	12.7

ADULT MALE
METRIC MEASUREMENTS

3/8 Life	1/3 Life	1/4 Life			1/6 Life	1/8 Life	1/12 Life
				ANTERIOR-POSTERIOR BODY MEASUREMENTS			
cm	cm	cm			cm	cm	cm
5.8	5.2	3.9	B24 D	Sternal Notch to Dorsal Spine	2.6	1.9	1.3
8.3	7.3	5.5	B25 D	Manubrium to Dorsal Spine	3.7	2.8	1.8
9.5	8.5	6.4	B26 D	Xyphoid Process to Scapula	4.2	3.2	2.1
6.7	5.9	4.5	B27 D	Umbilicus to Dorsum	2.0	2.2	1.5
8.6	7.6	5.7	B28 D	Pubis to Buttock	3.8	2.9	1.9
6.7	5.9	4.5	B29 D	Thigh to Gluteal Furrow	2.0	2.2	1.5
				VERTICAL BACK MEASUREMENTS			
cm	cm	cm			cm	cm	cm
9.5	8.5	6.3	B30 V	Vertex to 7th Cervical Spine	4.2	3.2	2.1
				7th Cervical Spine to:			
6.4	5.7	4.3	B31 V	Posterior Axillary Fold	2.8	2.1	1.4
8	7.1	5.3	B32 V	Inferior Tip of Scapula	3.6	2.7	1.8
17.8	15.8	11.9	B33 V	Post. Superior Spine Ilium	7.9	5.9	4
21.8	19.3	14.5	B34 V	Upp. Buttock Crease Midline	9.7	7.3	4.8
25.5	22.6	17	B35 V	Gluteal Furrow	11.3	8.5	5.7
39.8	35.4	26.5	B36 V	Popliteal Crease of Knee	17.7	13.3	8.8
59.1	52.5	39.4	B37 V	Sole of Foot	26.3	19.7	13.1
				TRANSVERSE BACK MEASUREMENTS			
cm	cm	cm			cm	cm	cm
13.3	11.8	8.9	B38 T	Inter Posterior Axillary Fold	5.9	4.4	2.0
5.7	5.1	3.8	B39 T	Inter Scapulae Medial Border	2.5	1.9	1.3
4.8	4.2	3.2	B40 T	Inter Post. Sup. Spines Sacrum	2.1	1.6	1.1
3.8	3.4	2.6	B41 T	Inter Post. Inf. Spines of Sacrum	1.7	1.3	0.9
9.5	8.5	6.3	B42 T	Inter Gluteus Maximus Muscle	4.2	3.2	2.1

ADULT MALE METRIC MEASUREMENTS

3/2 Life	4/3 Life (Heroic)	LIFE SIZE			3/4 Life	2/3 Life	1/2 Life
				UPPER EXTREMITY MEASUREMENTS			
cm	cm	cm			cm	cm	cm
274.2	243.7	**182.8**	U1 T	Span of Arms	137.1	121.9	91.4
34.3	30.5	**22.9**	U2 T	Sternum to Achromion Process	17.2	15.3	11.4
23	20.4	**15.3**	U3 T	Sternum to Shoulder Pivot	11.5	10.2	7.7
45.8	40.7	**30.5**	U4 V	Humerus Pivot to Elbow Pivot	22.9	20.3	15.3
57	50.7	**38**	U5 V	Shoulder to Elbow Flexed	28.5	25.3	19
53.4	47.5	**35.6**	U6 V	Acromion to Lat. Condyle Elbow	26.7	23.7	17.8
68.6	60.9	**45.7**	U7 V	Flexed Elbow to Finger Tip	34.3	30.5	22.9
38.1	33.9	**25.4**	U8 V	Flexed Elbow to Wrist Pivot	19.1	16.9	12.7
30.5	27.1	**20.3**	U9 V	Wrist to Finger tip	15.2	13.5	10.2
19.1	16.9	**12.7**	U10 V	Wrist to Thumb	9.5	8.5	6.3
16.8	14.9	**11.2**	U11 V	Length of Palm	8.4	7.5	5.6
13.4	11.9	**8.9**	U12 V	Length 3rd Finger	6.7	5.9	4.5
21.8	19.3	**14.5**	U13 V	Thumb Crotch to 3rd Finger	10.9	9.7	7.2
10.8	9.6	**7.2**	U14 V	Thumb Crotch to Thumb Tip	5.4	4.8	3.6
19.1	16.9	**12.7**	U15 D	Anterior-Post. Arm at Biceps	9.5	8.5	6.4
15.3	13.6	**10.2**	U16 D	Anterior-Posterior at Forearm	7.7	6.8	5.1
6.8	6	**4.5**	U17 D	Depth of Wrist	3.4	3	2.3
10.5	9.3	**7**	U18 T	Breadth of Wrist	5.3	4.7	3.5
17.3	15.3	**11.5**	U19 T	Breadth of Hand	8.6	7.7	5.8
14.3	12.7	**9.5**	U20 T	Breadth of Palm	7.1	6.3	4.8

ADULT MALE METRIC MEASUREMENTS

UPPER EXTREMITY MEASUREMENTS

3/8 Life	1/3 Life	1/4 Life			1/6 Life	1/8 Life	1/12 Life
cm	cm	cm			cm	cm	cm
68.6	60.9	45.7	U1 T	Span of Arms	30.5	22.9	15.2
8.6	7.6	5.7	U2 T	Sternum to Achromion Process	3.8	2.9	1.9
5.7	5.1	3.8	U3 T	Sternum to Shoulder Pivot	2.6	1.9	1.3
11.4	10.2	7.6	U4 V	Humerus Pivot to Elbow Pivot	5.1	3.8	2.5
14.3	12.7	9.5	U5 V	Shoulder to Elbow Flexed	6.3	4.8	3.2
13.4	11.9	8.9	U6 V	Acromion to Lat. Condyle Elbow	5.9	4.5	3
17.1	15.2	11.4	U7 V	Flexed Elbow to Finger Tip	7.6	5.7	3.8
9.5	8.5	6.4	U8 V	Flexed Elbow to Wrist Pivot	4.2	3.2	2.1
7.6	6.8	5.1	U9 V	Wrist to Finger tip	3.4	2.5	1.7
4.8	4.2	3.2	U10 V	Wrist to Thumb	2.1	1.6	1.1
4.2	3.7	2.8	U11 V	Length of Palm	1.9	1.4	0.9
3.3	3	2.2	U12 V	Length 3rd Finger	1.5	1.1	0.7
5.4	4.8	3.6	U13 V	Thumb Crotch to 3rd Finger	2.4	1.8	1.2
2.7	2.4	1.8	U14 V	Thumb Crotch to Thumb Tip	1.2	0.9	0.6
4.8	4.2	3.2	U15 D	Anterior-Post. Arm at Biceps	2.1	1.6	1.1
3.8	3.4	2.6	U16 D	Anterior-Posterior at Forearm	1.7	1.3	0.9
1.7	1.5	1.1	U17 D	Depth of Wrist	0.8	0.6	0.4
2.6	2.3	1.8	U18 T	Breadth of Wrist	1.2	0.9	0.6
4.3	3.8	2.9	U19 T	Breadth of Hand	1.9	1.4	1
3.6	3.2	2.4	U20 T	Breadth of Palm	1.6	1.2	0.8

ADULT MALE
METRIC MEASUREMENTS

LOWER EXTREMITY MEASUREMENTS

3/2 Life	4/3 Life (Heroic)	LIFE SIZE			3/4 Life	2/3 Life	1/2 Life
cm	cm	cm			cm	cm	cm
165.3	146.9	**110.2**	L1 V	Crest of Ilium to Sole	82.7	73.5	55.1
160.1	142.3	**106.7**	L2 V	Ant. Sup. Spine of Ilium to Sole	80	71.1	53.4
142.1	126.3	**94.7**	L3 V	Greater Trochanter Femur-Sole	71	63.1	47.4
124.5	110.7	**83**	L4 V	Crotch to Sole	62.3	55.3	41.5
132	117.3	**88**	L5 V	Gluteal Furrow to Sole	66	58.7	44
77.3	68.7	**51.5**	L6 V	Posterior Knee Crease to Sole	38.6	34.3	25.8
79.5	70.7	**53**	L7 V	Ant. Sup. Spine of Ilium to Knee	39.8	35.3	26.5
64.5	57.3	**43**	L8 V	Pubis to Knee at Patella	32.3	28.7	21.5
80	71.1	**53.3**	L9 V	Knee at Patella to Sole	40	35.5	26.7
72.3	64.3	**48.2**	L10 V	Tibia to Sole	36.2	32.1	24.1
15.3	13.6	**10.2**	L11 V	Med. Malleolus to Sole	7.7	6.8	5.1
11.4	10.1	**7.6**	L12 V	Lat. Malleolus to Sole	5.7	5.1	3.8
52.7	46.8	**35.1**	L13 T	Inter Both Mid Thighs	26.3	23.4	17.6
34.2	30.4	**22.8**	L14 T	Breadth of Both Knees	17.1	15.2	11.4
36.2	32.1	**24.1**	L15 T	Breadth of Both Calves	18.1	16.1	12.1
11.3	10	**7.5**	L16 T	Breadth One Ankle at Malleoli	5.6	5	3.8
22.8	20.3	**15.2**	L17 D	Mid Thigh, Anterior-Posterior	11.4	10.1	7.6
17.1	15.2	**11.4**	L18 D	Knee, Anerior-Posterior	8.6	7.6	5.7
19.1	16.9	**12.7**	L19 D	Mid Calf, Anterior-Posterior	9.5	8.5	6.4
12.3	10.9	**8.2**	L20 D	Ankle, Anterior-Posterior	6.2	5.5	4.1
15.3	13.6	**10.2**	L21 D	Ankle at Malleoli, Anterior-Post.	7.7	6.8	5.1
41.7	37.1	**27.8**	L22 D	Length of Foot	20.9	18.5	13.9
34.4	30.5	**22.9**	L23 D	Heel to 5th Toe	17.2	15.3	11.5
15.3	13.6	**10.2**	L24 T	Breadth Foot at Rest	7.7	6.8	5.1
17.1	15.2	**11.4**	L25 T	Breadth Foot Standing	8.6	7.6	5.7
10.5	9.3	**7**	L26 T	Width of Heel	5.3	4.7	3.5

ADULT MALE
METRIC MEASUREMENTS

LOWER EXTREMITY MEASUREMENTS

3/8 Life	1/3 Life	1/4 Life			1/6 Life	1/8 Life	1/12 Life
cm	cm	cm			cm	cm	cm
41.3	36.7	27.6	L1 V	Crest of Ilium to Sole	18.4	13.8	9.2
40	35.6	26.675	L2 V	Ant.Sup.Spine of Ilium to Sole	17.8	13.3	8.9
35.5	31.6	23.7	L3 V	Greater Trochanter Femur-Sole	15.8	11.8	7.9
31.1	27.7	20.8	L4 V	Crotch to Sole	13.8	10.4	6.9
33	29.3	22	L5 V	Gluteal Furrow to Sole	14.7	11	7.3
19.3	17.2	12.9	L6 V	Posterior Knee Crease to Sole	8.6	6.4	4.3
19.9	17.7	13.3	L7 V	Ant. Sup. Spine of Ilium to Knee	8.8	6.6	4.4
16.1	14.3	10.8	L8 V	Pubis to Knee at Patella	7.2	5.4	3.6
20	17.8	13.3	L 9 V	Knee at Patella to Sole	8.9	6.7	4.4
18.1	16.1	12.1	L10 V	Tibia to Sole	8	6	4
3.8	3.4	2.6	L11 V	Med. Malleolus to Sole	1.7	1.3	0.9
2.9	2.5	1.9	L12 V	Lat. Malleolus to Sole	1.3	1	0.6
13.2	11.7	8.8	L13 T	Inter Both Mid Thighs	5.9	4.4	2.9
8.6	7.6	5.7	L14 T	Breadth of Both Knees	3.8	2.9	1.9
9	8	6	L15 T	Breadth of Both Calves	4	3	2
2.8	2.5	1.9	L16 T	Breadth One Ankle at Malleoli	1.3	0.9	0.6
5.7	5.1	3.8	L17 D	Mid Thigh, Anterior-Posterior	2.5	1.9	1.3
4.3	3.8	2.9	L18 D	Knee, Anerior-Posterior	1.9	1.4	1
4.8	4.2	3.2	L19 D	Mid Calf, Anterior-Posterior	2.1	1.6	1.1
3.1	2.7	2.1	L20 D	Ankle, Anterior-Posterior	1.4	1	0.7
3.8	3.4	2.6	L21 D	Ankle at Malleoli, Anterior-Post.	1.7	1.3	0.9
10.4	9.3	7	L22 D	Length of Foot	4.6	3.5	2.3
8.6	7.6	5.7	L23 D	Heel to 5th Toe	3.8	2.9	1.9
3.8	3.4	2.6	L24 T	Breadth Foot at Rest	1.7	1.3	0.9
4.3	3.8	2.9	L25 T	Breadth Foot Standing	1.9	1.4	1
2.6	2.3	1.8	L26 T	Width of Heel	1.2	0.9	0.6

DYNAMIC SYMMETRY IN HUMAN PROPORTIONS

DYNAMIC SYMMETRY IN HUMAN PROPORTIONS

Our favorable reaction to the classical art and architecture of the Greeks and to the fine forms of later work in the Renaissance may be due to our unconscious appreciation of dynamic symmetry. It was manifest in proportions of the human body and incorporated into the beautiful shapes and rhythms created by artists of that period.

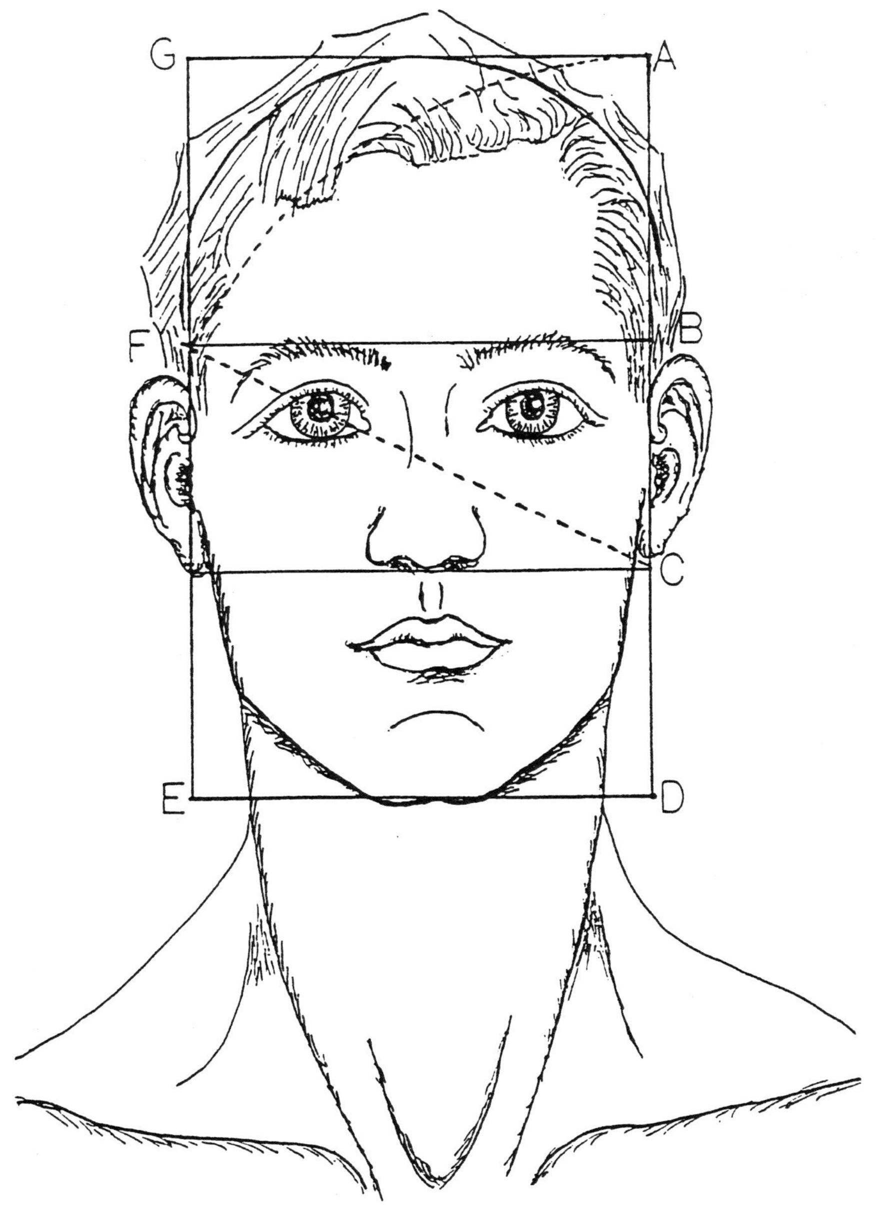

Fig. 57. Head proportions conform to the Golden Mean AD/AC = 1.6 = Φ

The study of human proportions is incomplete without a consideration of dynamic symmetry as it is expressed in the human body. Many names have been applied to this concept and considerable mathematical and geometric descriptions have been published. It is regarded as a significant factor of growth and development. Its presence in nature is widespread but seldom specifically recognized or appreciated. The ratios are pleasing because they are manifest in human form, as will be demonstrated. A more complete discussion of dynamic symmetry will be included the last section of the chapter on symmetry.

Fundamentally, dynamic symmetry is expressed in the Fibonacci series and in the golden rectangle. The Fibonacci series is a summation series of numbers in which any number of the series is the sum of the two previous numbers, as a + b = c; b + c = d. It starts with 1; 1 + 1 = 2; 1 + 2 = 3; 2 + 3 = 5; 3 + 5 = 8; 5 + 8 = 13. The ratio of a number of a sum divided by the proceeding number approximates 1.62..., and is called is Phi, Φ.

The golden rectangle begins with a square. A diagonal from the midpoint of the base to an opposite corner becomes the radius for an arc that intersects the line extended from the baseline. At that point a vertical line is constructed to intersect the line extended from the top of the square. This creates a golden rectangle. The ratio of the base of the rectangle to the base of the square is 1.62..., Phi, Φ. This rectangle is more pleasing than a square because many human features conform to it.

The ratio of the height of a human male head to breadth of head is approximately nine to five and one-quarter inches; 9 ÷ 5.25 = 1.61. The ratio of the vertex of the head to the umbilicus and from the umbilicus to the sole is nearly the same proportion.

Many other proportions of the human body correspond to or resemble this ratio. Since the reciprocal of 1.62..., (1 ÷ 1.62...), is 0.62..., it is nearly two-thirds of any unit measure. Whenever there is a two-thirds comparison, a dynamic symmetry relationship may be considered to exist.

These Phi (Φ) or approximate ratios, are present in the human body, and vary with individuals. Few people are aware of their significance. Several ratios listed here have a reasonable approximation to Φ, 1.62... or to the square root of 2, $\sqrt{2}$ = 1.414... Examples are listed using the charts of representative, prototype, proportions.

Feature measurement, approximately	**Female = Φ**	**Male = Φ**
Vertex to Sole ÷ Umbilicus to Sole	= 1.63	= 1.65
Umbilicus to Sole ÷ Vertex to Umbilicus	= 1.59	= 1.54
Vertex to Sole ÷ Vertex to Fingertip, at rest	= 1.64	= 1.66
Vertex to Fingertip ÷ Fingertip to Sole	= 1.57	= 1.57
Vertex to Fingertip ÷ Vertex to Umbilicus	= 1.57	= 1.55
Vertex to Elbow ÷ Elbow to Fingertip	= 1.61	= 1.65
Vertex to Elbow ÷ Vertex to Axilla	= 1.72	= 1.57

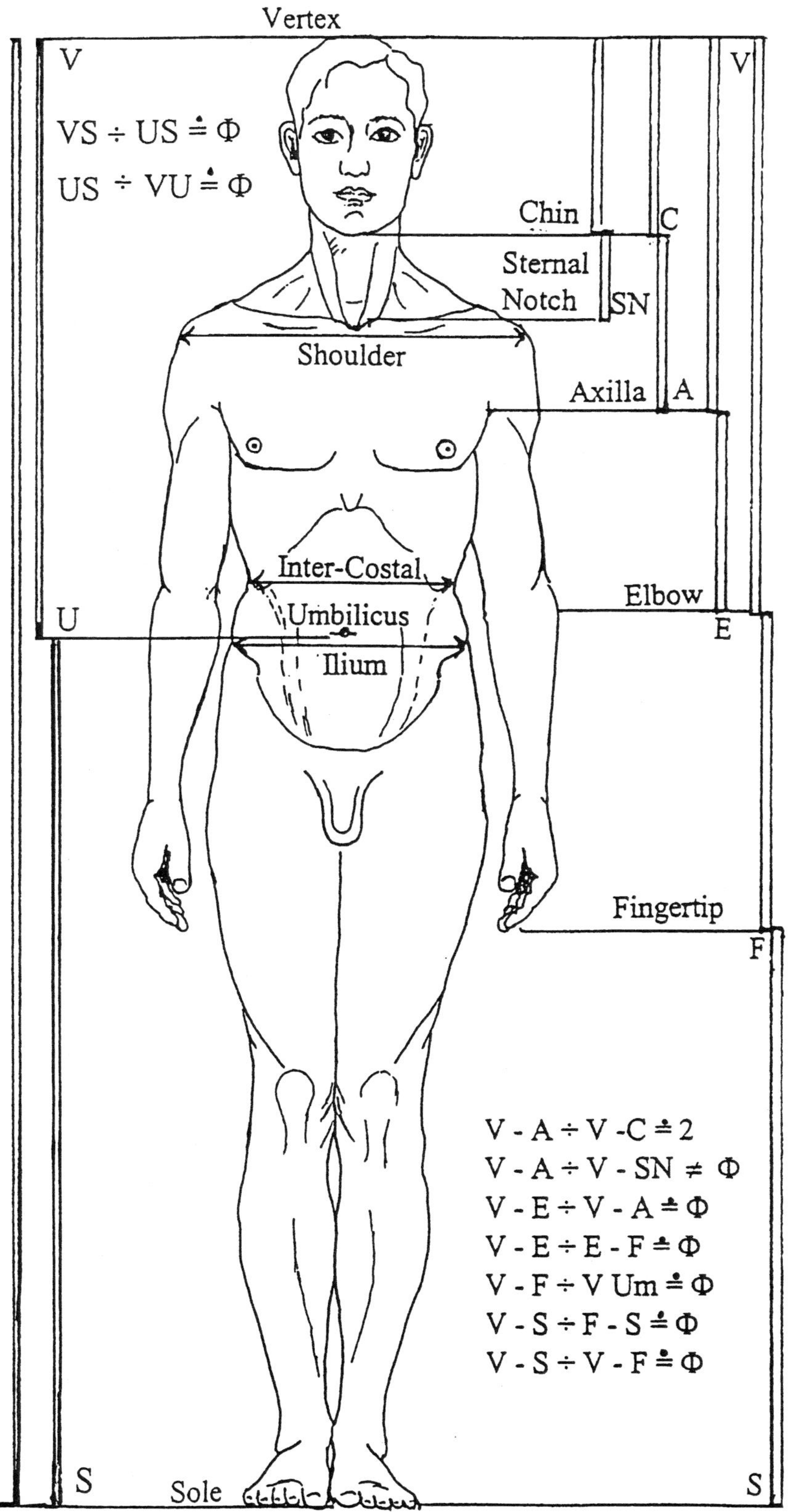

Fig. 58. Dynamic Symmetry in the human body vertical body measurements ratios approximating, (=) Phi.

TRANSVERSE BODY MEASUREMENTS RATIOS RESEMBLING PHI

	Female	**Male**
Vertex - Axilla ÷ Vertex - Sternal Notch	= 1.20 ≠ Φ	= 1.27 ≠ Φ
Vertex to Axilla ÷ Vertex to Chin	= 1.87 ≠ Φ	= 1.91 ≠ Φ
Shoulder Breadth to Inter-Costal Margin	= 1.88 ≠ Φ	= 1.87 ≠ Φ
Shoulder Breadth to Inter-Crest of Ilium	= 1.45 ≠ Φ	= 1.56 ≠ Φ

The waist on females is near the inferior rib margin while on males the waist is near the hip bone, or crest of the ilium, so the average is still only approximately equal to Phi.

After reviewing these calculations, one must therefore be cautious in applying Fibonacci ratios strictly to the human anatomy, since many factors are involved in human maturation. Young mammals like puppies and kittens may conform more closely to these ratios. We think of them as being cute. Zealous investigators have sought relationships where there is some coincidence or resemblance, but some of these are questionable for correlation.

Some other body segments do not invariably demonstrate this ratio. Although there is a gradation from the shoulder to the fingertips, the ratio is not always applicable. The male hand to the radius of the forearm is a ratio of 1 to 1.25. The radius to the humerus in the upper arm is a ratio of 1 to 1.2. This hardly approximates Φ. Furthermore, there is considerable individual variation of measurements and proportions.

Average measurements or representative proportions are not likely to be found in any one person, even when measuring a large group. When creating an image or a figure as an artistic endeavor, a live model is very important for accurate representation. Nevertheless, recognition and approximations of Phi ratios deserve appreciation to render pleasing configurations.

≐ is approximately equal to:
= is equal to:
≠ is not equal to:

DYNAMIC SYMMETRY IN THE FACE

Some Vertical Face Ratios Approximate Phi (Φ)

		Female	**Male**
Head height ÷ Head breadth		= 1. 45	= 1.51
Vertex to eyes ÷ Hairline to eyes	AD ÷ BD	= 1.32	= 1.29
Eyes to chin ÷ Nostrils to chin	DF ÷ DE	= 1.59	= 1.54
Hairline to eyes ÷ Eyes to nostrils	DB ÷ DE	= 1.6	= 1.67
Eyes to mouth ÷ Eyes to nostrils	DF ÷ DE	= 1.50	= 1.56
Nostrils to chin ÷ Mouth to chin	FG ÷ FG	= 1.45	= 1.46

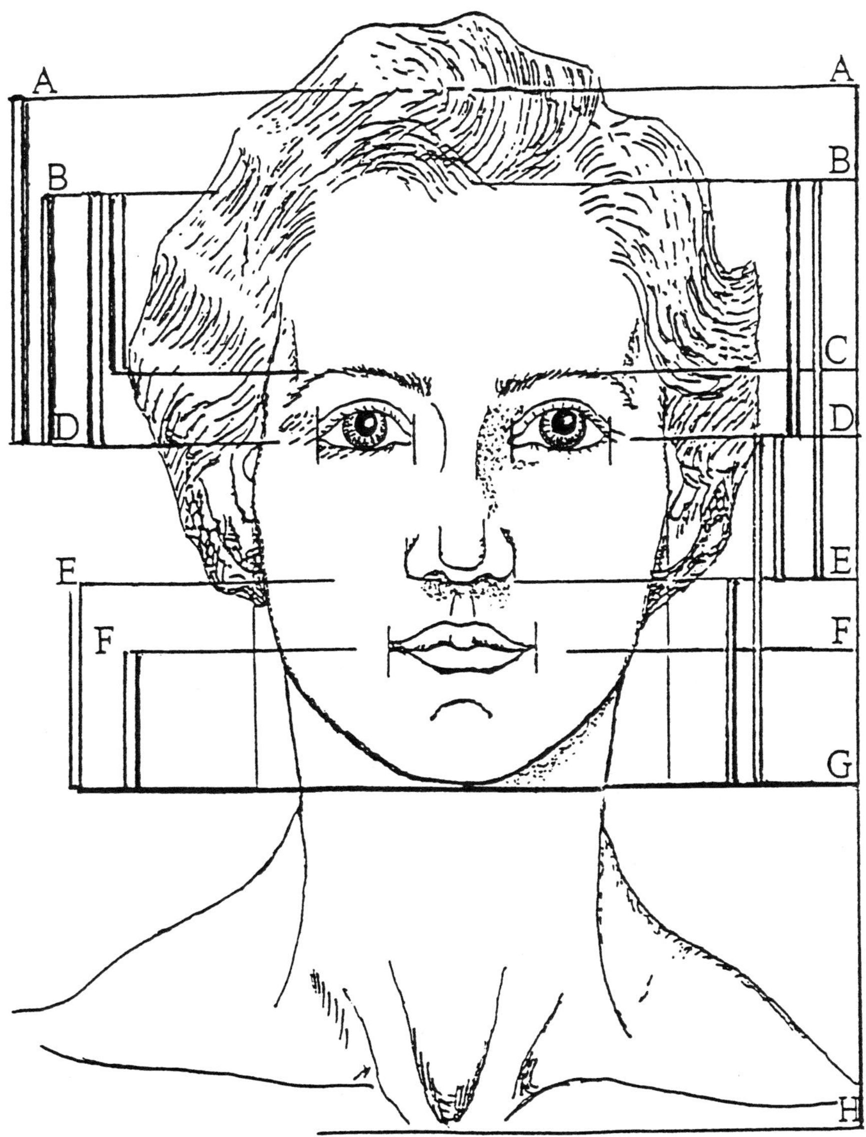

Fig. 59. Some vertical face ratios approximate Φ, 1.62.

DYNAMIC SYMMETRY IN THE FACE

Some Transverse Face Ratios Approximate Phi (Φ)

		Female	**Male**
Head breadth ÷ Lateral eye corners	gg’ ÷ dd’	= 1.56	= 1.49
Mouth breadth ÷ Nose breadth at ala	ff’ ÷ ee’	= 1.42	= 1.34
Lateral eye corners ÷ Mouth breadth	dd’ ÷ ff’	= 2.05	= 2.0

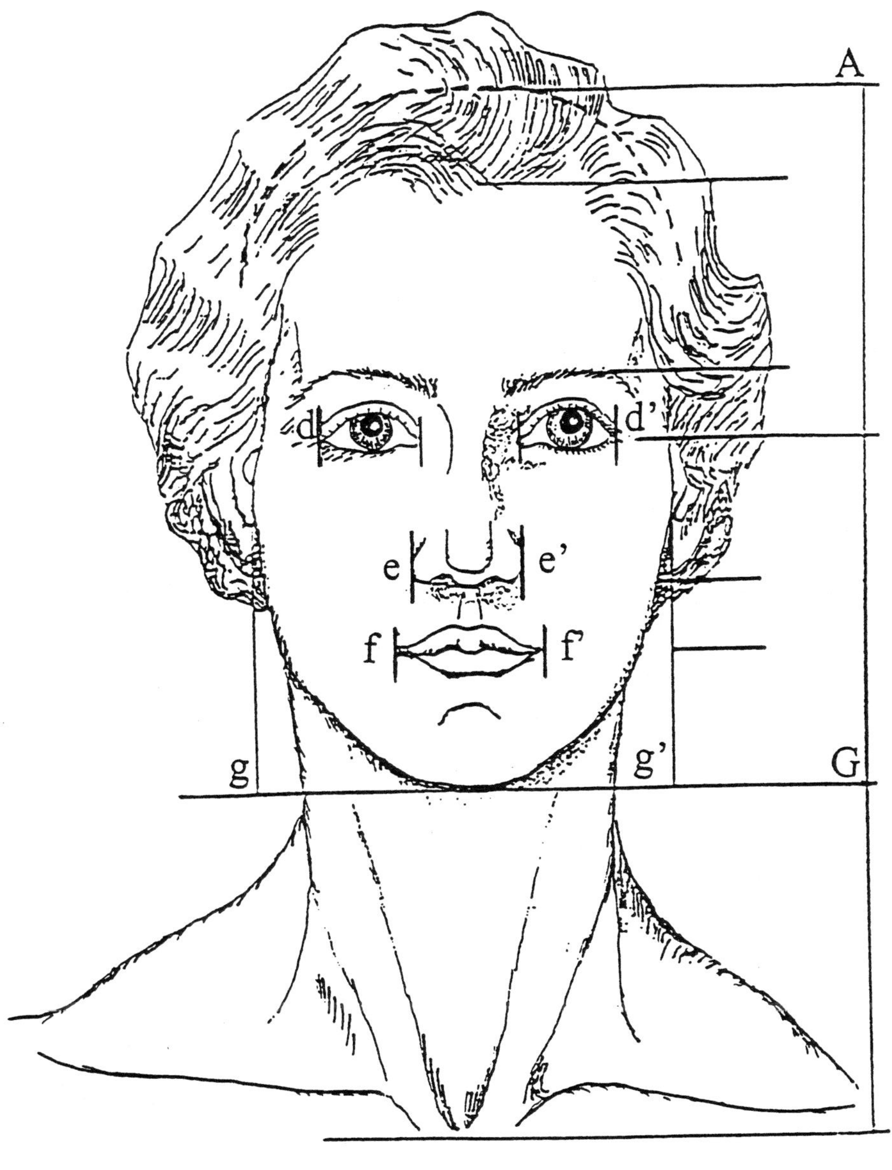

Fig. 60. Some transverse face ratios approximate Φ, 1.62.

FEATURES OF THE HANDS AND FEET

FEATURES OF THE HANDS AND FEET

For better comprehension, a few anatomical and technical terms are explained here. **Distal** means away from the body. **Proximal** means toward the body. **Phalanx**, or **Phalanges** are finger or toe segments or their bones. **Metacarpals** are the intrinsic bones of the hand in the palmar area. **Metatarsals** are the equivalent bones in the foot. **Dorsal** refers to the back of a hand and the top of a foot. These are opposite to the **Palm** of the hand and the **Plantar** surface or bottom of the foot

Parabolas and parabolic curves occur frequently in nature yet are seldom consciously appreciated. The mathematical equations for parabolas contain an $X = Y^2$ or equivalent in their formula but can also have other modifiers. When such an equation is plotted on a graph, a parabola has points on the curve equidistant from a focus. When a ball or other object is thrown up in the air, its trajectory is a parabolic curve. Water from a spout of a fountain follows the curve of a parabola. The waterfall of a stream pouring over a cliff into a plunge-pool resembles a half-parabolic curve. The outlines of many deciduous trees resemble a parabola. One of the most familiar forms is the paraboloid reflector of an automobile headlight. See Parabola, page 161.

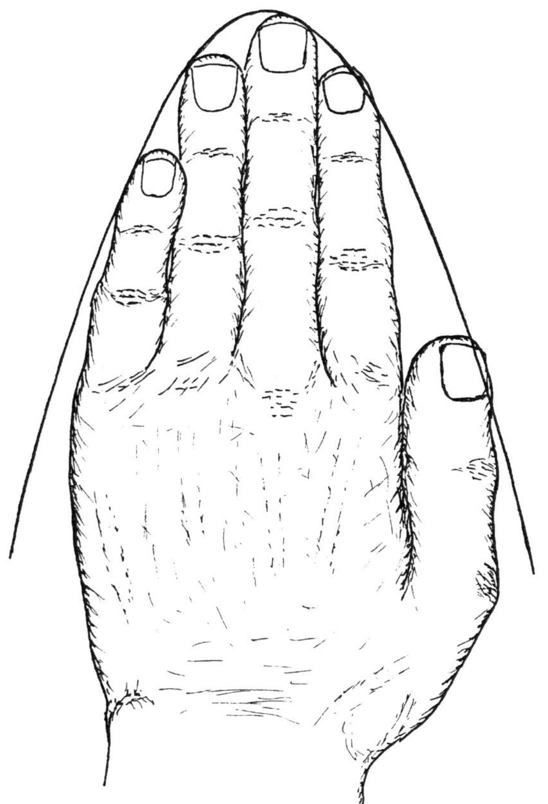

Fig. 61. The outline of a hand conforms to a parabola.

HAND FEATURES

Since the hands are an important part of the expression of an artistic endeavor, many details, often overlooked, become important. The three middle fingers are dominant, while the thumb and little finger are sub-dominant. Proportions have already been considered. Attention to other features can make a significant increase in the conveyance of an intended message or interpretation.

The overall fingertip outline of an extended hand with fingers together conforms to a parabola. Lines connecting the inter-phalangeal joints also resemble parabolic curves, Fig. 62. When the fingers are spread, the lines connecting the fingertips and the inter-phalangeal joints still conform to broader parabolic curves. Even when fists are clenched, there is still a broad parabolic curve evident.

On a top, or dorsal, view of the hand in a gently relaxed position, the fingers are generally in the same plane, but the thumb's axis is at about a 45 to 90 degree angle.

When all fingers of the hand are

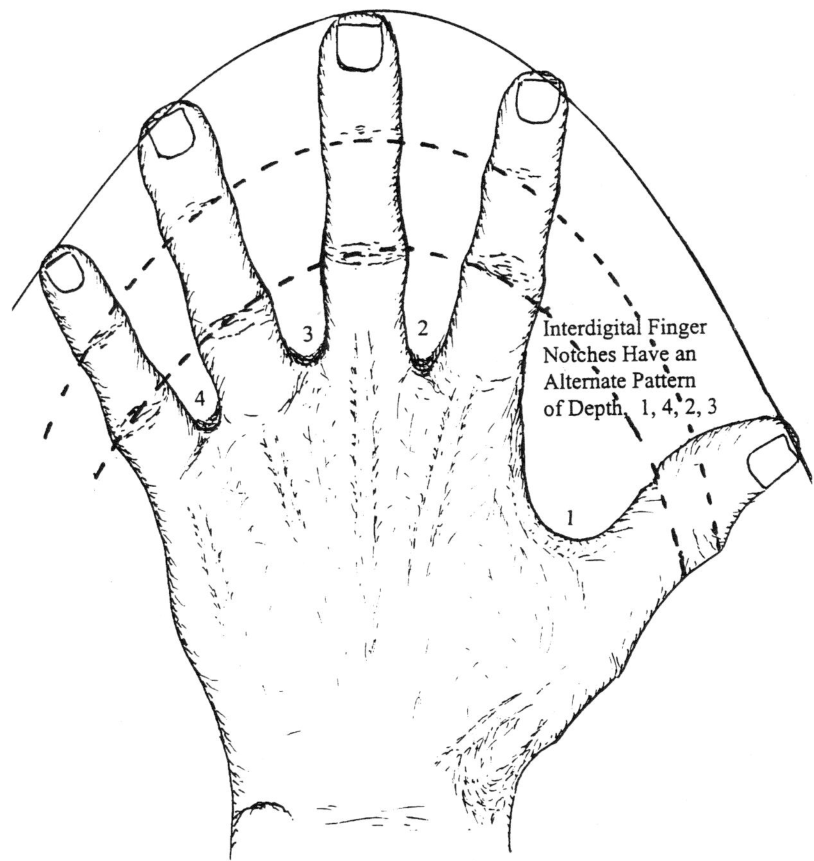

Fig. 62. The outline of fingertips of the spread hand conforms to a parabola.

extended, the index finger is gently curved toward the middle finger. The thumb's axis may be the same as the finger's, and the thumb tip is at the middle of the index proximal phalanx. When the hand is fully relaxed or neutral the thumb is oblique to the other fingers. The thumb is rotated to more than a 90 degree angle to the fingers when the fist is clenched.

The fingernails have an arch side to side and a slight curve from cuticle to fingernail tip. Fingernails are generally about half the length of the terminal phalanx. The terminal segment of the fingers have a slight downturn toward the tips except the thumb, which has a terminal segment upturn. The fifth finger may have a slight terminal upturn. In most men, the tip of a trimmed fourth fingernail is at the cuticle of the third fingernail, but in many women, it is halfway from cuticle to the trimmed fingernail tip. The fourth finger may be slightly longer on one hand than the other.

Note that the dorsal and palmar measurements differ. The wrist to the palmar-digital crease is longer than the dorsal measurement of wrist to third knuckle at the metacarpo-phalangeal joint. As a result, this dorsal joint to third fingertip is longer than the palmar third finger crease to third fingertip measurement.

The finger webs are slanted at about 45 degrees upwards, in a palmar to dorsal direction. The palm length is greater than the width, but is nearly equal to the width of the palm plus the thumb. This ratio varies with individuals, as some have narrow hands and others have broad hands. The thumb crotch is at 1/2 the length of the palm. The tip of the thumb reaches nearly the middle of the first phalanx segment of the index finger.

The finger notches, Fig. 62, demonstrate an interesting arrangement of alternations. The deepest notch is 1, the thumb crotch at one-half the length of the palm. The next deepest notch is 4, between the fourth and fifth finger. The next is 2, between index and middle finger, while 3, the notch between the third and fourth finger is least deep.

The palm of the hand has three main creases and four pads, Fig. 67. The proximal crease begins near the wrist at about midline of the palm and courses in an arc toward the thumb crotch to about two-thirds the palm length. It outlines the thenar eminence, a pad that contains powerful accessory muscles of the thumb. The middle crease is nearly diagonal across the palm to the base of the index finger. The distal crease begins proximal to the base of the fifth finger and curves in an arc to the web between the index and third fingers. The distal crease outlines the third pad that cushions the metacarpo-phalangeal joints or knuckles of third, fourth, and fifth fingers.

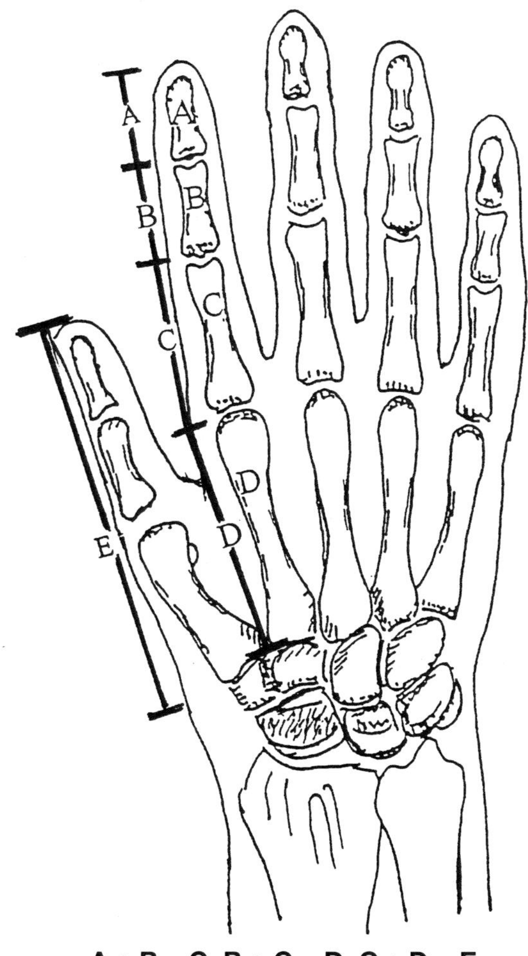

A + B = C, B + C = D, C + D = E

Fig. 63. The Fibonacci series is evident in the hand.

The lateral aspect of the palm features the hypothenar eminence, a pad that contains some accessory muscles for the fifth finger. The fourth and smallest pad, between the middle and distal creases, cushions index finger metacarpophalangeal joint. There are minor palmar creases below each joint of the fingers.

The dorsum or back of the hand has three planes, Fig. 65. The first plane is bounded by the first or thumb metacarpal and the second or index finger metacarpal. The second plane is bounded by the second and third metacarpal while the lateral plane is bounded by the third and fifth metacarpals. These planes are outlined by extensor tendons. Young women's hands have more fatty tissue that conceals veins and tendons, but adds to their beauty. When a vigorous male is portrayed, the extensor tendons of the fingers and veins should be apparent to emphasize virility. At the wrist, the spine of the distal ulna is prominent.

When the thumb is extended and the fingers are spread, a concavity is present between the base of the first metacarpal with its extensor tendon, the spine of the radius, and the extensor tendon of the thumb. It is called the snuff-box.

In addition to the segmental symmetry and poly-symmetry of the phalanges, dynamic symmetry is also present in the human hand, Fig. 63. A very beautiful example of a summation or Fibonacci series does exist. The sum of the distal two phalanges of each finger is equal to the proximal phalanx. See Fibonacci Series, page 216.

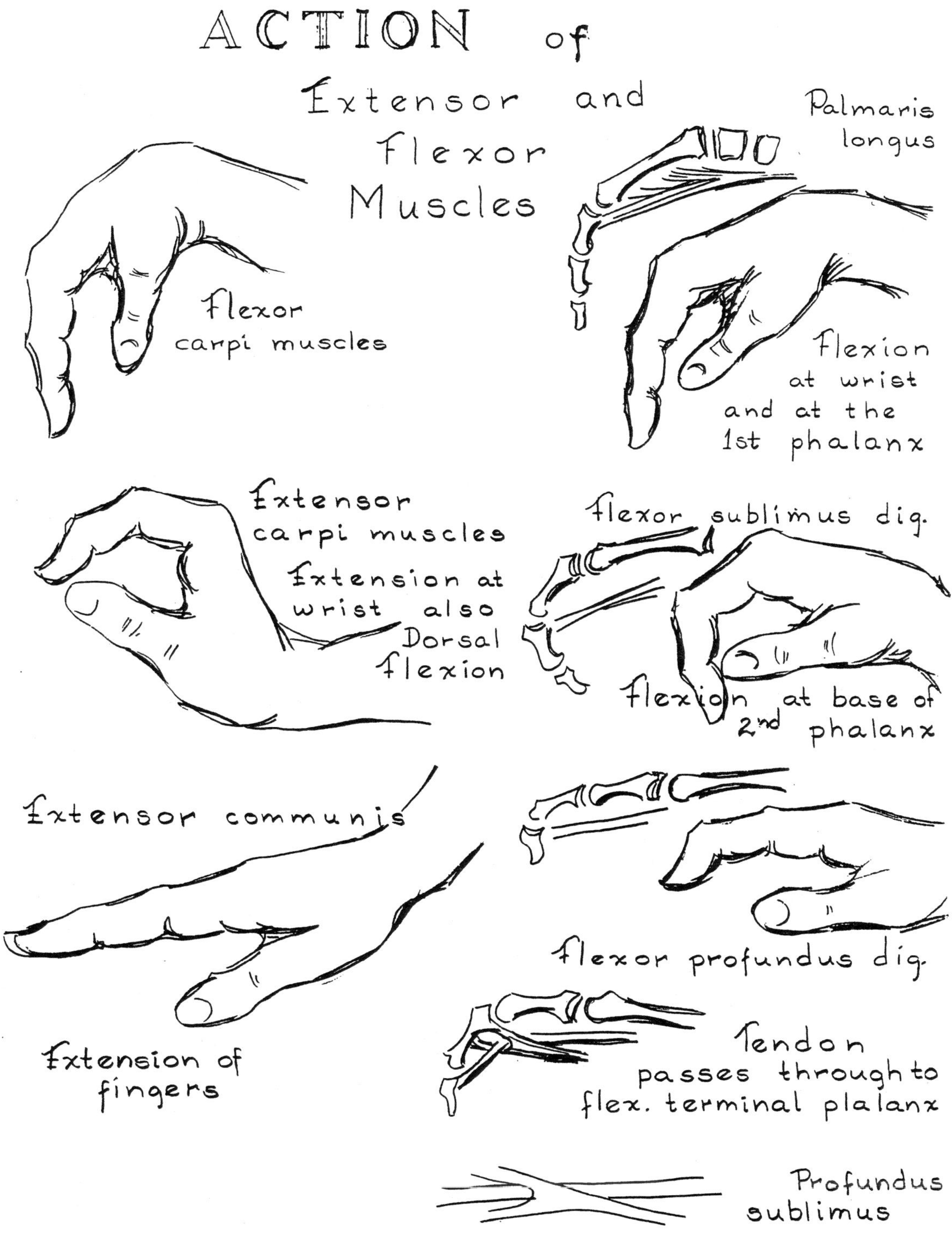

Fig. 64. Action of extensor and flexor muscles.

The proximal phalanx is one-half the length of a finger. The sum of the middle phalanx, B, and the proximal phalanx, C, equals the corresponding metacarpal, D, in the hand. This continues along the thumb; and the length of the thumb with its metacarpal nearly equals that of the second metacarpal and its proximal phalanx, see Fig. 63. When the fist is clenched, the fingers form whorls resembling a snail shell and the whirling rectangles of the golden rectangle. This configuration enables humans to grasp a tool or clench a fist. The hand functions with dynamic symmetry to develop an effective grasp.

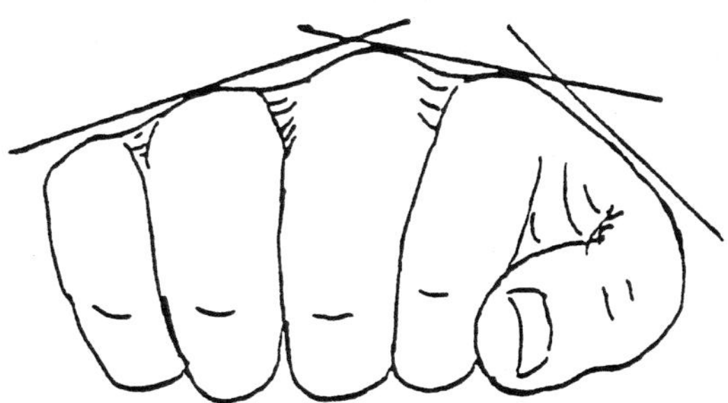

Fig. 65. The dorsum of the hand has three planes.

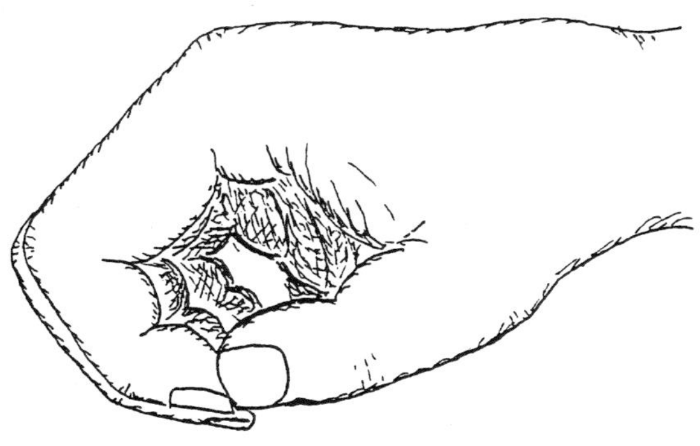

Fig. 66. The thumb opposes fingers when grasping.

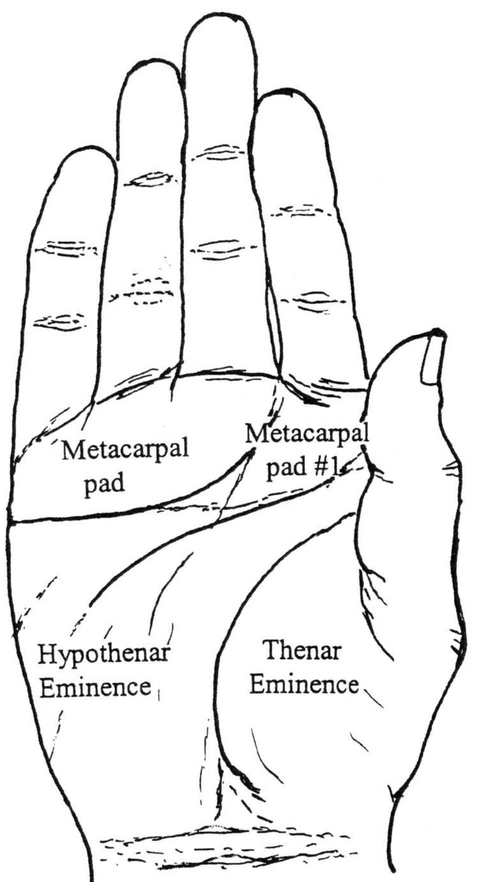

Fig. 67. Palm creases.

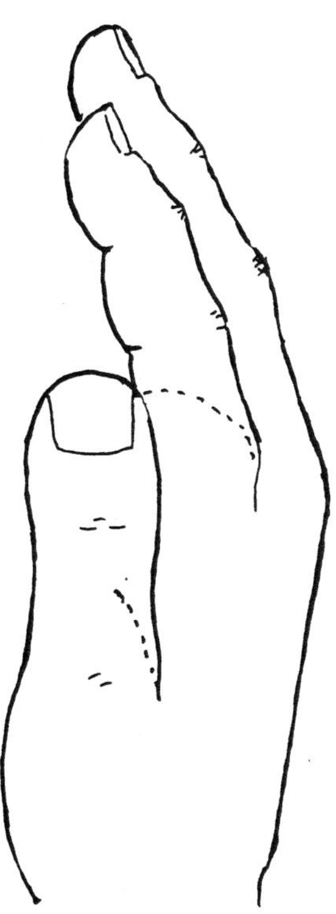

Fig. 68. Finger webs.

FEATURES OF THE FEET

When the two feet are together, the outline of the toes conforms to a parabola, Fig. 69. A hand is about equal to three-fourths length of a foot. The notches of toes have an alternation in a manner resembling the fingers. However, the deepest notch is the fourth to fifth toe and the next deepest is between the first and second toe. The third to fourth notch is nearly as deep as first to second and the shallowest notch is between second and third toes. As in the hand, the webs between the toes slope up, plantar to dorsal at about a 45-degree angle. The width of the toes are nearly equal except for the first toe, which is twice the width of any other toe. When modeling, divide the toes in three parts; one for the big toe and one part for each other pair of toes. The notches are then applied. Often, the second toe is longer than the big toe. The fifth toe is sometimes curled under the fourth toe.

Support to the body is effected by three parts of the foot, Fig. 70. These include the heel that has a large bone, the calcaneous, which is well padded; the ball of the foot, that includes the five metatarsophalangeal joints at the toes; and the head of the fifth metatarsal bone, a bony prominence along the lateral border of the foot. It is also well padded and gives lateral stability. The instep of the foot, or the medial aspect of the sole, has an arch, a dome-shaped concavity. Above it on the dorsum of the foot, is another arching plane sloping from medial at the first metatarsal bone to lateral and from the ankle to the toes. This con-

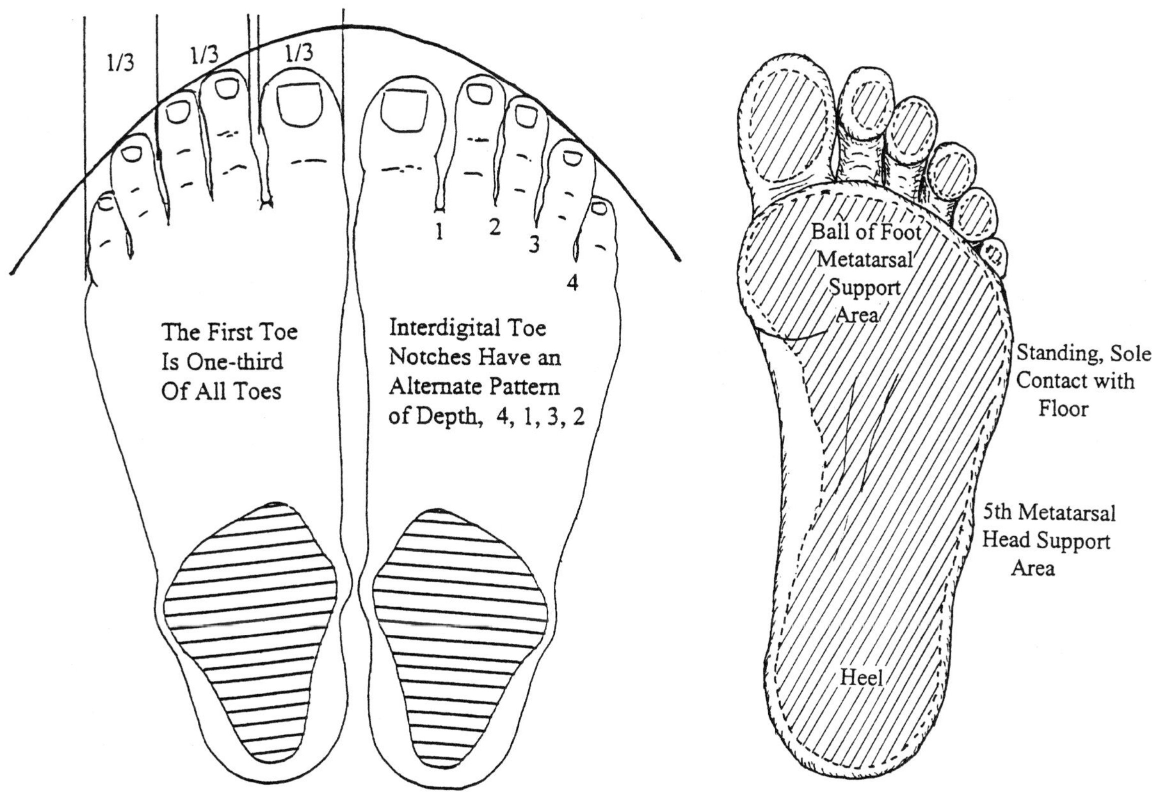

Fig. 69. The outline of the feet conforms to a parabola.

Fig. 70. The sole of the standing foot.

tinues to the big toe, which has a terminal up-turn. The other four toes interrupt this slope with first an up-turn and then a down turn. The big toe acts as a take-off when walking or running, and it is assisted by the other four toes.

Ankle flexibility and plantar flexion render some fine curving lines and planes. In the neutral position, a curved line with alternations begins concave with the Achilles tendon, reverses to convex around the heel to the instep where it is concave to the ball of the foot at the first metatarsal phalangeal joint. There it reverses again to convex. On plantar flexion, pointing the toes downward, these curves are accentuated. There are plantar creases, but they are less regular and prominent as on the palms. At each side of the ankle are bony prominences—the medial maleolus, a process of the tibia, and the lateral maleolus, the distal portion or end of the fibula. The tip of the lateral maleolus is lower than the medial maleolus. There is a concavity on both sides above the heel, bounded by the Achilles tendon and the maleoli. Attention to these details give more realism, but equally important, an expression of vigor and action can be manifest.

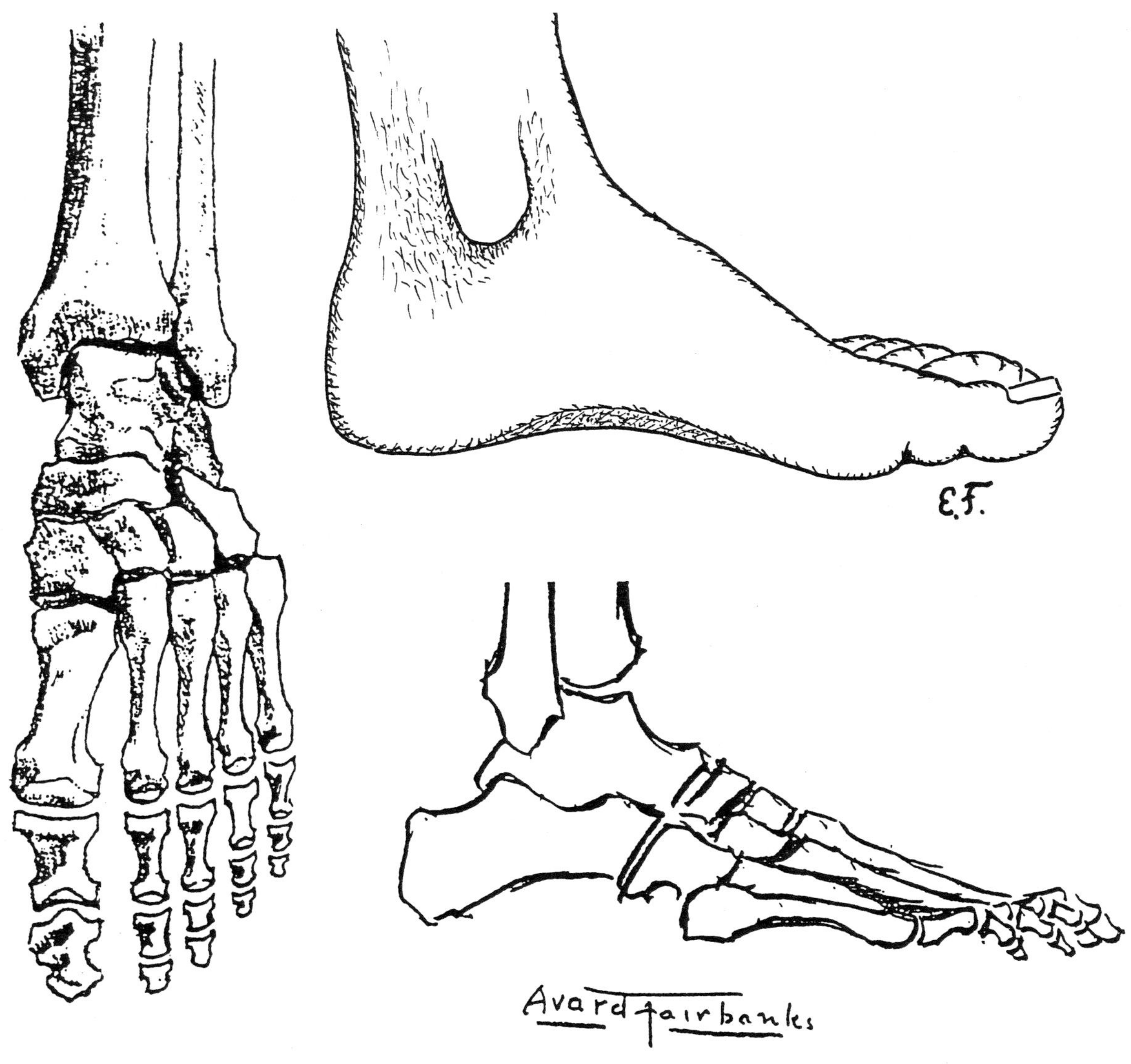

Fig. 71. Features of a foot.

A BASIS FOR DESIGN

It is the knowledge of law and order that leads the mind of man from chaos into a realm of reason, from mental bondage to freedom, and from mystery to understanding. There is often an assumption that design is a creation of man. However, design antedated man by eons. Elements of design were in effect at the dawn of time. There are five phases: The Energy Phase; the Media Phase; the Vegetal Phase; the Animate Phase; and the Psychic Phase.

The ENERGY Phase: Elements combined to become gases, liquids, and solids. The gases formed the atmosphere, and the liquids formed the hydrosphere. With a continuation of energizing forces acting on the atmosphere and the hydrosphere there is motion and activity, particularly with heat acting on substances to effect a state of agitation. This alters substance and reforms it to shape it according to some design. Consider weather, winds, rain, freezing, ocean currents and, waves. This Energy Phase also manifests itself in man. It is the creative impulse to be expressed through art.

The MEDIA Phase: This constitutes the existence of inorganic forms in gases, liquids, and particularly solids by which energy effects shape. In this environment, all forms acted upon by energy seek a proper relationship according to their designs. Water vapor rising by absorbed energy from the sun develops into appealing cloud formations. Streams and waterfalls show forces at work. The hills and mountains rise and are torn down by erosion. In this phase, geometric shapes are prevalent. All material substances acted on by energy strive to achieve the goal of their design. These include the materials that may be acted on by the artist in an effort of creativity. Their limitations are to be appreciated and respected.

The VEGETAL Phase: It designates the development of living, organic forms, primarily in the floral aspect by the action of cell growth, development, and proliferation. This characterizes both plant and animal life for growth, development and the will to produces and sustains life, adapting to the environment. Interest in life is expressed by the artist in simple patterns of symmetry, and the employment of floral decoration in a composition.

The ANIMATE Phase: This manifests a greater urge for freedom. Animal tissues form themselves into new types, seeking a release from the bonds of mineral and plant forms. These new forms began to move independently in the oceans and then on land. Animate forms in motion developed new designs with dynamic positions. Symmetry was broken or altered, and the elements of regularity and rhythm were adjusted to progressions and alternations. The development of a nervous system and many specialized organs manifest a high degree of arrangement. The shape of animals does not lend themselves for decorative patterns as does floral forms. Instead the appeal of action and movement encourages dynamic design.

The PSYCHIC Phase: With a further urge for freedom, the Psychic Phase manifests conscious thinking of an individual that strives to know and understand the environment. This may also be considered the creative phase of ideas. The artist with recorded knowledge, training, desires, and impulses can create designs for himself. It reflects the harmony, sensed by man, to surround himself with objects of design to gain physical comforts and mental satisfaction. The psychic phase is one in which thought finds expression through the higher orders of harmony.

The human form is more adaptable to this sphere of artistic design than to the decorative design that uses geometric and floral elements. This realm may be characterized by individuality, freedom, control, virtues, and harmonies. Individual realization can grow to a place where it is capable of creating forms and placing ideas in materials to be manifest in great masterpieces of art. Man can be the master of creative art with the power of developing harmonies and giving voice, a message, to substance. The purpose of **design** is to cause forms to harmonize

When one says **design**, the concept of decorative design often comes to mind. However, all masterpieces in a sense are the product of plans and a design. In the study of design, too much attention may be directed to the superficial or to the apparent. More stress should be given to the deeper knowledge that is available through scientific study.

Any complete **design** must result from the harmony of all of its parts. The goal of perfection is the design pattern, while the material form, that weaves itself into the order, renders the expression of the design.

Design, therefore is not only that which produces a sensory delight in one beholding objects, but something that leads to a conscious appreciation of the activity by which the artist created his work. It has been defined as the arrangement of parts, details, forms, and color, especially so as to produce a complete and artistic unit.

Design is the plan or pattern upon which inanimate or animate forms are constructed. It is inherent within the structure, not merely as a form or surface being applied to it. The highest order of design would be a more perfect unity of structure, significance, and harmony, which creates aesthetic delight.

In the beginning of civilizations, feelings awakened and gave stimulus to man's desire to know reasons for the reactions of the individual to life in a world of animate and inanimate forms. These same forces today give significance and harmony to a cultured existence, even though science has advanced remarkably.

Adapted from the doctoral thesis *Anatomic Design* of Avard Fairbanks, University of Michigan, 1936.

Several primary factors that are fundamental to design are basic; Content, Form, Balance, Rhythm, and Symmetry.

A. CONTENT: Art is a means of communication. It conveys a message, an expression, or creates a mood. It may record or re-create an event, an era, or portray a person. Besides the primary object, supportive accessories or artifacts generate added meaning. When depicting humans, these may include costume, uniform, helmet, headdress, tools, jewelry or other items that add to the impact of the creative effort.

B. FORM: A composition includes straight and curved lines that modify or are modified by plane and solid geometric figures, especially in sculpture. These blend or are subtly incorporated into a scene or figure so that only the very observant viewer may analyze their presence. These altered configurations may also be improved by change of tone, texture, and color. Various simple and fundamental forms will be discussed and illustrated to encourage better comprehension by students and amateurs. Appreciation of various forms and their inclusion can result in more vigorous portrayal.

C. **BALANCE:** That may be formal or informal, static or dynamic, but it indicates stability or anticipated stability as an expression of form in action. Additional discussion and illustrations are included in later pages to encourage recognition and application of dynamic balance in action.

D. **RHYTHM:** It is manifest by intermittent accentuation of repetitive elements.. In human life there are rhythms of breathing and heart-beat. Walking and running have their rhythms. We are creatures of rhythms and need to express it in our art and music. Additional discussion and illustrations are included in later pages.

E. **SYMMETRY:** The inclusion of its various forms that may be formal or informal. These can be altered by other factors to accomplish a symmetry associated with balance and rhythm as an expression of action and beauty. Examples and discussion will be included about primary categories of spherical symmetry, radial symmetry, and bilateral symmetry. Specialized symmetries as rotational symmetry, polysymmetry, multilateral symmetry, and dynamic symmetry will be included.

These factors may not be recognized by some people regarding human features, but on closer study, many examples are found. Bilateral symmetry is fundamental, yet there may be subtle asymmetries of face or extremities in various persons. An alteration of symmetry and balance develops in action and movement. Representations of dynamic qualities are significant to design.

The creative impulse of man to render beauty and charm to objects with which he intends to live, impels him to give permanence to those forms and designs that makes his existence a delight. Functional artifacts give way to more enduring ones carved in stone or painted on walls. Man's will is bent to leave his creative impressions in permanent objects of art.

As an actual object, the human figure is not appropriate for use in decorations, and consequently does not lend itself to being draped about pillars or pylons or to be thrown upon wall surfaces. However, as an object through which thought may be expressed, in works of art, the human figure becomes a voice of man's most treasured concepts.

In its use from the construction of idols to masterpieces of creative art, the human figure is admired because of its symmetry, its rhythm, and harmony, and because of the concepts that may be expressed through its representation.

In artistic design, raw materials that are acted upon by human intelligence, may be arranged into orderly patterns for the sake of awakening a sense of aesthetic delight in the beholder. These make up the ingredients that an artist uses. Two and three dimensional forms, created with balance and rhythms are akin to the word symbols of poetry. The greater values of artistic design lie in the power to bring persons into accord with harmonies of our environment and to arouse his consciousness. Like poetry, artistic design can and should deal with the most profound significance of life and existence.

BALANCE

Balance expressed in its simplest form is illustrated by two weights on a board balanced on a fulcrum. Formal balance shows two equal weights at equal distances from a fulcrum. Informal balance simply shown are two unequal weights at unequal distances from a fulcrum yet in equilibrium. This is the principle of the balance beam scale for weight measure.

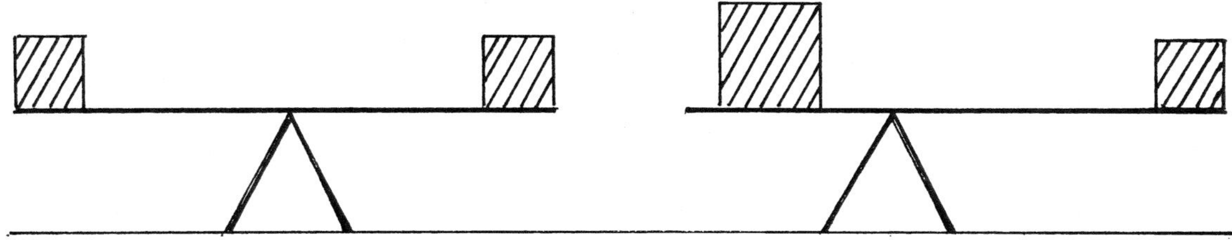

Fig. 72. Formal balance (left); Informal balance (right).

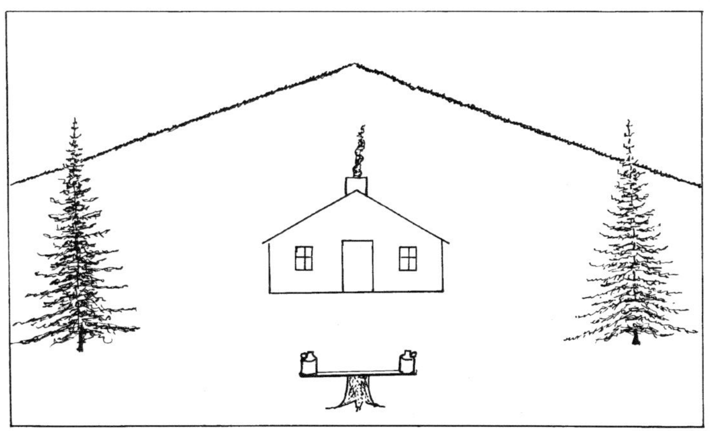

Fig. 73. Formal balance.

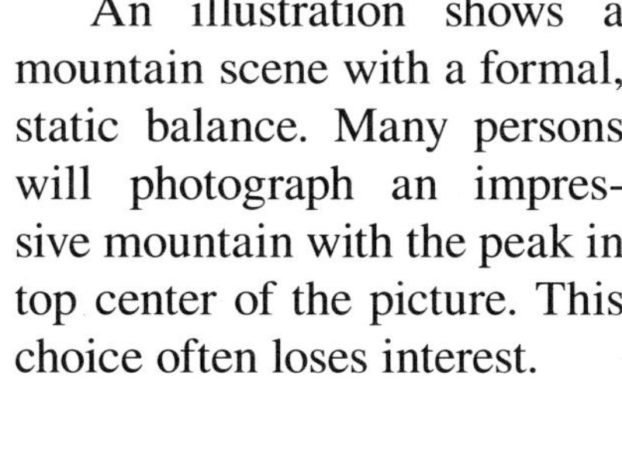

An illustration shows a mountain scene with a formal, static balance. Many persons will photograph an impressive mountain with the peak in top center of the picture. This choice often loses interest.

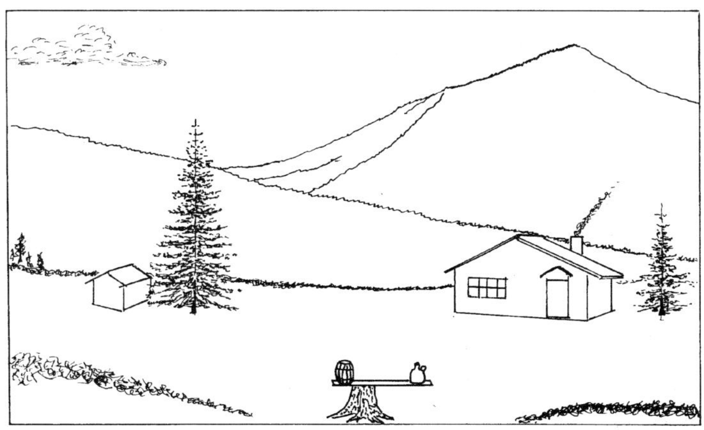

Fig. 74. Informal balance.

A second mountain scene is illustrated that has an informal balance. By adjusting the scene to have the peak off center and achieve an informal equilibrium with inclusion of other features improves interest in any similar composition.

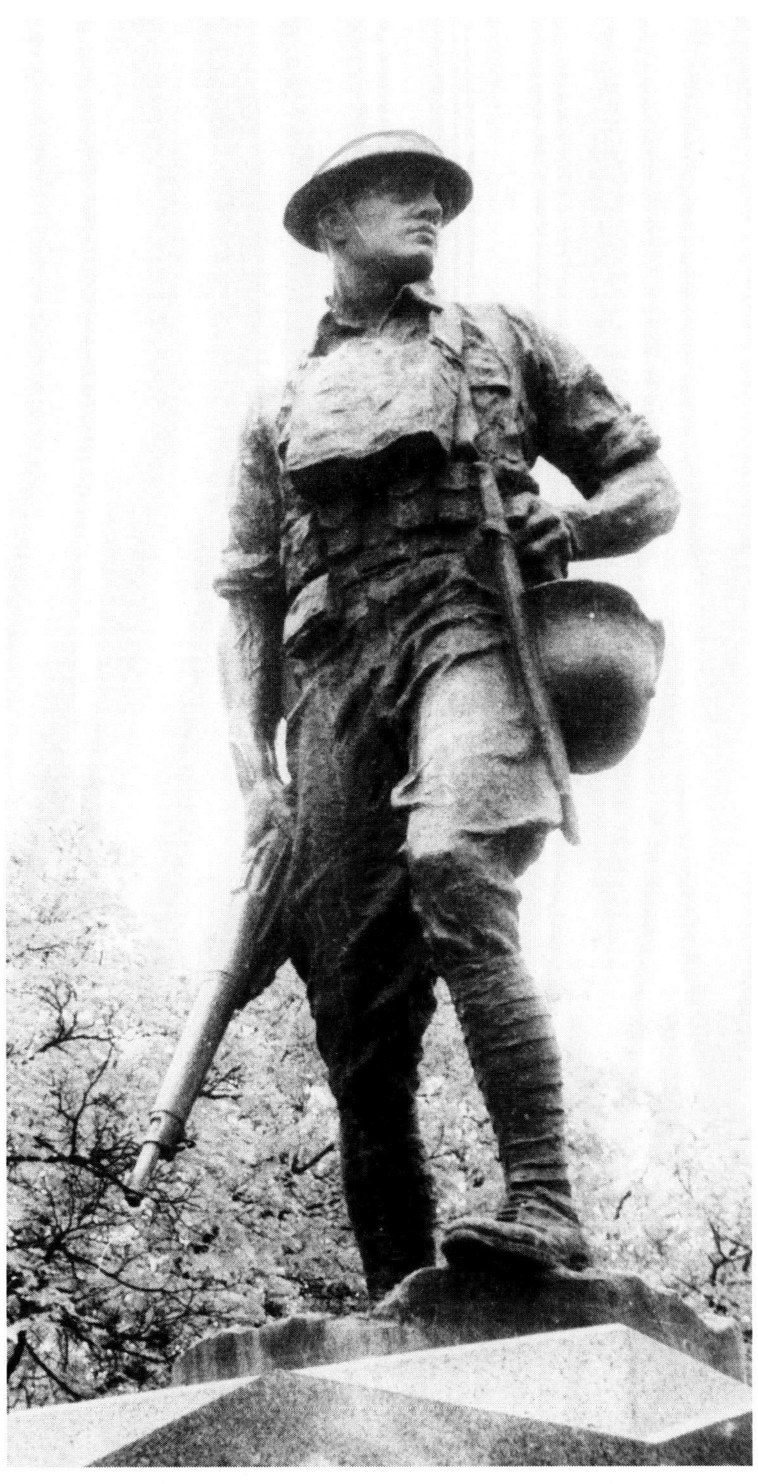

Fig. 75. The Idaho Doughboy by Avard T. Fairbanks, erected at Moscow and St. Anthony, Idaho.

Leonardo da Vinci noted that a human in a standing posture, with arms relaxed at the side, will maintain the ear directly over the ball of the foot. Weight will be supported equally by both feet. It is a state of equilibrium. Military drill emphasizes regimentation. The soldier at attention is appears motionless. A common phrase is, "stiff as a statue." Unfortunately many statues appear to have stiffness, especially some statues honoring the military. Some statues actually portray a soldier standing at attention.

The *Idaho Doughboy* monument, erected at Moscow and St. Anthony, Idaho by Avard Fairbanks, portrays a World War I soldier, alert and moving as if on patrol. There is an informal balance that anticipates movement and action.

When weight is shifted to one foot, there is a rotation and tilt of the pelvis. The shoulders tilt and rotate in the opposite direction. Equilibrium is re-established with an informal balance. Walking or running increases these changes. The adjustments occur spontaneously and impulsively.

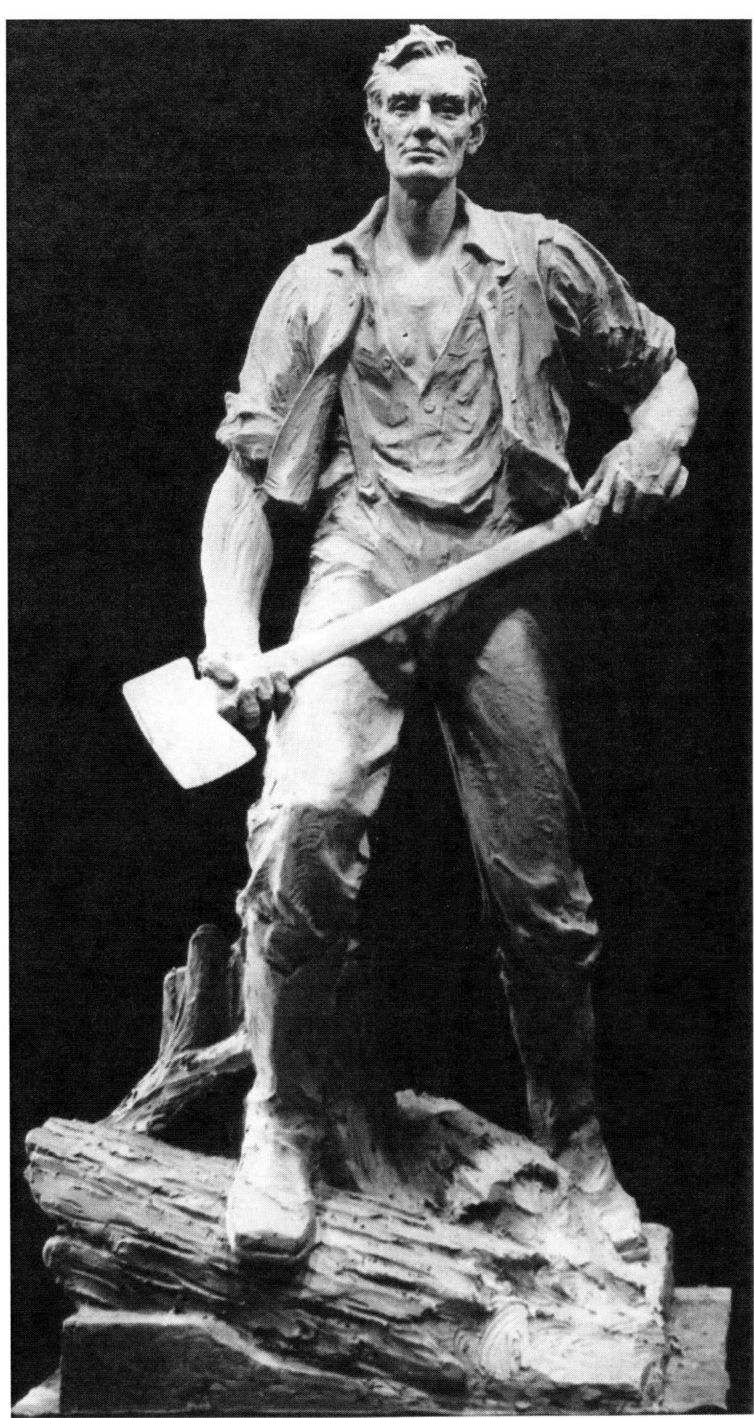

Fig. 76. Lincoln The Frontiersman, by Avard T. Fairbanks. Erected at Ewa, Hawaii

Alteration of balance with an anticipated return to an equilibrium that denotes action. A formal balance is static and it suggests security, but it may lack interest. An informal balance often expresses action and creates interest

There are many standing statues honoring Abraham Lincoln with a slight shift of a foot or a hand extended. The artists have incorporated a passive balance that is barely informal, but little action is anticipated. The illusion of meditation is suggested.

For contrast, a statue is illustrated here that is Avard Fairbanks' first Abraham Lincoln statue titled, *Lincoln The Frontiersman.* Informal balance is modeled with anticipation of him wielding an ax. This heroic bronze monument was placed at the Ewa School, Ewa, Hawaii. 1945.

RHYTHM

Rhythm involves an intermittent accentuation of repetitive elements. Rhythm is basic to cosmic forces that act upon the Earth. There are annual cycles with changes in seasons. There are lunar cycles with New Moon and Full Moon and the resultant fortnight tidal cycles. There is a day-night cycle with its rhythm. Fundamental to human life is the heart-beat. It is constant and fundamental on human appreciation to the impulses of rhythm. There are rhythms of breathing that are increased by activity. Walking and running have their rhythms with alternation of legs and rotations of shoulders and pelvis. We are creatures of rhythms and need to express the effects in our art and music. To create greater interest, modifications of rhythms are made. These are accomplished with changes in the repetition of elements as to their interdependent relationship, size, and position. These are illustrated, for brevity, with simple symbolism that is fundamental.

Additional factors modifying rhythms include:

1. A **progression** that has an increasing size of features, of height, volume, length, tone, or color. This gives a sense of positive action.
2. A **gradation** is the opposite. It demonstrates a decreasing size, height, volume, length, tone, or color. This is often noted when perspective is incorporated into the composition. Smaller features in scenes suggest greater distance. A gradation is present in the extremities of the human body. The arm to the forearm, to the hand, to the digits, and to the phalanges or segments of the fingers is a fine example of gradation. The thigh to leg to foot to the toes is another example.
3. An **alternation** of features has elements alternating from one side to another side of an axis, either apparent or implied. There is an alternation of the depth of finger webs of the hand. Thumb to index notch, 1, is deepest, followed by fourth to fifth, 4, then index to middle finger, 2, notch, and last is middle to fourth finger, 4, notch. Please see illustrations of the hand, Figs. 62, 69. Toe notches also have an alternation of 4, 1, 3, and 2. A combination of alternation with a progression or a gradation often increases interest in a design.
4. An **emphasis** of a dominant features of a series, with greater contrast or texture, is intended to render a stimulus to the senses and a concentration of attention. Greater detail should be modeled in face and hands. These are features of expression.

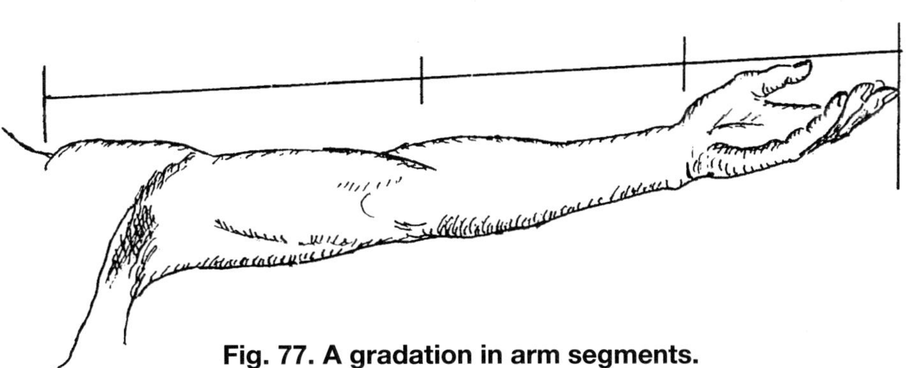

Fig. 77. A gradation in arm segments.

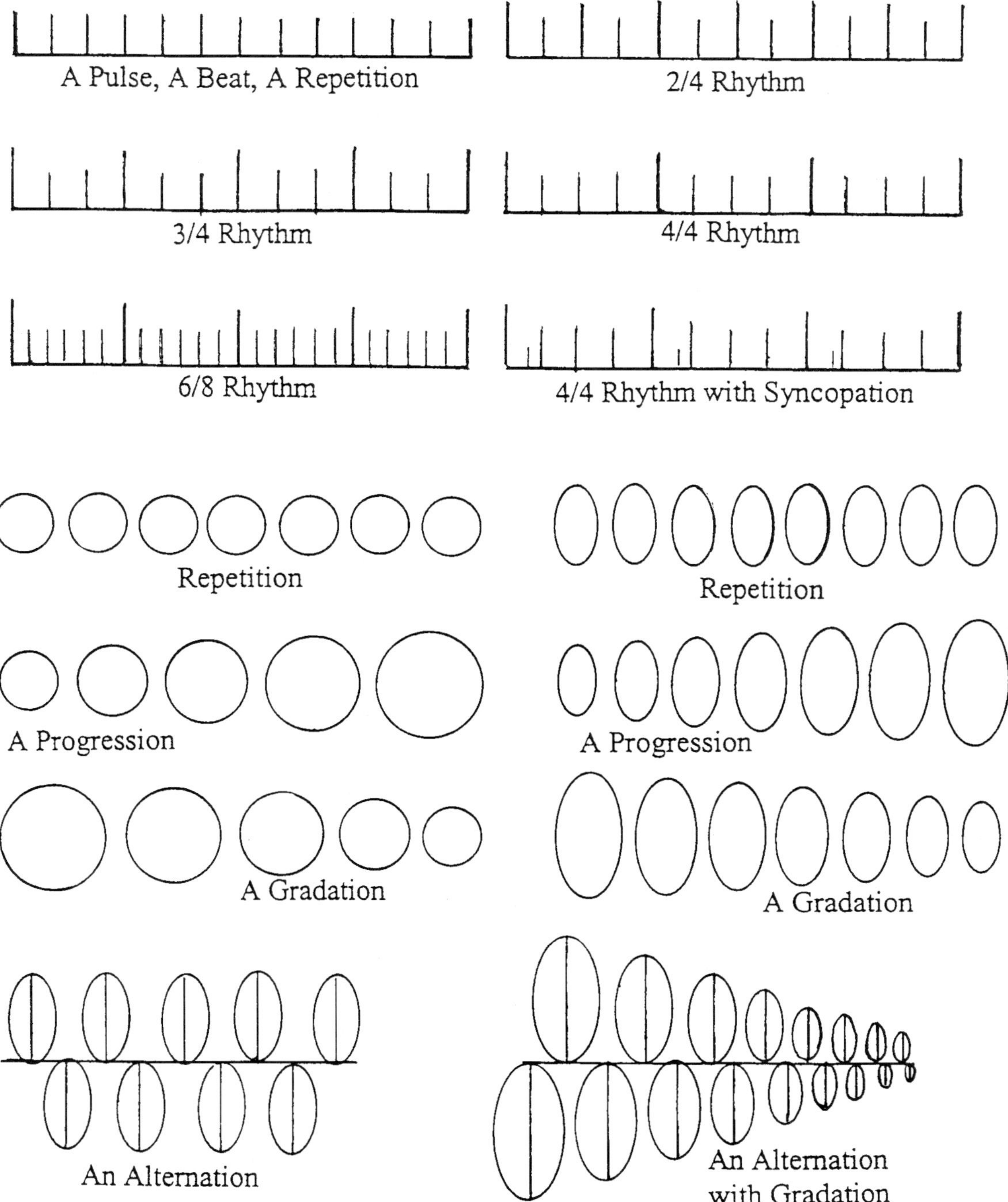

Fig. 78. Arrangements in design, repetition, rhythm, a progression, a gradation, and an alternation.

SIMPLE FORMS

Following a detailed study of human proportions, a review of elementary geometric forms might seem oversimplified. Various simple forms will be named, discussed, and illustrated to encourage familiarity and comprehension by students and amateurs. This is intended to help artists recognize these forms in human physique and to utilize this awareness when modeling or drawing. Appreciation of various forms and their modifications when creating artistic compositions can render more vigorous portrayal.

A line is essentially a single directional element that indicates a boundary or direction. Lines may be straight or curved. Form is indicated and bounded by lines, and constitutes an important component in design. It is the outward visible shape of an object. Other significant features that may involve lines are color, tone, and texture. Content and form are fundamental aspects for composition. Since art is a means of expression, form becomes the base or the substrate on which action can be applied for the content to convey a message. By studying simple forms and recognizing these various elements, that are present in nearly any scene, an analysis is facilitated. By learning the many configurations, a familiarity and a commanding knowledge allows the artist's awareness of forms to become natural and automatic. The composition can then be more readily synthesized with greater precision for rendering a vigorous expression.

Ars sine scientia nihil. This ancient statement reads, "Art without knowledge is nothing." A brief review of some aspects of form as it pertains to nature, the human body, and art is in order. The reader is urged to forgive some initial simplicity that is presented as a basis of more extensive discussion and analysis.

STRAIGHT LINES

Form involves a construction of lines and shapes. Lines are both straight and curved. A straight line is defined as the shortest distance between two points. It has only one dimension, the distance between the two points. Lines may be very short; they may be long as in buildings and road construction; or in astronomy where they can span millions of light-years. Yet straight lines are fundamental to our daily endeavors and culture.

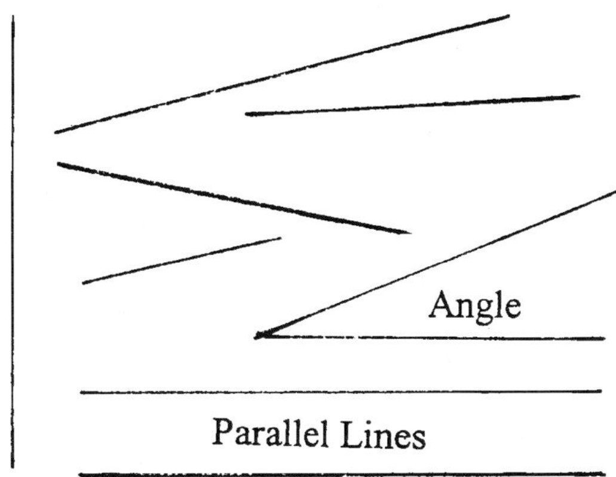

Fig. 79. Random straight lines.

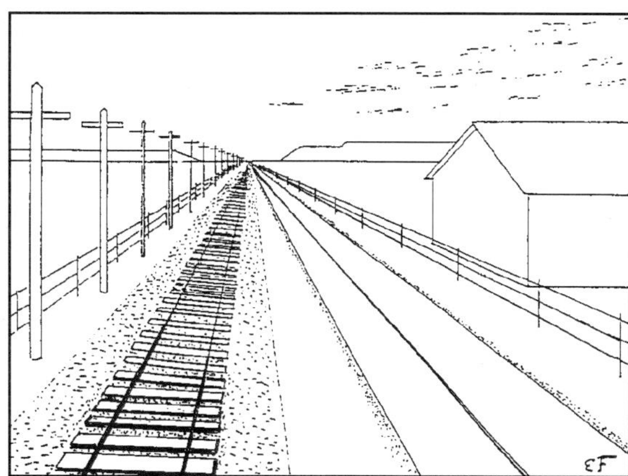
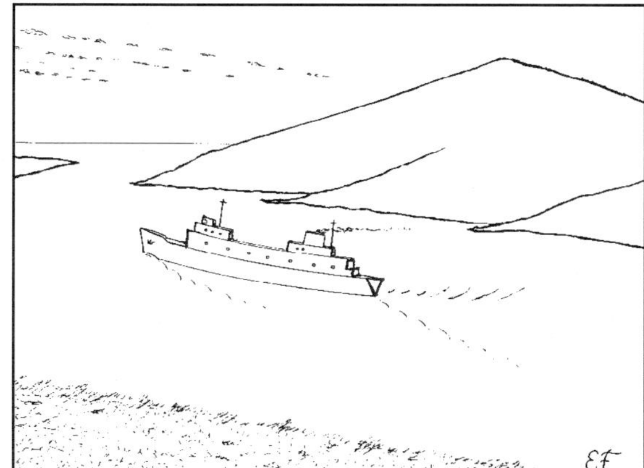

Fig. 80. Illustrated on the left is a western desert scene demonstrating one point perspective. A city scene with tall buildings and broad streets is also dominated by straight lines. The scene on the right demonstrates how obscure zigzag lines create interest in a composition.

Random straight lines command little interest or attention as noted in the illustration. An interesting composition can be designed using only straight lines. Lines in the same direction that do not intersect are parallel. When lines intersect, an angle is formed. This increases interest and awareness. There appears to be some purpose to the lines.

CURVED LINES

Curved lines have many categories and variations. Many are possible to describe or construct by mathematical formula, although some do not conform. A few deserve to be discussed here as portions of these curves are common in nature and many are significant to science and industry.

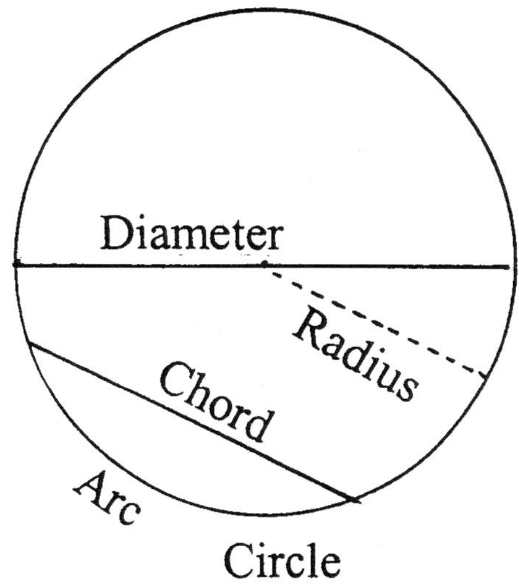

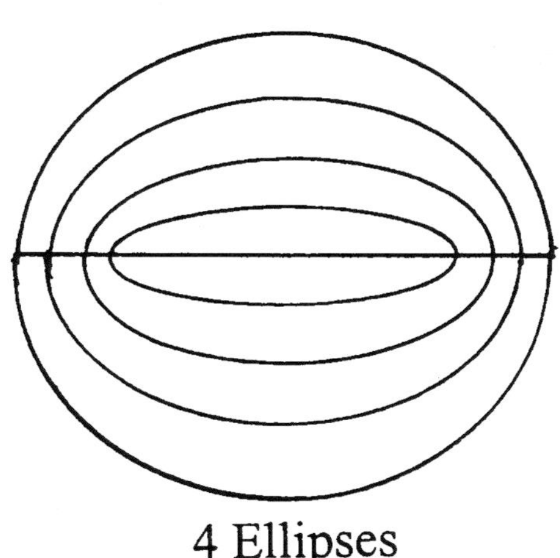

Fig. 81. Illustration of a circle and an ellipse.

A circle is formed by connecting all equidistant points from a single point. Like the equilateral triangle, square, pentagon, and hexagon, it is a fine figure, but is static. A segment of a circle is called an arc. A straight line connecting two points on a circle, an arc, an ellipse, or a curve is called a chord. An ellipse has 2 foci and the figure is the locus of all points on a plane such that the sum of the distances from the two foci is constant. It is less formal and more pleasing than a circle. There is an element of dynamics in an ellipse. The human face resembles an ellipse. Two other special curves are fundamental, the parabola and the hyperbola, and they also conform to mathematical formulas. Examples are common in nature.

A simple curve termed a "C" curve may be an arc of a circle of a segment of parabola, hyperbola, or of a spiral. Another beautiful curve is the reversal curve or "S" curve. Both are common in nature and lines of the human body. Their recognition, appreciation, and applications are fundamental to art. Combining a "C" and an "S" curve results in an "R" type of curve in which the "S" reverses the direction of the "C." These curves are often present in nature, although usually consciously ignored.

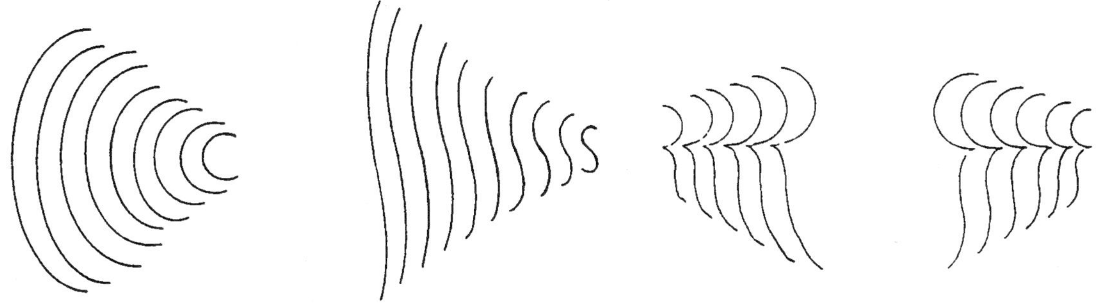

Fig. 82. Illustrations of "C," "S," and "R" curves.

The parabola, like the ellipse, is frequently seen in nature. It is one of the fundamental simple curves both in mathematics, science, and art. The standard mathematical formula is a curve equidistant from one point and a line. The simplest formula is $y = x^2$. There may be other modifiers in a formula resulting in broader curves or different direction of focus. This curve is observed when a cone is intersected by a plane parallel to the angle of the cone. A curve touching the tips of the digits of the hand resembles a parabola. Other parabolic curves cross the fingers at the interphalangeal or segmental joints. See pages 144-145.

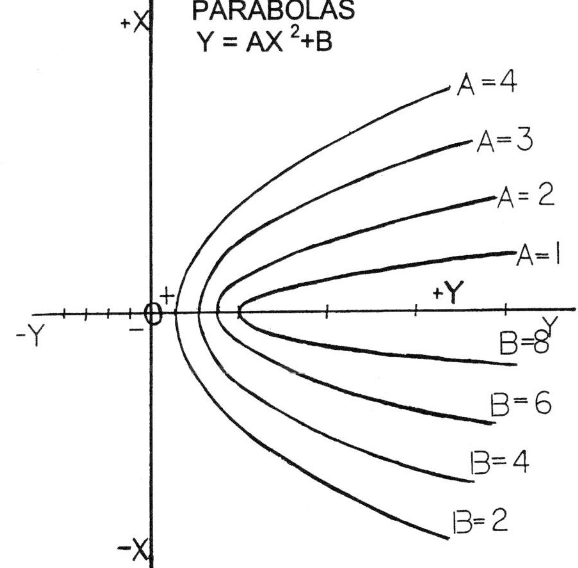

Fig. 83. Illustration of parabolas.

A hyperbola is plotted in paired curves on opposite sides of the ordinate (upright line) and abscissa (horizontal line) of a graph. The basic formula is x = m/y in which m is a constant and x varies with y. There may be other modifiers in a formula. This curve is observed when a cone is cut by a plane parallel to the axis of the cone. It is commonly observed when the border of a cone of light from a lamp with a shade strikes a vertical wall.

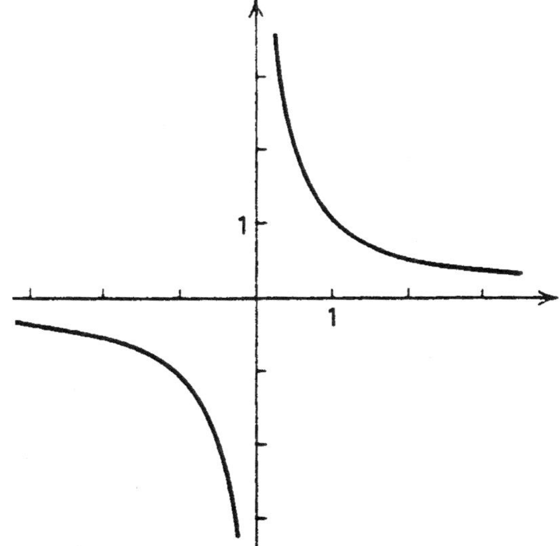

Fig. 84. Illustration of a hyperbola.

A cycloid is a curve generated by a point on a circle rolling on a straight line, either on the periphery or a point on a radius. This may be seen as the curve of a light on a rolling wheel, or it is perceived to follow or a mark on a bicycle wheel as it passes an observer. Walking also generates an unrecognized cycloid curve.

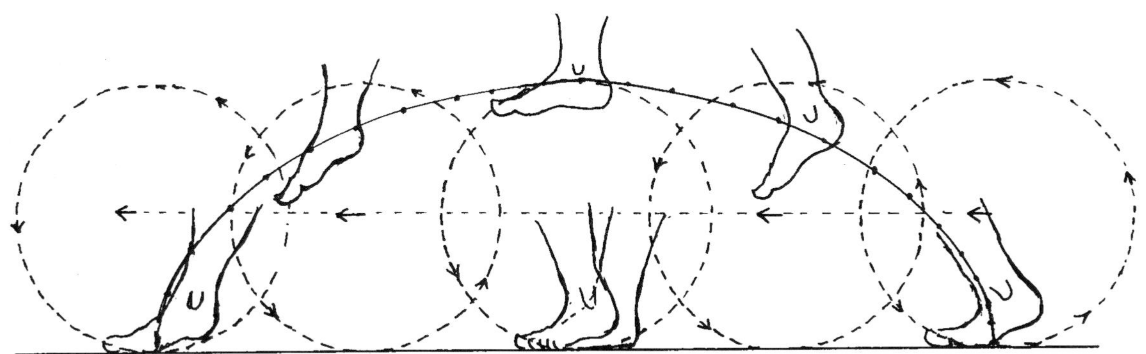

Fig. 85. Illustration of a cycloid.

An arithmetic or simple spiral progresses from a central point with a fixed increment of increase throughout each 360 degree rotation. A watch spring is a familiar example. A geometric spiral, by comparison, increases in logarithmic increments. The familiar example is a snail shell. This will be illustrated in a section on dynamic symmetry.

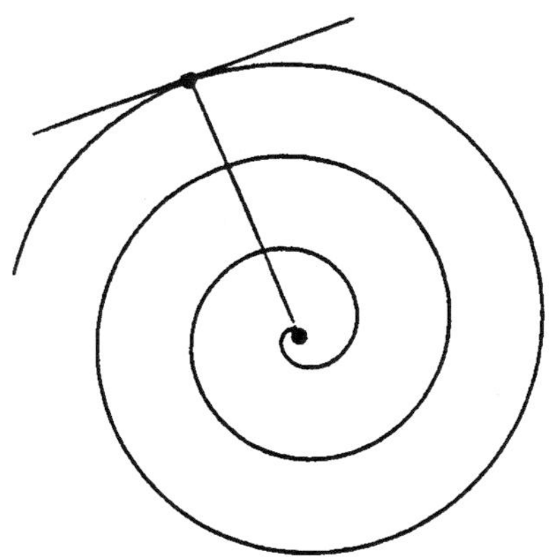

Fig. 86. Arithmetic spiral.

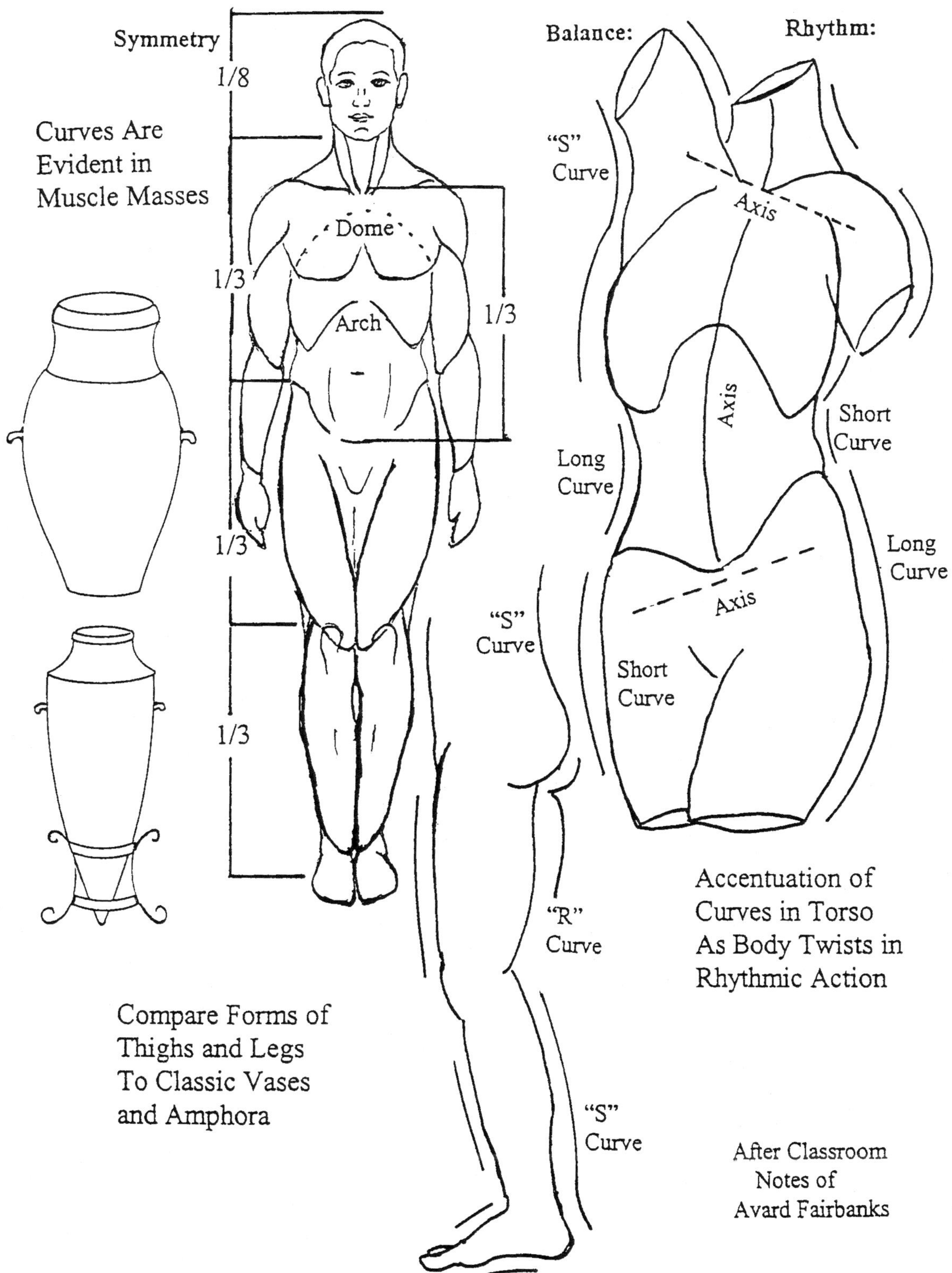

Fig. 87. Curved lines in human form.

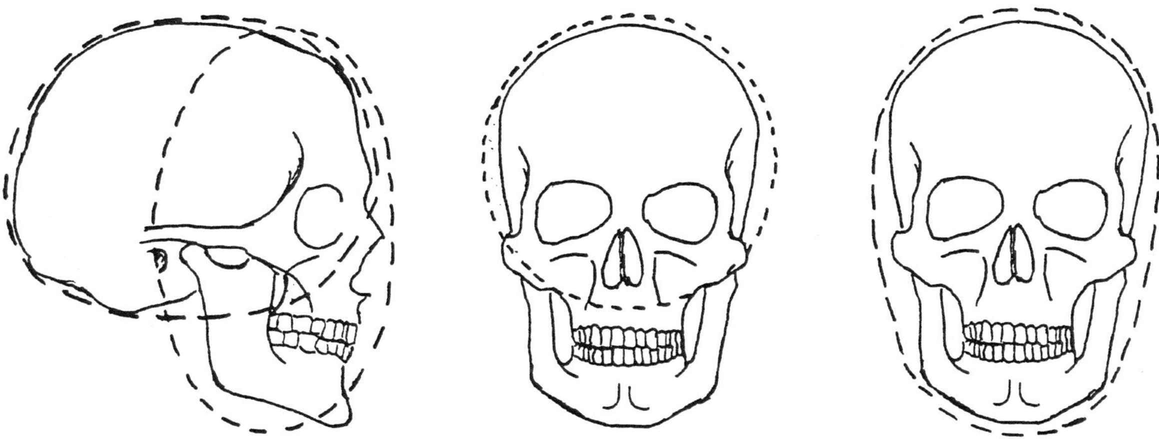

Fig. 88. The human skull resembles two intersecting ellipsoids.

Basic to form are lines, since forms are bounded by lines. Plane figures that are bounded by straight lines are called rectilinear figures. The plane figures bounded by curved lines are called curvilinear figures. Rectilinear geometric plane figures will be illustrated first .

Anatomists have recognized simple forms in the human body. Many names of human features recognize elemental form configurations. The deltoid, rhomboideus, trapezius, and scalenius muscles are prime examples named after geometric figures. The human head resembles a modified sphere. It is better compared to intersecting ellipsoids. Extremities resemble elemental solid geometric figures as cylindroids or long, narrow, truncated conoids. These will be noted in later paragraphs. The shape of clothing, with its folds and creases, assume combinations of geometric forms. Inclusion of the contours contributes to the action and expression of a masterpiece. Accessories to human endeavor in the form of tools of a trade or an intellectual pursuit render the correlating information to create a scene for the message expression. Most man-made articles conform to variations of simple form and deserve recognition. After analyzing a combination of forms or by attentive observation, they can then be incorporated into a drawing, a painting, or the modeling of a statue.

Skilled artists are constantly observing form, recognizing multiple config- urations, that generate interest. While graphic artists represent three dimensional forms on a two dimensional format, sculptors represent concepts with three dimensional figures. A review of form may seem redundant and over-simplified, but it should renew acquaintance with basic and fundamental configurations essential to art. The alert and enlightened mind can learn to recognize simple forms in nature and art, and by analyzing how these are incorporated into a design, then create a masterpiece that an observer may behold with an appreciation of beauty and rekindle an awareness about a scene or an event that is memorable. Many observers recognize a scene that is impressive but fail to appreciate details of the incorporated elements and combinations that elicit such a thrilling experience.

Simple forms of polygons will first be reviewed, followed by variations. Familiarity will facilitate recognition, and later, a mastery of knowledge about structure. It will promote the incorporation of various simple and fundamental forms into graphic or sculptural representation for an increased vigor and greater expression.

TRIANGLES

Regular angles are formed by two intersecting lines. Acute angles are less than 90°; right angles are 90°; and obtuse angles are greater than 90°, but less than 180°. A triangle is a plane figure bounded by three sides, and therefore has three angles. They are simple but pleasing two dimensional figures with a minimum of sides. Rectilinear triangles are constructed by three straight lines. They are rigid forms and consequently perform important components in structural design in bridges, trusses and cross bracing. There are several specialized forms. The equilateral triangle has all sides and all angles equal. Although it is formal, it nevertheless is appealing to the senses, a sense of stability. Its form can be adapted to attractive, decorative design. It was recognized by the Greeks who used it as the fourth symbol of their alphabet, the Delta.

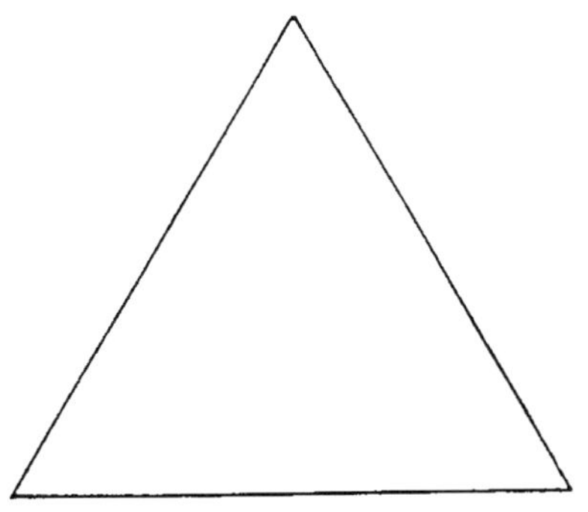

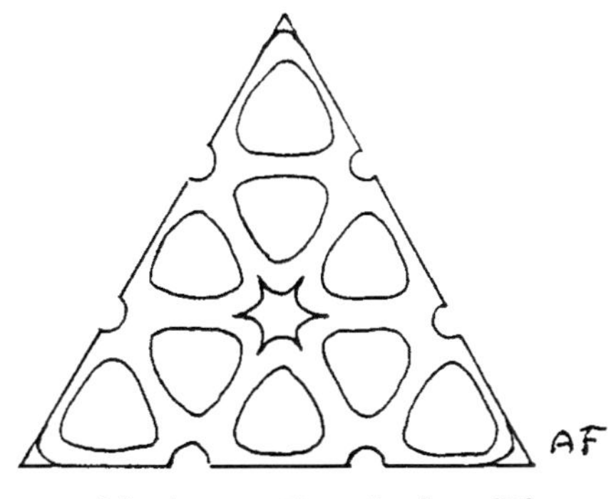

Fig. 89. Equilateral triangle (L); with decorative design (R).

Isosceles triangles have two equal sides, that may be variable in height, and the angles opposite the equal sides are equal. A right triangle has one right angle, while the other angles may vary. Two significant types include an isosceles right triangle with two 45° angles and the 30° – 60° right triangle, that is one-half of a bisected equilateral triangle.

A scalene triangle has no equal sides and consequently no equal angles. An acute triangle has three acute angles. An obtuse triangle has one obtuse angle.

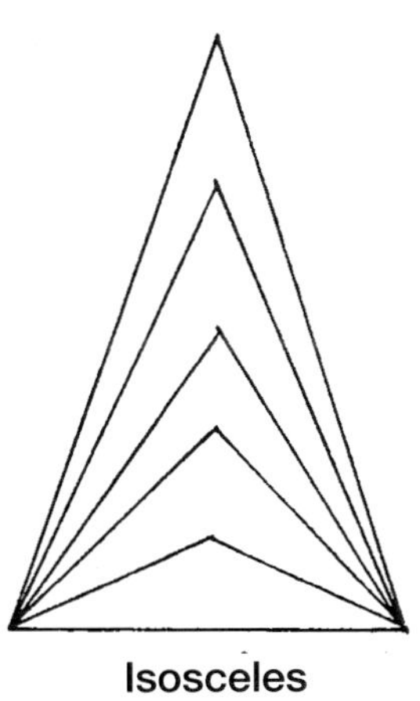

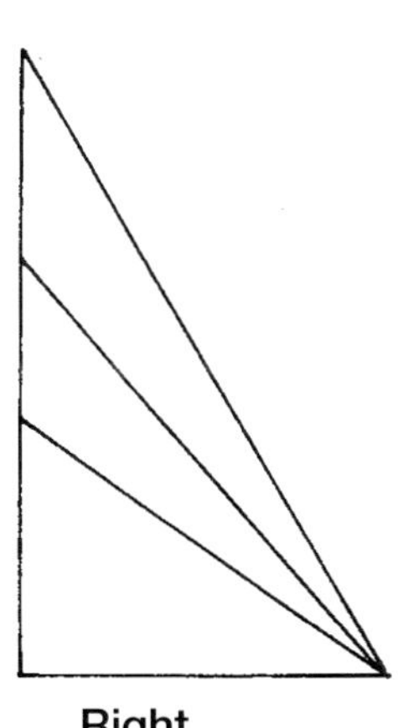

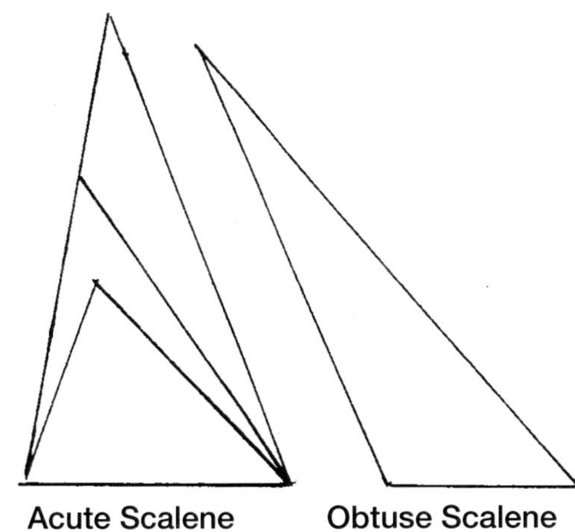

Fig. 90. A series of triangles.

When triangles are constructed with curved lines, they are called curvilinear triangles. These may add grace and beauty to form. These triangles can be drawn with convex or concave lines or combinations creating informality and interest.

Further variations can be observed when the lines are straight and curved. When triangles have mixed curved and straight sides they are termed mixtilinear. A few of the many varieties are illustrated. Triangles may also have reversal or "S" type of curves.

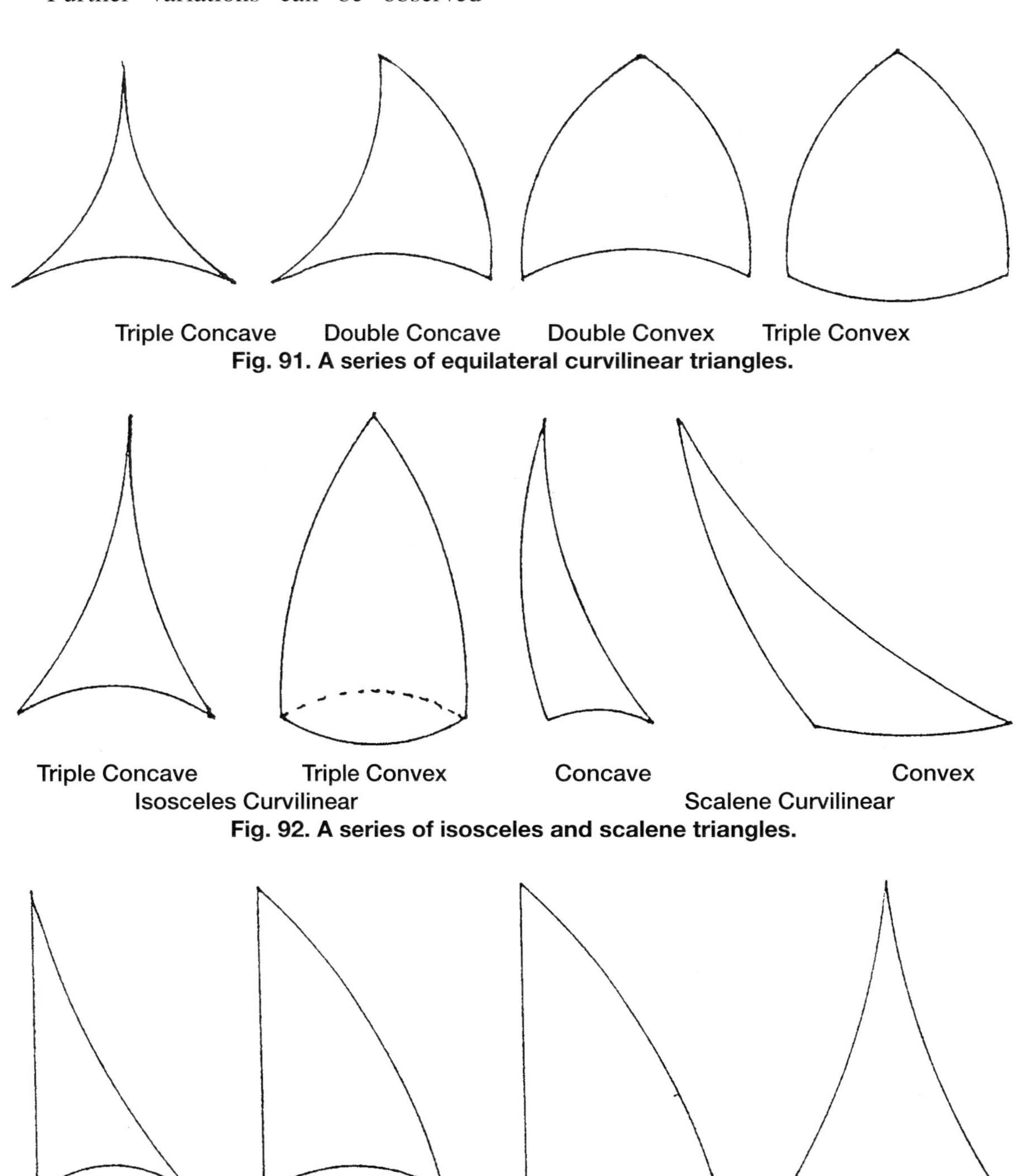

Fig. 91. A series of equilateral curvilinear triangles.

Fig. 92. A series of isosceles and scalene triangles.

Fig. 93. A series of mixtilinear triangles.

A study of various triangle forms is presented with rectilinear, curvilinear, and mixtilinear examples. Even more grace and rhythm are created when the curved lines have a reversal, such as an "S" curve for one or more sides. Three dimensional triangles are also interesting; since they outline portions of solid figures as spheres, ellipsoids, cones and cylinders. In the study of human anatomy, recognition and appreciation of these graceful forms adds considerable interest to a composition. They will be discussed later.

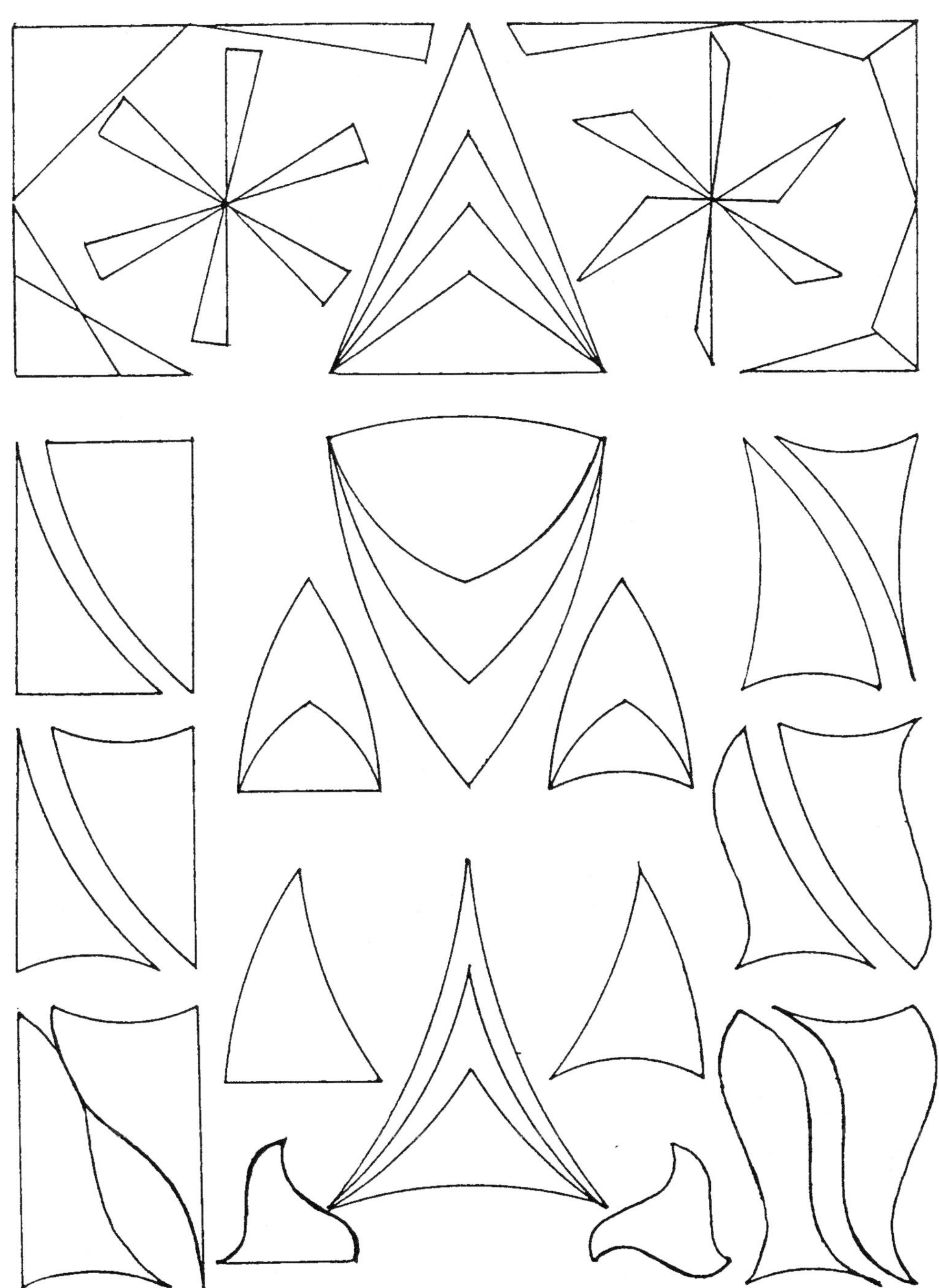

Fig. 94. A study of multiple forms of curvilinear and mixtilinear triangle configurations. Curved lines add grace. Reversal curves like "S" curves, add further interest and beauty.

QUADRANGLES

The square is the primary four sided figure with equal sides and equal angles, that are all right angles. We rely on this configuration for surface measurement, as square centimeters, square inches, and square feet, etc.. It is formal and static but fundamental and dependable.

Rectangles have four right angles and opposite sides that are equal and parallel. They are less formal and more pleasing to observe. The framing of most pictures are rectangles. Man-made structures as houses and buildings usually involve rectangles.

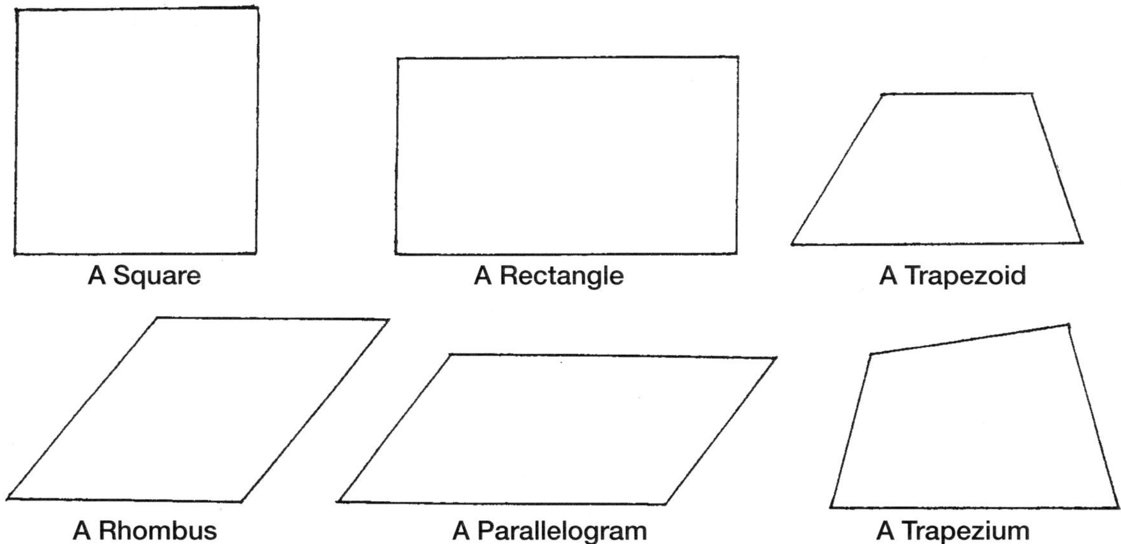

Fig. 95. A series of rectilinear quadrangle forms.

Parallelograms have opposite equal and parallel sides and opposite equal angles but no right angles. A special form, the rhombus, has equal sides with two acute and two obtuse angles. It is also called a diamond or a lozenge. A trapezoid has two parallel sides and two sides that are not parallel. A trapezium has no sides equal or parallel.

Squares and rectangles are not rigid figures. Before the use of plywood framing, houses had a diagonal shiplap sheath for framing that incorporated triangles into the construction, which act as cross bracing for greater stability.

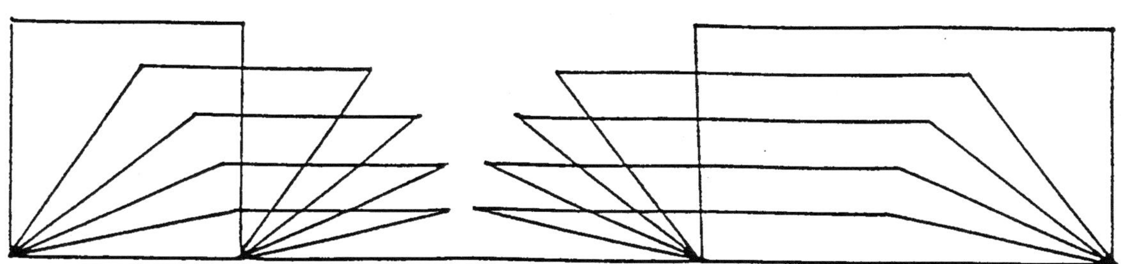

Fig. 96. Square, rectangle and parallelograms.

A deltoid is a quadrangular figure appearing to be two joined isosceles triangles. It is the familiar shape of a kite. A curvilinear form adds interest. When the opposite apices of the isosceles triangles point in the same direction, the shape of a harpoon or barbed arrow point is constructed, called a pheon and was popular in heraldry.

Quadrangular figures may also have curvilinear components, either convex or concave or combinations. Mixtilinear quadrangles have one or more straight sides and the other sides may have concave or convex lines.

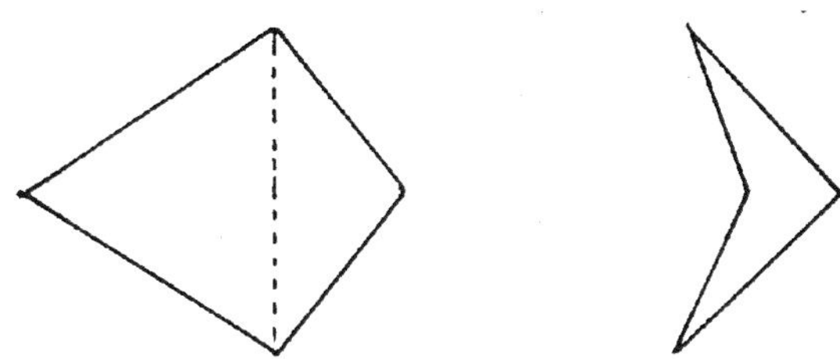

Fig. 96. A Deltoid (left); a Pheon (right).

Included is a study of multiple rectilinear quadrangle forms. Many of these familiar forms are often not consciously recognized as a discrete quadrangles.

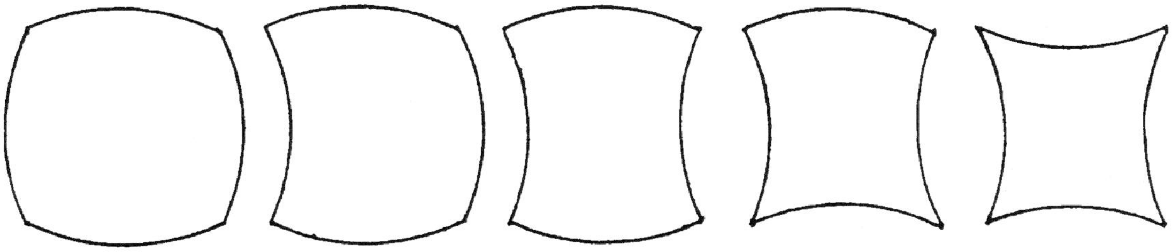

Convex and Concave and combinations of Equilateral Quadrangles

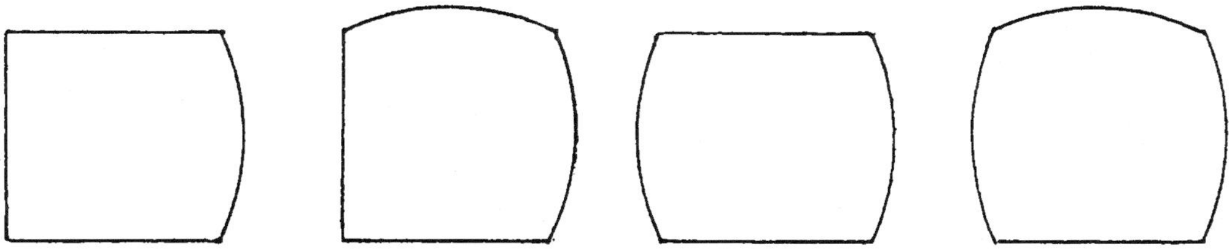

Mixtilinear Convex Equilateral Quadrangles

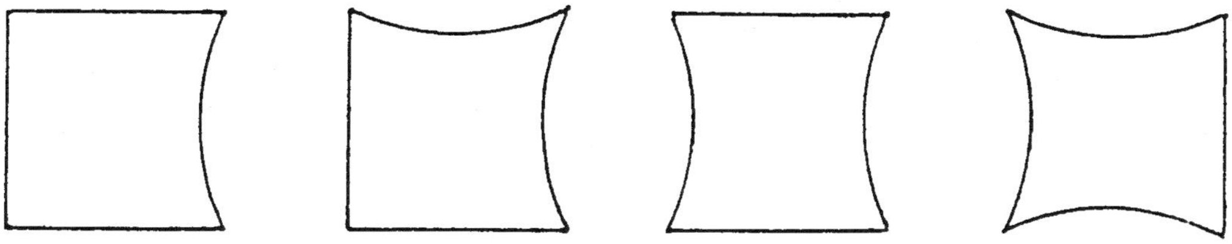

Mixtilinear Concave Equilateral Quadrangles

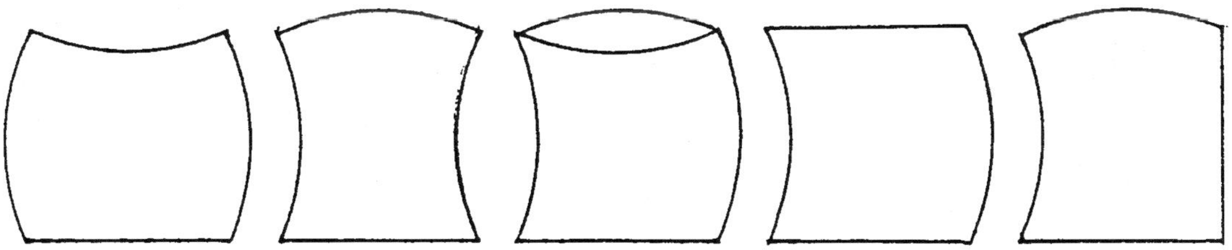

Fig. 98. Mixtilinear equilateral quadrangles with concave and convex sides.

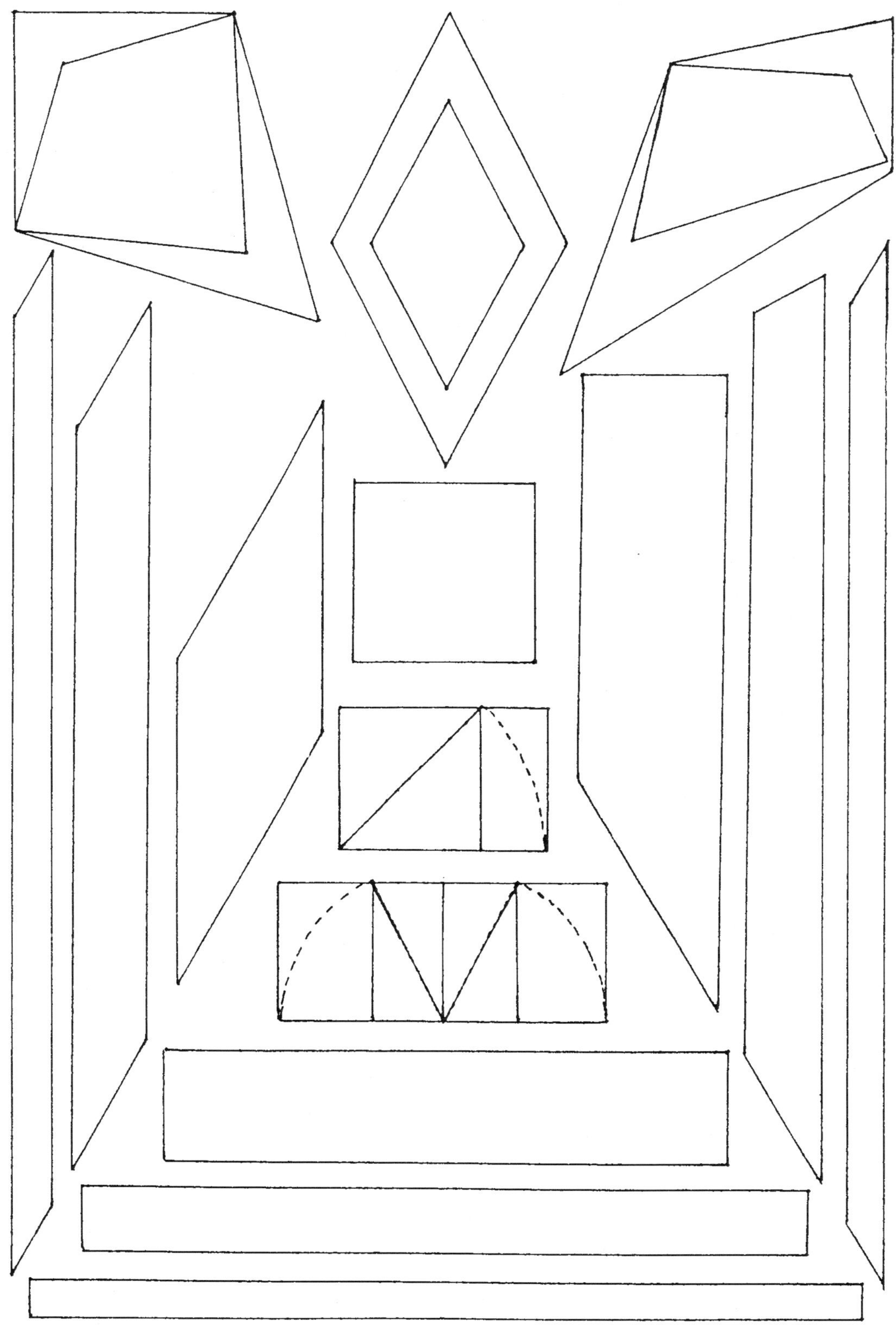

Fig. 99. A study of multiple rectilinear quadrangle forms. Many of these familiar forms are often not consciously recognized as a discrete quadrangles.

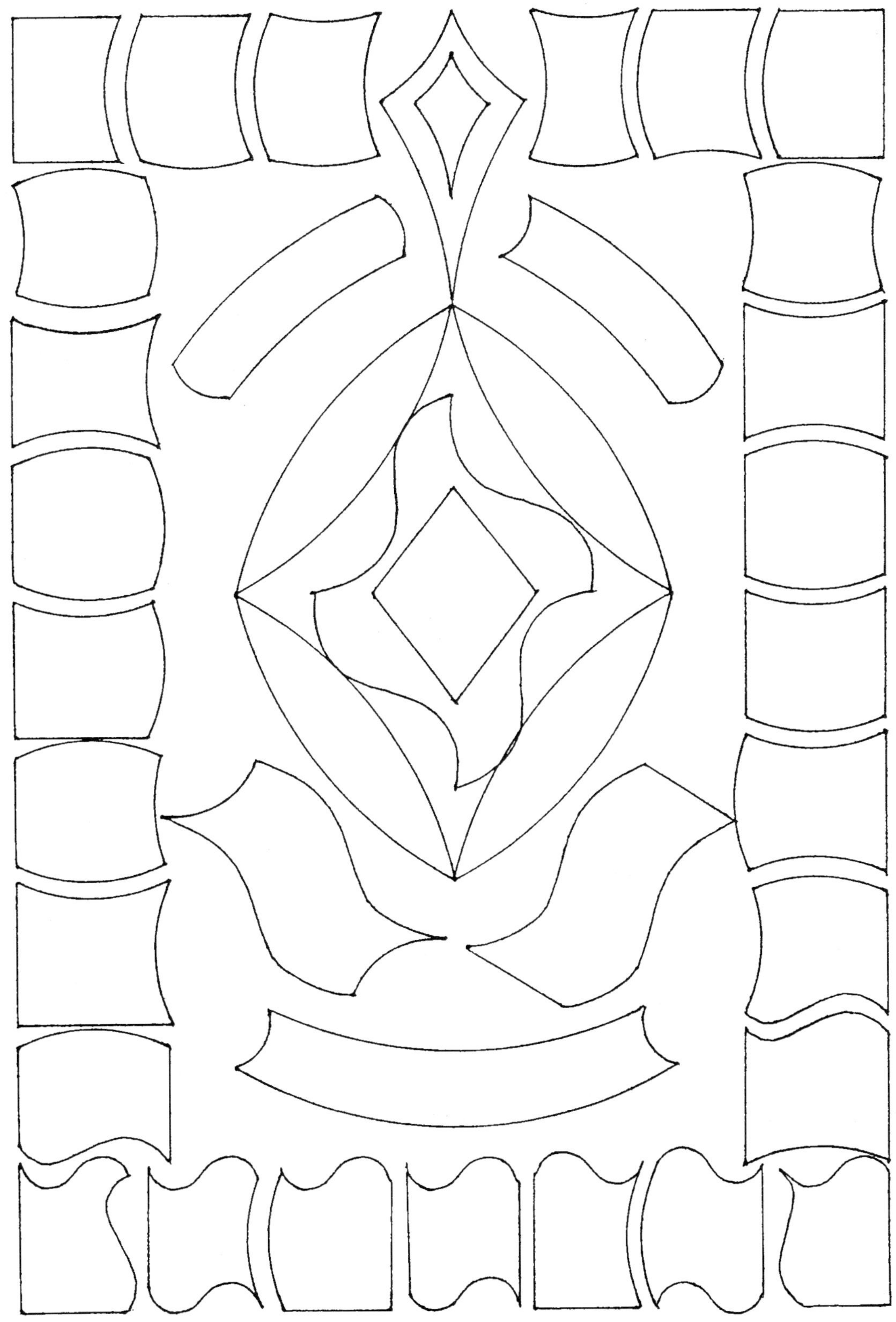

Fig. 100. A study of multiple forms of curvilinear and mixtilinear quadrangle configurations. Curved lines add grace. Reversal curves like "S" curves, add further interest and beauty.

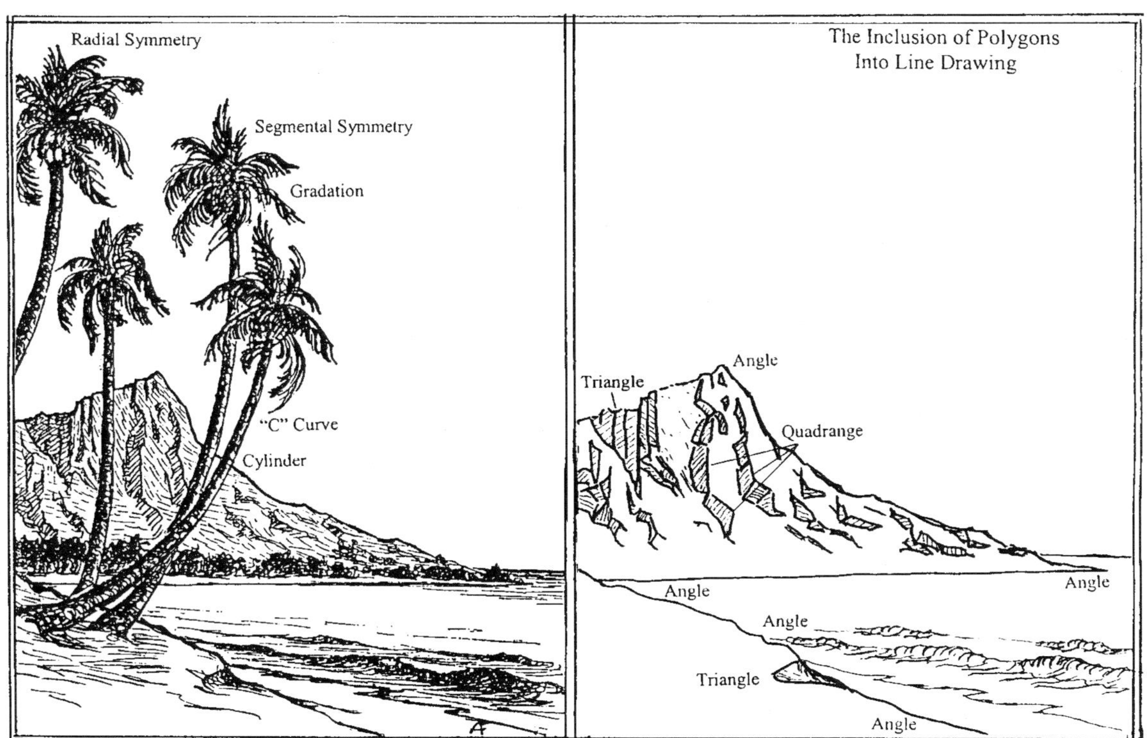

Fig. 101. Diamond Head on the Island of Oahu.

A pen and ink drawing of Diamond Head on the Island of Oahu in Hawaii is included, accompanied by an illustration with the diagram demonstrating how simple forms, angles, triangles and quadrangles are incorporated into the scene to accentuate rugged mountain features and enhance the composition. The cylindrical trunks of palm trees show "C" curves, while the cluster of fronds display an informal radial symmetry, viewed obliquely and modified by the Trade Winds. The fronds also demonstrate a repetition of leaflets with a gradation to the tips in graceful curves.

PENTAGON, FIVE SIDES

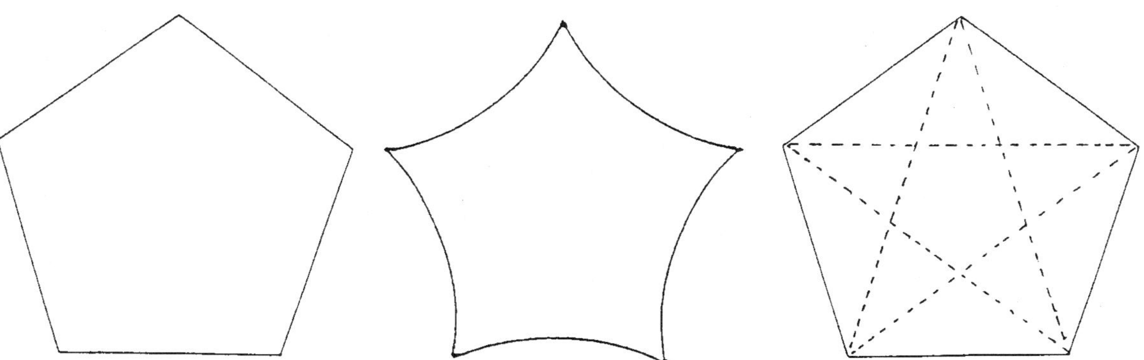

Fig. 102. A regular pentagon; a curvilinear pentagon; and a pentagon, pentagram.

The regular pentagon has five equal sides and equal angles and is also a pleasing, familiar figure. The number five corresponds to human architecture with four extremities and the head. The five pointed star, the pentagram, is the favored configuration, although it has ten sides. Five sided figures may have other configurations with unequal sides and angles. Curvilinear and mixtilinear pentagonal figures are present in nature and often used in design, but become less apparent when decorated or included in decoration.

Illustrated is a pentagon, a concave curvilinear pentagon and a pentagon with the construction of the familiar five pointed star, also called a pentagram. A study of a variety of pentagons is included on a following page

HEXAGON, SIX SIDES

The regular hexagon with six equal sides and angles, like the square, can fit in a continuous pattern. In nature it is seen in beehives, in basalt cliffs, ice crystals, and snowflakes. Informal six sided figures can also have grace and beauty. A chevron was popular in heraldry and persists in military rank emblems. Curvilinear and mixtilinear components may create interesting patterns. A special convex curvilinear configuration is the trefoil which resembles three leaves or petals, of a flower. A study of various hexagons is presented on later page.

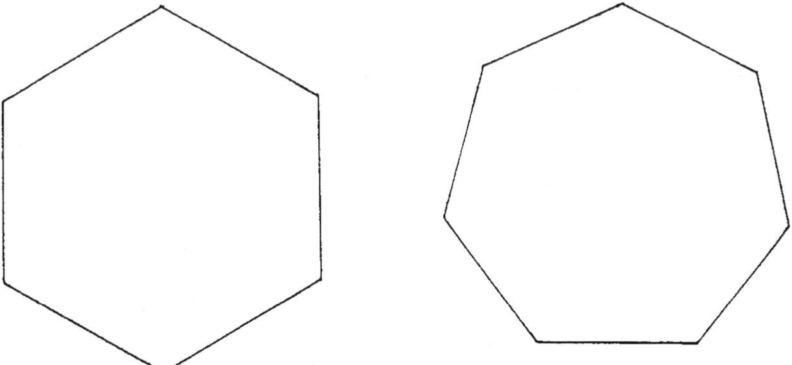

Fig. 103. A regular hexagon (left); a regular heptagon (right).

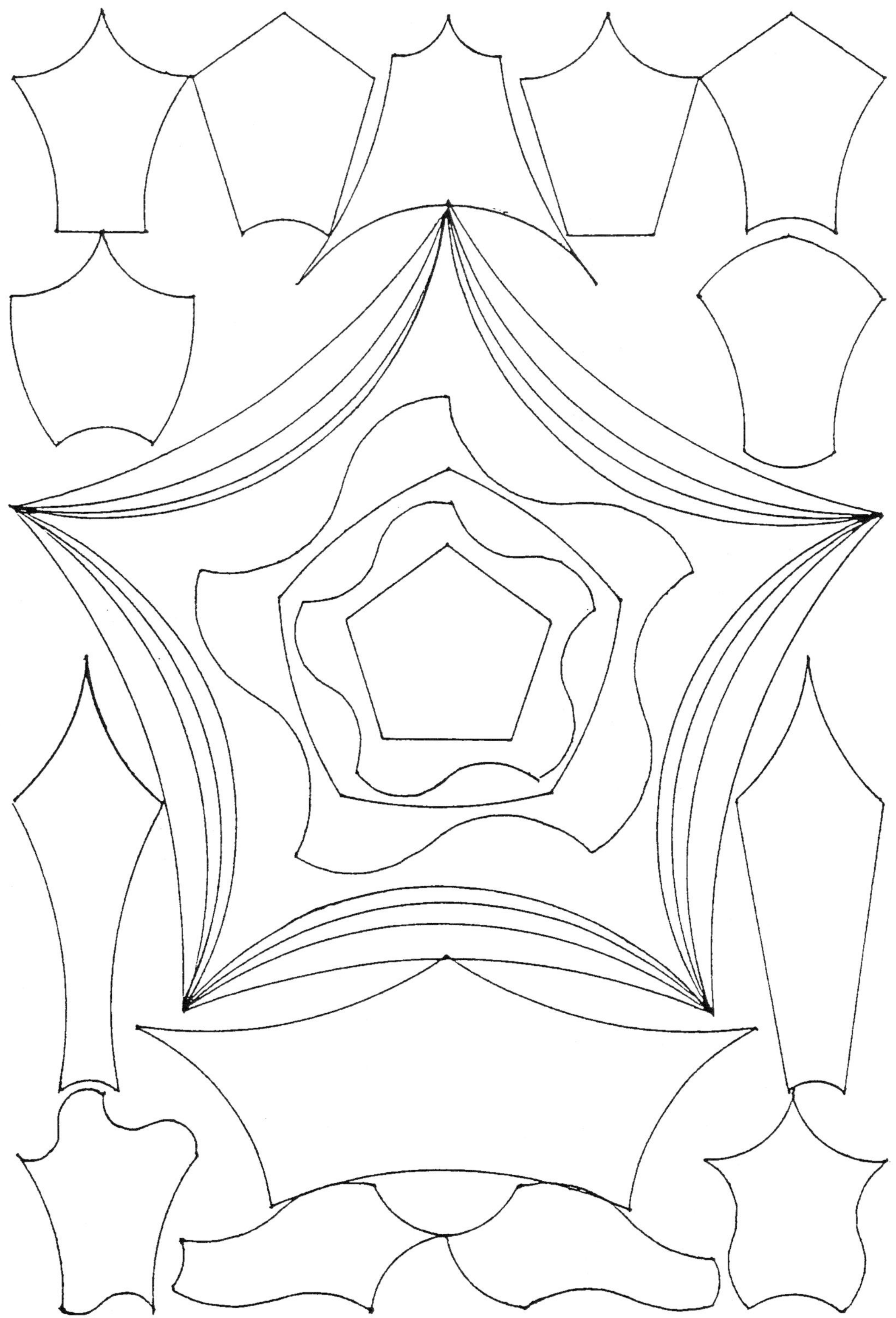

Fig. 104. A display of a variety of pentagons.

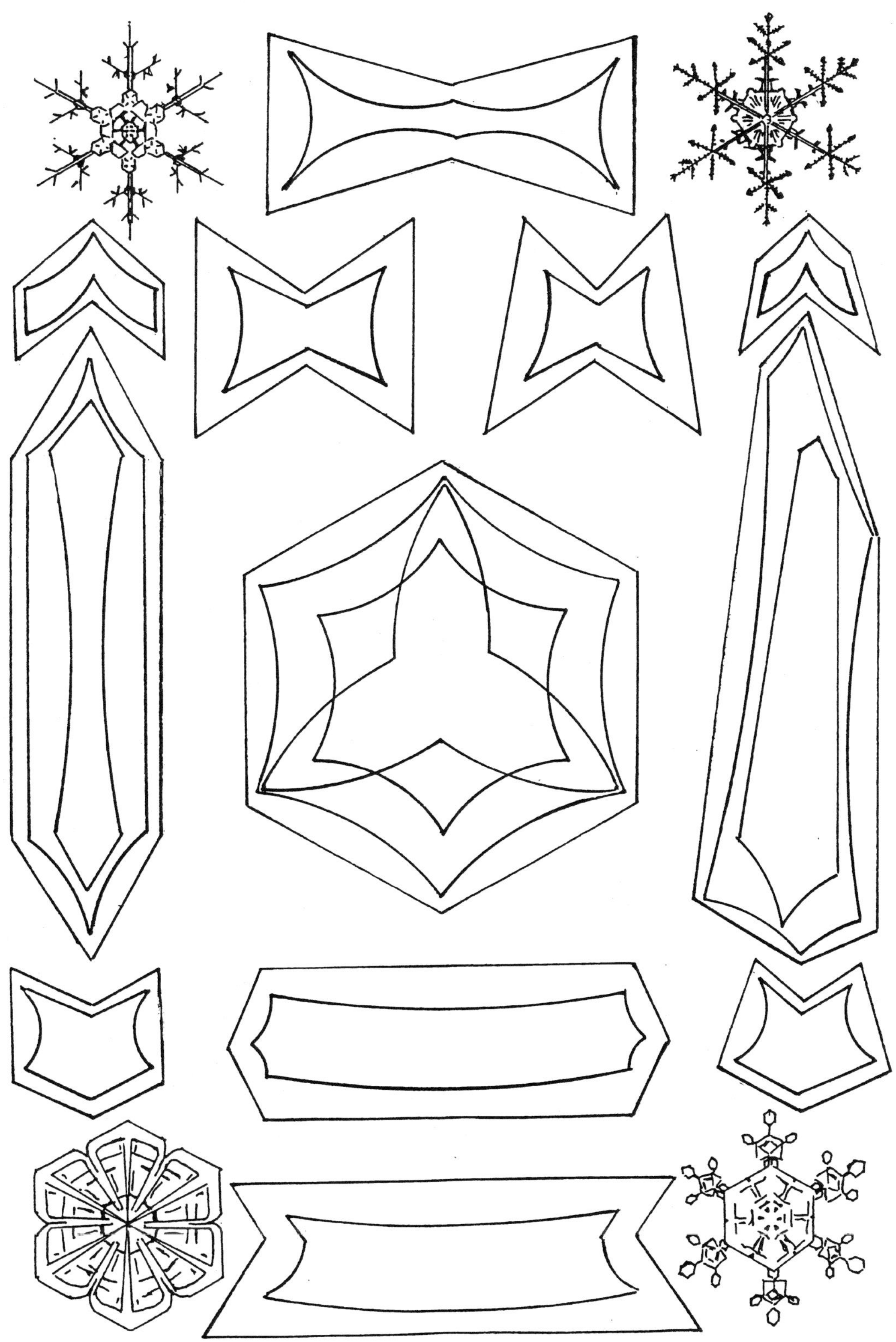

Fig. 105. A study of various rectilinear and curvilinear hexagons.

OCTAGON, EIGHT SIDES

A regular equilateral octagon is a familiar figure, probably best considered as a square with the corners cut off. This results in eight 135° angles. An octagon can be constructed with unequal lines and angles as well as with curved and mixed lines, adding grace and rhythm. Special forms include the four pointed star. A quatrefoil is a graceful curvilinear figure resembling four leaves or petals. A study of a series of octagon configurations is presented for added interest.

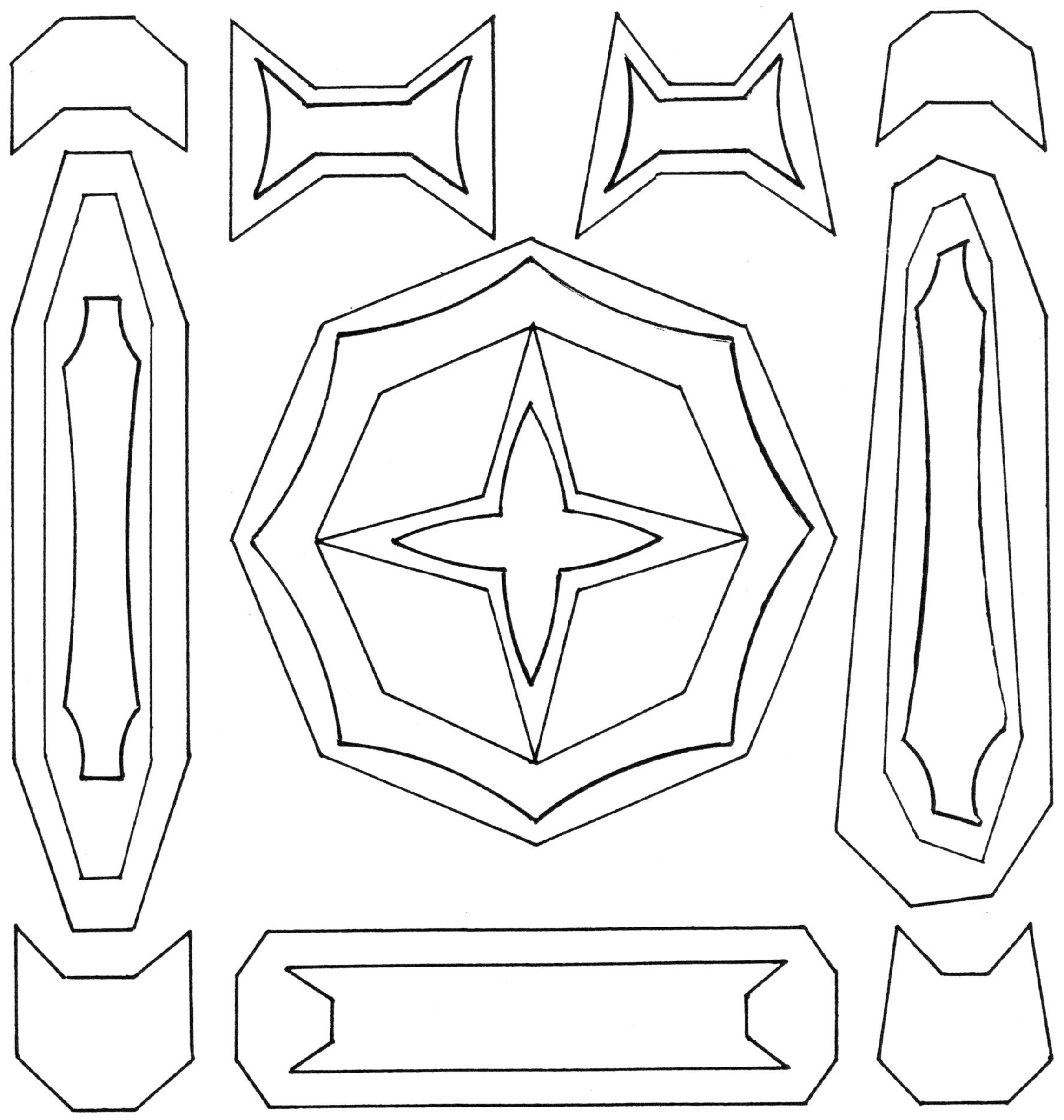

Fig. 106. A series of rectilinear and curvilinear octagons.

HEPTAGON, SEVEN AND NONAGON, NINE SIDES

Seven- and nine-sided figures are seldom seen in nature or decorative design. Heptagons are seven-sided figures, and are not easily constructed by geometric ratios. A circle is not easily divided into seven segments, as the angles would be 51.4°. A Nonagon, a nine-sided figure, is not readily distinguished from a ten sided figure. It is seldom referred to in geometry and is not common in nature. These will not be further illustrated.

DECAGON, TEN SIDES

The regular decagon with ten equal sides and angles begins to approximate a circle. A special form, the five pointed star, the pentagram, is a very familiar symbol, even more popular than a star with four points. There is a subconscious association with man. The four extremities and the head make five prominences. The cinquefoil, a curvilinear figure, suggestive of five leaves or petals, as in a wild rose blossom, is often used as a symbol. Curvilinear decagons with concave lines gives a pleasing fluted pattern. Eleven sided figures are rarely used.

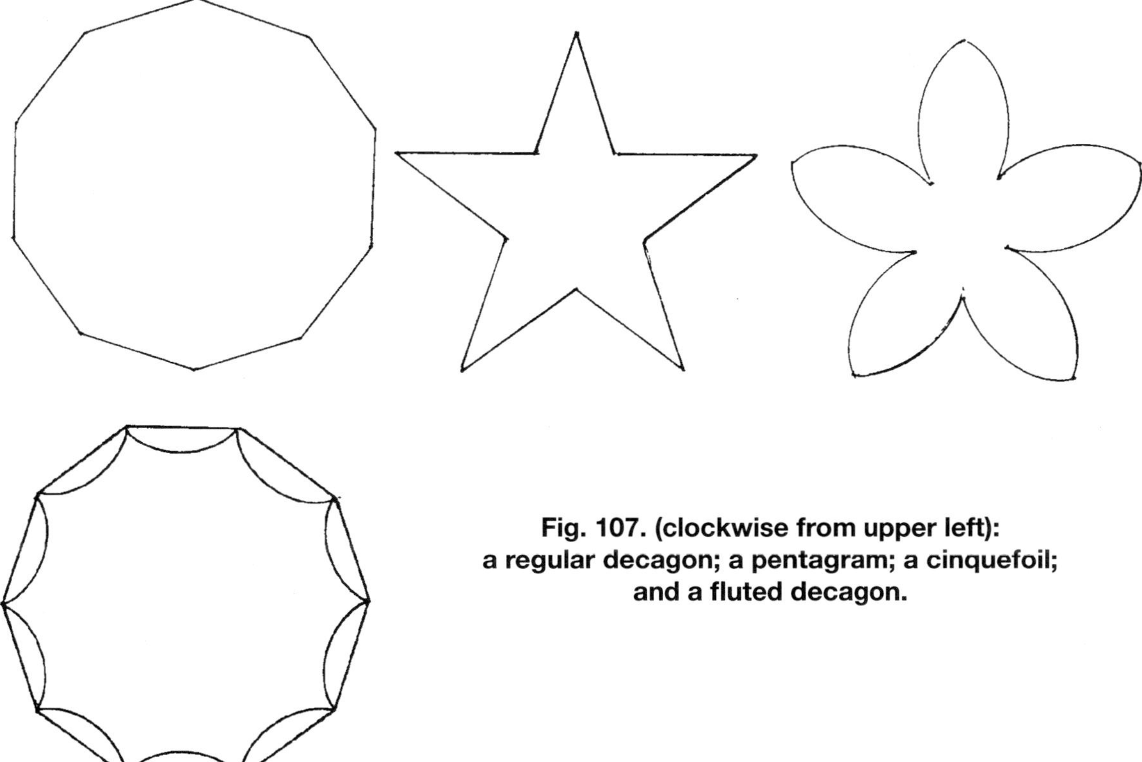

Fig. 107. (clockwise from upper left): a regular decagon; a pentagram; a cinquefoil; and a fluted decagon.

DODECAGON, TWELVE SIDES

The regular dodecagon with 12 equal sides approaches a circle even more than the decagon. One specialized form, the star of David, a symbol of Israel is formed by the super-imposition of two equilateral triangles. Concave curvilinear construction of dodecagons many create an interesting fluted figure. Curvilinear construction adds interest and beauty. Six petals are seen in the flowers of lilies, but A hexafoil with six petals did not become a popular symbol. An iris blossoms, with two sets of petals, three that curve up and three that curve down became a symbol, the *fleur de lis*, is prominently used in heraldry.

Interest may be lost with the increasingly greater number of components, especially when they are equal,. A sunflower is recognized as a disk with many petals. The mind easily comprehends small groups of numbers, but those greater than five appear too busy. Therefore components of 3 to 5 are preferred to the eights, tens, twelves, and sixteens. The mariners' compass is an excellent example where four points are dominant in a 16 point configuration. It is a functional tool and has beauty when components of the quadrants have varying prominences.

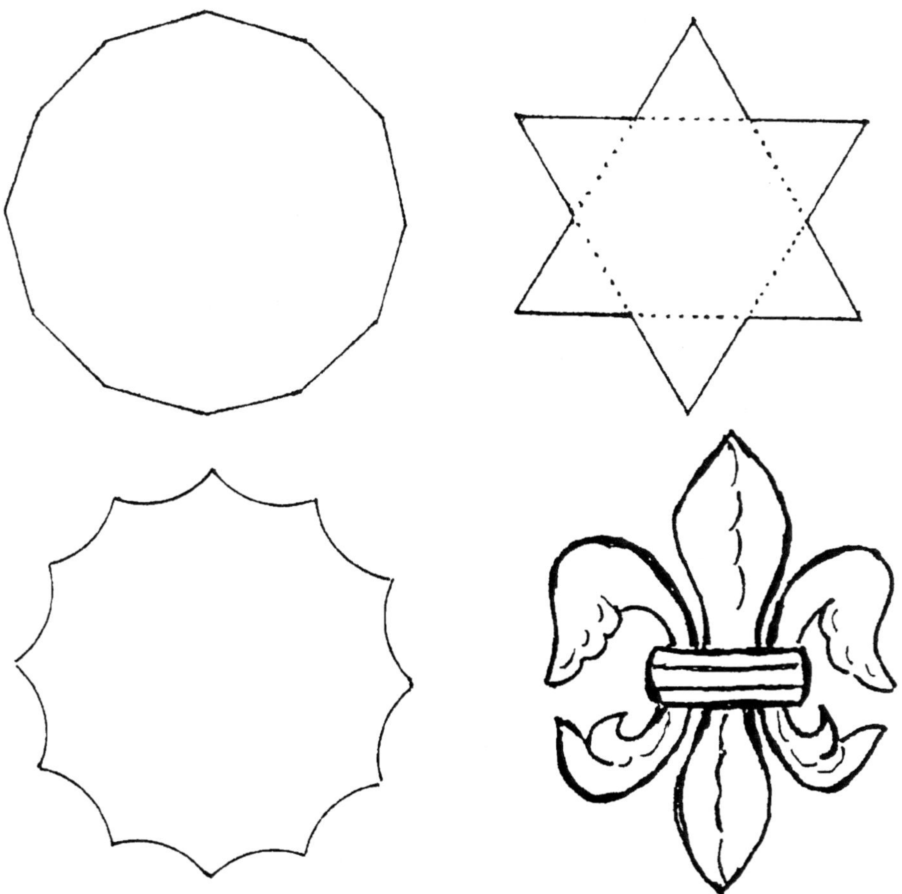

Fig. 108. (clockwise from upper left): a regular dodecadron; a Star of David; a fluted dodecagon; and a *Fleur De Lis.*

ARCHES AND THEIR SIGNIFICANCE IN THE HUMAN BODY

Arches are seriously studied in architecture and structural engineering, but they are very significant in art. An arch is a plane figure. The three dimensional longitudinal figure represented by an arch is called a vault. If an arch is rotated on its axis, a dome is formed. If it is inverted, it is a basin or a vessel. A series of arches is an arcade, while a series of columns is a colonnade. A cloister is a covered walkway, usually along a building, bordered by colonnade or arcade flanked by a plaza or an open space.

While arches are important for structural considerations, they are very significant in art and human anatomy. The neurocranium, although nearly a sphere, is a vault formed by an arch. The orbits of the skull. Sockets for the eyes have arches, and there are the supracilliary arches above and the infraorbital arches below the eyes. The palpebral fissure, the eye opening, bounded by the upper and lower lid has two intersecting arcs. There is a Zygomatic arch called the cheekbone. The palate of the oral cavity has an arch and is a vault. The rows of teeth form an arch and the lips conform to the horizontal dental arch.

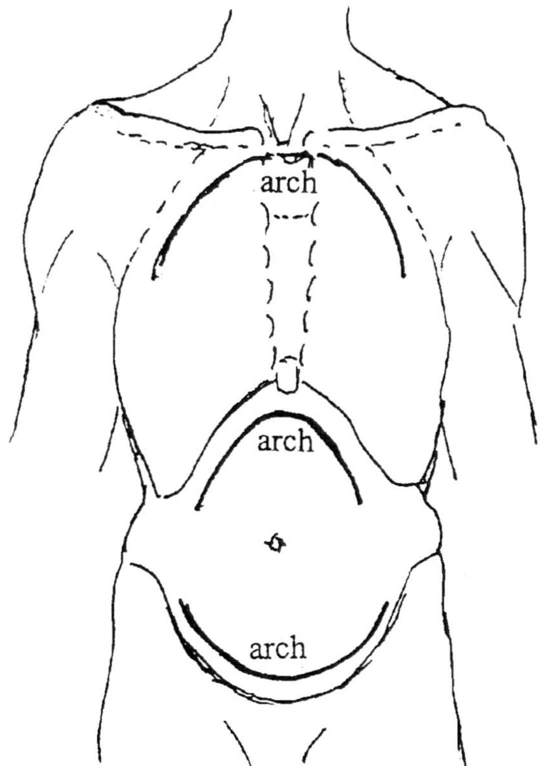

Fig. 109. Arches in the human torso.

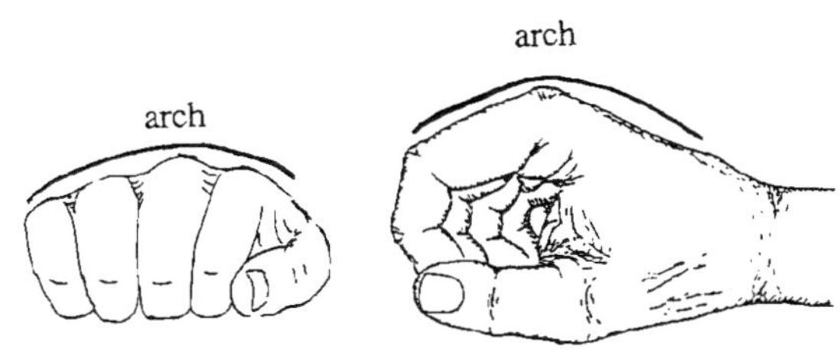

Fig. 110. Arches in the hand.

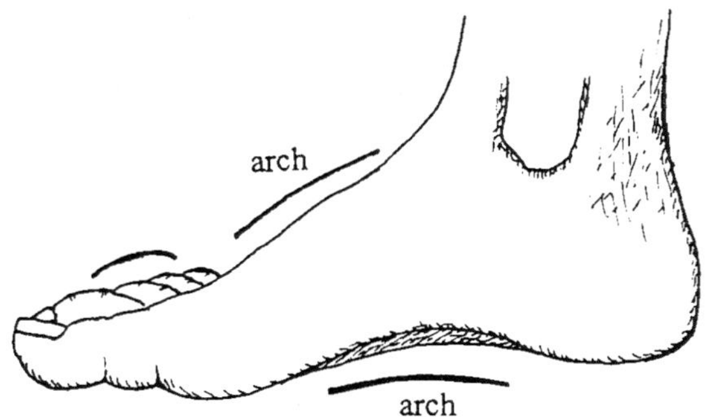

Fig. 111. Arches in the foot.

The thorax of the chest, composed of ribs, is dome shaped, outlined by an arch. The lower border of the thorax, the inferior costal margins, the rib borders, forms an arch with an apex at the xyphoid bone of the sternum. The anterior abdomen is bounded by this arch above and by an inverted arch of the pelvis, formed laterally by the anterior superior spines of the ilium and curving down medially to the symphysis pubis, or the joining of the two pubic bones at their anterior aspect.

There is a transverse arch on the dorsum, or back, of the hand. The palm of the hand has a longitudinal arch and a transverse arch. The palmar creases are curved lines resembling arcs.

The foot has a longitudinal arch and a less apparent transverse arch of the sole. There are arches in the popliteal fossa behind the knee bounded by the long tendons of the hamstring muscles. The buttocks are limited by a dense tendinous band forming the gluteal crease in the form of an inverted arch.

The artist, by studying lines, curves, plane figures, solid figures, and arches can more readily recognize these components of form and automatically incorporate them into design. It can facilitate more accurate portrayal, but may also increase accents and contrasts to emphasize the appearance of vitality, vigor, and action.

REPRESENTATIVE ARCHES

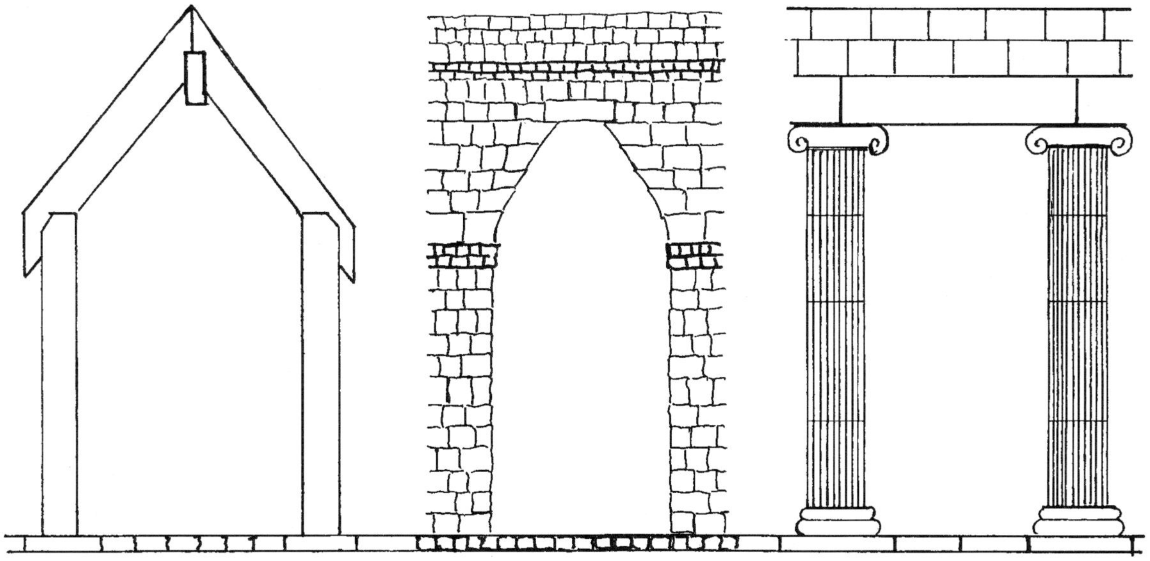

Fig. 112. Angled beams (L); a corbelled arch (center); and columns and lintel (R).

The spans over the space of doorways and windows are supported by beams that rest on posts. The width of a span over an opening depends on the tensile strength of the beam called a lintel.

When spanning a wider space, a primitive arch is formed by two posts and two intersecting beams at angles. The pitched roofs of houses are familiar examples. This configuration can span a greater distance using the same type of material. On a house this is called a gable.

Although ancient architects in Egypt, Greece, and Babylonia were familiar with the arch, they made great buildings with post or column and lintel construction. There the span between columns depended on the tensile strength of the stone lintels.

Corbelled masonry, with each layer of stones protruding farther than the stones underneath, was in common use in medieval castles of feudal lords. A window or parapet could extend out over a wall or a tower, making it easier for the defenders to drop cobblestones or boiling oil on their enemies or rioting masses of people below.

Corbelled arches and vaults are also common in Mayan architecture. Corbelled vaults are seen in many magnificent Mayan ruins. These arches could be high, but there was a limit in width, and the arch was usually capped with a short lintel. The Mayans also used post or square column and lintels for windows and doorways. These lintels were durable because they used a strong wood that was very decay resistant.

A post or column and lintel arch results in a rectangular opening. One of the most beautiful and impressive example is the Parthenon in Athens, Greece. Ancient Greek culture spread throughout the eastern Mediterranean nations, and many marble temples and other edifices were constructed in a similar manner.

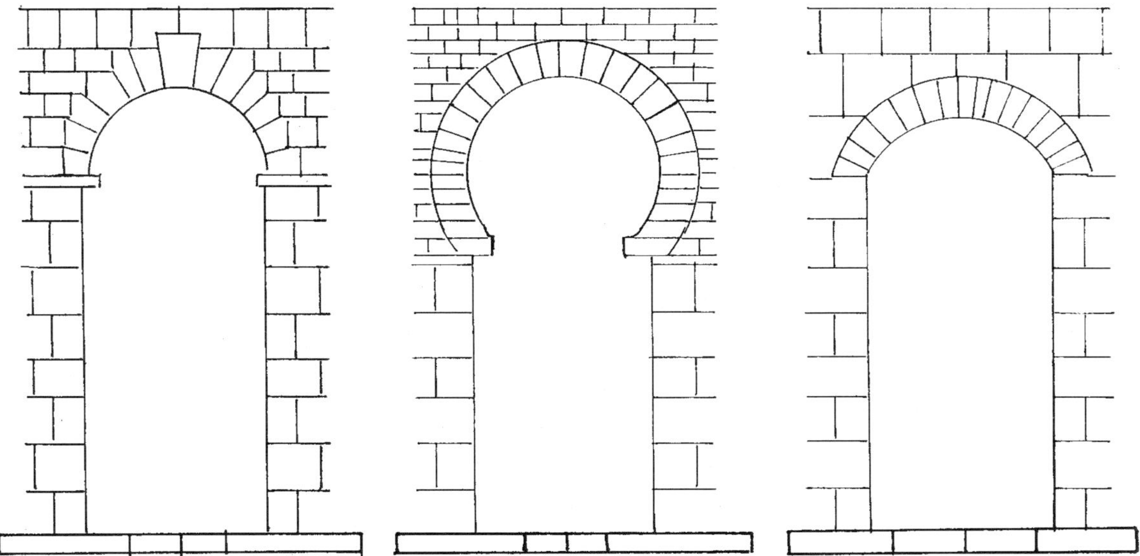

Fig. 113. A Roman arch (L); a horseshoe arch (center); and a segmental arch (R).

Curved arches include semicircles or arcs of a circle or an ellipse, or segments of other curves. Some arches involve two or more arcs of a circle. The Babylonian culture had developed an arch that was self supporting, and ancient cultures in Asia Minor developed vaulted underground aqueducts that brought water long distances. Many of these are still in use, supplying water to oases.

Large scale use of the semicircular arch awaited the Roman Empire. The semicircle is characteristic of the Roman arch. Their masons skillfully developed a semicircular arch with wedge shaped (actually trapezoid or trapezium shaped) stones, called vourrsoirs, and with a central keystone at the apex. Using this type of arch they could span a greater distance. It was a dominant architectural feature for many centuries, not only for buildings, but also for bridges and aqueducts.

Horseshoe arches are not common. They are designed having more than a semicircle with the diameter of the arch greater than the opening below. It is an infrequently seen style. A segmental arch is less than a semicircle. Modern materials with greater tensile strength, such as steel and reinforced concrete, allow a greater span, and these graceful arches are becoming more common.

GOTHIC ARCHES

During the Renaissance, artists and architects became interested in the golden section rectangle and the intersecting arcs. The pointed arch was a more graceful pattern. The equilateral arch is often called a Gothic arch, and it adds grace and beauty to a building. However, many churches built during that era still used semicircular arches.

When the intersecting arcs are narrow, the arch is called a lancet, and when the arcs are broad it is called a blunt arch. These arches are present in many churches, and are seen especially in the interior.

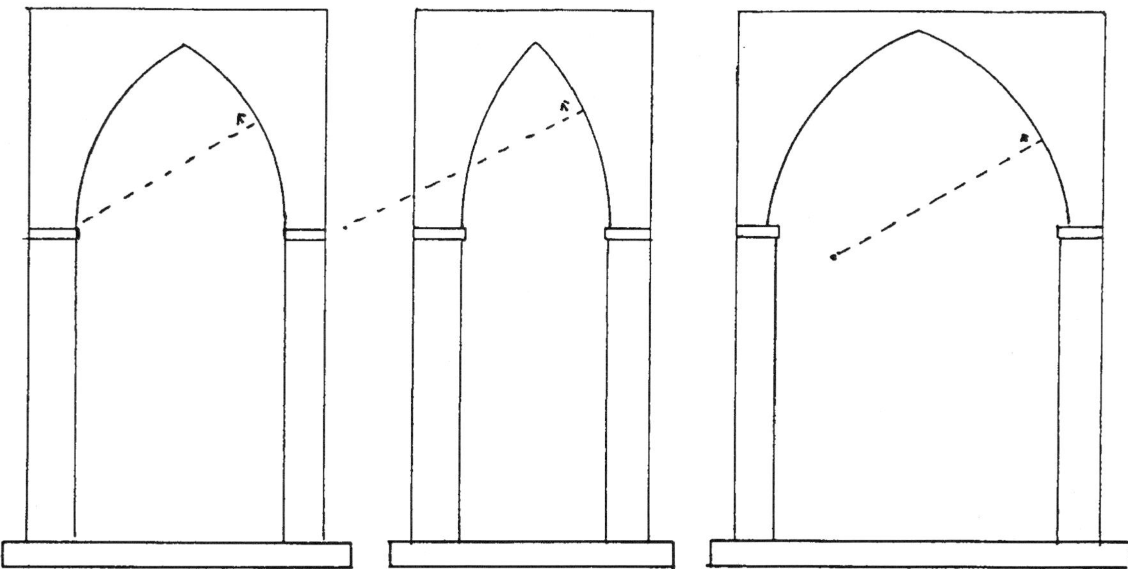

Fig. 114. Gothic Arches. An equilateral arch (L); a lancet arch (center); and a blunt arch (R).

Often lancet arches flanked an equilateral pointed arch. Modifications of these arches for embellishment included cusped arches and lacunate arches with circular voids. These decorative modifications were added to increase grace and beauty.

The Ogee or Saracenic arch is a combination of four arcs. It is often seen in Islamic architecture, expressing the cultural influence. The onion shaped domes of towers and buildings is another manifestation of that culture. Tudor arches are an adaptation of a blunt arch. Lateral portions are arcs and central portions represent slanting beams at a low angle to an apex. It became popular during the Elizabethan period. It may be seen in recent building that are described as College Gothic style. A catenarian arch is described as the arch formed by two curtains draped from a central point, sweeping down and retracted laterally by cords and then descending to a floor. It renders style and grace, but is rarely used in architecture.

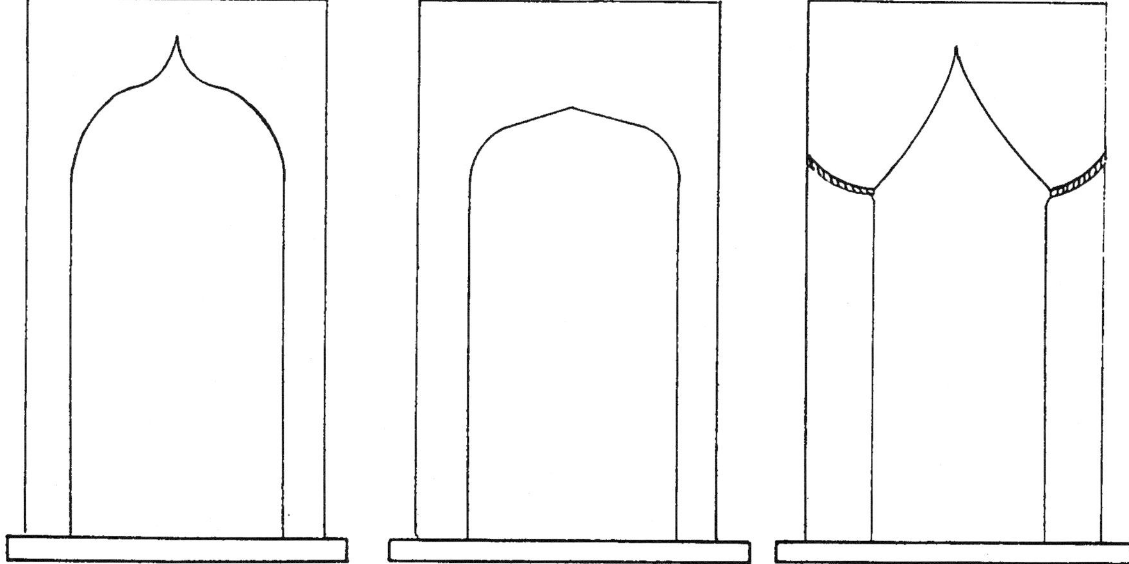

Fig. 115. A Sacracenic or Ogree arch (L); a Tudor arch (center); and a catenarian arch (R).

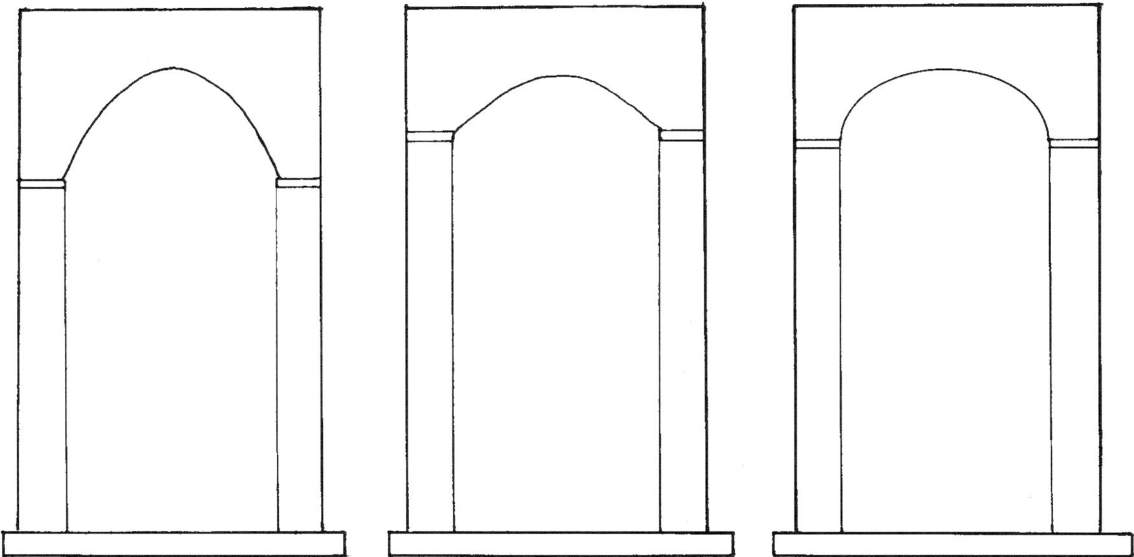

Fig. 116. A parabolic arch (L); a hyperbolic arch (center); and an ellipsoidal arch (R).

An ellipsoidal arch utilizes an arc of an ellipse rather than a circle. Since ellipses vary from nearly a circle to a narrow figure, this type of graceful arch is also variable. Occasionally other types of curves will be used such as a cycloidal curve, a parabolic curve, and a hyperbolic curve.

As transportation needs increased, rivers and gullies needed to be spanned. The truss was developed utilizing triangles that are rigid figures. After single truss structures, multiple truss structures were developed. Longer bridges spanned rivers, and multiple truss beams were used to support roofs of commercial and industrial buildings. When greater distances needed to be spanned, suspension bridges were devised. Again, an arch was involved. These have a graceful inverted arch, many of which are broad parabolas. Ancient suspension bridges were fabricated with braided ropes made of fibers, and some are still in use. Modern suspension bridges are formed by braided steel cables with vertical cables supporting a roadbed. The development and utilization of arches has been a great boon to mankind.

THREE DIMENSIONAL FORMS AND SOLID FIGURES

FORMS BOUNDED BY POLYGONS

The Graphic arts attempt to portray subjects and objects with the illusion of three dimensions on the plane surface of paper, canvas, or walls. Sculpture is a three-dimensional representation of subjects and objects to convey a message and a feeling. In order to better to prepare themselves to create plastic design, three dimensional rather than graphic design, students must appreciate and comprehend fundamental forms, such solids as polyhedrons with flat surfaces and other solids with curved surfaces.

SOLIDS

There are five regular polyhedrons called the platonic solids. The minimum is a four-sided figure called a tetrahedron composed of four equilateral triangles. A cube has six sides, which are squares. An octahedron has eight equilateral triangles like two pyramids joined at their bases. This configuration is found in crystals, notably the diamond when found in the natural state. A dodecahedron has 12 sides which are regular pentagons. Some crystals are found with this configuration. The icosahedron is composed of 20 equilateral triangles.

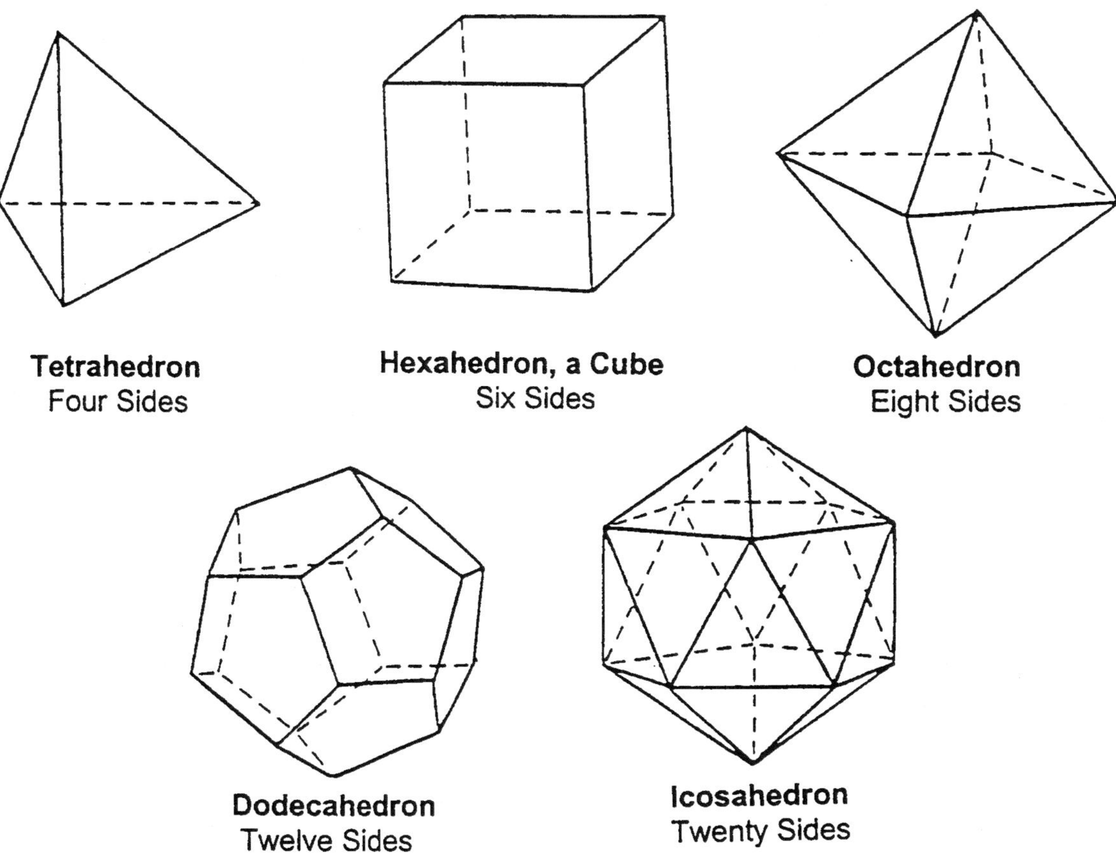

Fig. 117. The five regular polyhedrons, the Platonic solids.

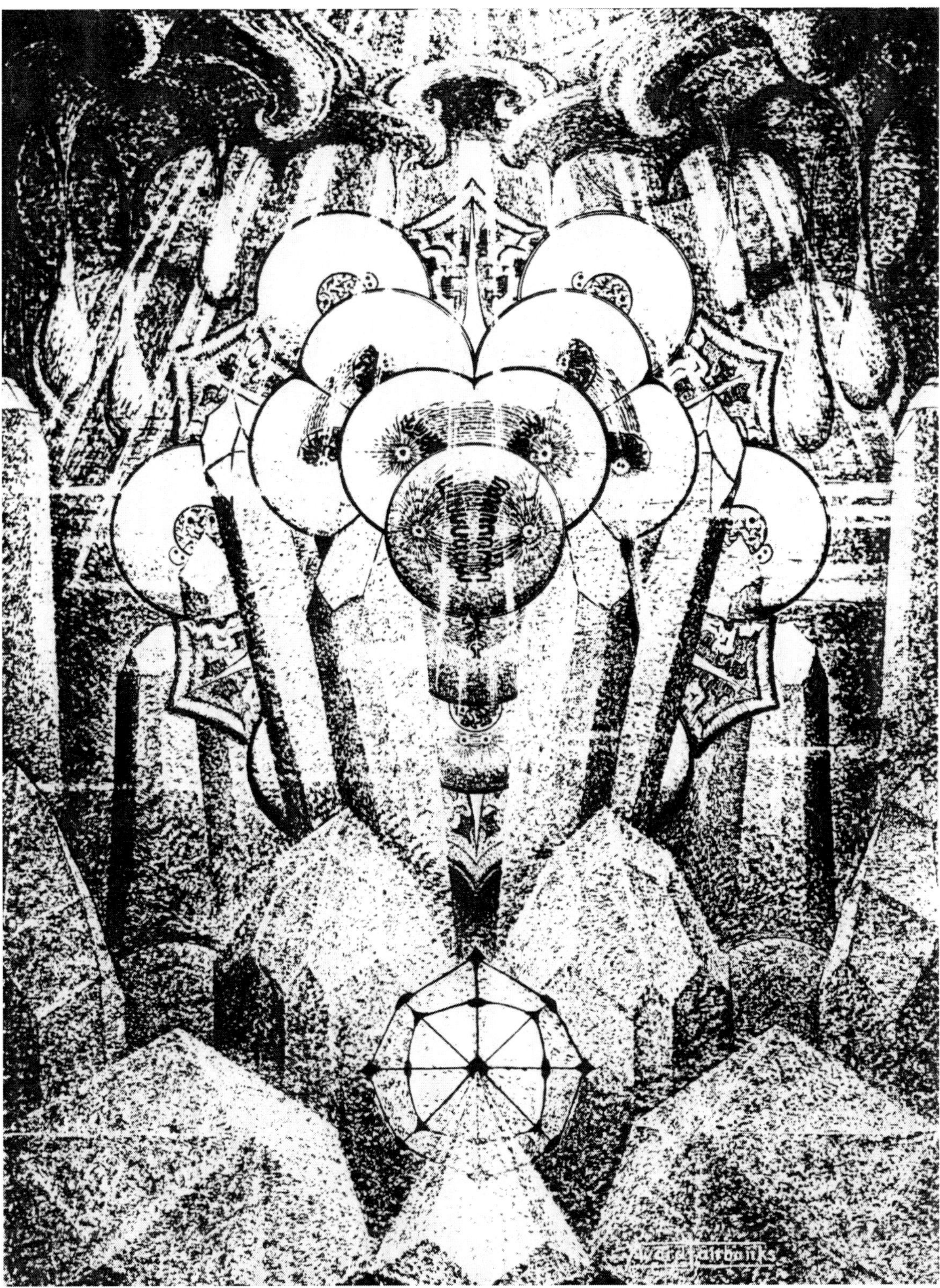

Fig. 118. A design in abstract about organic and inorganic forms demonstrating their struggle involving natural forces. Near the base is radio-activity. Crystals symbolizing minerals are thrust apart by dividing cells, the organic. Water crystal as a snowflake and stratified water are represented. Rain drops and storm clouds, are interspersed by radiance of the sun. **See pages 189 and 205 for explanation of symmetry.**

Other interesting figures are pyramids. The tetrahedron is a three-sided pyramid. The base of a pyramid is a polygon that may have four, five, six or more sides, but four is most common. The slanting surfaces in right pyramids are isosceles triangles. Irregular or oblique pyramids may have some variations, and sides may be constructed by triangles with unequal sides. By cutting off the top, a truncated pyramid is formed, and the remaining portion next to the base is called a frustum. An obelisk is a tall, slender, four-sided pillar, gradually tapering as it rises, having a top in the form of a pyramid.

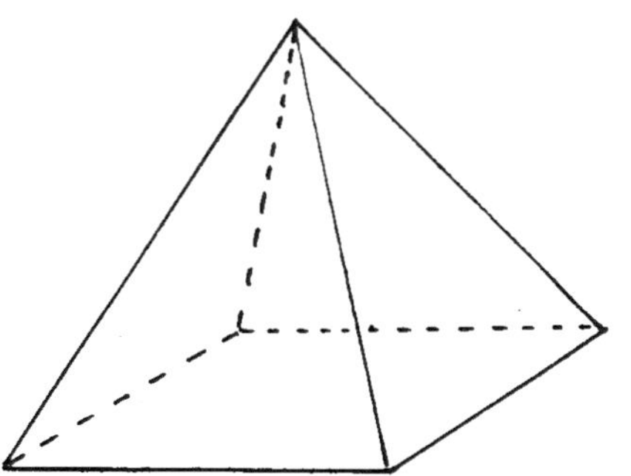
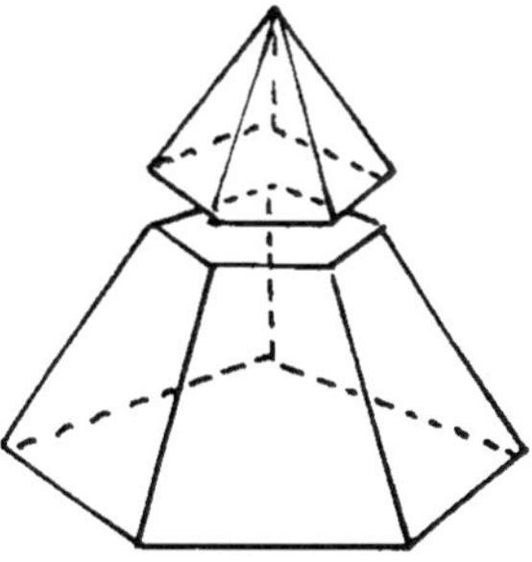
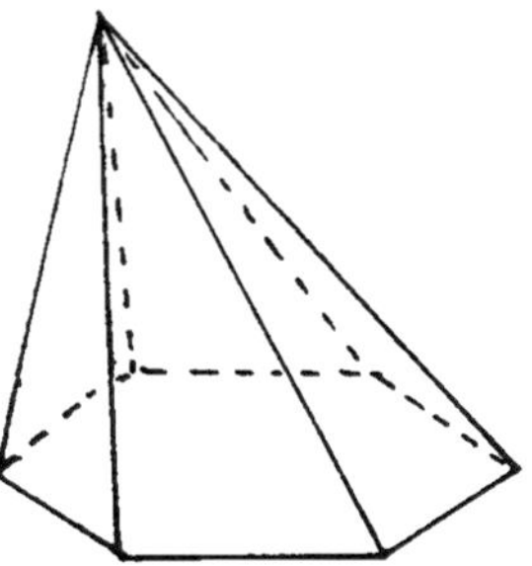

Fig. 119. A square pyramid (L); a pentagonal truncated pyramid (center); an oblique hexagonal pyramid (R).

Prisms may be seen in nature, but are usually fabricated. They have ends that are equal, similar, and parallel and have sides which are parallelograms. A wedge is a type of prism; it has five sides, three rectangles and two triangles. Other prisms have six or more sides. The triangular prisms are popular in chandeliers for dispersion of light, and in optics, prisms are integral parts of binoculars.

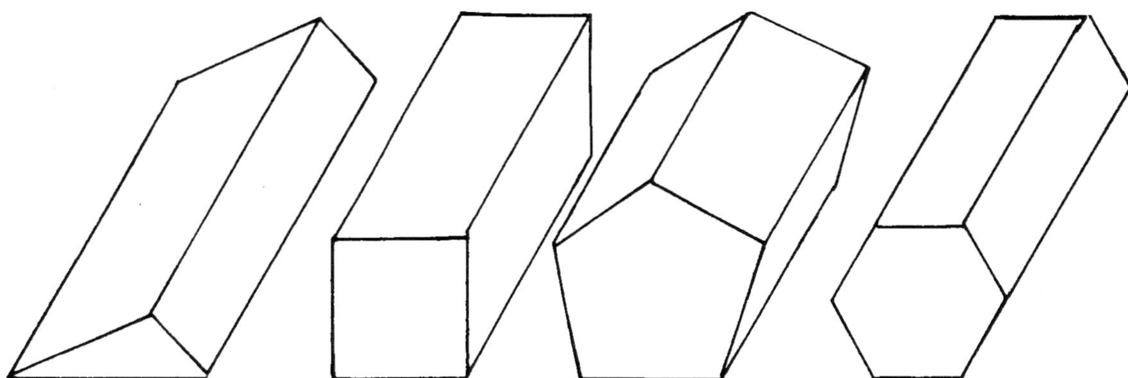

Fig. 120. Triangular prism; square prism; pentagonal prism, hexagonal prism.

A polyhedron composed of six square sides is a cube. Other right polyhedrons have rectangular sides that join at right angles. When the sides are parallel and consist of parallelograms with oblique angles, the figure is called a parallelepiped. These are often seen in nature as crystals and they are illustrated by the monoclinic and triclinic classification of crystal forms. Irregular polyhedrons may have some sides that are trapezoids or irregular polygons and have no regular relation for angles or shapes of other sides.

CRYSTAL FORMS

Crystalography is a fascinating science in which many beautiful forms with vivid colors challenge the imagination. In the formation of crystalline structures, atoms align themselves on definite axes. By continued growth, beautiful orders and patterns develop. Gems are a significant category that has thrilled mankind for centuries and served as one factor of wealth. Crystals are classed in six systems, subdivided into 32 classes. Only the six systems will be considered in this discussion. Many of the variations in other groups are interesting and beautiful.

1. **Isometric** system has three axes that are equal and at right angles, forming a cube. Examples are halite or common table salt, galena, a type of lead ore, and pyrite or fool's gold. These all have a cubic lattice of crystallization.
2. **Tetragonal** have three axes that meet in the center at right angles. The horizontal axes are equal, while the vertical axis is longer or shorter. Long square crystals with pointed ends belong in this system.
3. **Hexagonal** crystals have four axes and six lateral sides. The horizontal axes have equal length, meeting at 128 degree angles. The vertical axis is perpendicular. Quartz, ice, and basalt are examples.
4. **Orthorhombic** has 3 perpendicular axes of unequal length, similar to tetragonal, except one of the sides is either flattened or stretched out. All sides are rectangles.
5. **Monoclinic** has 3 unequal axes with one inclined or oblique, similar to orthorhombic except crystals have a tilted appearance. Common examples are satin spar.
6. **Triclinic** has three unequal axes in which all are oblique. Crystals have a lopsided appearance and seem to lack symmetry.

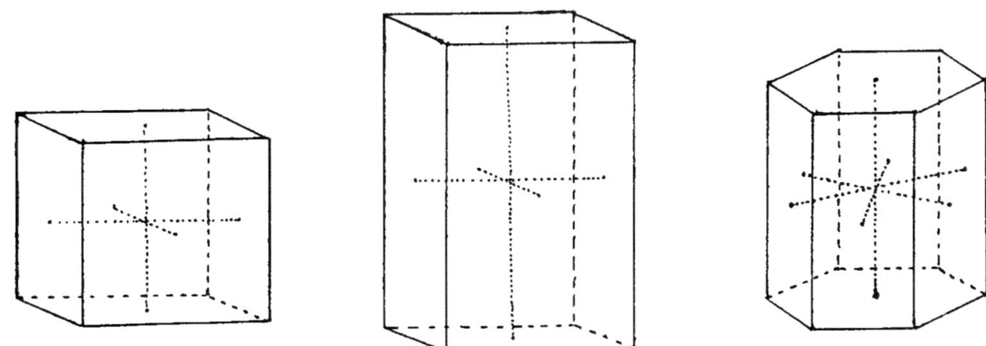

Fig. 121. Crystal forms: Isometic (L), tetragonal (center), and hexagonal (R).

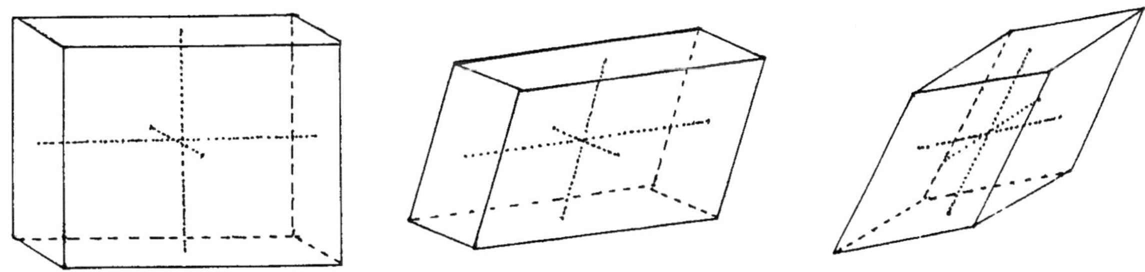

Fig. 122. Crystal forms: Orthorhombic (L), monoclinic (center), and triclinic (R).

SOLID FIGURES WITH CURVED SURFACES

Solid figures with curved surfaces include spheres, spheroids, ellipsoids, ovoids, cylinders, cylindroids, cones, conoids, torus, toroids, cochleate shapes, and helical forms. A sphere is a figure whose entire surface is equidistant from a central point. Familiar objects are numerous in society, including globes and balls. Many sports involve some type of ball in their contests. The human breast develops as a hemisphere, but weight alters it to a teardrop form. The eyeball is a sphere, but only a portion is visible.

An object that resembles a sphere is termed a spheroid. The suffix "oid" added to the end of a word means similar to. The earth is a spheroid, being slightly flattened toward the poles. A prolate spheroid is formed by an ellipse rotated on its long axis. A truncated prolate spheroid, with ends cut off, is familiar as a pickle barrel and a pot bellied stove. An oblate spheroid is generated when an ellipse is rotated on a short or minor axis. A familiar example is a doorknob.

An oval resembles the outline of an egg. It has three foci as compared to an ellipse with two foci. A three dimensional figure constructed by an oval rotated on its greatest diameter is an ovoid and is egg shaped. Generally it is broader at one pole.

A right cylinder is a solid body described by a rectangle rotated around a vertical axis. Both ends become circles. A disk is essentially a very short cylinder. A plane crossing the cylinder at any angle except perpendicular will inscribe an ellipse. An oblique cylinder's axis is at an angle to its base. A cylindroid is similar except that both ends are parallel ellipses.

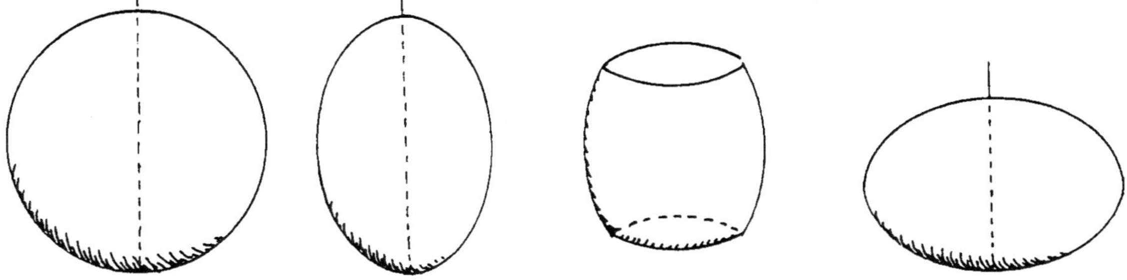

Fig. 123. A sphere, a prolate spheroid, a truncated prolate, and an oblate spheroid.

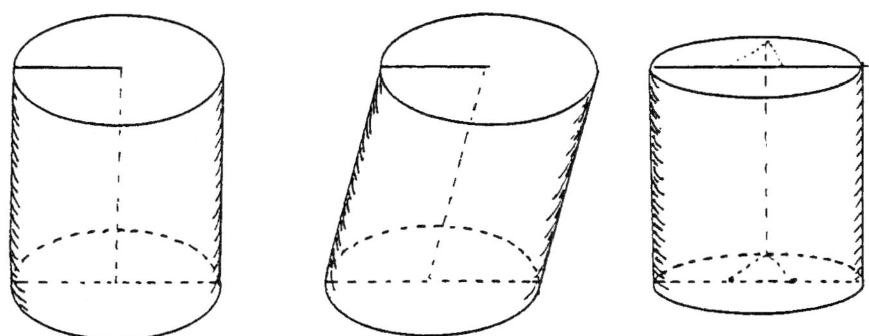

Fig.124. A right cylinder (L), an oblique cylinder (center), and a cylindroid (R).

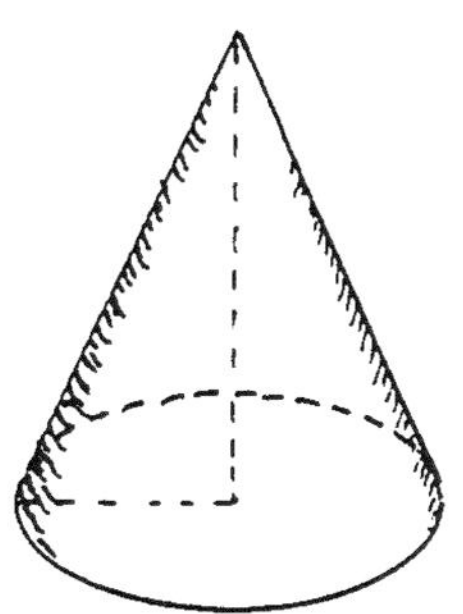
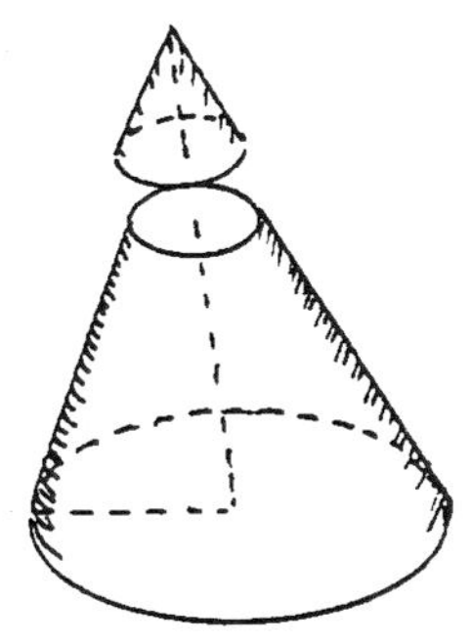
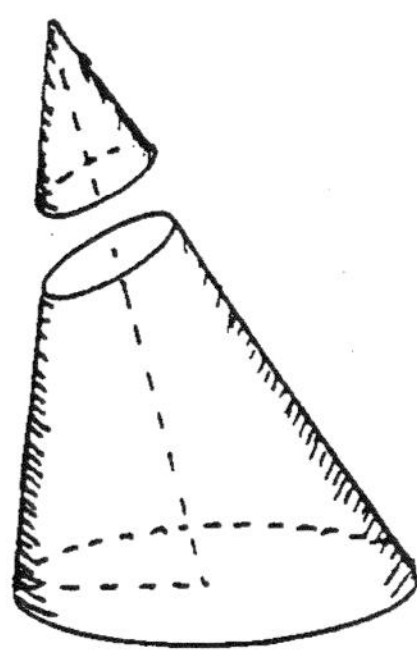

Fig.125. A right cone (L) a truncated oblique cone (center), and a conoid (R).

A cone is formed when a right triangle is rotated through a circle using a vertical leg as an axis. When a plane intersects a cone at perpendicular a circle is described. An angle other than perpendicular to the axis creates an ellipse. An oblique cone has an axis at an angle other then a right angle. A conoid has an ellipse for a base.

When a plane intersects the cone parallel to its axis, a hyperbola is outlined. When a plane intersects a cone parallel to an opposite side, a parabola is created. A conoid is formed when the base at right angles to the vertical axis is an ellipse. Like a pyramid, the portion near the base of a truncated cone is called a frustum. Segments of arms and legs resemble truncated elongated conoids, especially the forearm and the thigh.

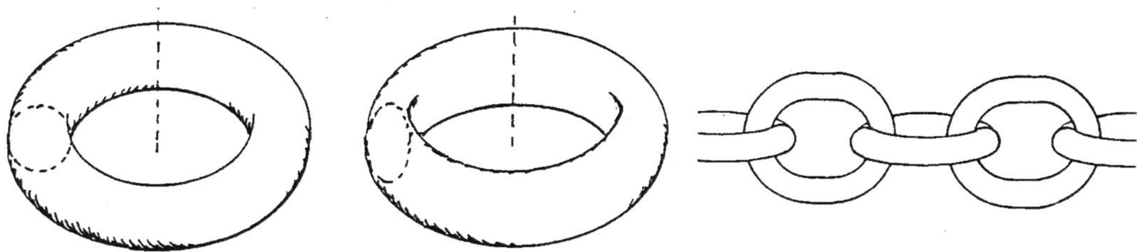

Fig. 126. A torus (L), a toroid (center), and chain links (R).

A torus is generated by a circle rotated perpendicularly about an axis. Familiar examples are links of a chain, a doughnut, and an inflated automobile tire inner-tube. The toroid is formed in the same manner using an ellipse or similar figure rotated about an axis.

A cardioid is formed when a C type curve is rotated on a vertical axis. A peach and plum are good examples. A paraboloid is a solid figure formed by a parabola rotated on its axis. Reflectors of automobile headlights, search lights and even mirrors of reflector astronomical telescopes, are practical examples. A hyperboloid is similarly, the solid figure generated by a hyperbola rotated on its axis.

Fig. 127. A cardiod (L), a paraboloid (center), and a hyperboloid (R).

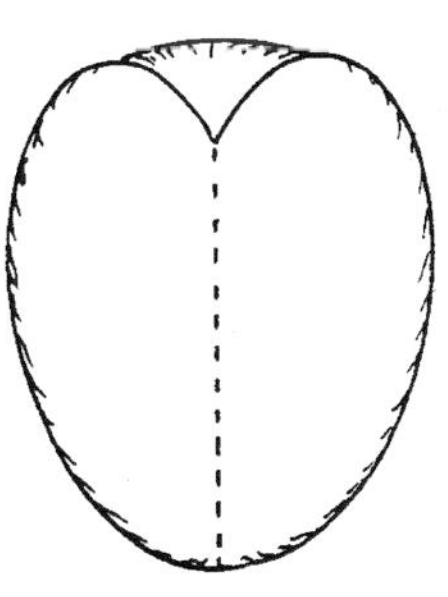
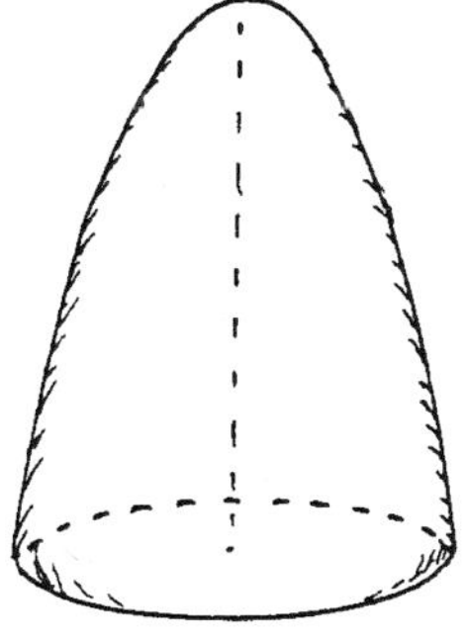
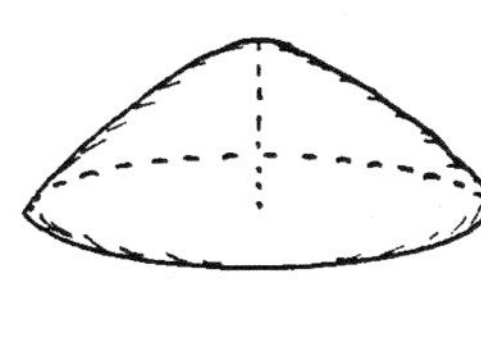

The three dimensional representations of spirals are the cochleate, flattened snail-like form, conchoid, elongate snail form and the helix. In nature the DNA protein molecule of the mitochondria, components of the chromosomes of cells, form a helix. More familiar examples are coil springs and the screw. These are discussed in a section on rotational symmetry.

A lens, is formed by the intersection of two spherical surfaces or a plane and spherical surface. There are several variable combinations of convex, plano, and concave configurations. The name was derived from Latin, *lens* the lentil seed. Pillows, bottles, and some balloons may assume this shape. These forms are often associated with optical instruments.

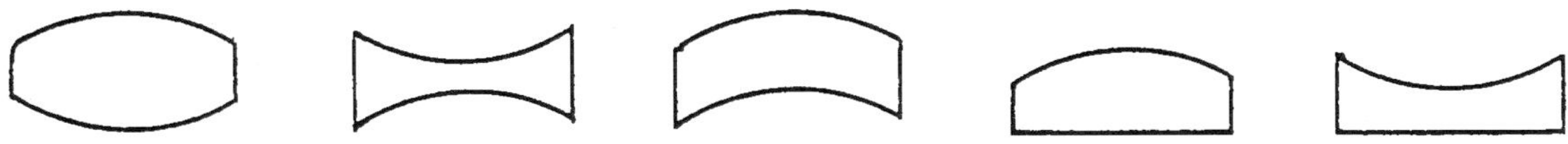

Fig.128. Double convex; double concave; concavo-convex; plano-convex; plano-concave.

THREE DIMENSIONAL POLYGONS

Rectilinear and curvilinear polygons have been discussed and illustrated. Plane surfaces in nature are observed on leaves in the Plant Kingdom but are seldom seen in the Animal Kingdom. Three dimensional surfaces are most common. The forms seldom conform to simple shapes or configurations, but instead are often combinations of forms. A circle cut by a line is an arc. A sphere cut by a plane results in a section. When a sphere has three arcs intersecting to form a triangle, a spherical triangle is outlined. Other polygons, such as squares, rectangles, pentagons, hexagons, and many more can be outlined.

Spherical polygons are formed by a series of connected arcs created by planes passing through the center giving an appearance of straight lines on the surface. Arcs that are oblique to the solid object give an appearance of curved lines on the surface of a sphere or other object. These forms are seen in nature, but the observer needs to be alert to recognize them. Look at your own fingernails and describe the form of a cylindrical polygon. Consider the lips with their curving surfaces and graceful lines. The iris of an eye is a circular section of a sphere. The human nipple is a circular portion of a hemisphere. Inclusion of discrete forms in a composition will render a greater realism and vigor to enhance a masterpiece.

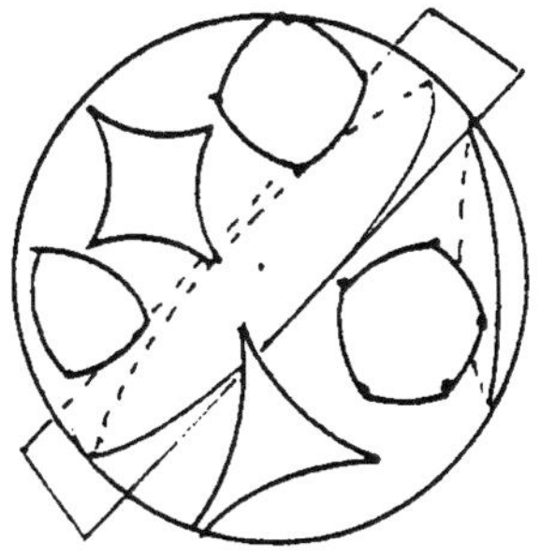

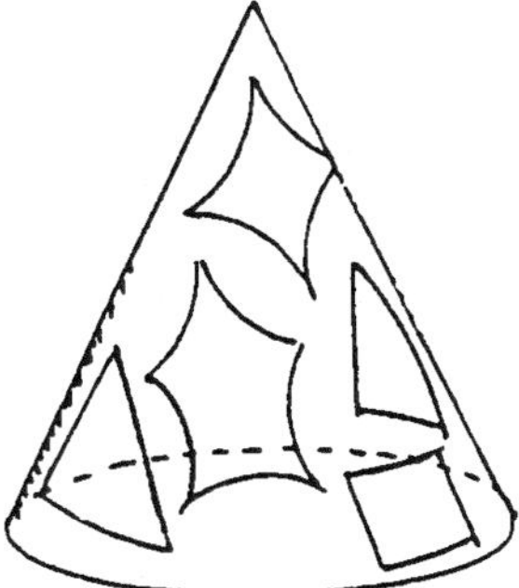

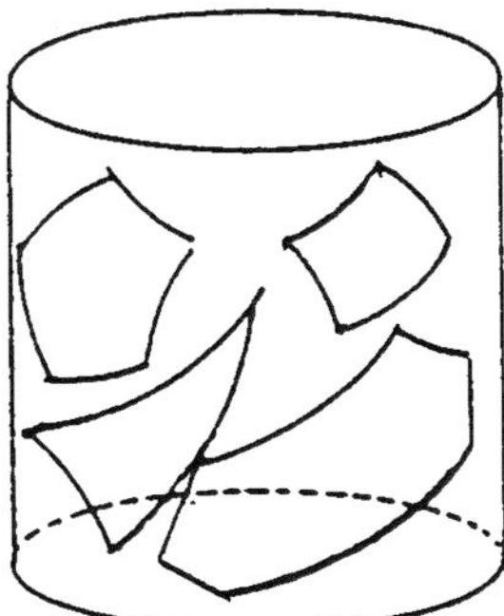

Fig. 129. Three dimensional polygons.

SYMMETRY

Symmetry is a word and concept that evolved through the French language (*symetrie*) from Latin (*symmetria*, due proportion) and Greek (*synmetros*, measure together). Its roots are metros—to measure—and a prefix syn—together. It literally means to measure together or compare dimensions and form. It is one of the major elements of design. Two others are balance and rhythm. Combining them leads to a development of dynamic harmony.

The term symmetry is also used in geometry, chemistry, and physics. It may be defined in biology and art as the corresponding arrangement or balancing of the parts or elements of the entire object in respect to size, position, form, and shape. This results in a balance on opposite sides of a central point, axis, or plane.

Frequently, there is a correlation of opposite parts with a balance of the proportions of the parts to the whole object. Symmetry may also include a similarity of units to each other in a regular repeated pattern, the arrangements of elements comprising a whole entity.

This is in contrast to asymmetry or non-symmetry, where there is no apparent organization, balance, or correspondence of parts. Inorganic forms and features often exhibit no symmetry. Many very primitive plants and animals, like an amoeba, are characterized by a total lack of symmetry. Others may change and develop asymmetry or partial asymmetry in adult stages as maturation of an organism conforms to a special environment.

In art, as in nature, there is an element of excellence or beautiful configuration that results from balance in an orderly and corresponding arrangement. Action results in a modified symmetry.

An illustration, Fig. 118 on page 183, represents many symmetries with organic and inorganic forms in their struggles involving natural forces. Near the base is radio-activity. Crystals symbolizing minerals are thrust apart by dividing cells, the organic. Water crystal as a snowflake and stratified water are represented. Rain drops and storm clouds, are interspersed by radiance of the sun.

AN OUTLINE OF SYMMETRY

After recognizing asymmetry, there are three elements of symmetry that have been described and classically taught in biology and art. These are spherical or universal symmetry, radial symmetry, and bilateral symmetry.

I. **Universal or spherical symmetry** is represented by a sphere. Equal halves may be created by any plane passing through a central point. It is the simplest and most fundamental form of symmetry, yet it is not necessarily static.

II. **Radial symmetry** includes plant and animal life with circular or disk-like form that can be divided in equal halves by many planes through a central axis.

III. **Bilateral symmetry** exists where the entity can be divided into two equal halves through a central axis by one plane, the mid-sagittal plane.

SPHERICAL SYMMETRY

Spherical symmetry has massive examples in astronomy, such as the sun, the earth, the moon, and the neighboring planets. Many stars, some even more massive than the sun, can be studied by telescopic observation. Spherical symmetry is represented by familiar globular objects like balls whose centers are points. Some primitive and colonial forms of microscopic animal life, such as radiolarians, exist in spherical form. Primordial forms often exhibit simple configurations, as spherical symmetry.

Some of the smallest organisms, the coccus forms of bacteria, are globular. Single cell plant life and some colonial algae are also globular. Organisms with spherical symmetry are passive forms not likely to alter their shape or exhibit self-propulsion. Examples in zoology are organisms that usually drift with currents or are carried by other higher forms of life. Noctiluca, a nearly spherical dinoflagellate that drifts in plankton, exhibits a bio-luminescence when disturbed, that is especially noticeable in the wake of ships at night. Many fruits, such as berries, cherries, peaches, and oranges approach spherical configurations.

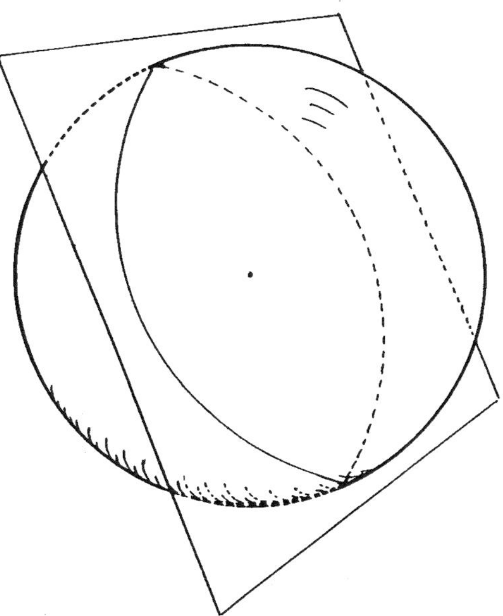

Fig. 130. A sphere with any plane passing through its center.

Spherical and radial symmetry are significant in the embryonic development of vertebrates, including humans. The human ovum is spherical with loosely attached adventitial cells. After fertilization, cell division proceeds rapidly, forming first a morula stage that is still spherical. As cell division continues into many smaller cells, a fluid-filled blastula develops, with cells forming a sphere. At one pole, cells accumulate in a cluster. At the other pole, a dimple develops, progressively moving inward to form the Gastrula stage.

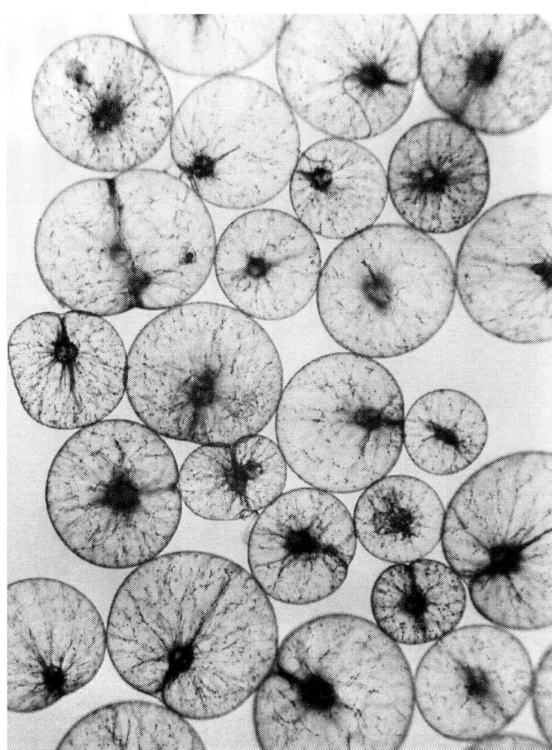

Fig. 131. Noctiluca.

An Ovum

A Morula

A Blastula

A Gastrula

Fig. 132. Above, early development of a human embryo.

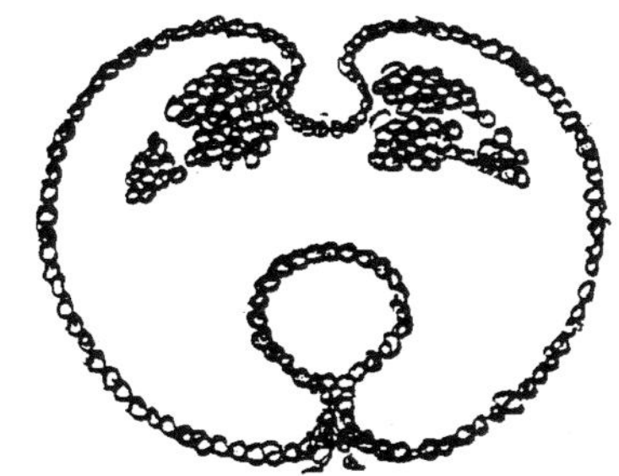

Later stages in the development.

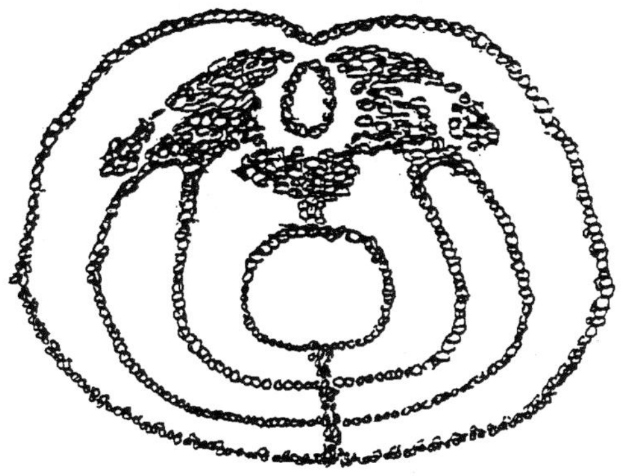

The next stage exhibits radial symmetry after a dimple begins on the sphere and progresses into a two-layered spherical cup, a gastrula stage with an opening at one pole.

There is a gradual transition from spherical to radial symmetry. As the embryo grows, it begins to develop into a three-layered organism and develops bilateral symmetry.[3]

The beauty of spherical and radial symmetry is not entirely lost in the mature forms of higher animal life or among humans. The human eyeball is nearly spherical. The head of the humerus and femur of the bony skeleton are partial spheres. Nipples, breasts, and the iris of the eyes are fine examples of retained radial symmetry. Many more examples of this beautiful symmetry are found when certain human tissues, particularly the liver and secretory glands, are examined under the microscope.

The sphere is important in athletic contests, particularly ball games, such as tennis, soccer, basketball, baseball, golf, and many more. As the world becomes more politically cohesive, discussions and illustrations of global commerce and travel become more prevalent. The sphere becomes a symbol of universality.

3. Williams, P. L., pg 19,20.

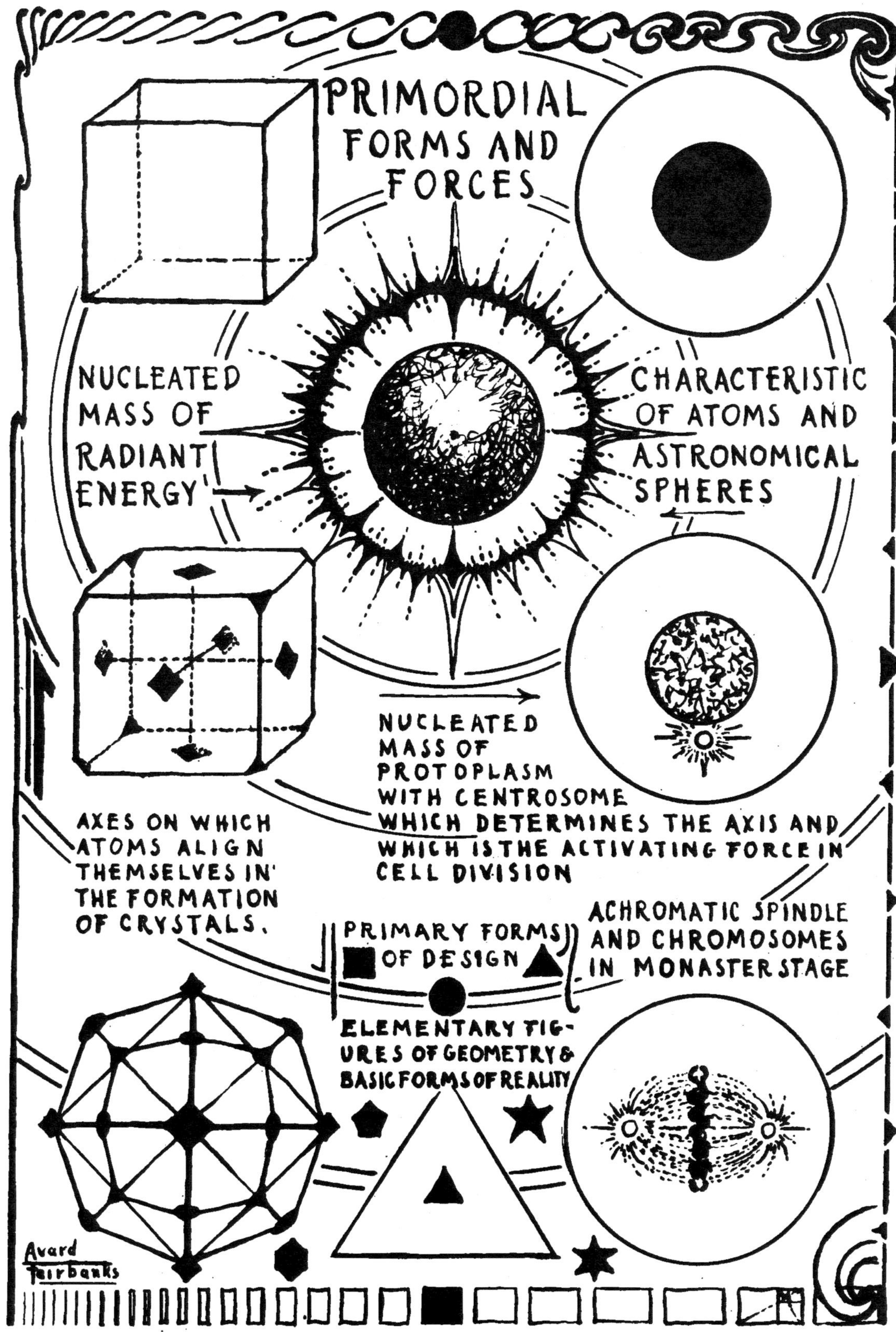

Fig. 133. Primordal forms and forces.

RADIAL SYMMETRY

Radial symmetry is represented by a circular or a disk-shaped entity when equal halves may be created by any plane passing through a central axis. In zoology, organisms that exhibit radial symmetry may be active forms capable of alteration of their configuration to effect some slow locomotion. Radial symmetry is present in many forms of marine life somewhat higher on the phylogenetic scale. Sponges, hydra, hydroids, sea anemones, sea jellies (jelly fish), sea stars (star fish), and sea urchins are well known examples of marine life that serve as beautiful examples of radial symmetry.

These animals may be either attached to underwater structures or may be slow moving. Those that are free floating are capable of some locomotion, but swim weakly and primarily drift with the tide or current. These are still primitive forms of life, yet they often exhibit grace and beauty, see Fig. 135 illustrations of Sea Star, Cyanea capillata, anemone, and basket star.)

Radial symmetry is often portrayed in art. An example is the illustration of Roman and Egyptian designs.

Radial symmetry is also abundant in the plant kingdom. Most flowers are beautiful examples of radial symmetry, as the Rose, the radiating limbs of evergreen trees and the scales of pine cones. Among the minerals, many crystals form their lattice on a longitudinal axis. Snow flakes, although tiny, demonstrate an exquisite hexagonal filigree with lacy, radially symmetrical patterns.

In commerce and industry, examples of radial symmetry are numerous and include vehicle wheels, gears, river boat paddle wheels, water wheels of mills during pioneer times, turbines, propellers, and many other structures involving rotational energy.

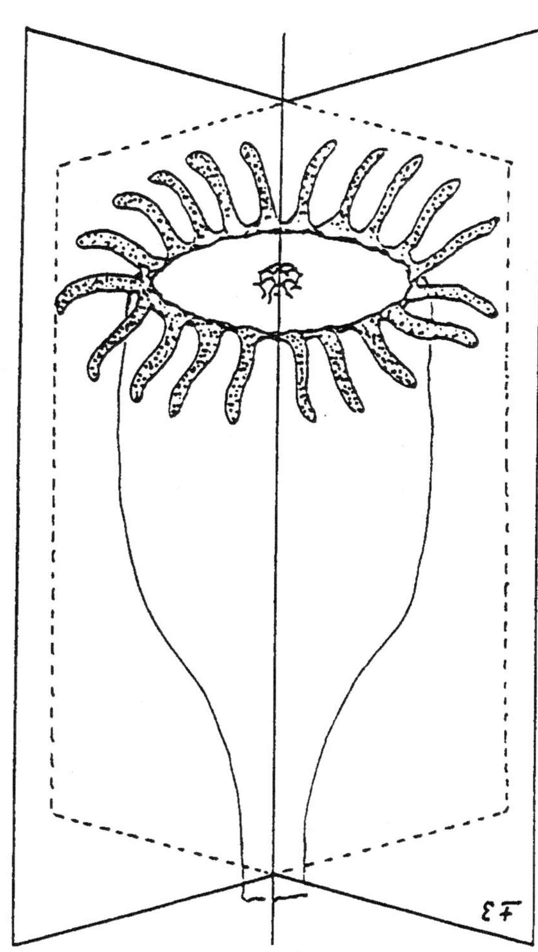

Fig. 134. A hydra polyp with two planes passing through a cental axis.

Illustrations are presented in Fig. 135 of four marine specimens exhibiting radial symmetry: Cyanea capillata, a sea jelly (jelly fish); Anthropleura artemesia, a sea anemone; Gorgonocephalus eucnemis, a basket star; and Evestarias troschlelii, a sea star (starfish). Examples are also abundant in plant life, as flowers like a lily, a chrysanthemum, a dahlia, and a sun flower. Fig. 136, *Symmetry and Balance*, is an illustration demonstrating natural and artificial forms, is included for artistic representation.

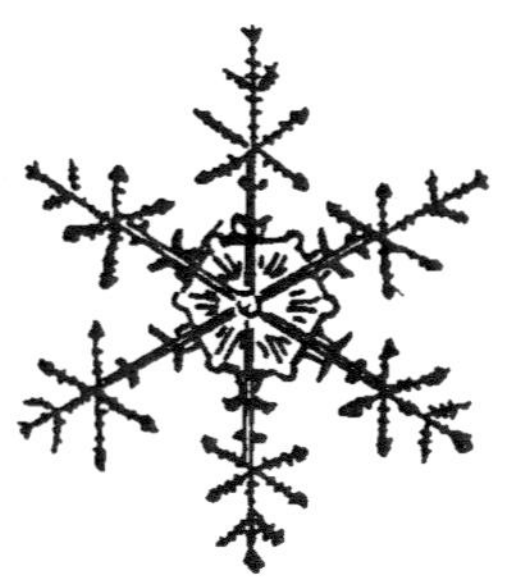

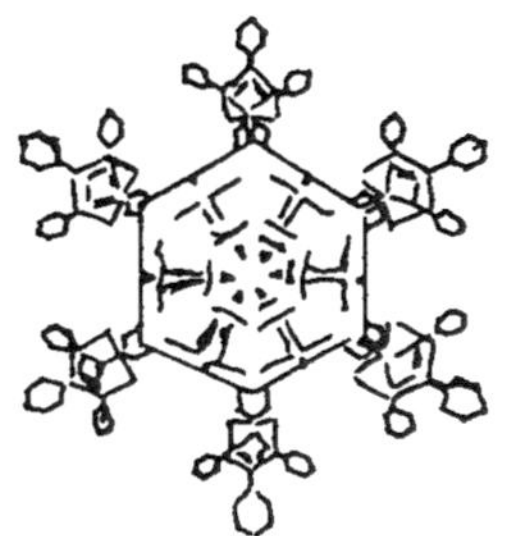

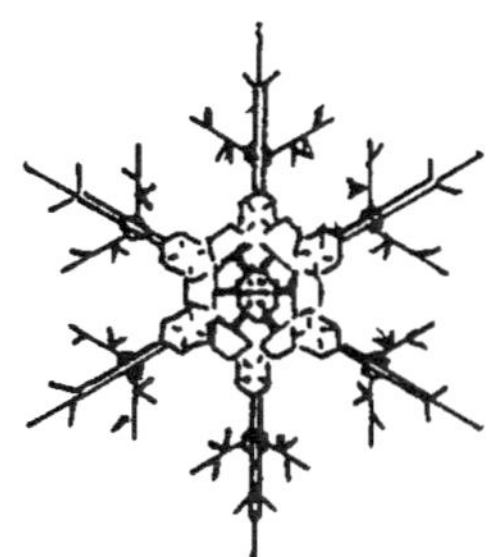

Snowflakes.

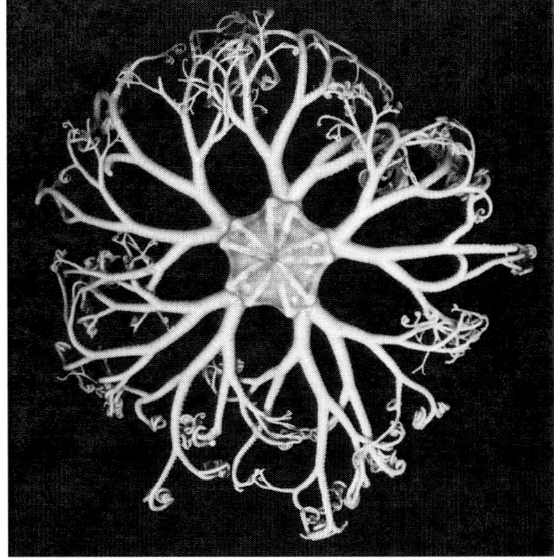

A basket star, Gorgonocephalus caryi.

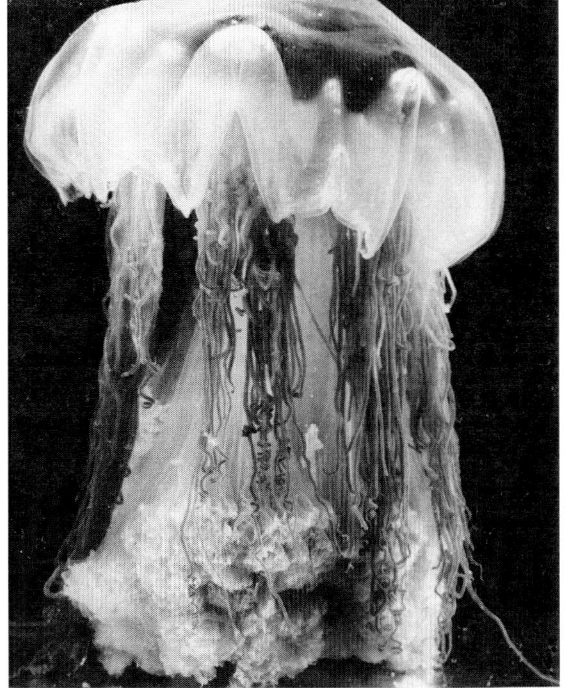

Sea jelly, Cyanea capillata.

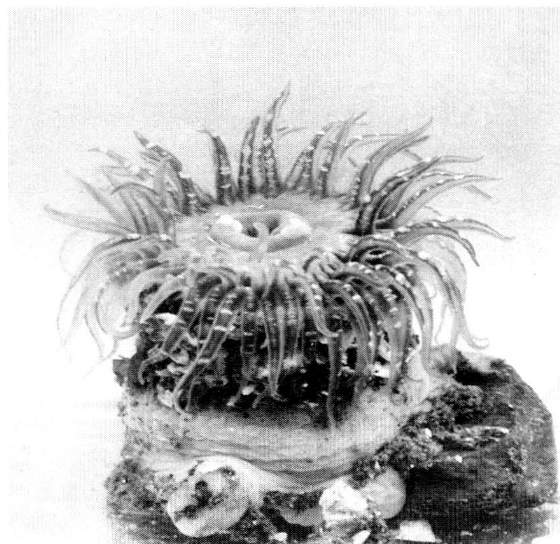

A burrowing sea anemone, Anthropleura artemisia.

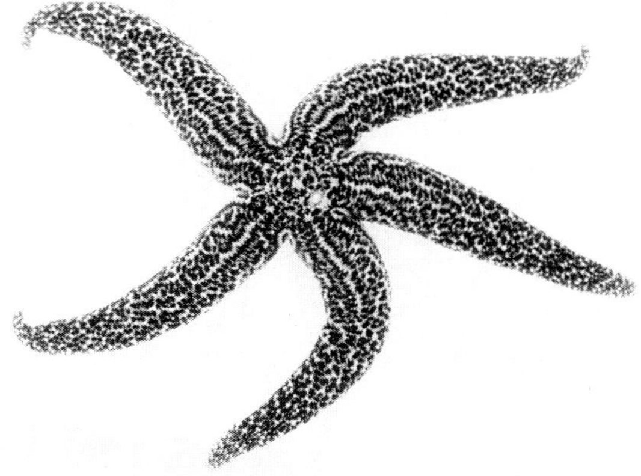

A sea star, Evasterias troschelii.

Fig. 135. Radial symmetry examples: Snowflakes; a basket star, Gorgonocephalus caryi; a sea jelly, Cyanea capillata; a burrowing sea anemone, Anthropleura artemisia; and a sea star, Evasterias troschelii.

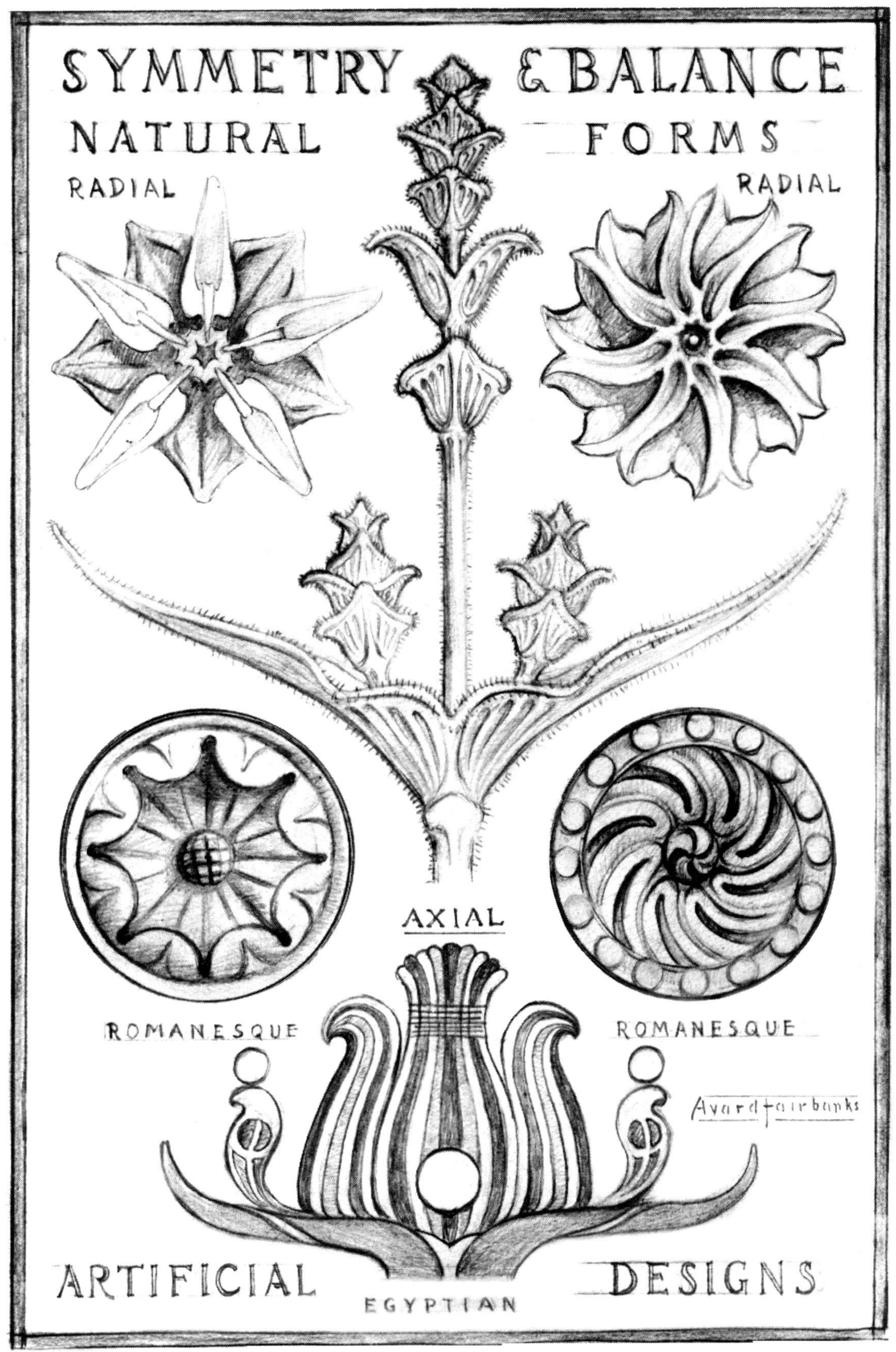

Fig. 136. Symmetry and Balance, Natural Forms and Artifical Designs, by Avard Fairbanks.

BILATERAL SYMMETRY

Bilateral symmetry exists when the entity can be divided into equal or similar halves by one plane through a central axis, essentially a mid-sagittal plane. This symmetry is seen in animal life that has greater potential for movement than those possessing radial symmetry. Efficient locomotion needs one end to go first. Therefore specialization has developed head and tail ends. This symmetry has developed in some primitive animal phyla. Arthropods, such as crustaceans, spiders, and insects, exhibit it; mollusks, particularly octopus and squid, have this symmetry Vertebrates that include fish, amphibians, reptiles, birds, and mammals manifest this symmetry.

This is noted even in primitive animals such as terrestrial and marine worms. Illustrated is a beautiful green, iridescent, three foot-long polychete marine worm, Nereis brandti, that demonstrates bilateral symmetry and polysymmetry. In higher animals, bilateral symmetry is accompanied by a greater differentiation of dorsal and ventral areas of the body. Appendages, such as fins, then arms and legs, developed for balance and assisted locomotion. Static bilateral symmetry is then altered for action. Many higher vertebrates depend entirely on their appendages for movement. Important human features with bilateral symmetry are the extremities and the paired structures of the face—the eyes, ears, and nostrils.

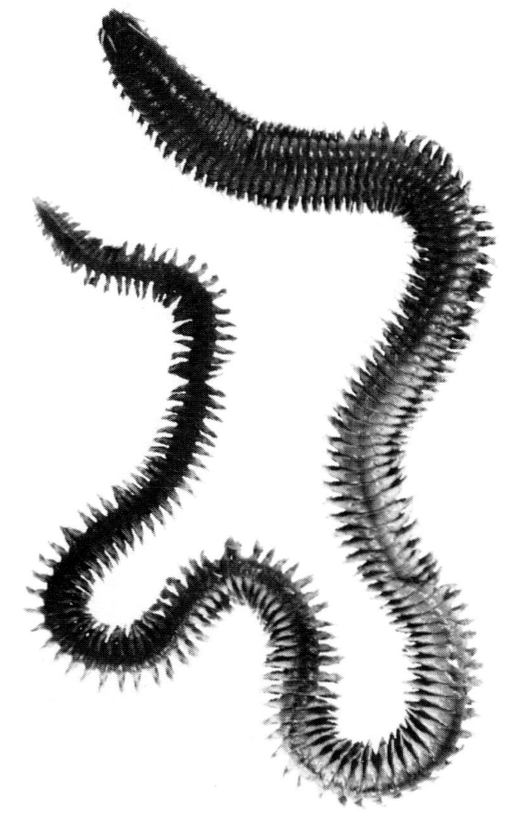

Fig. 137. A marine polychete worm, Nerieis branti.

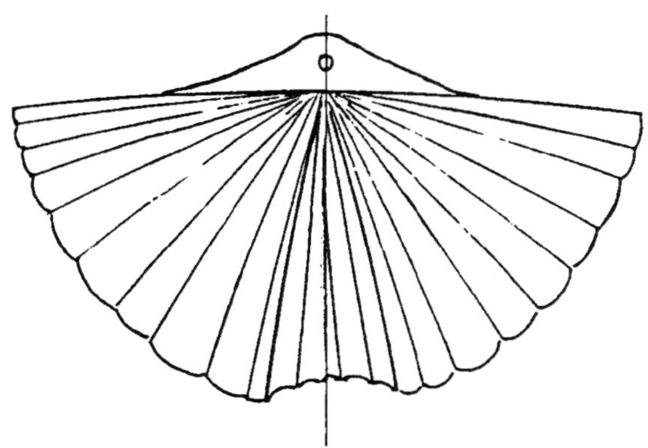

Fig. 138. A brachiopod.

Bilateral symmetry is present in mollusks and in many other primitive animals. One illustrated is a brachiopod. Although there are now only about 300 living species, thousands of species are found in fossiliferous, Paleozoic rocks. These primitive lampshells have a dorsal-ventral symmetry in contrast to clams and oysters that have a side-to-side symmetry of their shells. Bilateral symmetry is most apparent in the vertebrates.

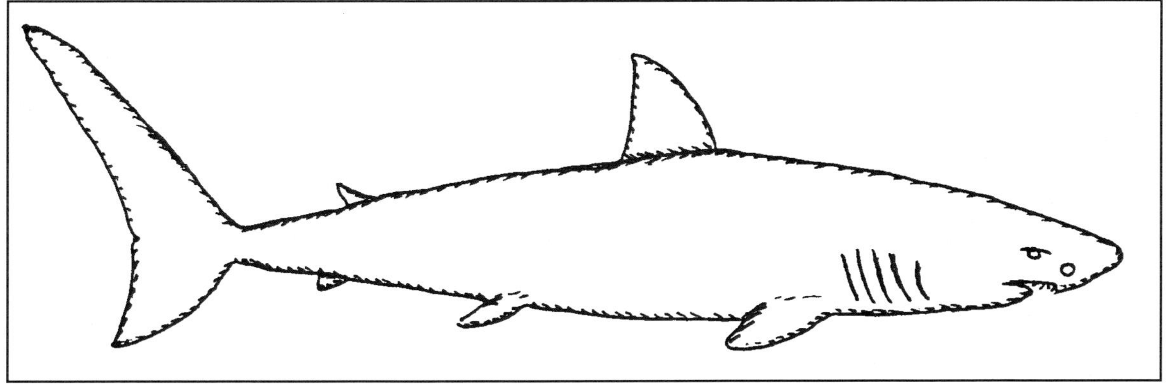

A shark, lateral view.

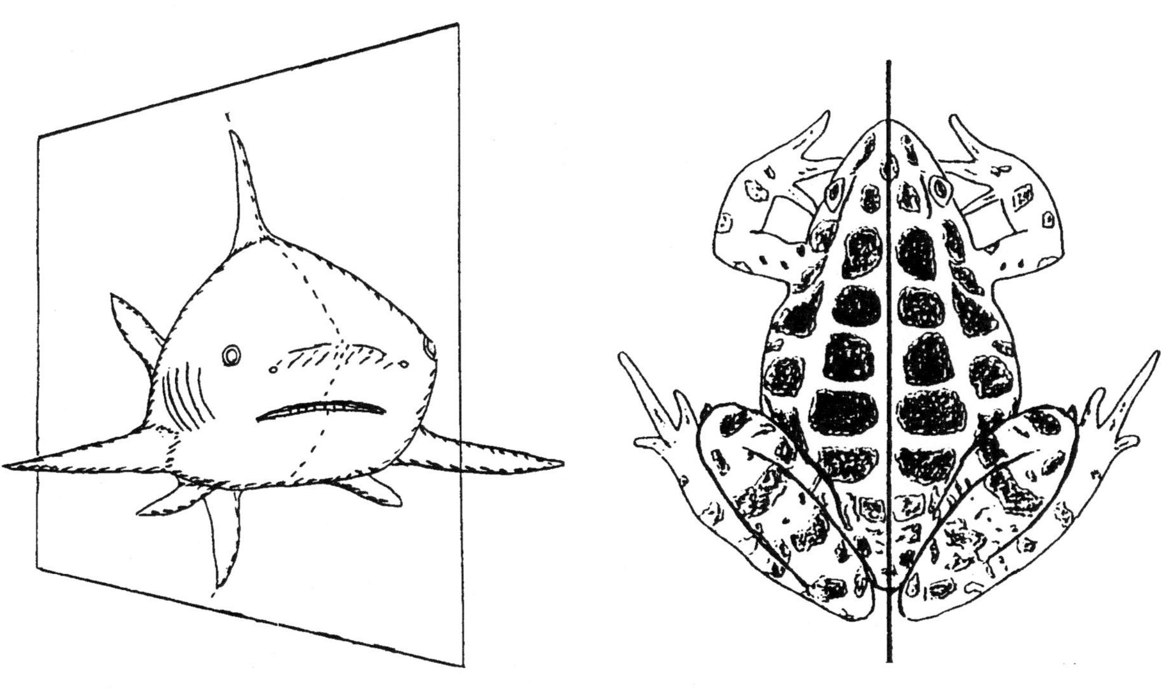

Bilateral view showing a shark with only one plane creating equal halves.

A Pickeral frog showing bilateral symmetry.

Fig. 139. A shark and a Pickerel frog demonstrating bilateral symmerty.

A shark is used here as an illustration with a dorsal-to-ventral mid-saggital plane. A pickerel frog is also illustrated. A similar dorsal-ventral, mid-saggital plane can be described in quadruped mammals and in humans that are bipedal and have erect posture.

OTHER SPECIALIZED SYMMETRIES EVIDENT IN FAMILIAR FORMS

In addition to these three main classifications, there are several specialized types of symmetry to be considered. Rotational symmetry is present in spirals. Multilateral symmetry is evident in the many-sided, three-dimensional solid figures such as crystals. In biology, polysymmetry, segmental or zonal symmetry, and dynamic symmetry are also recognized. These types, with variations and in combinations, are important to form, life, and function. Appreciation and understanding these concepts are important for the enhancement of artistic expression.

1. **Rotational Symmetry** is noted in a coil, a whorl, or a helix, and is a form of radial symmetry, altered for action.
2. **Multilateral symmetry** is present in crystals with many equal or similar sides, with some being parallel.
3. **Polysymmetry** is present with multiple repetitions of similar specialized forms.
4. **Segmental symmetry** is demonstrated by many segments that are similar in form.
5. **Dynamic symmetry** is represented by a similarity in form, but with a geometric progression in size or position, as in a whorl resembling a snail shell.

ROTATIONAL SYMMETRY

This symmetry is a modification of radial symmetry. A figure of three radiating forms such as leaves, is a trefoil, and is somewhat static. Add a curve to each petal or a right angle line to each leg gives a sense of rotational motion, as in the triskelion, a symbolic figure in heraldry with three bent branches or flexed arms. With four legs, it is a swastika. Other figures may have five, six, or seven legs with feet at right angle projections to render a sense of rotation.

Prior to recent times these figures have had mystical significance. The swastika is an ancient Hindu symbol of good fortune. It was reversed to become the hakenkruez, or broken cross, and was chosen as a symbol of death and destruction by Adolph Hitler and the Nazi Party prior to and during World War II.

Rotational symmetry is seen in the vortex of a whirlpool. It is present in the coil of a clock spring. An arithmetic spiral on a plane adds a constant sum to its diameter as it increases, like string wound around a point or an axis. A three-dimensional example may be called a spiral, as a spiral staircase, but is more accurately termed a helix. Essentially, this form of a coil or a spiral is a three-dimensional type of rotational symmetry. It is a form shaped

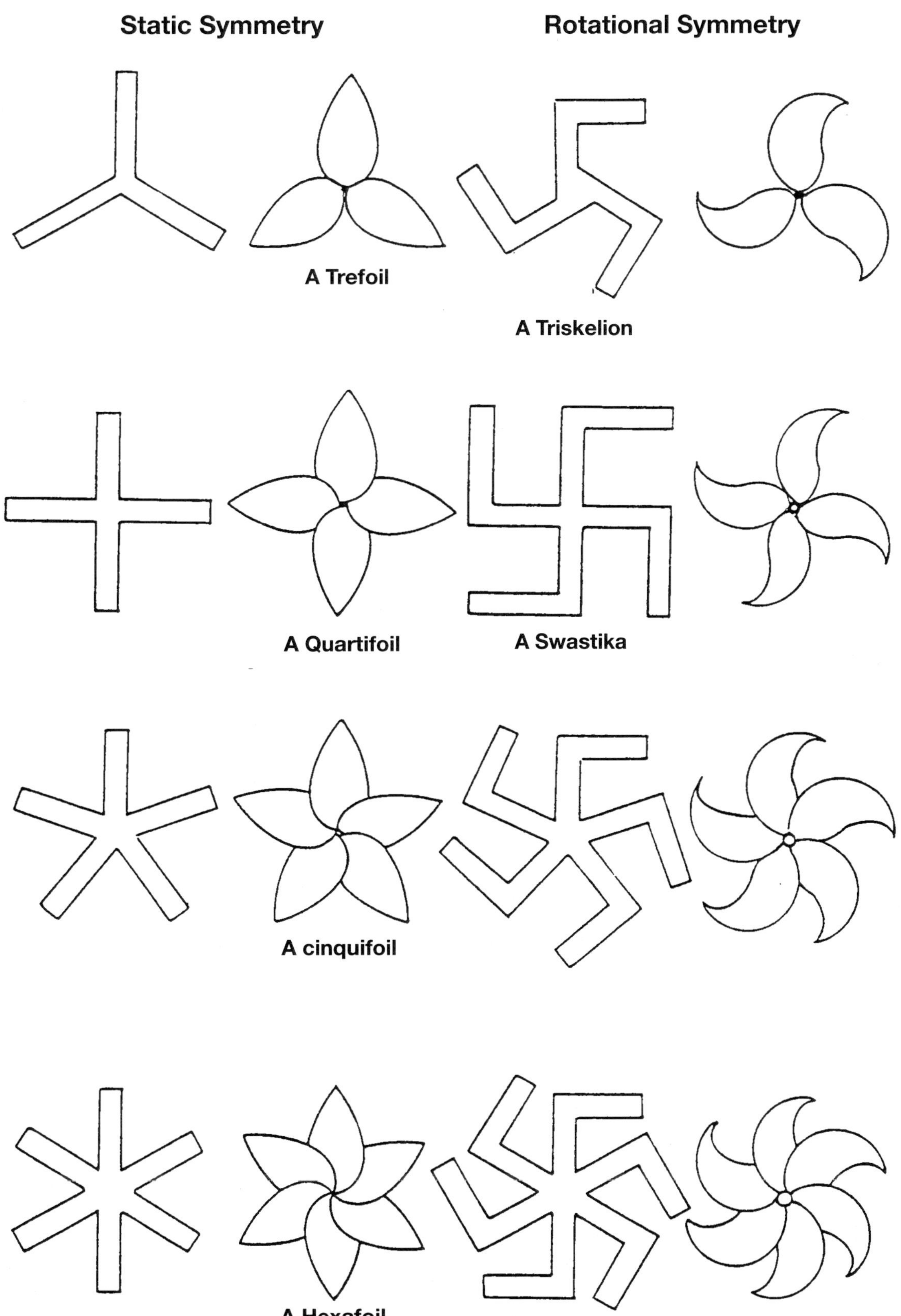

Fig. 140. Static and rotational radial symmetry in design.

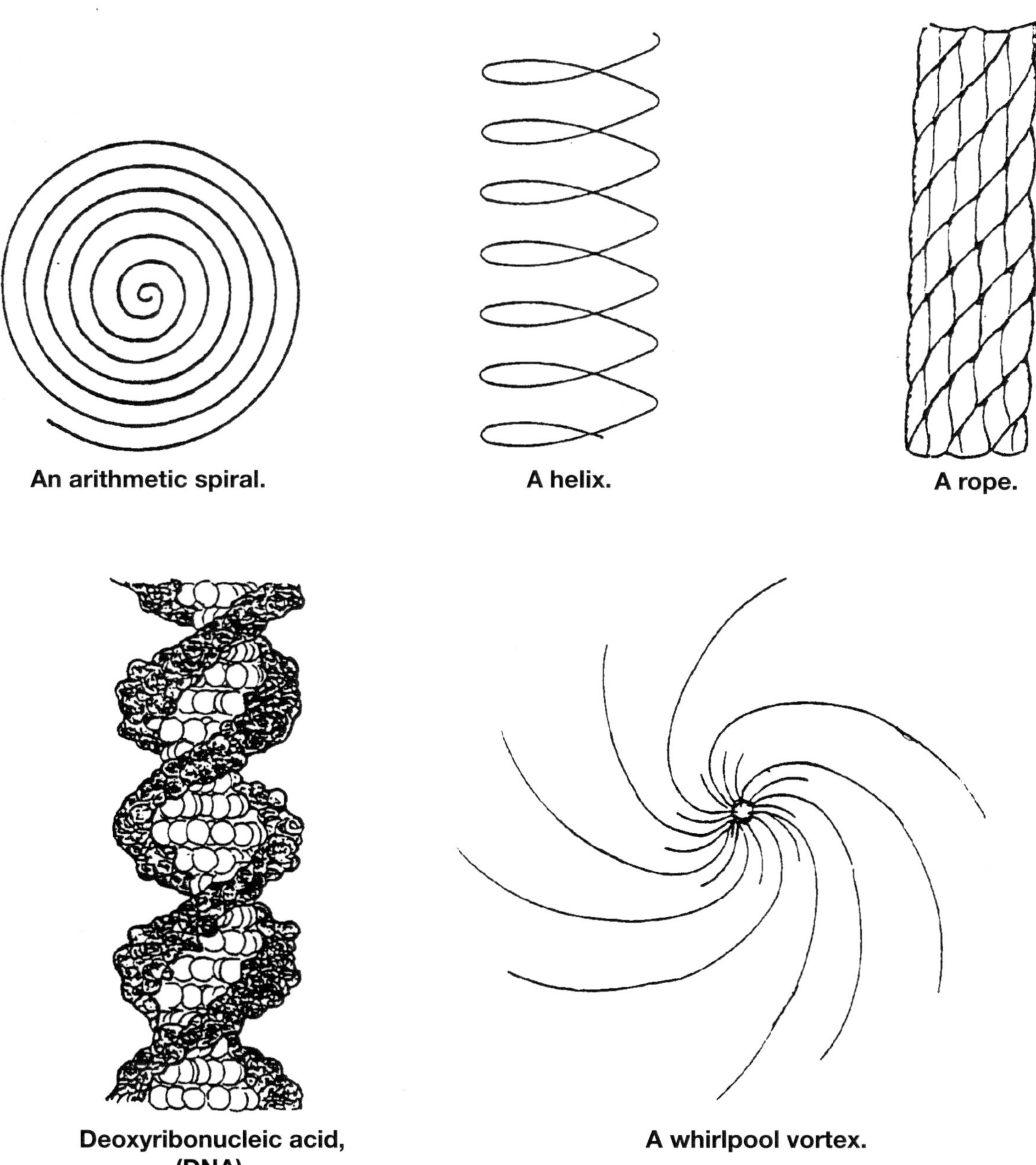

An arithmetic spiral.

A helix.

A rope.

Deoxyribonucleic acid, (DNA).

A whirlpool vortex.

Fig. 141. Examples of rotational symmetry.

as if wound around a upright axis, cylinder, or cone. Familiar examples are a screw, a coil spring, a propeller, and a rope with inter-twisted strands. Twentieth century advances in cellular and molecular biology have demonstrated that DNA (deoxyribonucleic acid), important to life and development, exists in cells as a double helix. It has been demonstrated in the mitochondria of chromosomes of cells in the body and is significant in genes and the protein structure.[4]

4. Yanofsky, pg. 278-279

MULTILATERAL SYMMETRY

This is not common in biology, since plane surfaces seldom occur. Although plane surfaces are common in leaves of plants, polyhedrons are rare. They are seldom seen in animal life. Multilateral symmetry is often seen in crystals that assume the shapes of polyhedrons or solid geometric figures. The sides may be polygons or simple plane figures like triangles, squares, rectangles, or parallelograms. Six common crystal forms are recognized with many variations and are included in an illustrated diagram in a previous section on three dimensional forms.

Many crystals are found in sand or stream beds. They have been worn by glacial or flowing water action and have a rounded appearance that alters their original shape. Some crystals have interesting forms and have fascinated humanity for several millennia. Those with hardness, color and transmit light are called gems. Some have been chosen as birthstones. Mystical significance has been attributed to some of them and some are even used in religious ceremonies. An artist should become familiar with these beautiful configurations, as they may be incorporated in a design for contrast or to represent inorganic forms. Jewelry design is also a very fine expression of art.

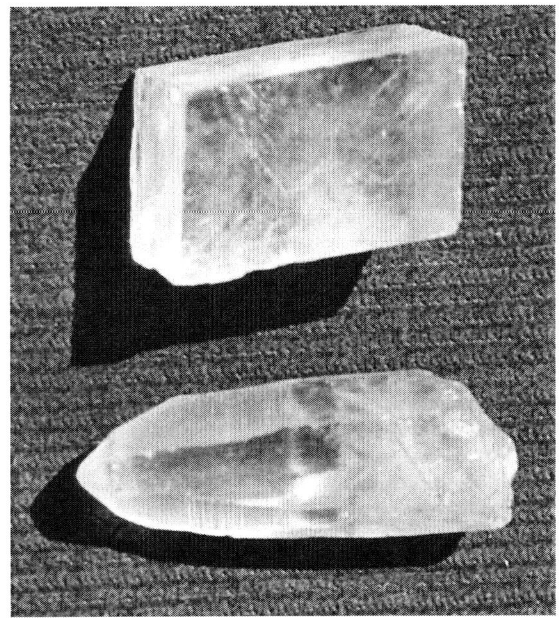

Fig. 142. Crystals With multilateral symmetry.

POLYSYMMETRY

In biology, a special symmetry is recognized, termed polysymmetry, and is manifested by repeated patterns. This may also be recognized as a repetition, an important element of design. In flowers, besides the radial symmetry of the placement of petals, there is also a polysymmetry, since the petals are nearly duplicates of each other. The flower parts show a repetition of form.

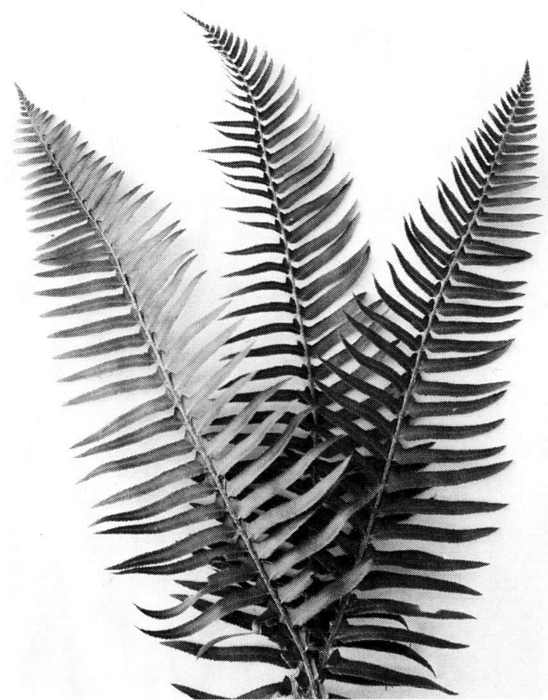

Fig. 143. Fronds of a sword fern.

A familiar example of combined radial and polysymmetry is represented in flower blossoms.

This design principle of repetition is characteristic of most flowers, and the leaves of plants and trees. The leaves are also essentially duplicates. Even the notches and serrations on the borders of leaves show polysymmetry. Examples in nature are too numerous to list, but others among them are: the kernels of wheat and corn, the fruit of trees, pine needles and cones, and the mosaic created by the ivy leaves on the walls of venerable buildings. Man-made structures often display a repetition and polysymmetry, such as the columns on a Greek temple, windows in a cathedral, and the tiles on a roof. We recognize that repetition can be pleasing if monotony is avoided.

In animals, there are many examples of repetition and polysymmetry. A striking example is the scales of a fish. Other examples include the teeth of sharks, reptiles, and other vertebrates; the feathers of birds; and the hair and claws of mammals. Likewise, in humans, the hair, teeth, digits, and fingernails are examples of polysymmetry with various slight modifications.

SEGMENTAL SYMMETRY

Another form of symmetry is serial symmetry, sometimes termed segmental or zonal symmetry. This form has a strong element of repetition. In botany, it is most strikingly represented in the living fossil called joint grass or horse tails (also called scouring rushes), genus, Equisetacia, a survivor of the Carboniferous Age. During that period, articulated or segmented plants were abundant. The stalks of these living plants are made up of multiple segments that can be easily pulled apart, Fig. 144 illustrates horse tail or joint grass. Serial symmetry is also evident in the radiating clusters of leaves on some plants and the branches on evergreen trees, each of which arose early in spring from a terminal bud cluster at the apex. The trunk may show three to six branches in a cluster at each annual level, six to eighteen inches apart, depending on the growth rate of the tree. This effect is also present in the branching of broad-leafed trees, but is not as evident.

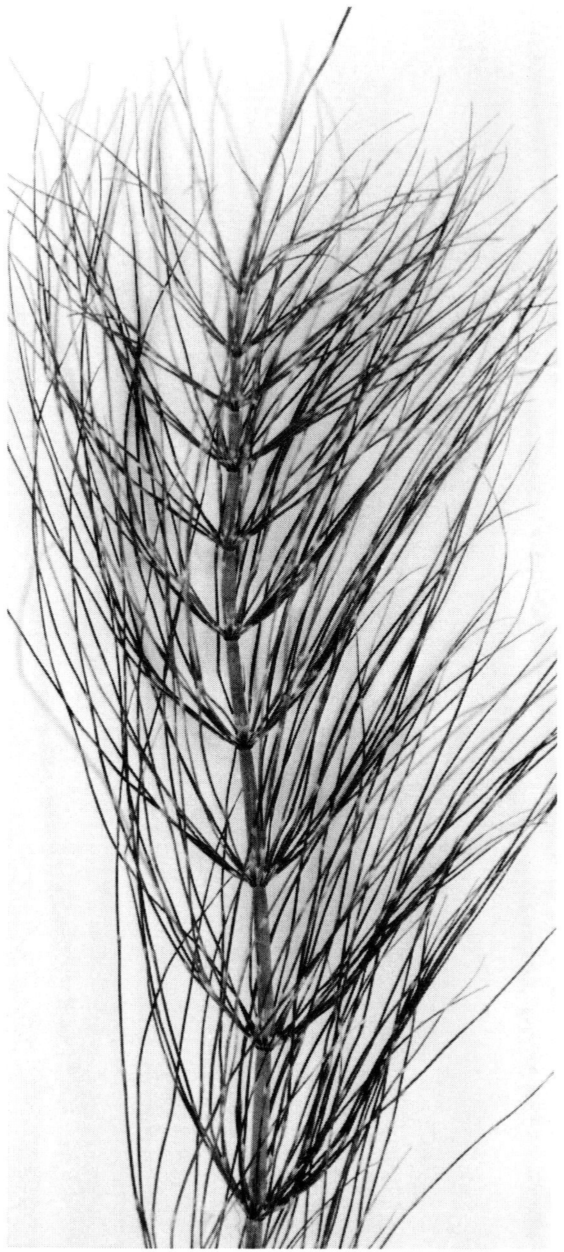

Fig. 144. Joint grass (or Horsetails, equisetacia), demonstrating segmental symmetry.

Examples of segmental symmetry and poly-symmetry may also demonstrate the principle of design called a progression, in which segments or elements may be progressively longer or larger. A gradation is the opposite design principle, where segmented elements become gradually shorter or smaller. The arm to forearm to hand to digits and to finger segments demonstrates a gradation. It is important that the artist be aware and recognize these symmetries in combination with repetitions and a progression or a gradation.

In the animal kingdom, segmentation and repetition are very obvious in marine worms and earthworms. It is also noted in many arthropods, including the centipede and millipede. It is present in insects and evident in caterpillars and dragonflies. The examples in nature are countless when one is alert and perceptive. Many vertebrates also show evidence of segmental symmetry.

The skeleton of a fish reveals a beautiful repetition series in the vertebrae, dorsal rays, ribs, and ventral rays. These are attached to and activated by segmental muscles, called myomeres, controlled by segmental nerves. This pattern is present in all vertebrates, but has been modified in many species.

In the developing human embryo, segmentalization is also very prominent, as the vertebrae, ribs, and muscles begin to develop. It is evident in adult forms of higher vertebrates, including humans, in the vertebrae and ribs (note the vertebrae and ribs in the illustration of a skeleton, pg. 53-55). The digits of the human hand demonstrate a modified segmental symmetry.

Up to this point the discussion of symmetry has dealt with many beautiful but relatively static forms. Balance with a change in form allows for a deviation from a rigid symmetry. When a larger deviation occurs from the formal symmetry and equilibrium, an off-balance situation develops. A reversion seeks to balance itself again, and if another imbalance occurs, the order of rhythms results in alternative attempts toward a continuous restoration of balance. The order of rhythm results in repeated balances and off-balances, bringing dynamics into play.

In dynamic design, principles are found in actions of the human body. In order to portray movement, the body's formal symmetry must be thrown into an off-balance situation. The weight is thrust to one foot, then to the other, by means of exerting force. There is a consistent endeavor to keep returning to equilibrium. With alternating repetitions and return to balance, dynamic motion is set into action. It can then be maintained in an even rhythmic cadence or one that can be accelerated or diminished in progressive repetitions under control. An illustration is included showing a lizard and a human body with alternating actions generating rhythms.

Ancient and primitive cultures generally represented human figures in a stiff or rigid pose. A big change occurred in the Greek classics, demonstrating a weight shift to a one point or a dynamic balance. By placing all of the weight on the leading foot, there is a high hip and a low hip. This causes the vertebral column to bend and twist, creating a low shoulder with the high hip on one side and a high shoulder with the low hip on the other side. The sternal notch continues to be over the center of gravity when the figure is at rest.

When the foot without the weight is put forward, the weight must go forward and alter the balance. The figure appears to be ready to take a step as if it were moving. Normally, when one foot is forward, the opposite shoulder goes forward. When this is included with weight shift it was known by Italian sculptors, including Michelangelo, as contraposto. It puts the body into alternating rhythms that are the rhythms of movement such as walking and running. In the Renaissance there was a reawakening of intellect and pursuit of knowledge. Ancient teachings became available. The artists became aware of a dynamic representation of life and put it into their creative efforts. The Renaissance masters and their students have subsequently been appreciated and praised for their magnificent representation of people, events, lore, and action.

An illustration of a lizard and a human, Fig. 145, demonstrate how the motion requires an alteration from a static symmetry to a dynamic state. Graceful curves result as the shoulder and pelvic girdle responds to motion. Forms in action create inequalities, disturb balance, and initiate movement.

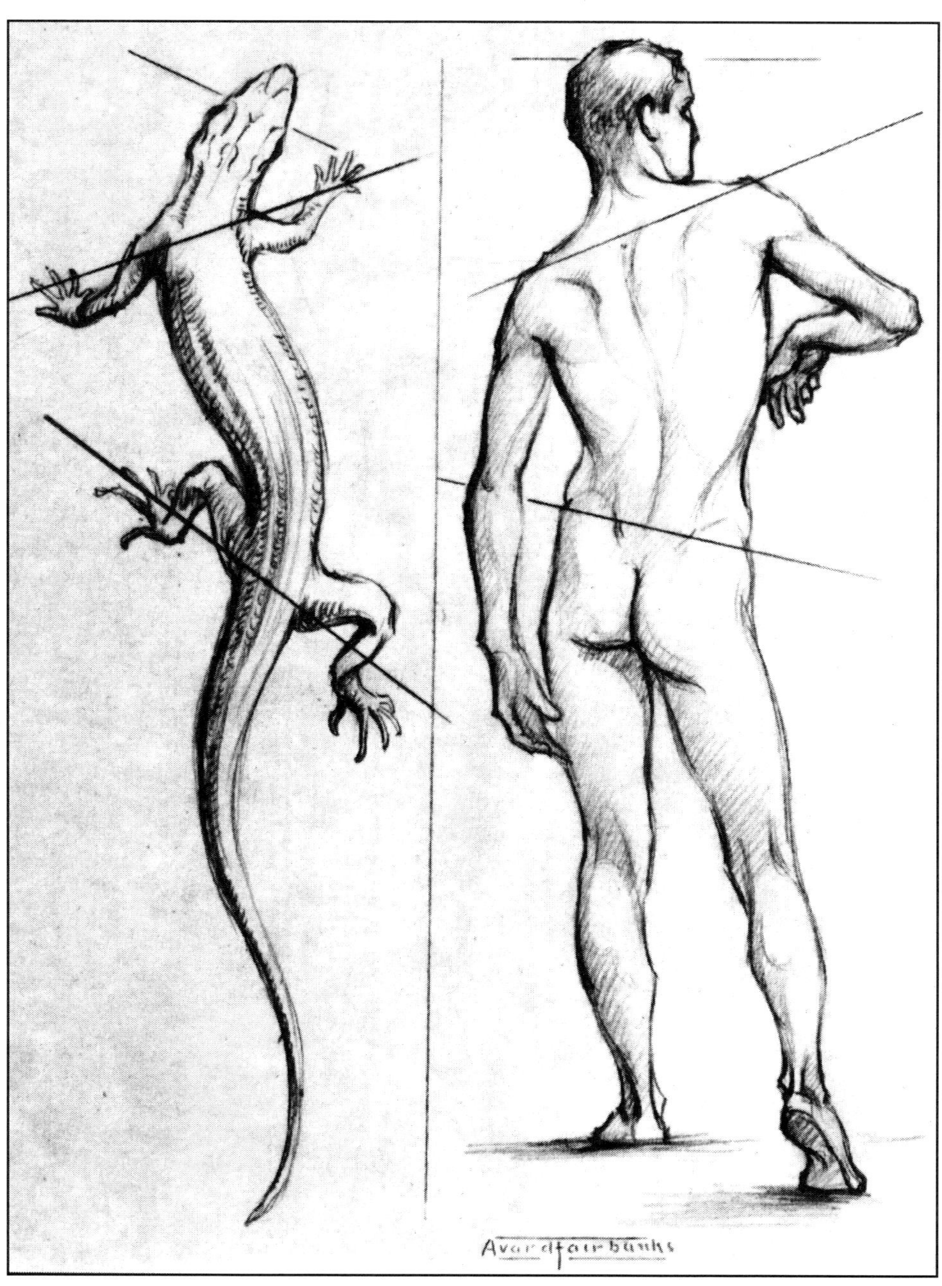

Fig. 145. Forms in action; inequalities disturb balance and initiate action; similarity of a lizard and human while walking.

DYNAMIC SYMMETRY

Over the centuries, even millennia, many names have been applied to dynamic symmetry. Among them are the divine proportion, the golden mean, the golden rectangle, and the golden triangle. This is a special type of symmetry in which there is an orderly arrangement of similar parts manifesting simple ratios of dimensions of the parts in an obvious progression. There may be inequality of elements, but there is a similarity and a proportional progression often resulting in a whorl, the most familiar example of which is a snail shell. Besides being a form of symmetry, it also manifests a progression from small to larger dimensions.

The concept of dynamic symmetry is not new. It was known to the Egyptians in the 6th century BC, who used rectangles in planning their temples and in decorating their tombs, even though they built pyramids with a square base. The Greeks may have borrowed concepts of dynamic symmetry from the Egyptians and further developed its principles and application in art and architecture. Euclid, in ancient Greece, described its geometric fundamentals. It was recognized by the Greek sculptors and architects who applied it to their sculpture and temples, particularly the golden section rectangle

Geometrically Φ, a ratio of 1.62... to 1. It is demonstrated by forming a golden rectangle from a square. Various cultures in several previous millennia recognized that a rectangle was more pleasing than a square, and it is evident in their art and architecture.

The golden rectangle is constructed, starting with a square, ABCD, then by a diagonal starting at the midpoint of the base at E, extending upwards to an opposite corner, D. An arc is drawn by a protractor from D to the baseline at F. The line BF has a Φ ratio, 1.62, to BC. A vertical line is drawn from F up to an extension of AD, to G. This resulted in a figure, ABFG, called the golden rectangle. When another square is constructed adjacent to the golden rectangle using the longer dimension of the rectangle, AF for a base, another similar but larger rectangle is formed. By repeatedly adding progressively larger squares, whirling rectangles result. This is a geometric summation series. A logarithmic spiral may then be inscribed by a curve connecting the diagonals at the corners of the rectangles. The example of whirling rectangles is illustrated here.[5]

A golden triangle with similar progression and curves is also described in dynamic symmetry texts. It is an isosceles triangle formed with a base of one unit and the other two equal legs are 1.62 times the unit. This produces a triangle with an apex angle of 36° and base angles of 72°. Whirling triangles may then be created that will inscribe a geometric spiral. Curves connecting corners of the whirling rectangle and other similar geometric spirals are involved in the curves of life. The most apparent example in nature for comparison of these curves are the coils of snail shells and other mollusks. One of the most beautiful examples is the shell of a chambered, or pearly, nautilus, Nautilus pompilius. Not all curves of living organisms conform to the Fibonacci series, or Phi ratio, but there are many variations and other ratios that result in beautiful forms. The example shown of whirling rectangles and triangles, is a geometric expression of the Fibonacci series, to be discussed later.

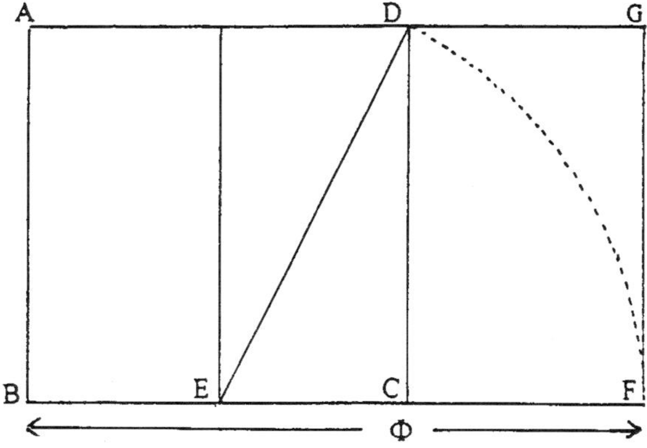

Fig. 146. A golden rectangle.

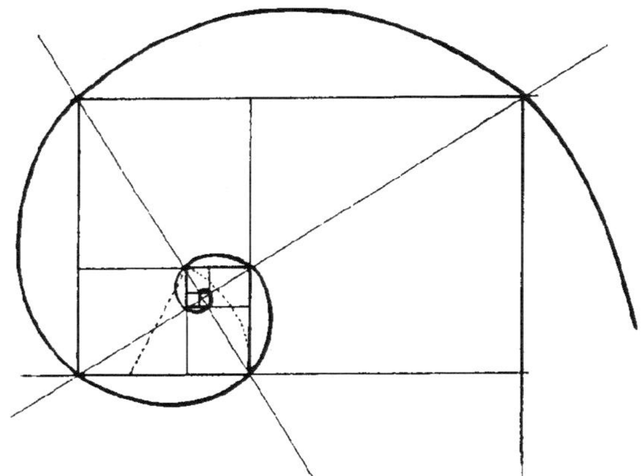

Fig. 147. Whirling rectangles and a logarithmic spiral.

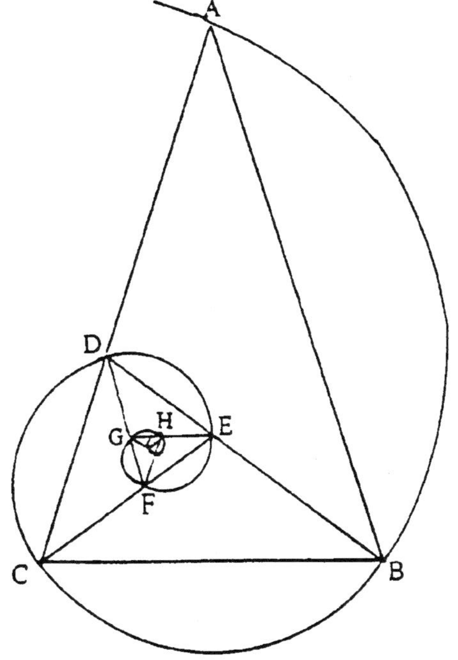

Fig. 148. Whirling golden triangles.

5. Ghyka, p. 10; Huntly, p. 61

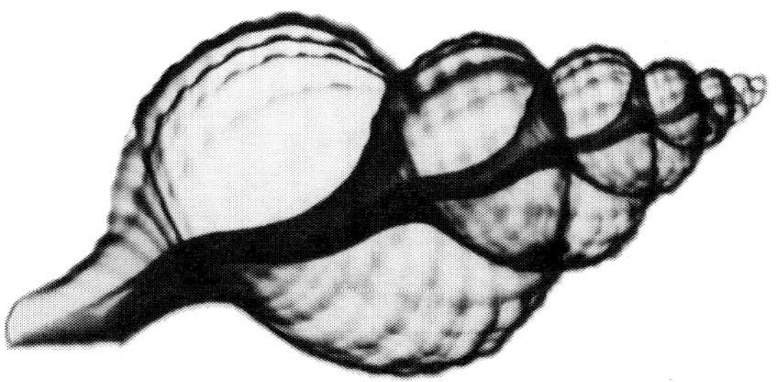

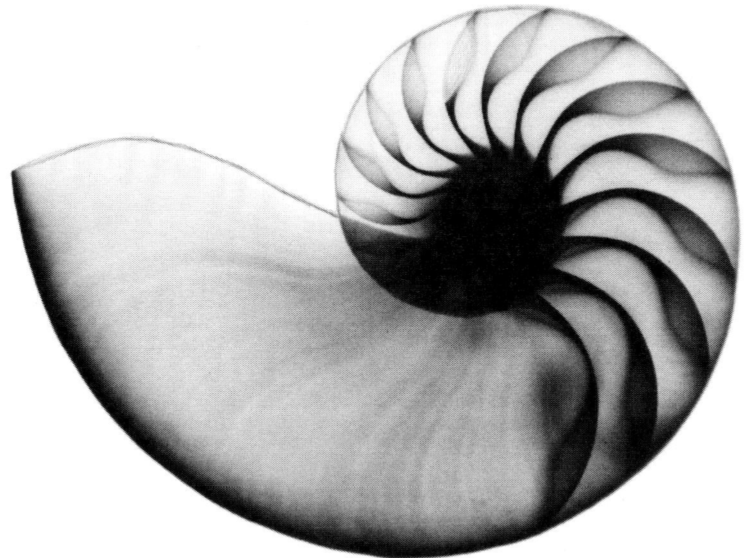

Fig. 149. An Oregon triton and a chambered nautilus, x-ray images of shells, examples of dynamic symmetry.

A rectangle ABCD of nearly any ratio of base to upright side may have a rectangle spiral constructed. A diagonal, BD, is drawn. From an opposite corner, A, a line is drawn perpendicular to the diagonal and it strikes the base, BC, at E. This line is called the reciprocal. The intersection of the diagonal and the reciprocal is called the eye of the rectangular spiral. A similar rectangle can then be drawn by a line at E, vertical to the base, BC to an intersection at the diagonal, F. By connecting diagonals and reciprocals at right angles, a rectangle-based spiral results. By connecting these corners with arc like curves, a geometric spiral can be inscribed.[6] Whorls may vary from tight to expanded forms.

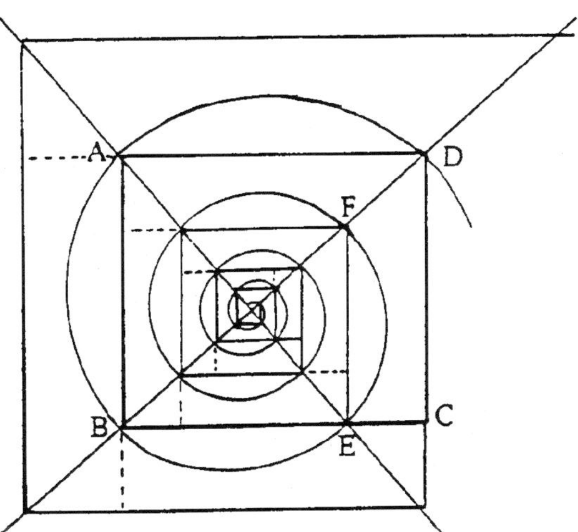

Fig. 150. A tight whirling rectangular and a tight spiral.

6. Hambridge, p. 30, 31.

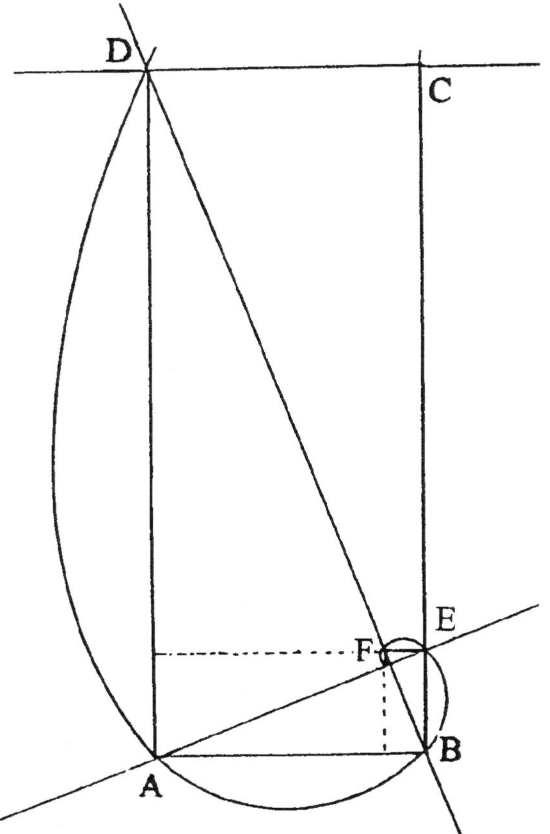

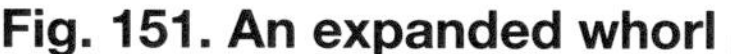

Fig. 151. An expanded whorl .

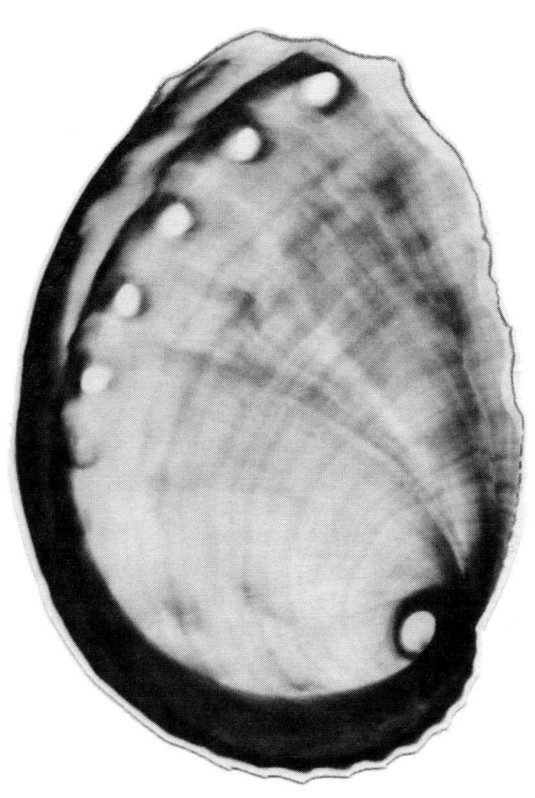

Fig. 152. An X-ray image of a northern abalone, Haliotis kamschatkana.

Many snail shells, as examples of a form of dynamic symmetry, have outlines conforming to other whirling rectangles of different ratios. Their forms are geometric spirals that vary from tight whorls, as a snail, to expanded whorls. One rectangle illustrated, has a ratio of base to upright of 1 to 1.125. The other, an elongated rectangle, has a base to upright ratio of 1 to 2.5. The resulting whorl resembles the pattern on the shell of an abalone.

A pentagon may be inscribed using the phi ratio or the golden section. Plot a 1 unit as the base, AB, for an isosceles golden triangle. The other two equal, upright sides are 1.62 units or Φ times the unit. These join in an apex angle of 36° at C. At 1 unit distances from the base AB, on the longer, upright sides, mark points D and E,. Draw a straight line, FDEG parallel to the base, measuring 1.62 units extending equally across the apex angle. Connect F to A and C. Connect G to B and C. The resulting figure is a regular pentagon. By additional connecting lines, FB and GA, a five pointed star or pentagram is constructed within the pentagon.

The golden triangle or Φ series is significant in animal form and growth. Many of those animals with radial symmetry have modified pentagon configurations in fives or multiples of five as recognized in sea stars and urchins. The pentadactyl, five fingered, architecture of vertebrate hands

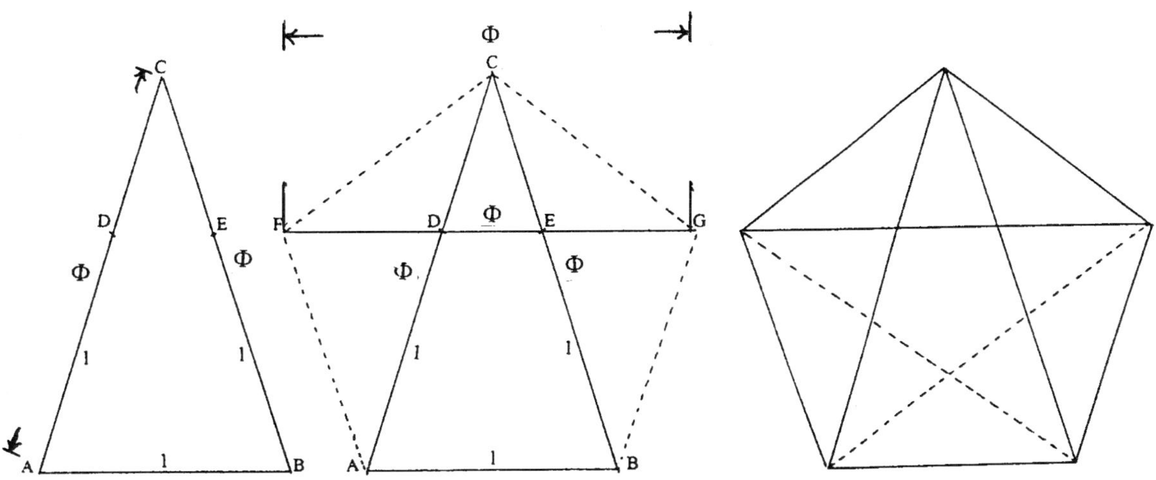

Fig. 153. A pentagon constructed using a golden triangle.

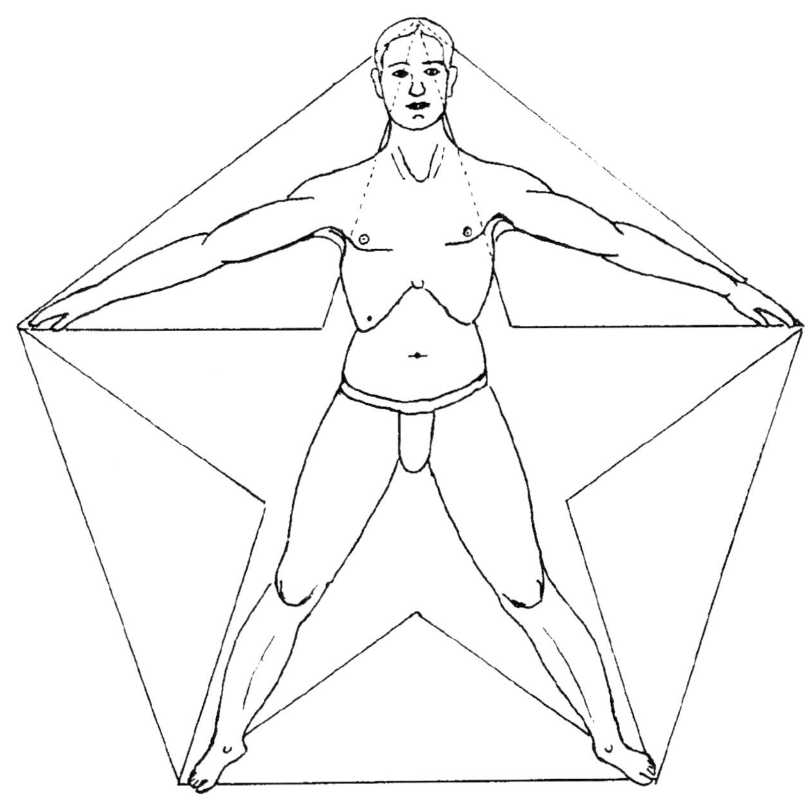

Fig. 154. The human body compared to a star and a pentagon.

and feet is another significant example. The human body form, four extremities and a head, also conforms to the number five. The face, with two eyes, two nostrils, and a mouth, also conforms. The pentagon as a simple figure is compatible with three dimensional expansion, modification, growth, and development.

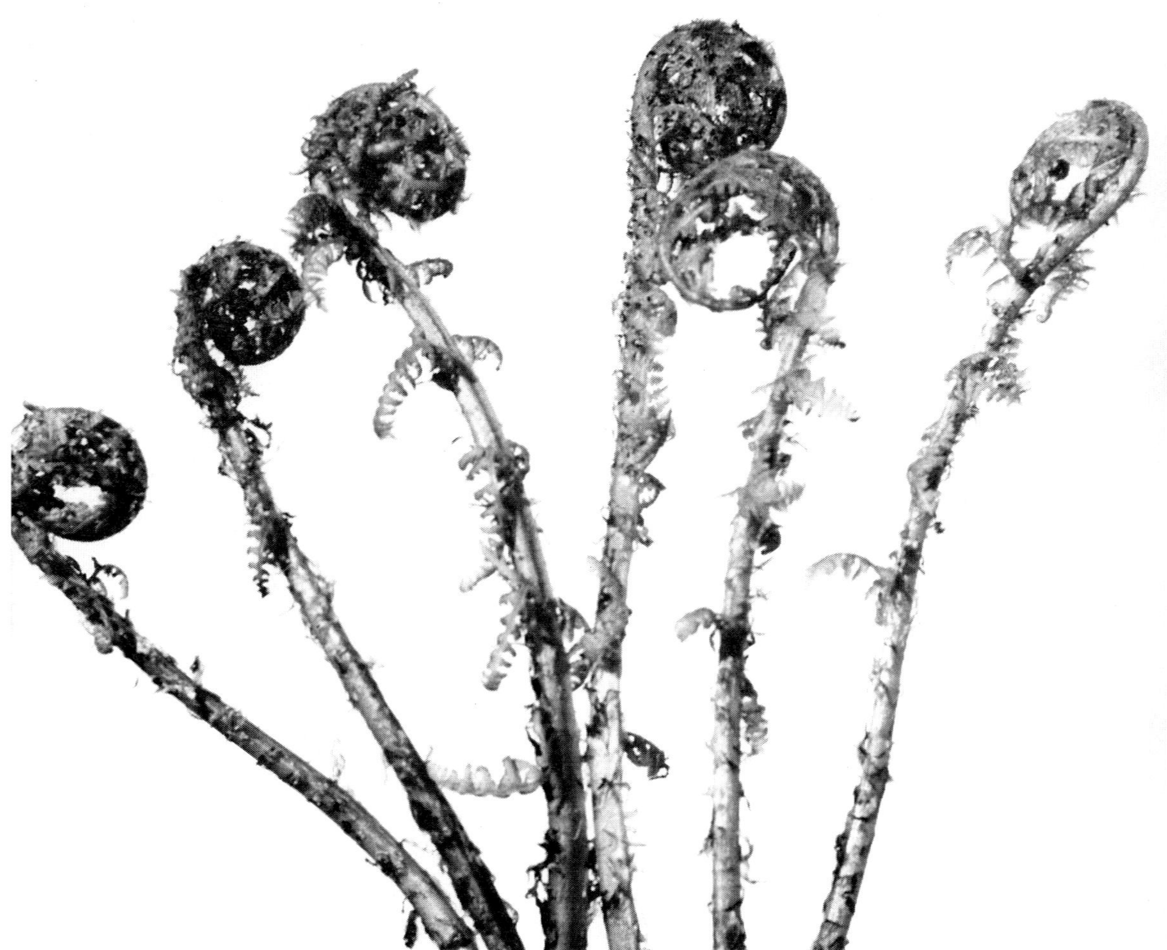

Fig. 155. Fiddle heads of bracken ferns unfolding in the spring.

Dynamic symmetry was less recognized by the Romans, who used a semicircular arch. The concepts were gradually ignored or lost and did not resurface in western culture until about two centuries before the Renaissance and Gothic periods, when Greek principles and philosophy were reintroduced and again studied. (Illustration Roman and Gothic Arch) Dynamic symmetry continued as a motivating factor for decorative design through the Renaissance and even in later periods.

The Gothic Arch is the prominent feature of many chapels and cathedrals of the Renaissance and the following centuries. It is compared to a Roman arch.

The growth of plants, the unfolding of leaves, the fiddleheads of fern fronds, the expansion of buds into blossoms, and the curved horns of bighorn sheep are logarithmic curves. These depend on the principle of continued proportionate growth and on similarity of form with respect to size. All these are manifestations of some form of dynamic symmetry. Other examples in nature include the swirling lines of whirlpool and eddy currents in rivers or of tides surging through narrows. Ocean waves also have action. As a wave breaks over a reef, the crest curls upon itself in a splendid and graceful form of dynamic symmetry.

In astronomy, spiral nebulae mani-

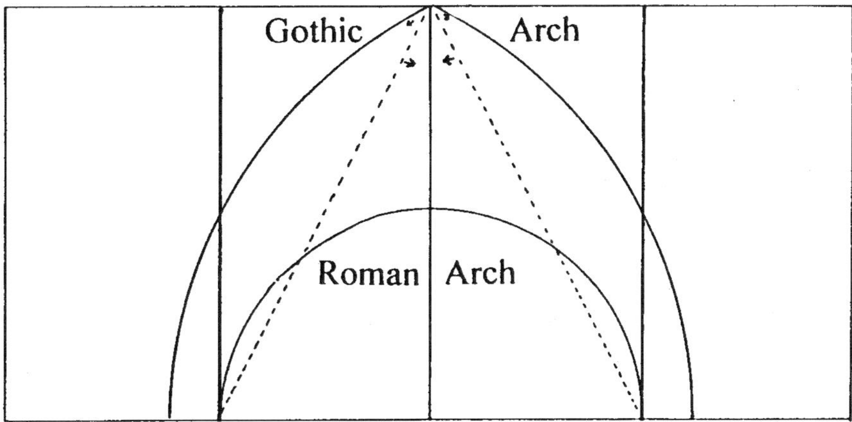

Fig. 156. The golden rectangle and the Gothic arch.

fest dynamic symmetry with an illusion of motion and action.[7] It is seen in the clouds as they billow upwards, particularly in thunderheads. It is seen in dunes, where the wind creates waves in the sand.

It is seen in the mammalian embryo as the segments grow and the caudal or tail end begins to develop. It persists in adult mammals with a prehensile tail, such as the opossum, whose babies curl their tails around the mother's tail when going for a ride on her back. Many new-world monkeys also have prehensile tails for grasping branches, to assist their tree climbing and swinging from branch to branch.

Architects have appreciated for many centuries that rectangular buildings are more pleasing than square structures. A prime example is the Parthenon in Athens, Greece. Other Greek temples in eastern Mediterranean archeological sites have similar ratio dimensions. Most homes and residential buildings conform to or resemble some elements of dynamic symmetry for an appeal to the human sensitivity. Since ancient times, the golden section rectangle has been recognized as more pleasant than a square object.

Mystics have been enchanted by dynamic symmetry. Many artists have appreciated its application to human form and action. It has been consciously and unconsciously incorporated, often with modifications, into decorative design in architecture as observers sense a form, a contour, or rectangular arrangement that is pleasing to view.

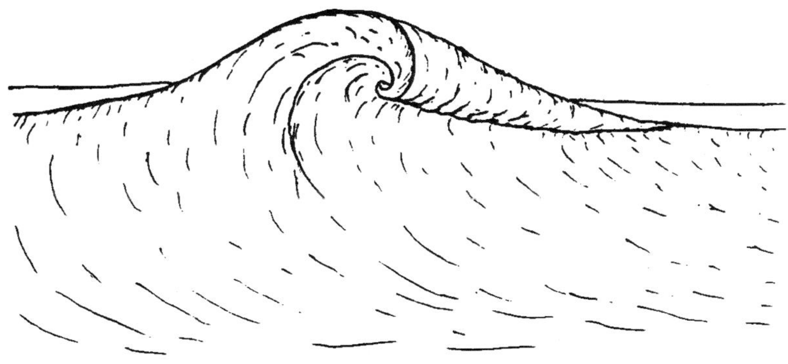

Fig. 157. A cresting ocean wave.

7. Livio, p. 53.

THE FIBONACCI SERIES

The geometry of dynamic symmetry is mathematically expressed by a summation series of numbers called the Fibonacci Series. These numbers were involved in a hypothetical puzzle about how many breeding pairs of rabbits would result at the end of a year if someone began with one breeding pair that had two to a litter and a litter each month. Answer: 233 pairs.[8]

It was noted in a book written by Leonardo of Pisa (1180-1250), who used the nickname Fibonacci, meaning Filis (son of) Bonacci. His father was an affluent merchant, and Leonardo traveled extensively around the Mediterranean Sea. He was able to study mathematical concepts in Islamic ports where the Greek knowledge and teachings had been maintained over many centuries during the dark ages of Europe. When he returned home to Pisa, Italy, prior to the beginning of the Renaissance, he was able to reintroduce some of the lost classic knowledge to Italy. He also became conversant with the Hindu-Arabic numeral system and recognized its advantages over the commonly used Roman numerals. He published a book entitled, *Liber Abaci* (meaning book of abacus, a calculator), promoting the system of numbers, and influenced the introduction in Europe of the numerical system we use today.

The Fibonacci series is a progression of summations of numbers. The progression of this is:

1, 2, 3, 5, 8, 13, 21, 34, 55, 89, 144, 233, etc.

8. Huntly, p. 159.

The series consists of each number being the sum of the two previous numbers:

1+1=2, 1+2=3, 2+3=5, 3+5=8, 5+8=13, 8+13=21, 13+21=34, 21+3=55, 34+55=89, 55+89=144, 89+144=233, etc.

The ratio of any number to the preceding number is about 1.6..., and in larger sums it eventually averages 1.618..., the same as the ratio of the two sides of the golden rectangle. That ratio is termed Phi, designated by a Greek letter Φ. (Please do not confuse this with Pi, $\pi = 3.14...$, which is the circumference of a circle divided by the diameter.) The reciprocal of Phi, $1 \div \Phi$, is 0.62... or nearly 2/3.

A redirection of attention occurred during the 20th century, and many authors have discussed and described dynamic symmetry with extensive mathematical analysis. Mathematicians have studied, described, and elaborated on dynamic symmetry. Some have used it to analyze many human features. Forms and characteristics of other species in the animal and plant kingdoms have also been analyzed. After studying several texts, it becomes apparent that a few mathematicians have progressed into a state of mathematical and geometric ecstasy with sophisticated equations that are difficult for many people (including this author) to follow and are beyond the needs of most artists. It may be better to let the beautiful concepts be recognized by those striving for mastery, and unconsciously appreciated by most observers, than to pursue an overly enthusiastic exercise in the analytic process.

Dynamic symmetry cannot be simply described in ordinary words or easily explained, since its fundamentals are mathematics and geometry. However, when understood, the concepts are both logical and beautiful.

"In nature it is the orderly arrangement of members of an organism in plant and animal life.... It was the Greeks who in about the fifth century B.C. made the astounding discovery that this symmetry was the symmetry of growth in man."[9]

For a more comprehensive appreciation, the serious student will enjoy further study of books listed in a special bibliography at the end of this chapter.

Other rectangles have been selected for their aesthetic appeal. Many forms in common use are rectangles of the same or similar ratios for their dimensions. File cards are made with a ratio nearly equal to or similar to Φ, 1.62... :

3 by 5 ratio is 1.66,
4 by 6 ratio is 1.5,
5 by 8 ratio is 1.6,
Legal stationery is 8.5 by 14, with a ratio of 1.64;
Office stationery is 8.5 by 11, with a ratio of 1.29.

Other common picture sizes have various ratios that approximate significant geometric numbers.

The square root of 2, $\sqrt{2}$, is 1.4142... ,

and the square root of 1.5, $\sqrt{1.5}$, is 1.23....

Familiar rectangles with ratios approximating these are informal and appealing.

5 by 7 ratio is 1.4
8 by 10 ratio is 1.25
9 by 12 ratio is 1.33
11 by 14 ratio is 1.27
12 by 16 ratio is 1.33
16 by 20 ratio is 1.25

Many of the measurements of these commonly used rectangles are adapted to the convenience of inch measurements, but approach or resemble the golden rectangle, the root 2 rectangle (1 to 1.414...), or the root 1.5 rectangle (1 to 1.23...). These are less formal than a square and appeal to sensitivities. Like a square, a circle is formal while rectangles and ellipses are informal. A golden ratio ellipse has 1 unit for a vertical axis and 1.62 units for the horizontal axis. It is less formal and more pleasing than a circle, because it resembles the outline of a face.

While artists may not be expected to model geometric figures, they can and should appreciate correlations with the observed form and be aware of variations and combinations of forms. When students have learned how to recognize various symmetries and how to describe or classify those symmetries, they may discover them in many unexpected places. They may then observe many more examples of the role they play throughout nature, art, and life. They should appreciate the beauty rendered and recognize the advantages of incorporating symmetries into their artistic creations.

There are many other manifestations of the various forms of symmetry for which numerous examples could be cited, but the text would be too lengthy. Clearly, it is important that the artist appreciate the different forms of symmetry, recognize them when evident, and note their variations in form, size, and contours. When a natural object or an artistic creation is viewed that displays the unconsciously anticipated combinations of form, balance, rhythm and symmetries, it is pleasing and satisfying to the human sense of order.

9. Hambridge, p. xv.

BIBLIOGRAPHY

Pearl, Richard M. *Rocks and Minerals.* New York: Barnes and Noble, Inc., 1956.

Williams, P.L, Wendell Smith, C.P., Treadgold, Sylvia. *Basic Human Embryology.* Philadelphia: J.B. Lippincott Company, 1969.

Yankofsky, Charles. "Gene Structure and Protein Structure." The Chemical Basis of Life: An Introduction to Molecular and Cell Biology: Readings from Scientific American. San Francisco: W.H. Freeman and Company, 1973, 278-287.

REFERENCES

Church, *Relation of Phyllotaxis to Mechanical Laws.* Oxford: 1901,1903.

Cook, Theodore A. , *The Curves of Life.* New York: Dover Publications, 1979.

Coleman, *Nature's Harmonic Unity.* New York: G.P. Putnam Sons, 1912.

Edwards, Edward B., *Pattern and Design with Dynamic Symmetry.* New York:, Dover Publications, Inc., 1967.

Garland, Trudi H.. *Fascinating Fibonaccis.* Dale Seymour Publications, 1987.

Ghyka, Matlia, *The Geometry of Art and Life.* New York: Dover Publications Inc., 1977.

Hambridge, Jay, *The Elements of Dynamic Symmetry.* New York: Dover Publications, Inc., 1967.

Huntley, H.E., *The Divine Proportion, A Study in Mathematical Beauty.* New York: Dover Publications Inc., 1970.

Livio, Mario, "*Searching for the Golden Ratio;* A Geometric Proportion Discovered in Antiquity Turns Up in Sculpture, Botany, Planetary Orbits and in the Thermodynamics of Black Holes." *Astronomy,* Vol. 31, No. 4, (2003), 52-57.

Livio, Mario. *The Golden Ratio.* New York: Broadway Books, 2002.

THOUGHTS ON THE MEANING OF ART

In a discussion of Art, one naturally wonders why this seems so important and why so much attention is directed to this phase of our lives. Briefly, Art makes living seem more worthwhile. Art does not portray life as a bare matter of fact existence, but it sees beyond life's mechanics, materials, and form. It strives to see and express the spirit of life, to find and present the transcendent essence of being. The artist selects, and with the media in which he works, he organizes and forms, by means of skillful techniques, something that expresses the significant concepts and makes his creation a part of life objectified. We may call it an essential aspect of culture. Thus, we may conclude that:

ART IS THE MEASURE OF THE CULTURAL ACHIEVEMENT OF OUR CIVILIZATION

If we have pride in our cultural development, we cannot help but be deeply concerned about the art that we encourage. Furthermore, if we are anxious for our period of time to measure up to those important ages of the past, our art must, likewise, be the expression of the culture that we encourage and promote. Let it become the standard, and the evidences of our hopes, our ideals, our aspirations. Let it become an expression of our attitudes toward people, to nature, and our striving toward the finer things of life.

If we deny the significant and beautiful aspects of living, then Art sinks to a low ebb, and it tends toward degradation. However, if we lend encouragement to the better things of life and aspire to present them with excellence, with skills, and with more efficient methods, then Art arises to great heights. The production of such, done with great mastery, then leaves fine masterpieces for the world to appreciate. In the social mind of the people there is left a heritage of great musical compositions, worthy accomplishments in drama and dance. An age of great literature may occur. Outstanding architectural achievements, masterpieces of painting, and great monuments of sculpture in bronze and stone may be created as records of our age. It is the care and sensitivity that makes for ***great art,*** not just getting production done fast. Granted, the technical skills and noteworthy content are important to emphasize in the production of truly Fine Art. There are those who have trained well and who have struggled to gain that sensitivity to our life and culture and to that of all nature. It is through the dexterity of such persons and their arts that they can render important contributions to our part of history and civilization.

It can be stated without reservation that one of the purposes of Art is to elevate mankind into the higher realms of thinking and feeling. Therefore, Art has a very definite place in the life of our people. When people draw near to and greet each other, they become quite civil. To be civil means harmonic relations between individuals. These are unities. In the expression of such relationships there can be harmonies between family units, community units, and national units, achieving a dynamic work harmony.

The great principle of harmony is also one of the objectives of Art. The use of materials, shapes, colors, tones, and their organization into harmonies can produce studies that evoke the admiration and ambitions of the spirit. Likes and opposites may be adjusted achieving unity with variations until patterns of delight and excitement can result throughout any art forms. Art deals with orderly arrangements of elements together in the most expressive way of conveying profound thoughts Therefore, the thinking must be of the highest order that man can achieve. We may here conclude that Art and Life itself function on similar deep universal principles. As Art expresses Life, then Life also expresses Art. Art and Life with our reasoning can come into intimate and sympathetic responses. In the expression of a great universal harmony, artists can produce important treasures and masterpieces that become a cultural achievement for our civilization.

Some have expressed the attitude in our nation that Art can be put aside until we can afford to spend for luxuries. But Art never grows to heights of true greatness in times of extravagance or in periods of lavishness when the vanities and expressions of excessiveness become popular attitudes. Such influences occur during periods of art decadence.

The sincere arts and those with great concepts develop with a struggling people. When artists struggle along with the people of their own times to express their own spiritual aspirations, they create an indigenous culture which fares well to become a significant contribution to the world's growth and development.

When Greece was laying the foundations of the Democracy of Western Civilization, Art flourished along with the ideals and concepts of its people.

When Rome was struggling to bring uplift and the benefits of organized government to the peoples of Europe, Art also grew and developed in proportion to other activities.

When the Renaissance was at its height, Columbus discovered the western continents. Michelangelo was also giving his masterpieces to the world. These events helped inspire many nations still in their infancy, and some yet to come into existence.

With the revolutions of America and France and struggles for freedom, there came forth new influences and vigorous art forms. As one outstanding example we may point to America's colossal bronze statue in New York Harbor, the Statue of Liberty (a gift from France). It is a symbol of hope for people everywhere.

Thus, the new, the adventurous, the spirit of hope, the pioneering movement, the daring of your youth, and other aspects of the nation can create heroic art forms of significance. We can leave monumental examples of our aspirations to the world and express our struggles to achieve them.

It is important that we develop art here in the nation that will inspire, influence, and lead our children and their children. Their imaginations in their formative years should be guided with sincere and profound creations of art that can secure their admiration and cause them to develop constructive and aesthetic concepts.

Like pilots that guide great ships from their moorings out through the harbors to the vast expanse of the open ocean, it should also be the responsibility of the artists of our day to pilot the imaginations and motivations of our youths as they venture forth on the great open sea of knowledge and understanding, accessible to the mind. To them, reliable charts should be made available for the challenging opportunities ahead. The Arts, thus hold important responsibilities for the future culture of society.

~Avard Fairbanks

At the conclusion of a philosophic discussion of Art, a definition seems appropriate. A search of dictionaries reveals that there are many definitions that hope to comprehend all forms of artistic expression. One that impressed me most was: "Art is an endeavor towards perfection."

~Eugene Fairbanks

GLOSSARY

Acromion process: the lateral point of the shoulder

Ala, ala nasae: the lateral border of the lower third of the nose, literally, wings of the nose.

Anterior aspect: ventral, it is the front of a standing human figure.

Anterior superior spine of ilium: a prominence of the pelvic bone anterior to the crest of the ilium. It is often used and referred to as a point for measurement.

Anthropometric, anthropometry: measuring the human figure.

Aperture: an opening, as the parting of the lips for the mouth.

Axilla: arm pit.

Axillary: reference to the arm pit.

Axillary folds: anterior, formed by the pectoralis muscle; posterior, formed by the latissimus dorsi muscle.

Axillary pivot: the center pivot for extension or raising of the arm.

Biceps muscle: a large muscle on the anterior aspect of the upper arm.

Braccio: an old Italian measure from the shoulder to the wrist.

Brachychepalic: a head configuration that is short, width to height, with a cephalic index of 80 to 86 .

Brachymorphic: short body build.

Bridge of the nose: a notch just below the brow at the upper part of the nose.

Buttock: the rump or protuberant hinder part of human.

Canthus: the corner of an eye where the lids join, the inner canthus and outer canthus.

Caudal: toward the tail in most vertebrates or towards the coccyx in humans.

Central: is toward the center axis, the vertebral column which is generally vertical and generally but not entirely central. The axis is on a plane, but is not a plane, it is a theoretical straight line, but in body development it has developed gentle curves.

Cephalic: also Superior: toward the head.

Cervical: refers to the neck.

Chryselephantine: sculpture carved in elephant ivory.

Clavicle: the collar bone; it is attached to the acromion process of the shoulder and to the sternum at the sternal notch.

Costal margin: costal refers to ribs and the costal margin is the lower border of the ribs of the thorax, starting in back near the vertebrae and forming an arc attaching to the sternum in front.

Crest of ilium: a prominent ridge of the pelvis bone on the lateral aspect of the abdomen.

Crotch: the apex of the angle where the legs join in the midline.

Cubit: ancient unit of measure from the tip of the flexed elbow to the tip of the middle finger of the straightened hand.

Deep: inside and deep to the surface.

Deltoid muscle: a large triangular muscle at the lateral aspect of the shoulder.

Distal: a part of an extremity away or farther from the body; compare to proximal.

Dolicocephlic: a type of head that is long and narrow with head width to height about index of 70 to 75.

Dolicomorphic: tall and slender body form.

Dorsal aspect: posterior, it is the back of a standing human figure.

Dorsal spines: posterior vertebral spinous processes of vertebrae.

Epicondyle: prominence at lateral aspects of a joint, especially on the humerus.
Fathom: a span of the out-stretched arms, finger tip to fingertip.
Fibonnaci series: a summation series of numbers in which a number is the sum of the previous two numbers, as: 3, 5, 8, 13, 21, 34… .
Frontal plane: any theoretical plane that intersects the erect human body from side to side, parallel to the central axis and perpendicular to the mid sagittal plane.
Frontotemporal: a junction of a frontal bone of the forehead with a temporal bone on the lateral aspect of the skull.
Gluteal cleft: the crease between each buttocks.
Gluteal furrow: a prominent transverse crease below a buttock.
Gluteus maximus: prominent large muscle of the buttocks.
Gonion: an anthropometry term for the angle of the jaw bone.
Greater trochanters: the widest prominences of the femurs, thigh bones at the hips.
Helix of an ear: the lateral, outer border of an ear.
Humerus: the upper arm bone.
Ilium: a prominent bone of the pelvis.
Infra-: below, compare to supra, above.
Infranasal point: the junction of the base of the nose and the upper lip.
Labium: lip; labial, pertaining to a lip.
Larynx: the voice box or Adam's apple, an anatomical feature of the neck composed primarily of the thyroid cartilage.
Lateral: is away from the mid-sagittal plane.
Mandible: a jaw bone.
Nasion: at the bridge of the nose, see selion.
Malleolus: a bony prominence at the ankle, either medial or lateral.
Manubrium: the upper part of the sternum.
Mastoid process: a bony prominence just behind an ear.
Medial: is toward the midsagittal plane.
Menton: chin.
Mesocephlic: medium head, a head width to height index of 75 to 80.
Mesomorphic,: medium body build.
Mid-saggital plane: a theoretical plane that intersects the human body from front to back through the central axis, perpendicular to frontal planes and creating two equal halves.
Occiput: the low posterior prominence at back of the skull.
Olecranon process: the tip of the flexed elbow.
Orbit: the bony socket of the skull for an eye.
Patella: knee cap.
Pectoralis muscles: anterior chest muscles inserting on the upper part of a humerus.
Phalanx, phalangeal: segments of digits, fingers or toes.
Popliteal crease: the popliteal fossa is a cavity behind the knee and when bent forms the popliteal crease.
Posterior aspect: dorsal, it is the back of a standing human figure.
Proximal: a part of an extremity near or closer to the body; compare to distal.
Pubis: a bone of the pelvis fused to the ilium. It is prominent at the base of the genitals.
Radius: a bone of the forearm parallel to the ulna.
Rod: an English measure of sixteen feet.
Scapula: shoulder blade.
Selion: a junction of the nasal bones with frontal bones at the bridge of the nose.
Sternal notch: the top of the sternum, or breast bone, between clavicles or collar bones.
Sternocleidomastoid muscle: a prominent muscle of the anterior neck originating

at the sternal notch and inserting on the mastoid process behind an ear

Sublabial: below the lip.

Supercilliary arch: the brow ridge that is above the orbit or eye socket.

Superficial: toward the surface; compare to deep.

Supra-: above; compare to infra-, below.

Symphysis pubis: a midline pelvic junction of both pubic bones of the pelvis, also considered a base of the genitals.

Thorax: the chest, composed of vertebrae in back, ribs, and sternum in front.

Thyroid cartilage: the prominent cartilage structure of the larynx or voice box in the anterior part of the neck.

Tibia: the shin bone of the leg.

Tragus: a cartilaginous prominence or flap anterior to the ear canal.

Tragion: a point on the tragus of an ear, just anterior to the ear canal.

Transverse plane: any theoretical plane that intersects central axis at right angles; in most vertebrates, top to bottom; in the erect human body, from front to back.

Ulna: a bone of the forearm parallel to the radius.

Umbilicus: belly button.

Ventral: in most vertebrates inferior or abdominal aspect; in humans, anterior, or the front of a standing human figure.

Vertex: the highest part of the human head.

Xiphoid process: a midline bony prominence below and attached to the sternum or breast bone.

Zygomatic arch: a lateral cheek bone in front of an ear.

Symbols:

- $=$: Equal to
- $\doteq$: Approximately equal to
- $\neq$: Not equal to
- Φ : Phi, ratio 1.62…

ABOUT THE AUTHOR

AVARD T. FAIRBANKS, SCULPTOR

Avard Tennyson Fairbanks was born 1897 in Provo, Utah, to a family profoundly interested in art. His father and oldest brother were professional artists. He began to study sculpture at the age of twelve and in 1910-11 received scholarships at the Art Students' League in New York City where he had James Earl Fraser as an instructor. His work was exhibited at the National Academy of Design in 1911. Two years later he went to Paris to study at *Ecole des Beaux Arts* with Injalbert, at *Academie Colorossi,* and at the *Ecole de la Grande Chaumiere.* The outbreak of World War I forced him to return to the United States.

At the beginning of his professional career he created a number of large statues at the Latter-Day Saints Temple at Laie, Hawaii. While in Hawaii, he sent for his sweetheart, Maude Fox, and they were married in Honolulu. His career of teaching sculpture at the college level began in 1920 at the University of Oregon. In 1925 he earned a Bachelor of Fine Arts degree from Yale University. In 1927 he was awarded a fellowship by the Guggenheim Foundation, which enabled him to pursue further studies in Florence Italy. In 1929 he was awarded a Master of Fine Arts degree by the University of Washington. He was appointed to the Institute of Fine Arts faculty at the University of Michigan in 1930, and while teaching, earned a Master of Arts and Doctor of Philosophy degree in Anatomy there. The human proportions study in this book was a part of his doctorate thesis, titled, *Anatomic Design.*

During 18 years at Michigan while teaching sculpture he created many fine portraits, garden figures, and monuments. In 1948 he moved to the University of Utah where he was appointed Dean and asked to organize a College of Fine Arts. Many of his impressive portraits and heroic monuments were created in Utah. After being designated Emeritus Professor, he was appointed Resident Sculptor at the University of North Dakota for two years.

He has erected nearly one hundred public monuments and has created nearly another fifty significant portraits, garden figures, and bas reliefs. Many honors were awarded him during his career, including two honorary degrees. In 1982 he was honored for 75 years of professional sculpture. He died in 1987 at nearly ninety years of age. He left a legacy of creative, dynamic, and expressive fine art that is carried on by family members, students, and others. Many have benefited from his teachings and have utilized his principles.

Regarding family affairs, Maude and Avard were proud parents of eight sons and two adopted daughters. Two sons studied engineering, two became artists, and four became doctors of medicine. One daughter is a housewife and the other is a teacher of music. All retain an active interest in art.

ABOUT THE AUTHOR

EUGENE F. FAIRBANKS

Eugene Fox Fairbanks, the second son of Maude Fox and Avard T. Fairbanks, was born 1921 in Eugene, Oregon. He was involved in the studio at an early age. When the family was in Florence Italy, he modeled his first sculpture under the direction of Dante Sodini, one of Italy's most famous sculptors at that time. When Sculptor Avard Fairbanks was appointed to the faculty of the University of Michigan in 1930, his sons often helped at the studio. They did some modeling, assisted the plaster caster, retouched casts, and were taught photography for sculpture. There was a progressive increased expectation in skill and responsibility. This continued from grade school through high school and into college. An older brother chose engineering as a vocation. Younger brothers studied engineering, art, and medicine.

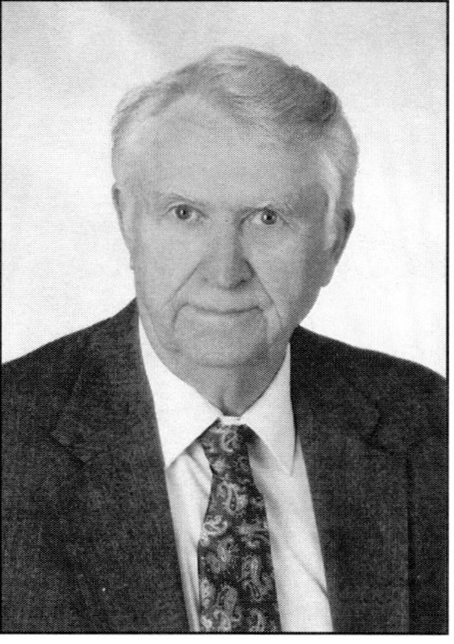

Eugene chose to study Medicine. He married Florence Sundwall in 1944 in his last year of the University of Michigan Medical School, and graduated in 1945. He interned at Wayne County General Hospital near Detroit, Michigan. Subsequently, he served in the Army Medical Corps as a transport surgeon on a troop transport which sailed from the Seattle Port of Embarkation. Following military service he practiced medicine as a family physician in Pasco and Kennewick, Washington. After an Anesthesiology residency in Seattle, he moved to Bellingham, Washington, and practiced Anesthesiology and Family Practice. He was certified as a diplomat of the American Board of Anesthesiology and the American Board of Family Physicians. In time Florence and Eugene became the proud parents of five sons and five daughters. He practiced medicine in Bellingham, Washington, until retirement in 1995.

With Dr. Charles J. Flora he has co-authored an invertebrate marine biology species identification handbook, published in 1966 and 1977, titled *The Sound and The Sea.* His first book about Avard Fairbanks' sculpture, titled *A Sculptor's Testimony in Bronze and Stone,* featured sacred sculpture. He has collected photographs and made many enlargements of Fairbanks sculpture for projected publications. In 1995 he was asked to create a heroic bronze monument honoring fishermen of Bellingham who have been lost at sea. This was titled, *A Safe Return,* and was dedicated on Memorial Day 1999 in Zuanich Point Park in Bellingham, Washington. A second book, titled *A Sculpture Garden of Fantasy,* was published in 2001. A third book titled, *Abraham Lincoln Sculpture Created by Avard Fairbanks,* was published in 2003.

Other planned publications about Avard Fairbanks' creativity include the modeling of statuettes, portraits, and relief sculpture. A documentary about Avard Fairbanks' many public monuments is also considered and is in progress. Children's proportions using similar format to the adult proportions is another study in progress.